AN END TIME LOOK AT GOD'S REDEMPTION PLAN

By
Lynette Carrington-Cox

World rights reserved. This book or any portion thereof may not be copied or reproduced in any form or manner whatever, except as provided by law, without the written permission of the publisher, except by a reviewer who may quote brief passages in a review.

The author assumes full responsibility for the accuracy of all facts and quotations as cited in this book. The opinions expressed in this book are the author's personal views and interpretations, and do not necessarily reflect those of the publisher.

This book is provided with the understanding that the publisher is not engaged in giving spiritual, legal, medical, or other professional advice. If authoritative advice is needed, the reader should seek the counsel of a competent professional.

_____

Copyright © 2014 TEACH Services, Inc.
ISBN-13: 978-1-4796-0472-2 (Paperback)
ISBN-13: 978-1-4796-0473-9 (ePub)
ISBN-13: 978-1-4796-0474-6 (Mobi)
Library of Congress Control Number: 2014956700

Published by

CONTENTS

An End Time Look at God's Redemption Plan 1
Chapter One 112
Chapter Two 117
Chapter Three 124
Chapter Four 127
Chapter Five 130
Chapter Six 135
Chapter Seven 138
Chapter Eight 180
Chapter Nine 186
Chapter Ten 222
Chapter Eleven 224
Chapter Twelve 236
Chapter Thirteen 257
Chapter Fourteen 322
Additional Study Topics 330

AN END TIME LOOK AT GOD'S REDEMPTION PLAN

Every now and then a new book is released and with great anticipation people stand in long lines, some even camp outside the bookstore overnight waiting to purchase a copy. Television news sometimes captures the picture of people pushing and shoving into the stores to get their hands on that book and within a few days they have read every line. As I look at these lines of people I have often thought, "now what book can get me so excited that I would stand in line for hours to get a copy and then lose sleep trying to read every word?" It would have to be a book filled with essential, long lasting, lifesaving information. Its author has to be lovable and all-knowing and the information has to be crucial to my existence now and in the future. Then the thought flashes through my mind, there is such a book available free, for the asking, and there are no long lines of eager excited people waiting to get their hands on it. Is it possible that most people really do not know what is in this book? I know that if they truly understood the depth and scope of knowledge that this book offers there would be long lines outside bookstores and people would spend a lot more time studying it.

This book is none other than the Bible. The Bible is the most important book that has been written and the most important book that we will ever read. This book reveals the history of God's plan of redemption. It tells us who, and whose, we are, where we came from and where we are going. More than any other book, it gives us a lifetime of never ending discoveries about God. The information is inexhaustible. The more you study the more you get out of it.

Why should anyone read the Bible?

The Bible has extremely important things to say to every human being on Planet Earth and the information is life changing. The author of this book is God and He is the only one who truly knows everything, made everything and has everything. In this book He promises an abundant new life which begins now but culminates in an eternity of happiness. The Bible was written by men but God inspired it. In Selected Messages, book 1 pp.416, 20, and 21, my favorite author states "It is not the words of the Bible that are inspired, but the men that were inspired. Inspiration acts not on the man's words or his expressions but on the man himself, who, under the influence of the Holy Ghost, is imbued with thoughts. But the words receive the impress of the individual mind. The divine mine is diffused. The divine mind and will is combined with the human mind and will; thus the utterances of the man are the words of God."

The Holy Spirit impresses the prophets, they chose the words that they express the messages given by God. The prophet's education and background plays an important role in how these messages are written. This is seen throughout the Bible where the prophets use the language of others to express the message which is the word of God. Much of the language in the New Testament is borrowed from the Old Testament. It is still God's words to us. The Bible is God's instruction book to us. With the exception of the Ten Commandments the words of the Bible were not written by God in his own language instead He used imperfect human beings to express His will for us.

To really know God and to develop a deep personal relationship with Him we must read his book to obtain the knowledge we need to fulfill his expectations of us. Of all the books that have been written in this world this book is by far the most important because it is the book that most comprehensively reflects who God really is and in it God outlines how we should live. Since the entrance of sin on Planet Earth all things have deteriorated and are still getting worse but the Creator of Planet Earth has a plan of redemption and restoration not only for inhabitants of Planet earth but for Planet Earth itself. God has miraculously outlined His divine plan of salvation for the human race in the Bible. This book is filled with hidden truths that can only be discovered by diligent studying and the more you study the more treasures you will find. It contains simple and complex truths written in many literary styles. God uses life stories, prophecy, history, poetry and parables to reveal Himself to us and to teach us the various aspects of his salvation plan for us. The Bible is our guide to the highest achievements in this life and its knowledge is essential for true success. In this book are numerous hidden treasures that no other book can offer. As we trace the history of God's salvation plan we will see the picture of a loving God who is guiding and leading His people from the beginning of this world to the end of it.

A book of Communication

Created in every human being is the need to communicate. Losing one's ability to communicate is a devastating loss. Communication is vital to relationships and a civilized world. Through this Book more than any other book God communicates with us. Communication with God is vitally essential to our lives both physically and spiritually. When we cut off communication with God we become separated from the source of our light and truth. The Bible teaches us how to communicate with God who is holy. How does a sinful human being communicate with a Holy God? The Bible tells us how to. The Holy Bible is one of the most important tools God uses to communicate with us. A study of the Bible helps us to understand how God communicates with us. There are some people who claim that God is always talking to them and advising them on all the issues of their lives. How can you tell if God has really spoken to someone? When someone says to you "the Lord gave me a message for you," how do you know that that it is truly a message from God? How can you tell whether or not the Lord is communicating with them? The Bible instructs us in Isaiah 40:8 that in order to tell if someone is speaking the truth you examine them to the law and to the testimony given in the Bible and if they do not speak according to the word of God they have no light in them. To know if someone does not have the inspiration of the Holy Spirit you must study the word of God to be familiar with the law and the testimony of the Bible.

God powerfully communicates with us through two main books, the Bible and through the book of nature. The Bible portrays God as a powerful, loving God who protects, sustains and provides for us. Genesis chapters 1&2 reveals that when God placed the first man and woman on Planet Earth he had daily direct face-to-face communication with them. Sin entered Planet Earth and ended that direct communication so a Holy God chose other methods of communication. Some of these methods are described in the Bible. Some are *(1) by voice (2) from angels, (3) Through Dreams (4) Urim and the Thummim in ancient Israel. (5) Through God, the Holy Spirit who lives in every child of God (6) in nature (7) In the person of Jesus Christ (8) Through Prophets.*

1. **By voice** – The Bible describes instances when God communicated to us with a voice. Some examples are Exodus 19:19 states that God descended on Mt. Sinai and answered Moses by a voice. In Matthew 3:17 at the baptism of Jesus as Jesus came out of the water God the Father's voice was heard saying "This is my beloved son in whom I am well pleased." God spoke to Saul by voice saying "Saul, Saul why are you persecuting me."

2. **Through angels** – Hebrews 1:4 says that angels are ministering spirits sent forth to minister to those who will inherit salvation. Throughout the Bible there are many documented evidences of angels communicating with man, some examples are Job,

Daniel, Joseph and Mary, Zacharias the father of John the Baptist etc. Every human being is assigned a guardian angel at birth and only in eternity would we know how they have protected us during our lives.

3. **Through dreams** – The Bible shows that God communicates through dreams e.g. King Nebuchadnezzar, Joseph, Jacob, Pharaoh, many of the prophets etc.

4. **The Urim and the Thummim** – In ancient Israel God communicated to the High Priest through the *Urim and the Thummim.* These stones were placed on the High Priest's garment and when God gave a positive answer there was a light on the stone, when the answer was no a shadow covered the stone.

5. **Through the Holy Spirit** – who works within us to convict us of sin and lead us back to God.

6. **Through Jesus Christ** – God gave us a vivid demonstration of Himself in the person of Jesus Christ. God became a man and revealed to us who He really is.

7. **In nature** – In the beauty of nature that is still found in this sin cursed earth to the majestic splendor of the Heavenly bodies God communicates to us that we have an awesome creator. Romans 1:20 tells us that "for the invisible things of God from the creation of the world are clearly seen, being understood by the things that are made, even His eternal power and Godhead, so that they are without excuse." The Heavens are telling us that there is an intelligent designer.

8. **Through his prophets** – God has chosen these human beings and revealed Himself to them and many of them have recorded these communications in the Bible. 2 Peter 1:21 "For the prophecy came not in old time by the will of man but holy men of God spoke as they were moved by the Holy Spirit." The Bible is the word of God as revealed under the inspiration of the Holy Spirit. 2 Timothy 3:16 states that "all scripture is given by the inspiration of God." The Bible is a God inspired book. If there is one book on Planet earth that every human being should become familiar with, it is the Bible. Ignorance of God's word is no excuse. If you are capable of reading the Bible do so without delay.

Studying the Bible

A lot of people find it difficult to read the Bible. The standard King James Version can be challenging because it uses words and phrases that we do not use today. We are a privileged generation in that there are many modern day translations that make the Bible easier to understand e.g. the New International Version, the Good News Bible, the New King James Version. The more versions you read the more information you have available to understand what the text is saying. The Old Testament was originally written in Hebrew and Aramaic and the New Testament in Greek. If you are not versed in these languages, the many translations help you to see the picture better. It is like looking at an object from different angles, it broadens your understanding. When you open the Bible pray earnestly for understanding and God's Holy Spirit will guide you into the truths of the Bible. One does not need to be a biblical scholar to understand the Bible. God's admonition to us is to study the Bible diligently for ourselves and his Holy Spirit will guide us. God wants us to diligently study His word for ourselves. Do not rely on others to interpret God's word for you. People can lead you astray if you do not read it for yourself. So develop a Bible study plan that fit your needs. I do not suggest that you start reading from cover to cover as you would soon get lost in the details of the early books but develop a study plan over a period of time. Start to read the stories of the Bible they reveal the main point of the Bible which is God and his redemptive plan for us. Develop a study plan around that and see how all of the stories in the Bible revolve around this main theme. Find out why Jesus told a story, to whom He told the story and what does He want you to learn from the story. Another approach is to pick a theme in the Bible e.g. grace or sanctification and develop a Bible study around that. Later in this book I will discuss some of the great themes of the Bible and show you how they reveal an awesome loving and patient God who is ever reaching out to save us. When you develop a love and appreciation for the Bible, reading it gives you a deep joy and a peace that passes all human understanding. No one can feel that for you. You can deal much better with the issues of life that you encounter every day because of the biblical insights God has given you to deal with these issues. The Bible provides protection against temptation. When tempted by Satan Jesus often quoted the scriptures e.g. "it is written man shall not live by bread alone but by every word that comes out of the mouth of God."

The Bible is the inspired authoritative word of God. It is the most remarkable and incredible book. The Bible is a unique book containing 66 books bound into one book. Twenty-one of these books are mostly prophetic, 22 mostly historical, 21 written in the form of letters and two in poetic form. The Bible reveals God's sovereign will for mankind. In book after book, chapter after chapter, story after story, verse after verse, God lovingly and patiently works out His divine plan of salvation for us. In every story Satan has tried to destroy the plan but God miraculously gets it back on track. It's amazing and so educational to read these stories of how God can restore that which has gone far astray from His divine plan.

The Bible is the Creator's manual for His created beings. It is our moral authority, our guidebook and compass in this life as we prepare for eternal life. It reveals our past, our present and our future. God's divine hand has miraculously preserved this book written over thousands of years ago from about 1500 BC to AD 100 by inspired men from all cultures and walks of life, from a wide spectra of education and social background from kings, statesmen, fishermen, military General, prisoners, Prime Minister, prophets, exiles, priest, tax collector, herdsmen, an ex- Pharisee, poets, physician, scholars etc. The Bible was written by inspired men in their own style of writing under the guidance of the Holy Spirit. The Bible was written in at least 3 languages and from palaces, prison, dungeons, deserts, and exile in at least 3 continents. It is inspired by God and written by 44 authors over a period of 1500 years. Despite the differences in time, geography, race, language, culture etc, these writers under the influence of the Holy Spirit left us with a guidebook with incredible harmony. All of these writers with such widely different backgrounds over thousands of years are all telling the same story of God and His salvation plan for the human race. Mere human effort could not have produced this book now thousands of years old yet more relevant with each passing hour.

The Bible is the infallible enduring unchanging word of God. It is the Revelation of God's thoughts towards us. The Bible stands forever and should not be changed or altered in any way. In Deuteronomy 4:2 God said "you should not add to the word which I command you, neither shall you diminish anything from it, that you may keep the commandments of the Lord your God which I command you." Revelation 22:18 and Proverbs 30: 6 also warns about taking away from the word of God. The Bible claims that it is indestructible and it has survived incredible attempts to destroy it. The prophet Isaiah declares in Isaiah 40:8 that the grass withers, the flower fades: but the word of God shall stand forever. The Bible is thousands of years old. It has worn out many a hammer that has beaten up on it down through the centuries. Philosophers have tried to discredit it, kings have burned it, and emperors thought they had destroyed the last copy, societies have banned it, and great scholars have dissected it and declared its contents false. Its numerous critics claim they have found many discrepancies. Many people think that it is a book of fables. Some keep it in their homes for sentimental reasons maybe it was grandma's Bible. Most people simply ignore it and dust it off when they are cleaning. The Bible annoys some people. In the second century the Roman Emperor Diocletian ordered death for any person seen with the Bible, twenty-one centuries later you can still be killed in some societies if you are seen with a Bible.

Why does God's Holy Work bring on such terrible reactions in some people? Skeptics have long combed its pages looking for errors or inconsistencies, and many people despise and ignore it. Despite numerous heroic efforts to destroy it and generation after generation of its critics have long gone and forgotten the Bible is still a best seller and perhaps the least read bestseller for centuries now. You can probably find a Bible in most homes in America today, yet most people are unaware of the contents of its sacred pages. Many who read it still do not understand and misinterpret its messages to us. There are too many preachers teachers who really do not know the Bible and their sermons reflect that. The Bible is God's instruction manual for our lives. The Bible has the answer for all of our needs and it is important to read it for and do not depend only on other people's interpretation. Read the Bible for yourself to be informed, get a good Bible dictionary and a Bible concordance, read various commentaries on the Bible, listen to various interpreters but most importantly read it for yourself to be informed so that you can discern truth from error. This is important because Satan's most successful weapon against God's people is that he dresses up error with some truth and we fall for his errors. Most importantly believe in the Bible to be wise and put into practice its admonitions.

The Bible is not a science book nor is it a history book but it has been proven by history, true science, and modern archeology to be accurate. This strong external evidence helps validate what the Bible says and boosts faith for those who need external evidence to validate their faith. The Bible is not just an accurate historical book it stands as a witness of God's plan of salvation and a moral guide to Godly living. The critics and skeptics of the Bible have long doubted these biblical accounts and call them fairy tales but that is changing in the world of modern archeology because the archeologists are digging up these biblical places many of them mentioned in the Bible only. The stones are crying out that the Bible is true.

God authenticates the Bible

You are in good company when you believe the Bible. Jesus the creator of the universe believes the Bible. When Jesus came in human form he validated what the Bible writers penned. In John 5:39 Jesus says, "Search the scriptures; for in them you think you have eternal life for they testify of Me." Jesus authenticated the accounts of the Old Testament and quoted many of them to support His teachings. For example In Luke 24:27 right after His resurrection Jesus appeared to two dejected disciples walking to Emmaus and He began to enlighten them by giving them a Bible study beginning with Moses and all the prophets, He expounded unto them in all the scriptures the things concerning Himself. In Mark 10:6 Jesus authenticates the creation as described in Genesis. Jesus states in Matthew 19:6 "Have you not read that He who made them at the beginning made them male and female. For this cause shall a man leave his mother and father and cleave to his wife and they two shall be one flesh." In Matthew 24:38 Jesus talks about Noah's flood and in Matthew 12:40 He mentions Jonah in the belly of the whale. Jesus the creator of the universe believed and quoted the Bible. The Bible is a Revelation of Jesus and His plan of Salvation. In Matthew 7:24–27 Jesus warns that whosoever hears the word and does what it says is likened to a wise man who builds his house on a rock but if you hear his words and do them not is like the foolish man who builds his house in the sand. The Bible reveals God's will for us and He wants us to obey His will. The entire Bible is relevant to all cultures regardless of time. Jesus quote from the Old Testament writers and the New Testament writers frequently quoted from the Old Testament. Most of the symbolic language used in the book of Revelation can be found in the Old Testament. This is not plagiarism, which is a modern concept; this is the work of the Holy Spirit the common thread of inspiration that created the unity of the Bible written over a 1600-year period.

The Bible reveals our origin

Every human being can trace his or her origin back to God, our creator. He created the first man and woman and they are the origin of all subsequent races. It does not matter if you are a king, a beggar, educated or uneducated, it doesn't matter what culture, or religion or race you call your own; everyone's original heritage can be traced back to Adam and Eve and the Bible states that God created them. Therefore we came from God and our lives and our future destiny is finally determined by God based on the choices we make in this life. When we truly come to the realization that we all have the same origin and destiny it should matter how we treat each other and how we live our lives. Throughout the course of this Bible study we will trace the destiny of mankind and how God is always involved in our salvation and how He uses His foreknowledge to reveal the details of history to us as He communicates His salvation plan for us. You will get a greater insight into the world of the Bible and the plans God has made for you.

Our God is not an absentee Landlord. He powerfully, yet gently, communicates to us through all the works of His hands which includes everything -nature, science, the Bible. Let us briefly look at how God communicates through Science. The wise man Solomon says in Proverbs 1:7 "The fear of the Lord is the beginning of knowledge, but fools despise wisdom and discipline". Science is but one aspect of the handiwork of our great creator. God has also revealed Himself to us through the works of his hands, the firmament and this vast universe. The glory of God is displayed in the works of His hands. In Psalms 19:1 King David states that "the Heavens declare the glory of God and the firmament shows his handiwork." In Romans 1:20 Paul tells us that since the creation of the world God's invisible attributes are clearly seen being understood by the things that are made, even his eternal power and Godhead, so there is no excuse for not believing in

God. God has a vast universe which runs in perfect order. Sin and its' devastating effects on Planet Earth are an aberration to the perfect order of God's universe. All of the laws that make possible our understanding of science and all other disciplines were ordained by God. God's has laws that govern all of His creation as evidenced by the preciseness and the order of things in nature. When you look at the visible things of creation does it seem to just happen or does it seem to be the hands of a master designer? Which seems more logical, someone created everything from nothing or no one created everything from nothing? If when you return home from work one day you notice that all of your belongings in your house were lined in perfect order in your front yard would you say that that your belongings put themselves there or would you more appropriately think that someone did that. If you went to the bank and all your money was missing would you assume that the money moved itself? Similarly when you look at this highly organized vast universe and even our solar system do you think that such precise organization just happened from chaos? Can you really accept the theory that this vast universe and all of life organized itself from chaos? Did the big bang give rise to this limitless highly organized universe? The Bible tells us no way. There is nothing random about this universe. The Bible tells us that God the infinite creator created and sustains His universe. He is big and powerful enough to rule this vast universe, yet He condescended and mysteriously became one of His creation to save us from eternal extinction. This great big God of the universe has chosen to live in the humble hearts of those who make Him their Lord and savior.

We are part of God's creation

God is an awesome creator whose works are beyond our greatest discoveries. From His scientific lab out of human reach He speaks and galaxies are formed. He is awesome He can create and destroy. God's infinite power to create is a mystery to us. I have always been baffled by the fact that so many scientists refuse to discern God in His creation. When science is rightly understood it is in harmony with its creator. The Psalmist David in Psalms 14: 1 indicates that only a fool would say that there is no God. His son Solomon writes in Proverbs 1:7 "The fear of the Lord is the beginning of knowledge: but fools despise wisdom and instruction." The things that God has revealed to us in this life are ours to know. Nature all around us attests to an infinite creator. The beauty of springtime and the innumerable variety of flowers and blossoming trees shows how lavish our Creator is. The beauty of nature reveals that He is altogether lovely. The universe reveals that He is more than awesome. Recent scientific discoveries have shown that the Bible is correct our universe is limitless. This unending limitless universe does not create or sustain itself. Long before the Hubble telescope was invented, the Bible unmistakably states that God created and sustains this vast universe. The Bible tells us that there are three heavens, the atmospheric Heavens that surround our Planet Earth (Genesis 1:20), the starry Heaven above that where the stars are (Genesis 1:14-19), then Heaven itself or paradise (2 Chronicles 12:4), where God's lives, way out there beyond the bounds of human perception or ability to reach or see. Only God's mighty creative energy and His infinite power can create and sustain this never ending universe in space and to sustain billions of Heavenly bodies all doing their appointed tasks in perfect order. We know very little about this vast universe of which we are but a minute speck. God suspends planet earth in space and designed that it should move an average of 67,062 miles an hour as it orbits the sun. Planet Earth is a tiny speck of cosmic dust in this vast universe that is limitless. It would take 1.3 million earths to equal the size of our sun. Our sun is miniscule in comparison to Antares another star in our solar system and Antares is nothing in size in comparison to Pistol Star a star in the center of the Milky Way which releases 10 million times the power of the sun. It is estimated to be about 25,000 light years away from Earth and it is still in the center of the Milky Way. Traveling at the speed of light at 186,000 miles per second it would take 4 light years to get to our nearest star and there are billions and billions of stars. This universe is so vast it is beyond man's perceptive abilities. We can only come up with man-made theories about God's universe. Greater and more magnificent than anything in this universe is the God of the Universe and the more of the universe we see is the more we can understand how the works of His hands reveals His magnificence.

The Bible reveals our origin

We do not need to speculate or come up with incredible theories regarding the origin of life or the origin of Planet Earth or the universe. Under the inspiration of the Holy Spirit, the writer of the book of Genesis has given us the history of our origins. Genesis 1:1 states "in the beginning God created the heaven and the earth," the Bible does not give us the date of this beginning when this earth was just a floating mass in space in what we now know as the Milky Way. The Milky Way is but one of the billions of galaxies in the universe. It is the home of our solar system; As far as we can tell it is about 120,000 light years in diameter and 300,000 light years in circumference. It is estimated to have about 400 billion stars and their planets. The Bible tells that the stars cannot be numbered. In Jeremiah 33:22 the prophet states that the host of Heaven cannot be numbered. We now know that space is endless with more than billions of planets, more stars than the sands of the sea, it takes billions of years for light from distant planets to reach us traveling at the speed of light.

Did all of this happen by chance? Who created all of these amazing things and gave us eyes to behold them? Who created the stars? Who created and sustains us? Acts 17:28 states for "in Him we live, move and exist", we are His children. A super intelligent, loving God whose intelligence far exceeds His created beings created everything. Psalms 33:6 "by the word of the Lord were the Heavens made; and all the host of them by the breath of His mouth. He spoke and it was done He commanded and it stood fast." God speaks and energy turns into matter. God is the creator of science and true science agrees with its creator. Today in too many centers of education science is separated from its creator and often placed above its creator. Most of the misunderstanding or confusion in the scientific world comes from inadequate knowledge of God and His creation. Eventually when more discoveries are made Science agrees with the Bible. It has to because it has the same creator. As more and more of this universe is discovered more and more scientists today are coming out of the cold and admitting that there has to be an intelligent super designer. You would have to be in a state of deep denial not to realize that this complex unending universe in not self-existent or self-propagating. Science is not God, it reveals God's creative works. Science cannot tell us who our creator is and what He expects of us. God uses the Bible to tell us what He is like and what He wants us to do. Hebrews 1:1-3 "God, who at sundry times and in divers manners spoke in time past unto the fathers by the prophets hath in these last days spoken unto us by His son, whom He hath appointed heir of all things, by whom He made the *worlds*." This same Jesus who died on a wooden cross is the same God who created and sustains this universe. God created worlds and there is life in other worlds who worship their creator God; we are not here alone. The prophet in Nehemiah 9:6 says "Thou, even thou, art Lord alone, thou hast made Heaven, the Heaven of Heavens, *with all their host*, the earth, and all the things therein, and thou preserve them all; and the host of Heaven worships thee." Job 26:7 "He stretches out the north over the empty place, and hangs the earth upon nothing." God the Holy Spirit reveals this to the prophets and now science is confirming these statements.

Putting science in its proper place

Much more important than discovering science is the discovery of the God who created science. Scientists like Bohr and Ernest Rutherford did not create the atom; they discovered the existence of the atom and more modern physicists today are discovering the existence of even smaller subatomic particles. We have only just begun to discover God's handiwork. God's creativity is never ending and true science leads us to more and more discoveries of our awesome Creator. The Theory of Relativity existed before and after Einstein, the Law of Gravitation existed before and after Newton. This expansive universe was there long time before Hubble and man will make better telescopes than Hubble and discover more of God's handiwork. We are blessed by the knowledge of these scientists who are discovering what the true scientist has made. Scientists of the 17th century believed that they were discovering the handiwork of God. In more recent centuries scientists have not acknowledged God as the Creator. One of the discoveries of modern science is that most of the universe is made up of things that we cannot see. God created all of these things a long time before man discovered them. The Principles of Mathematics were created by God and discovered by man. Life is dependent on the laws of mathematics. Without cell division we cannot reproduce. God made it so.

Every discipline of Science teaches us more about the Great Creator and Master Designer. The numerous disciplines of science attests to the depth and wisdom of God and it is an insult to the Great Creator to attribute such intricate and complex functions that we are ever discovering to chaotic evolution. How silly would it be to say that New York City with its numerous buildings, parks, bridges and highways is the result of some cosmic accident? How incredible it is to believe that the human body is the result of chaotic evolution. Well, the human body is infinitely more complex that anything on Planet earth and the evidence is blinding that we are created and sustained by a powerful God. There are so many disciplines of science such as physics and mathematics that function harmoniously and we are able to study them because of constant God given laws. There is nothing random about these laws. God's universe is governed by His laws.

The biblical prophets acknowledge that God is the creator of this universe. The prophet Nehemiah declares "You alone are the Lord who made Heaven, the Heaven of Heavens, with all their host, the earth, and all that are therein and Thou preserves them all" (Nehemiah 9:6). David writes in Psalms 102 "of old you laid the foundations of the earth and the Heavens are the work of Thy hands." The apostle Paul in Hebrews 11:3 writes "through faith we understand that the worlds were framed by the word of God, so that the things which are seen were not made of things that are visible."

Moses recorded the story of our creation in the book of Genesis. The Holy Spirit inspired Moses as he wrote the first five books in the Bible and Jesus in John 5:47 states "for had you believed Moses, you would have believed me: for he wrote of *me*. But if you believe not Moses writings, how shall you believe my words?" Here Jesus who is the creator of all things authenticates the words of Moses. Moses affirms Jesus as God of the Old Testament. The Godhead is one. The prophet Isaiah in Isaiah 42:5, writes "Thus saith God the Lord He that created the Heavens, and stretched them out; he that spread forth the earth, and that which cometh out of it." Isaiah 40:28 "Has thou not known? Has thou not heard that the Everlasting God, the Lord the creator of the ends of the earth, fainteth not, neither is weary? There is no searching of his understanding." In Psalms 33:6 David states "that by the word of the Lord were the Heavens made and all the host of them by the breath of his mouth…. He spoke and it was done he commanded and it stood fast." God can do anything but fail. He can create a world instantly if He wants to. God does not need existing matter to create anything. *God can do anything that He wants to.*

The true origin of the species

Under the inspiration of the Holy Spirit the apostle John living in the first century AD writes in John 1 that Jesus is the word and the creator of everything and He was there at the beginning with the Father. He is not a created being. He is the creator of everything.

The first day of creation

The prophet Moses who lived about 1500 to 1400 BC under the same inspiration of the Holy Spirit wrote in Geneses 1:1 that in the beginning God created the Heaven and the earth. In Genesis 1:2 he continues to describe the creation of our world and it states that in the beginning this earth was without form and void and darkness was everywhere on this earth. It further states that God the Holy Spirit was present at creation of this earth and the Holy Spirit of God moved upon the surface of the waters. Then God, who is light, said let there be light and he commanded light to come forth from the darkness and it did. God called the light day and the darkness night. The end of these activities God called the first day of creation of Planet Earth. The Bible clearly states in Genesis 1:8 that the evening and the morning were the first day. God created the day to begin at sundown, that is the way it was at creation, the evening and the morning were the first day. In Leviticus 23:32 God admonishes "from even to even shall ye celebrate your Sabbath." It is clear that God created a day beginning at sundown to the next day sundown. This twenty-four hour period of night and day has not changed since God placed man on Planet Earth some 6000 years ago. *This is the origin of day and night since the first week of creation.*

In the beginning of habitation of Planet Earth God spoke light into existence. He is the source of all physical and spiritual light. God saw the light and declared that it was good and he separated the light from the darkness. When God shine His light on you, you will no longer be in spiritual or physical darkness. Second Corinthians 4:6 states "For God who commanded the light to shine out of darkness, hath shined in our hearts to give the light of knowledge of the glory of God in the face of Jesus Christ".

The second day of creation

On the second day God divided the waters into two parts, the atmosphere with its water vapors and clouds and the water on the earth such as seas, rivers. God surrounds the earth with this atmosphere and He created the physical laws that govern its' operation. The sequence of creation indicates He prepared the right environments to sustain His subsequent creation.

The third day

On the third day, God caused all the waters on the earth to be gathered in one place so the dry land which God called earth was separated from the water, then He ordered the earth to grow grass, herbs to produce seeds, and seed bearing trees to bear fruit after their kind suggesting different plants within the same species and God saw His creation and called it good. Today 6,000 years after God's creation was marred by sin we still see plants and trees reproducing after their own kind. A tomato plant is still a tomato, carrots are still carrots, grass is still grass and today we enjoy a variety within the species as God had ordained in the genetic makeup of these original plants and trees. This is a very simplistic overview of this aspect of creation because the wisdom of God is past human understanding and His creation works are beyond our full understanding.

The fourth day

On the fourth day, God appointed two great skylights the greater light called the sun to rule the day and the other lesser light the moon to rule the night. (Remember that night and day were created on the 1st day). These lights were not only to control the day and night 24-hour cycle but also to control the seasons and years. The earth makes a complete rotation on its axis in a day; the earth makes a complete revolution around the sun every year according to God's physical laws. This has continued in its God ordained orderly manner since creation week. God appointed these Heavenly bodies for His own purposes. They are not to be worshipped as gods as many have done; they fulfill God's purposes for Planet Earth.

The fifth day

On the fifth day God, after God had created the proper environment to sustain life, He created the sea creatures, the great whales to the tiniest fish etc and the birds of the air.

The sixth day

God created a vast number of animals. the land animals, the cattle after its kind, the great dinosaurs and every creeping thing after their kind suggesting that God created a lot of different kind of animals and plants. This has not changed since creation, today we still see dogs having dogs, fowl having fowl, monkeys having monkeys, and baboons having baboons. We do not see evolution from one lower species to another and the account of Genesis does not support an evolutionary process but a creation of distinct kinds and variation within species as dictated by the Laws of Genetics. 6000 years later we cannot cross one species with another. You cannot cross a cat and a chicken. Within each species we still see the fascinating display of the genetic information that God created. The God of Genetics created these genes and placed them in his creation and we are able to discover them because of the basic laws of genetics that God created in the beginning. God's word has remained the same forever. The Bible declares that God speaks and worlds are formed. He command and they come forth. God said it is so and it is so. God did not leave us without information. He told us that he is the creator of everything and left an account of creation in Genesis.

On the sixth day of the creation of Planet Earth the Godhead, having prepared the right environment during the preceding five days, did what is called the Crowning Act of Creation. In Genesis 1:26 God the Father said to God, the Son *"Let us make man in our own image and in our own likeness. This* includes not only a physical appearance but also mentally and spiritually. Man was able to love and communicate with God and with each other on a much higher level than the animals but on a little lower order of created beings than the angels (see Hebrews 2:7). God could have spoken man into existence but according to Genesis 2:7 God took the inanimate dust of the ground and formed animate man. God took a lump of clay and molded it into a complex human being that He named man. When he was finished man lay lifeless before Him and God stooped over and breathe into the first man the breath of life and the lungs filled up with air and man started to breathe, the heart start pumping blood around the body, the brain and every other organ started to function, the eyes behold its' creator and the ears heard his voice and man became a living soul. The process reverses at death, the breath leaves body and man is no longer a living soul, his body decomposes and returns to dust from which he was made. Every element in man's body can be found in the dust of the earth. Ecclesiastes 3:20 says "all go unto one place; all are from dust and all turn to dust again." This is an undisputable fact for all mankind.

Just imagine when man saw his creator and they first conversed. Just imagine the first conversation. God may have said "Your name is Adam and you are the first man." God put Adam in charge of all the earth and Adam named the living creatures, there were two of each. The creatures were created male and female. God created man with a photographic memory. There was no need for books or computers. On the same day he took a rib from the man and created another human being. When Adam saw her he said she came out of man and so she shall be called woman. This is the origin of the first man and woman. Adam and Eve were joined together in holy matrimony and became one flesh on the sixth day of creation. This institution of marriage created in the beginning has been under constant fire and attack by Satan and he has destroyed so many marriages. In the beginning man was created in the image of God perfect in beauty and character. Every human being is of royal descent. We can trace our roots back to the Divine Creator. We did not come from a blob of slime or a monkey, as Satan would like us to believe. We are the handiwork of the Divine Creator of this universe who has infinite wisdom, infinite knowledge and infinite power. The concept that man evolved from a lower form of life is a major deception of Satan as he wages his great controversy against God. The opposite is the truth man came from the hand of an awesome infinite powerful Creator.

God infinite power

God has infinite power and can destroy us instantly. The Bible portrays that God so love us that He died to save us from sins destruction rather than destroying us with His mighty power. He patiently and gently calls us to Him. He uses the trials of this life to refine our character and make us fit for a place in His home that He is preparing for His redeemed. Mortal man cannot begin to understand the infinite power of God. Jesus addressed this issue in Mark 12:19–25. The Sadducees were a group of religious political Jews who thought they were intellectuals. They only believed the first five books of the Bible, they did not believe in the resurrection, or angels or the Holy Spirit. Jesus was in the temple on the Tuesday before His crucifixion and instead of realizing they were in the presence of the awesome God who created the universe and who in three days would die to save lost humanity; they did not accept Jesus as God and they tried to stump Jesus by asking Him this question, if a man dies and leave his wife behind and left no children and this is repeated over and over so that she marries the seventh brother and still left no children, in the resurrection whose wife should she be? Jesus could read their insincerity but always ready to save lost humanity He gently replied, "you are in error and do not know the scriptures, neither do you know *the power of God.*" Jesus continues that in the resurrection there will be no marriage, the resurrected saints will be like angels there will be a higher state of affairs and relationships like marriage will pale in comparison. God has greater things in store for us, eyes have not seen or ears heard the great things God has for the redeemed of Planet Earth. The point that Jesus made that should not be missed is that they had *no clue how powerful God is.* These were supposed to be learned men of understanding and yet Jesus said they did not know the scriptures. The God who created this universe can do anything; the idea that God needs billions of years to create is another deception of Satan and not consistent with the biblical account of creation. God can speak this world into existence in an instant. As high as the Heavens are from the earth so are Gods ways higher than our ways and His thought higher than our thoughts. God created this vast universe eons before the existence on man on this planet.

The seventh day of Creation

Genesis 2:2 and 3 "And on the seventh day God ended His work which He had made; and He rested on the seventh day from all his work which He had made. And God blessed the seventh day and sanctified it: because that in it He had rested from His work which God created and made." God finished His creative work on Planet Earth in six days and He saw everything that He had made and it was very good. On the seventh day of Creation God rested from all the work that He had done and set the seventh day apart from the other days and sanctified it as a permanent commemoration of His creation. Sanctified means that God made this specific 24hour block of time holy. This seventh day He called the Sabbath. On this day once a week since the creation of this world man has a divine appointment with His creator and do not let Satan or anyone else tell you otherwise. On this day once a week man rests from his daily labor and develops his intimate relationship with God and acknowledges God as the creator of all things. In the beginning God blessed this specific day and gave it to Adam and Eve and all subsequent mankind as a weekly reminder of His creative power and He commanded that mankind remember to keep it holy every week. The seven days of creation are the origin of the weekly cycle that we have today; this weekly cycle, unlike the day, the month and year does not revolve around God's creation such as the sun and moon but around God Himself. The Sabbath institution and the marriage institution that were created in Eden before the entrance of sin has been under constant attack from Satan and he has been successful in undermining and destroying both institutions. Satan hates God's seventh-day Sabbath and he hates the institution of marriage.

It took God one week to create our world. He could have created it all in an instant but He took one week. It was all done for our benefit so we can appreciate His creative and his redemptive plan. Six days He gave us to work and play but the seventh day He gave us to keep holy and worship him as creator. This is the simplified biblical version of creation that was written by the inspired writer of Genesis. Under the influence of the Holy Spirit God's prophet Moses recorded the book of Genesis. Is there a more complicated, more scientific version of creation? I believe so. I believe that through the ceaseless ages of eternity God's children will study God great scientific works, which include the creation of our planet and the creation of this vast limitless universe. I believe that one day the redeemed of this world will learn from the master designer Himself and we will be able to fill in many of the blanks that we are not told now.

The Bible was not written as a history book giving us the perfect chronology of the creation and the history of mankind. It contains instructions how we can live a life that is acceptable to God. It is meant to portray the great controversy over Planet Earth, the lives of people in this great controversy and most importantly the story of our redemption and Gods plan to save His faithful children from this doomed planet. It tells us how to live Godly lives. In 1 Corinthians 2 Paul stated here that he was determined not to know anything except Jesus Christ and him crucified. Paul declares that the wisdom of this world and the princes of this world would come to nothing but the wisdom of God is a mystery, even the hidden mystery, which God ordained before the world for our glory. He further states "eyes have not seen, ears have not heard neither has it entered in to the mind of man the things that God has prepared for them that love him." God, the Holy Spirit has revealed these things to us because the Holy Spirit knows the deep things of God. The natural man does not accept spiritual things; they are foolishness to him; he cannot know these things because spiritual things are spiritually discerned. You cannot appreciate the Bible unless the Holy Spirit leads the way. The apostle Paul admonishes us to spend our time wisely and concentrate on Jesus and His great salvation plan for us. On this side of heaven and at this time in our history God want us to concentrate mainly on the essentials of salvation not on the science of creation. We will have an eternity to study the details. It is quite evident that we are not here by accident. God sustains this planet and he has physical and moral laws that govern His vast creation, including us.

Man the crowning act of creation week

The creation of man on the sixth day of creation is often referred to as the crowning act of the creation week. God created man and put him in charge of His earthly creation. The advent of sin on Planet Earth has wreaked havoc and we see the deterioration of man and the Planet Earth and today we have vivid evidence that our planet is deteriorating faster than we think. The prophet in Isaiah 51:6 told us that the earth will wear out like a garment and its inhabitants will die likewise but the salvation of the Lord will be forever and His righteousness will never fail. We will all die but our God ever exists and it is only through Him that we can live on and obtain eternal life and its rich inheritance. Genesis 2:7 states that God formed man from the dust of the ground and after man sinned God said in Genesis 3:19 for dust thou art and unto dust shall you return. God created this intricate human body from dust and when we die we return to dust. This is an obvious fact from the greatest to the least of us when we die we return to the dust from which we were formed. It's astounding to me that man can believe they evolved from a lower form of life. The evolution of man is another deception of Satan. It is mind boggling that this complex human being returns to mere dust.

The formation and operation of this complex body is beyond human understanding. The study of our complex human body is humbling to say the least; it cannot be mastered by the most brilliant mind. The scientific discoveries about the human body are inexhaustible. I cannot keep up with the scientific information that I get in the few medical journals that I subscribe to. The information in these journals is constantly changing as man discovers more of God's creation. Anyone with a working knowledge of the body from a microscopic to a macroscopic viewpoint can only marvel at the intricacies of its design and it shows beyond the shadow of a doubt that there is a masterful designer and an awesome creator. It is mind boggling when we think that every second there are trillions of chemical actions and reactions taking place in the estimated trillions of cells that make up our body. At rest we effortlessly breathe about 12–16 breaths a minute (16,000–23,000 times a day) through a mechanism that involves complex respiratory physiology that allows us to breathe in oxygen and eliminate carbon dioxide from our bodies. We cannot exist without oxygen for more than a few minutes; we can exist without water for days and food for weeks but not oxygen. How does a normal heart continue to beat 100,000 times a day and pump blood through thousands of miles of arteries every minute? Who created this enduring cardiac muscle and electrical system that conducts the heartbeat. God created each with about 35 trillions of cardiac cells with automaticity, excitability and conductivity. Automaticity means the cell can begin and maintain its rhythm on its own. Excitability means the cell can respond to an electrical stimulus. Conductivity means a cardiac cell can conduct an impulse to another cell so fast that all areas of the heart respond or depolarize at the same time. The transfer of an impulse in the heart cells vary. An impulse can transfer in the AV node about 200 mm per second, 400mm per second in the ventricular muscle, 1000 mm per second in the atrial muscle and 4000 mm per second in the Purkinje fibers. Every Cardiac cell in its resting position has a negative charge on the inside and a positive charge on the outside. When a cardiac impulse is initiated there is a movement of sodium, potassium and calcium across the cell membrane. This excites the cell and depolarizes it by causing the exchange of these ions. This spreads from cell to cell until the cardiac muscle is depolarized. The reverse then takes place and is called repolarization so that the cell can get back to its resting state for the arrival of the next impulse. This whole process can occur is less that a second and this is occurs 60 to 100 times a minute in the normal heart for up over a hundred years in some people.

The SA node of the heart does not require a signal from the brain to beat, God created it with automaticity. In the embryo the heart begins to beat before the brain is formed and in some illnesses the heart continues to beat even after brain death is declared. Soon we are going to have to revise our textbooks on how the heart works. Current research indicates that the heart has a brain of its own. It has about 40,000 neurons in the atria. The heart is a sensory organ and it communicates with the brain biochemically through hormones, and neurotransmitters, neurologically through nerve impulses, biophysically through pressure waves and energetically through electromagnetic field interactions. We frequently measure the heart's electrical field from the body surface by the electrocardiogram. The heart's electromagnetic field is estimated to be 5,000 times greater than that of the brain and it can be measured in all directions several feet from the body. This area of research is very exciting from a biblical standpoint and we can now expand our understanding of many biblical texts such as "create in me a clean heart of God and renew a right spirit within me." The Bible has always indicated that the heart and brain were connected. The heart has emotional intelligence and the researchers has coined the phrase Heart Intelligence which describes numerous attributes of electrical and magnetic energy waves radiating from the heart that influence functions and systems including the brain. Mankind has only just begun to unravel some of the science of creation. There are trillions upon trillions of other cells in the brain, the kidney, the lungs, the gastrointestinal tract, the skin and all the other organ systems that have their unique very complex functions and together they function in unity to promote a healthy body. This is just a bird's eye look at a speck of the human body function. It is inconceivable to me that these trillions of cells working in harmony to produce a functioning human being organized itself from chaos. This is the handiwork of an infinite creator. Give Him the honor and praise.

The human body is just one example of God's creative handiwork and it takes a lifetime of study to understand the basics which is ever expanding. We have been studying it for centuries and yet we have only just begun. There is still so much more to know. In 2003 the Human Genome Project was completed. A genome is an organisms complete set of DNA. A bacteria has about 600, 000 DNA base pairs while a human has about 3 billion DNA base pairs. In the human genome DNA is arranged into 24 chromosomes. Each chromosome contains genes but genes make up only about two percent of the human genome. Our genes contain our hereditary code. Of the genes discovered we still do not know the function of 50% of these genes. We know that certain genes are associated with certain diseases. It is estimated the human genome has about 30, 000 genes and that these genes and proteins along with all the other components of the body work harmoniously together to produce a healthy human being. Every cell in the human body carries these complex codes of genetic information. This complex genetic code is called the language of God. God created these millions of nucleotide bases that comprise the human genome.

When the great geneticist created Adam his DNA had the potential for all the races of the world. He created a perfect DNA with no diseases. Sin entered our planet and caused subsequent DNA mutations and diseases. Genetics is just one field of study and we have only just begun to unravel its' complexity. The study of one organ can take a lifetime to master what is known about it. Just think of the creation of the human eye a billion times more sophisticated than any camera, the billions of nerve cells, the blood vessels of the eye, the ability to process objects and present it as a picture to the brain, and eyelids to protect the eye, tear ducts that bathe the eyes, an eye socket that protects the eye, the muscles, the lens – the creator of the eye is an awesome creator. The brain is another masterpiece that is wonderfully made. How these 100 billion brain cells can work harmoniously to conduct its numerous chemical reactions. How does a brain cell develop the ability to produce and process thoughts, numerous ideas, reason, and describe itself? How does it remember things, how does it display the myriad of emotions like happiness, sadness and laughter? How does it have desires? How does it love, hate, smile, or frown? This is not happenstance but the handiwork of an infinite creator. We are just now beginning to understand how the condition of our heart physically and emotionally can affect brain functions. Over 3500 years ago King Solomon wrote in Proverbs 17:22 that a merry heart doeth good like a medicine: but a broken spirit dries the bones. Today we know that laughter boosts the immune system and depression has the opposite effect. The Bible teaches that when the Holy Spirit takes residence in our hearts our minds will be transformed. God created us this way. The question is what has God placed in our hearts? Are there receptors that yearns for him and eternity? Is that why we are not satisfied with life and we keep searching for more and more? Some people saturate their receptors with drugs, some with pleasures, money but they are still not satisfied. Did God place within us these receptors that only bring full satisfaction when they are saturated with the love of God and our fellowmen and not with other earthly achievements? Is that why we are not satisfied not matter how much we have achieved?

The study of the Human Body alone should overwhelm us with the fact that there has to be a Creator. This can only be the work of an infinite beyond intelligent mind. If you understand the human body and how it works you can only marvel at the handiwork of a Great Creator. God's has placed His fingerprint is on all of His creative works. The harmonious functioning of the body attests to the unity of the Godhead who created us.

God is the creator of all of these fields of study and this complex human body is an export from His universal scientific lab that extends throughout this vast universe. To attribute such scientific marvel to random happenstance is to deny the great creator the praise and honor that is due to Him and that is just what Satan wants. Only someone who wants to deny the existence of this Great Creator would attribute this great design that is still beyond human understanding to mere chance. The Great Creator gave us so much evidence of His great creative ability that the psalmist King David proclaimed only a fool would say in his heart that there is no God. He also said we are fearfully and wonderfully made. Today there are specialists for every part of the body. There is Internal Medicine with its numerous specialties. I can think of at least fifteen of them and these specialties have subspecialties. There is surgery with its numerous specialties such as vascular, abdomen, trauma, ear nose and throat specialists, the breast specialists, the head and neck specialists, and neurosurgery. There is Neurology, dermatology, ophthalmology, dentistry, gynecology and their various subspecialties. There are specialists for everything and the reality is despite the remarkable advances of medicine there are so many people today with troubling diseases for which no specialist has the answer. The specialists themselves are afflicted and many of the specialists die from the same diseases that they specialize in. What a humbling thought. I know a well-loved cardiologist with whom I worked for many years who died suddenly from a heart attack leaving hundreds of his cardiac patients with no doctor. There are so many patients today with chronic diseases going from specialist to specialist with no cure in sight. Many are strung out on pain killers because there is no medical cure for their illness so they settle for the amelioration of the pain. Millions are seeking alternative medicine for help. Our urine is rich with dietary supplements that we take to feel better and live longer. Every year we come up with more diagnostic test and equipment. We have more sophisticated diagnostic and surgical equipment today than ever before but we still cannot cure so many of society's ills because we left God out of the equation.

When God created the human body, He made a complex system whose various chemistries come to life and work together when His breath of life was given to it. He created a body that can be affected by many factors that are under the control of the human will. For example a complex structure like the brain, the heart and the major blood vessels are affected by the food we eat, by exercise and other factors like stress. Hence you can be the most famous heart doctor or brain specialist and understand many of the physiologic laws that govern the function of these organs but if you are not aware of the interrelated principles of health and practice these principles in your lifestyle you can be affected by the diseases that affect these organs. On the other hand you can be totally ignorant of the structure and function of these organs and know the principles of healthy eating and not have these diseases. While it is true that many of us inherit diseases through our genes our lifestyle plays a significant role in the disease process. It is said that genetics loads the gun but lifestyle pull the trigger. God combined the body, mind and soul for the optimal function of the human being.

We certainly appreciate the great advances of modern science. We are now able to prevent and ameliorate the effects of many diseases today and our life spans have increased over the past 100 years. Our knowledge has improved tremendously in these last centuries but let's be real, there is nothing like the real thing that God created. Artificial limbs and transplants are merely a human effort to help suffering and they do help, but let's not get carried away, they are what they are, human efforts. The true author of science, God the Creator condescended and became human. He lived among us and left us with substantial evidence of His creative powers. We were not present at creation but the Bible has revealed many eyewitnesses to God's creative and recreative powers. Read 2 Peter 1: 15–21. There are many accounts in the Bible of Jesus demonstrating that He is the Creator. Over 2000 years ago he clearly showed that he knew the interrelationship between body, mind and soul. God who created the human body knew the connection between the mental and the physical and he never healed the physical without first healing the mental. Today medical science is just appreciating the connection between the physical and the spiritual and they are actively studying the effect of the spiritual on the healing processes of the body. When you read the Bible you realize that Jesus didn't separate them, after healing a person from their physical disease he would say go and sin no more lest a worse thing happen to you. Jesus combined the psychological, the spiritual and the physical.

During his earthly sojourn Jesus on numerous occasions demonstrated his creative powers in so many ways. He showed his control over every element. The Bible records numerous evidences of God recreative power of the human body. There are many accounts in the Bible of Jesus demonstrating that He is the Creator. He clearly showed that he knew the interrelationship between body, mind and soul. Jesus never healed the physical without healing the mental and is actively studying the effect of the spiritual on the healing processes of the body. When you read the Bible you realize that Jesus did not separate them. After healing a person from their physical disease he would say "Go and sin no more lest a worse thing happen to you." Jesus combined the spiritual, the psychological and the physical.

During His earthly sojourn, Jesus on numerous occasions demonstrated His total control over every element including the human body. John 5 records the incident when Jesus healed a man paralyzed for 38 years. What a difference it would make in the field of neurology if neurologists could do that for their patients today. Two thousand years ago Jesus completely healed a man with a stroke for 38 years. Today if you can get to a stroke center within three hours we can give you a drug but cannot guarantee that you will get considerable better and sometimes there are devastating side effects from the drug. The Bible says in John 21:25 that if all of the works of Jesus were recorded there would not be space on earth to contain the books that should be written.

Luke, a physician, was one of Jesus' disciples. He described numerous diseases that Jesus healed. In the presence of the Creator diseases had no power over the human body. Time and time again He proved that He controlled nature and he controlled the human body. In Luke 5 a man diseased by leprosy fell on his face and asked Jesus, "Lord, if you will, you can make me clean." Jesus touched the man saying, "I will: be thou clean." Immediately he was healed. Jesus healed many people from leprosy. He is the same God who healed Moses' sister Miriam in Old Testament times. In Matthew 8:28 and 29 after calming a tempest on the Sea of Galilee, Jesus and His disciples came to the country of Gergesenes. Two wild fearsome looking demon possessed men rushed upon Jesus and His disciples, Jesus was not afraid of them. The demons recognized Jesus, Satan knows that Jesus is the Son of God. The demons asked Jesus, "If you decide to cast us out, allow us to go into a herd of pigs in the distance." The pigs soon perished and the men were completely healed of their demonic illness. After Jesus was arrested and was about to be crucified one of His disciples, Peter, could not tolerate the mistreatment of the Lord and in his anger he cut off the ear of the high priest servant Malchus. Jesus picked it up and with spit replaced it and it was as if had never been severed. Jesus healed Peter's mother in law and Roman centurion's servant. He brought back to life the son of a widow from the dead. He brought the leader of the synagogue's daughter back to life. He healed a woman suffering for years with a gynecological problem, beyond help of Medicine. He healed numerous blind people. One of his greatest miracles was raising Lazarus from the dead after four days of death and decomposition. This is no fable, Jesus will bring to life again all the righteous dead at His second coming. He already raised several people from the dead when He arose from the tomb. He took those back to heavy as first fruits of those who will be raised from the dead at his second coming. I can go on with case after case recorded in the Bible but the point is that Jesus has clearly demonstrated that He is the Creator and Restorer of all things. He has ability to restore our bodies totally, if it is according to His divine purpose. It should be noted that not everyone who asks for physical healing is healed physically; most people die from some disease or another. This is often very difficult for us to relate to. We are not given biblical answers why this is so but when this mortal body becomes immortal we will live with Jesus and we will understand it better then.

God's Lifestyle Recommendations

At creation God determined the genetic composition of man. It was perfect with no mutations and hence no diseases. Sin had not yet appeared. The entrance of sin has affected everything on Planet Earth. Our DNA has mutated and we have all manner of diseases. 6000 years after our creation we have just finished unraveling the human genome in the hope that we can understand diseases better. Every cell function whether it is a heartbeat, a thought or any metabolic process, is governed by an *innate process created by God*. God's physical and moral law has significance relevance to our very existence. God ordained simple diets to keep this most complex of machinery the human body in optimal health and He left the instructions for use in his holy word, the Bible. Adherence to God's health care plan is essential for healthy living and would solve the world's heath care crisis.

Healthy Eating

Healthy eating is essential to a healthy lifestyle. Sometimes diseases afflict you no matter how well you eat but there are many diseases you can prevent by choosing the right lifestyle. God has outlined the essentials for healthy living and eating in the Bible. He wants us to read and follow His instructions. Today there are many people getting rich on health care plans while God's free and simple plan is ignored. Who should you listen to the creator of the human body or someone else? How would you know if someone is wrong unless you compare what they say to the Gold Standard of the Bible? In Leviticus 11 God gives detailed instructions on why certain foods should not be eaten. God advises us that of all the beasts on the earth do not eat the ones that have divided hooves, and chew the cud. Specifically mentioned are the camel, the hare, and the pig. The pig is unclean because it does not chew the cud although it divides the hoof. God wants us to obey Him and the prophet Isaiah is given messages on the same subject. In Isaiah 65:2 God said, "All day I reach out to a rebellious people who walk in a way that is not good, and follow their own thoughts. In my face they do things that provoke me to anger like making sacrifices in gardens and lodging in the monuments on graves trying to communicate with the dead and eating pig's flesh." In Isaiah 66:15–17 God warns "Behold, the Lord will come with fire and his chariots to render His anger and fury, and will rebuke with flames of fire. On that day (at the second coming of Jesus) the slain of the Lord will be many. In verse 17 God said He would destroy those who practice strange things by purifying and sanctifying themselves in strange ways, those that eat pig's flesh, and those who eat the mouse will be consumed. In Leviticus 11:12 God gives instructions about the fish that live in the water. You are to eat only the fish that have fins and scales. The ones without fins and scales are an abomination unto you. Examples are lobster, shrimp, scallops, crab, crawfish, scallops, clams, squid, and oysters. Next God describes the unclean fowls and flying insects that are clean or unclean. God gave these health laws to His people.

Some people think that these are only relevant to God's people at that time and that God has cleansed everything. These health laws are relevant to God's people in every generation. When these laws were given those people did not have the knowledge that we have today and they obeyed God's instructions. Today we know that these creatures are scavengers. God made them to clean up the environment and they carry toxic chemicals and parasites. Recently I admitted a woman to the hospital with new onset seizures from a parasitic infection called cysticercosis. She contracted it from eating pork that was not properly cooked. It appears as though God labeled the animals that eat unclean food and the contaminants of society as unclean and we now know that they are the ones that transmit diseases.

It is a mistake to think that the principles of healthy living outlined in the Old Testament are not relevant to God's people today. We can look at the health care industry today and see the major shift towards preventive medicine. That was God's health care plan for us at creation. Satan is seeking to destroy us but God has lovingly given us a healthy lifestyle plan.

Our lifestyle contributes greatly to many diseases such as heart attacks, strokes, Diabetes, Hypertension, cancer and so many gastrointestinal diseases. Our foods contain too much animal fat, too much cholesterol, too much sugar, and too much salt. Many of the clean meats and fish that we eat are contaminated with toxins and antibiotics making them unhealthy for eating. Healthy living and eating can go a long way in solving the health care crisis. Hospitals are inundated every day with people sick because of the abuses of drugs, alcohol, sugar, salt, and fatty foods. He who designed this awesome body left instructions for us in the Bible on how to care for our bodies. In the creation record of Genesis 1:29 God said to Adam and Eve "behold I have given you every herb bearing seed, and every tree in which is the fruit of a tree yielding seed, to you it shall be for meat." God recommended a diet of fruits, vegetables, then nuts, and grains as the original diet. Note that it did not include the flesh of animals. It has taken us 6000 years to prove scientifically that God's original diet that was given to Adam and Eve is the best. Health enthusiasts all over this world are promoting God's original health plan and making a lot of money on the advice that God has freely offered to us. Many refuse to acknowledge God as the originator of this plan. God has given us many natural remedies for health. They are proper nutrition, exercise, water, sunlight, temperance, fresh air, rest and trust in God's divine power. Those who by faith have followed God's blueprint for living have been living longer and healthier lives.

Since the creation of man we have seen a deterioration of the human condition, and the mutation of various genes causing many deadly diseases. The advances in modern science have increased the lifespan of modern man but we are not living healthy lives and living for centuries as was the case shortly after creation. Many of us have inherited genetic diseases. We have also developed bad lifestyle habits such as smoking and drinking, overeating. These can shorten out life span significantly. The lifespan of man shortly after creation was several hundred years. The fruit of the tree of life in the Garden of Eden prolonged life. When man sinned they were barred from the Garden of Eden. Noah's grandfather Methuselah lived 989 years. Then came the great flood. God instructed Noah what he should take in the ark-seven pairs of every clean animal and one pair of every unclean animal. The distinction between clean and unclean animals was told to man by God long before the Jewish nation came into existence. Noah was not a Jew; he lived long before Jews came into history. After the flood of Noah's time Planet Earth changed drastically. It is important to note that after the flood of Noah's day, the vegetation was destroyed and man was given permission to eat the flesh of clean animals. Man's life span changed drastically. There is convincing data that vegetarians live longer than meat eaters. God loves us enough to give us instructions in every aspect of our lives.

There is no question that the optimum functioning of the human body depends on healthy eating and living. The optimum functioning of this complex machine depends on simple God given rules. He made the human body to be subject to his moral and physical laws. Those who are knowledgeable about this amazing human body with its complex cellular structure and function must admit that this has to be the work of a super intelligent Creator. He made the human body to be subject to his moral and physical laws. Those who are knowledgeable about this amazing human body with its complex cellular structure and function must admit that this has to be the work of a super intelligent Creator. It is inconceivable and frankly impossible that these trillions of cells and hormones just randomly got together and produce this complex intricate thinking human being with the ability to love, think, feel, reminisce, talk, laugh, cry and learn. It was not random; God's fingerprints are all over His creation.

There is consistency in God's handy work all over Planet Earth. Everything in this universe points to a Great Creator and He is in control of His vast creation. One day, in God's own time when this sin problem is behind us we will study God's creative handiwork from the Master Creator himself. There would be no confusion and then we will see God clearly because there will be no deceiver. Satan and his deceptions would have been forgotten history. In the meantime God has not abandoned His creation; He is fully in charge and one day soon everything will be back in perfect order. Satan does not want you to know that he is the enemy of God's plan or that he has been undermining God's plan for some 6000 years now. To fully understand why there are so many problems in this world we must understand the enemy and why he has chosen to destroy God's creation.

Satan destroys a perfect creation?

On the sixth day of creation God created the first man and woman, Adam and Eve. They came from the hand of their Creator perfect in beauty and with no genetic defects. God made a special home for them called the Garden of Eden. Genesis 2:10–14 indicates that the Garden of Eden was probably in Iraq. Two of the four heads of the river that came out of Eden are split into the rivers Tigris and Euphrates. This was a beautiful place; they had a great life there that included taking care of the beautiful Garden of Eden. There is something about working in a garden that soothes our nerves and gives us great satisfaction. God gave them permission to eat the fruit of all the trees in the Garden of Eden but in the center of the Garden of Eden, God placed a Tree of Knowledge of Good and Evil. God warned them to stay away from this tree. This place was the testing ground for Adam and Eve's obedience to God. Satan was not given open access to Adam and Eve except for one place in the garden at the tree of knowledge of good and evil. They were warned about this and they were to be on the lookout for him. He knew that God had warned them not to eat of the fruit of the tree of life in the midst of the Garden of Eden. In Genesis 2:17 God told them that 'of the Tree of the Knowledge of Good and Evil, you should not eat of it: for in the day that you eat of it you will surely die." Evidently there was the potential for disaster at this tree. They were not given immortality and God wanted to test their loyalty and obedience to Him and so God placed this tree in the Garden and this was the only place where Satan was allowed access to them. They were permitted to eat of the myriads of trees in the garden but God had warned them in Genesis 3:3 that "of this tree that is in the midst of the garden you shall not eat of it, neither shall you touch it, or you will die."

Satan studied the situation intently and came up with a masterful plan of *deception*. Satan then implemented his plan. He disguised himself in the serpent and perched on the tree of knowledge and began eating the fruit. Eve wandered away from Adam and began gazing at the fruit on the forbidden tree. This was Satan's grand opportunity. The pair was separated and he stood a better chance of deceiving them. He engaged the woman in conversation and Satan speaking through the serpent outright lied to the woman saying "you shall not surely die God knows that when you eat it you shall be as God knowing good and evil." Eve, not suspecting that he devil had disguised himself in this beautiful animal believed the lie and ate the fruit. She did not even ask the question why an animal that was not supposed to talk was talking to her. She listened, believed and was deceived. While in the bliss of Eden they were oblivious of sin, although God forewarned them of Satan's plans to overthrow God's kingdom and to destroy them, Eve found herself at the forbidden tree and there Satan, masked as a serpent, deceived her with a lie. She then gave the fruit to Adam. He knew that she was deceived but because of his great love for her, and seeing that she did not instantly die when she ate the fruit he too disobeyed God and ate the fruit. In the end they both died. The Bible says that a day is a thousand years to God and a thousand years a day. Neither of them lived to be a thousand years. God cannot lie. Satan knows the scriptures and knew that God had told them that the soul that sinned would die. Satan was able to convince Eve that she would not die and that her soul would live on and she would be like God. Satan started this belief that the soul is immortal right here in the Garden of Eden. God said the soul that sins will die. Satan says that the soul is immortal and the soul continues on at death. It is an attractive lie. He deceived Eve with this lie and it still works for him today. Despite the downfall of Adam and Eve with this lie, millions today still hold on to that belief. Satan wrapped the deception so attractively that Adam and Eve bought it. It seemed true but it was an attractive lie.

Eve, and then Adam disobeyed God and temporarily railroaded God's original plan for Planet Earth. Their access to the Garden of Eden was restricted so that they could not gain access to the Tree of Life and be perpetual sinners. Satan now had full access to them to tempt them continually. Pay strict attention to the way Satan deceived Eve He did not identify himself. Instead, he used the most beautiful animal in the Garden. Satan is clever; he studied the situation and came up with a successful plan of deception to overcome Eve. He was successful because Eve did not follow God's plan. Satan studies our situation diligently and he along with his evil angels devises their most successful plan of attack and gets us to stray away from God's plan for us. He carefully packages his deceptions so he can snare his victims. You have to stay with God's plan always or Satan will deceive us.

It was in the Garden of Eden that Satan gained control of Planet Earth. He told her that contrary to God's command, if she ate the fruit she would not die. He told her that God knows that in the day that she eats thereof your eyes would be opened, and she would be like God, knowing good and evil. Satan succeeded again in his deceptions. First he had deceived Heavenly angels into disobeying God's law and now he got Adam and Eve to do the same. Eve then Adam fell for Satan's deception. The serpent was used by Satan as his camouflage. God cursed the serpent and it could no longer fly from tree to tree. It was made lower than the other animals and was limited to crawling on its belly and eating dust. It has been on his belly ever since and is a dreaded creature. When Adam and Eve sinned everything changed, life was no longer a bed of roses. The ground was cursed and brought forth thorns and thistles, the woman was cursed and she had pain in child birth. Satan had more access to them and was now permitted to tempt them. Their natures were changed to a sinful ones and the human race came under the curse of sin and death. Every subsequent human being was born with this carnal nature that is prone to sin.

When man sinned it grieved the heart of his Creator. God did not abandon man; God came down, to commune with Adam and Eve but they hid from Him. Prior to sin communion with God was a daily-anticipated event for them. That changed drastically after sin. We do not know how long Adam and Eve lived in the Garden of Eden before sin. It seemed to have been a short time because they were told to be fruitful and multiply and this did not happen before they succumbed to sin. Sin marred God's perfect creation but the all-knowing God had a plan to deal with sin. God initiated the plan of salvation that was devised long before this world was created. The all-knowing God foresaw that man would sin and He had a plan prepared before man was placed on Planet Earth. Sin changed human nature. Romans 5:12–14 says that because Adam sinned a sinful nature was passed on the every human being, and we all have a death sentence on our heads for all of us have sinned. The good news is that because of God's atoning sacrifice and resurrection those who accept the atoning sacrifice of Christ on their behalf have passed from death into life and what was lost in Adam was redeemed in Jesus Christ.

The redemption of man came at a great price to the Godhead. In an effort to teach man how offensive sin is and the great price that it would cost to redeem man, God instituted the sacrifices of animals that pointed to the coming of the true sacrifice at Calvary. Adam offered animal sacrifices for sin. Abraham offering up his only son as a sacrifice, foreshadowed the coming of the Messiah, the true sacrifice. God initiated these sacrifices to teach the plan of salvation that He was the ultimate sacrifice that these sacrifices pointed to. The entire Bible is story after story of the unfathomable love of God for His creation, His plan of redemption and His second coming. Story after story, century after century reveals God's love and plan of redemption for man. This redemptive plan has been sidetracked, railroaded, harpooned, and misconstrued by Satan but it is still on track. God is patient and is working things out to save anyone who believes and chooses to be saved from this doomed planet.

Satan Kidnapped God's Creation

In six days God created a perfect world with perfect human beings. Satan deceived our forefathers and gained the control of Planet Earth that was given to Adam and Eve in the beginning. Since then things have steadily gone downhill. Deterioration, death and destruction of all things have been the result. Satan is so rampant in the world today and there is so much senseless crime and violence that it defies logic. Sometimes it seems that hardly a day goes by without hearing about a vicious crime or an abused child. Innocent lives are destroyed every second on Planet Earth. Innocent children are killed or kidnapped frequently. Some of their kidnappers hold them for years constantly violating them. Many of these disturbing kidnapping cases hit the national headlines. Every now and then some of these children are found and their kidnappers brought to justice. In 2002 a fourteen year old girl was abducted from her peaceful, sheltered life while sleeping in her bed one night. An intruder entered her bedroom and kidnapped her at knifepoint. We watched the anguish of another family. Months went by with no news of her whereabouts. Many of us counted her off as another statistic. Some of us had even forgotten her name and had moved on. While we moved on to the next headline, there was a family who was deep in pain. They held out hope that she was alive. They maintained their strong faith in God despite their ordeal. They kept praying. They kept trying even when it seemed hopeless. They also kept the authorities informed so they could keep searching for her. Thousands of tips came in; none led to a break in the case. Several months went by and hope seemed to be slipping away when the little sister had a revelation; "Daddy", she said, "I think I know who took my sister". This loving dad did not ignore this thought. When you truly love someone and is desperately trying to find them you would take every hint seriously. This father went to the authorities with this information. He publicized it on America's Most Wanted and someone who saw the show recognized the abductor and surprise, the little girl was found with him.

When she was found she did not look the same because her kidnapper had disguised her as well as himself. We sat watching the evening news. The family was very thankful to find her alive. We were overjoyed with happiness for them. The story does not end here. There were press conferences and there were so many people who wanted to know all the gory details of what happened, when it happened, why it happened, and why she did not escape. The reporters' questions were endless. The ending to this all too often-tragic event was happy but the story was disturbing to say the least. Why do these horrible things happen? Why do they happen to innocent children? As I looked at the reunion of this child with her family, the thought came to my mind that there is something familiar about this story. This is the story of our lives. Satan has been doing this to the human race for 6000 years now.

In a sense just like that innocent little girl before her kidnapping; we were created by a loving God, and placed in a perfect Edenic environment. While basking in the bliss of it all, totally oblivious of evil and sin, we were deceived and kidnapped by a disobedient, contentious, deceptive, destructive, deranged, lawless and evil devil. A loving Father could not bear to see our degradation and eventual destruction so He gave everything. He emptied the treasure chest of Heaven and He gave the best heaven had to offer to rescue us. God knew that we could not save ourselves and so He put everything on the line to redeem us. He sent His only begotten Son, the Creator of this universe, the Alpha and the Omega, the Great I Am. God Himself in every respect came and died so we could be restored back to His image. We can never understand how this great God, who created a universe so vast that is beyond human conception, would condescend to come to this minute seemingly insignificant planet to save wretched lost sinners like us. We are thankful and we praise Him for this wonderful act of love and mercy.

Like a lost sheep wondering on the mountains of sin; Satan takes us from one hiding place to another, from one homeless shelter to another; from one abusive situation to another, from one illness after another, from one prison cell to another, from one bad relationship to another, from one drug abusive situation to another, and from sin after sin while hiding from us the security and joys of the Father's house. Satan tries to hide us from the outstretched arms of our loving Savior. He distorts the truth and feeds us junk food and worst of all he fills our minds with his rebellious ways thus weakening our mental powers and destabilizing us. Jesus our Creator and Redeemer saw our lost and hopeless condition and divine love sprung into action. In Luke 15 Jesus told the parable saying "What man of you, having an hundred sheep, if he loses one of them, doth not leave the ninety and nine in the fold, and go after that is lost, until he finds it? And when he has found it he lays it on his shoulders, rejoicing. When he brings the sheep home he calls all his friends and neighbors saying 'rejoice with me for I have found my sheep that was lost.' Jesus says similarly there is more joy in Heaven over one sinner that repented than the ninety and nine just persons that need no repentance.

When Satan took this world and made it captive to sin and suffering, our loving Shepherd and Savior left heaven and all of the unfallen worlds and came to Planet Earth on a risky mission to save this one world that was taken captive and lost on the steep mountains of sin. We could not save ourselves but a loving Father gave the best He had. The beloved of Heaven adored by countless angels came to earth and rescued us from certain death and destruction. Many of us are hopelessly lost and do not know it. When God's sweet message of salvation finds us and we make it back home into the fold of safety, He does not ask us any questions. He knows our past. He knows that we have been wounded and disgraced to the point that we do not want to return home. We have been changed by our traumatic experience and are not the same. God understands our situation. We do not need to put it in words for Him. The important thing is that we are found and He gently puts us on His shoulder, welcomes us back home and pardons us by His grace. He knows the minutest details of our captivity; but he does not reveal them, He buries all of our misdeeds and sins in the bottom of the ocean and puts a sign up that reads 'No fishing allowed here.' He does not encourage us to wallow in our past sins or blame anyone for them. He works with us to overcome our past and press forward to the mark of the high calling in Christ Jesus. That is what a loving Father does. He does not care where we have been, how long we have gone, what we have done, or how messed up we have become. He takes us back, cleans us up and gives us a new life in Him. He has been doing just that since the advent of sin on Planet Earth. The many stories of the Bible reveal ours is a God of love and restoration.

God never gives up on us, no matter what we have done. In Jeremiah 18 God sent the prophet Jeremiah down to the potters house and there Jeremiah observed the potter as he worked with the clay. When the vessel did not turn out the way the Potter wanted it to be, he did not discard it. He made it into something else. God the righteous potter wants to take our lives and put them back together the way he wants them to be. The truth is that one way or another Satan has kidnapped us all, lied to us and has led us all astray but God has made a way of escape for us. God's arms are always open wide for us to return home. There is security from every snare in the Father's arms. There is love and joy and happiness in the Father's arms so when troubles rise hasten to the Father's arms and find shelter and security in the Father's House.

In Luke 15 Jesus tells the parable of a young man whom Satan enticed to leave the security of his father's home. The father in the story had two sons. The younger son got bored at home and wanted freedom. He perceived freedom to be far away from the rules and regulations of home and so he asked for his inheritance and went far away from home. There was no one to tell him what to do. He had plenty of friends and harlots to spend his money and he quickly squandered it in riotous living, living it up with his friends. Soon the money ran out and seemingly so did his friends. He found himself broke and lonely and far away from home. There arose a famine in the land and this young kosher man took a job feeding pigs. He was so hungry that he ate the pig's food.

Like Jonah, in the belly of a fish in the depths of the sea, he remembered God and cried out to Him. He realized that he was not free. That freedom was a deception of the devil. True freedom cannot be found outside of the security of the father's house. True love cannot be found outside of the father's house. The father's rules are protection against self-destruction from intemperate living. The father's rules are a demonstration of his love. One day the young man finally woke up and came to himself and he said, 'My father's servants have extra food and I am starving. I am going home. I am going to tell dad how sorry I am, ask for his forgiveness and beg him to take me back as a servant.' The young man came to his senses and went back home. No longer the innocent kid who left home, he was now filled with bad memories of his recent adventures. He set out on his way back home. He was going back to find the true love and security that he had left behind. He was not the same well-kept lad that left home. His garments were tattered, and his body tired and worn, hungry, weak and broke. He pressed homeward.

He had no idea of the pain that he had caused his father when he left home. There was a void in the heart of his father and this loving father had not forgotten his son. Day after day, he sat by the window looking for his son to return. One day the father saw the faint form of a man coming in the distance. Although he was a great distance away he recognized him as his son and ran to meet him. He had compassion on him and kissed him. The son said "Dad I have sinned against Heaven and in thy sight I am no longer worthy to be called your son." The father did not ask any questions because he understood the situation. He put his best robe on his son and threw a big party and restored him back as though he had not left home. The older brother was angry and had many questions. "How could you do that dad? He left home and spent all his money with prostitutes and now you throw a party for him. That is not fair to me. I have been here with you all this time, working faithfully. My brother took off with his share of the money and blew it." The father knew what his son had done; He did not need to be reminded. This angry son did not feel the pain of a father. He did not sit by the window, day after day, waiting for his brother to return home. The father did not give a long explanation to the angry son; he merely reminded the angry son that there was plenty a room in the father's house for all his children, even the prodigal ones. The father said to his angry son, "Your brother was dead and is alive again; he was lost and is found, that is the bottom line." The father was not so interested in the details of his son's riotous life. He was interested in his salvation and restoration. He restored his son to full son-ship again.

Our Heavenly Father is like that, He knows our individual stories intimately. He knows every sin we have committed against His instructions and He has opened the doors of Heaven. He will clean us up and restore us to Himself if we would accept and follow His leadings.

He knows that we cannot do this on our own. When we accept Jesus' atoning sacrifice for us on Calvary and surrender our will to the will of God; God the Father sees us as though we have never sinned. We are forgiven by our faith in Jesus. God does not expect us to behave like the brother who never left home. He wants us to extend this forgiveness to others. Since He has forgiven us for so much we ought to forgive others and treat them as though they never sinned. Calvary covers all our sins. That is the reason why Calvary has such tremendous significance for us. It gives us the opportunity for redemption back to God. Without Calvary we are dead in our sins. God knew that since the fall of Adam and Eve that we, on our own, could not overcome sin, because we are born with sinful natures. The penalty for sin is death but God stepped in and took our place. When we accept Jesus as our personal savior from sin, we are restored into fellowship with God and by His grace we live according to His will.

When God finds us and we are restored to fellowship with Him, Satan does not leave us alone; He constantly tries to get us back into his captivity. He lies to us and tells us that we are nobody. He wants us to look at the things we have done and believe that we cannot be saved. He works on our minds because that is where the battle is won or lost. Each of us has a story to tell. The story of redemption is being played out in our individual lives every day. Some of the redemption stories are more dramatic than others. One day in our Father's Kingdom, far beyond the reach of Satan, we will share our redemption stories. There are many dramatic stories to tell. There are people today whom have suffered much for the cause of Christ and have been imprisoned, tortured and killed. Only in eternity we will hear all of these stories. Stories of how they made it to glory and the work that Jesus had to do in their individual lives to make it all possible. A sad truth is that most people do not realize they have been kidnapped and are living far away from the father's house. Many are born into captivity and have no clue what it is like to live in the Father's house. Many have been kidnapped so long that they no longer recognize it. They have been gone so long that they do not know the way back home. They have gotten so used to an alien life that they have no desire to abide in the Father's house. Some of the kidnapped are sympathetic with and have joined hands with their kidnapper. Satan does not care about us. The emotion he knows best is hate. You can serve Satan from now until eternity and he will still hate you and kill you in the end. The depths of his evil are unimaginable. There are many whom the devil have convinced that there is no God and there is no Father's house. Do not let Satan lead you astray; God is preparing an eternal home for His children.

Satan may have worked on our minds, lied to us, deceived us, mesmerized us, clouded and confused us. We may have done the worst things possible and ended up on death row; but God is constantly searching for us. Sometimes He sends His messengers in the dungeons of our hideout because sometimes we only listen to Him when we are in the dungeon. He brings us the sweet message of salvation and when we listen and accept and cry out to God, "abba father.' He is there for us. He put His arms around us in our dirty kidnapped clothes and welcomes us back. A loving Father does not sit at home and hope that we will return. He puts the information out everywhere by radio, internet and word-of-mouth that His child is lost and He sends His messengers out to find us. That is why He gives us the gospel commission to go out into all the world and preach the gospel baptizing them in the name of the Father, The Son and the Holy Spirit. For centuries now people have left their comfortable homes and have gone out into the mission fields to take this life saving gospel to the remote corners of this planet and millions have found their way back to God.

The Origin of the Sin That Marred God's Creation

Sin started in Heaven in the heart of Lucifer, a highly decorated angel. It festered for a while and caused a war in Heaven. Revelation 12:7–9 says that "There was war in Heaven: Michael and His angels fought against the dragon; and the dragon fought and his angels, and prevailed not; neither was their place found any more in Heaven. The great dragon was cast out, that old serpent, called the devil, and Satan, which deceives the whole world: he was cast out into the Earth, and his angels were cast out with him." Before Satan's rebellion in heaven he was an angel. He was the highest anointed, highly decorated angel dwelling in the very presence of God. His name means light bearer. Lucifer was a covering cherub, denoting the order of angels dwelling near to the mercy seat of God. The mercy seat is located in the Most Holy Place of the Heavenly sanctuary where God dwells. He dwelt in the very presence of God. With the exception of the Godhead, he occupied the highest place possible in Heaven.

In Ezekiel 28:12–17 we are given interesting information about who Satan is and how he controls our minds. Satan often works behind the scenes to disguise his deceptions. Satan is a shrewd operator and works behind powers, political and religious to deceive us. He can disguise himself behind your favorite preacher or person or music or whatever it takes to deceive you. Here in Ezekiel the veil is taken away and the prophet Ezekiel is given a behind the scenes glimpse at the Satanic power that controlled men like the King of Tyre. Tyre was a Mediterranean city and the Lord revealed to the prophet Ezekiel that the King of Tyre thought he was God. The prophet was shown the power that controlled the king of Tyre. The King of Tyre was a front for Satan and God gave us a behind the scenes look at sin. The King of Tyre was exhibiting the character of Satan who controlled him and the prophet was given this insight. This is very important information because here Satan's deception is exposed and in Ezekiel 28:12 God describes Satan through the prophet Ezekiel. The prophet is shown that Satan was created with perfection, full of wisdom, perfect in beauty, and he had everything going for him. He lived in the Heavenly Eden, in the very garden of God and had close communion with God. He could wear every precious stone, rubies, diamonds, beryl, jasper, sapphires, topaz, emeralds, onyx, turquoise, and the gold. Every precious stone was his covering; his pipes were prepared in him the minute he was created. Some interpret this to mean that he was quite a singer and probably directed the Heavenly choir. He lived in the fire of God's presence and walked up and down on the holy mountain of God. What a privilege!

Ezekiel 28:15 states "He was created perfect until sin was found in him." The origin of this sin is a mystery to us. There was no cause or justification for sin in Heaven. How could evil begin in a perfect being dwelling in the very presence of God? The prophet in Isaiah helps in our understanding of this issue. Isaiah 14:12 says "How art thou fallen from heaven,

Oh Lucifer, son of the morning! How art thou cut down to the ground, which did weaken the nations? For thou hast said in thine heart, I will ascend into Heaven. I will exalt my throne above the stars of God. I will sit on the mount of the congregation. I will ascend above the heights of the clouds; I will be like the most high". Lucifer developed an "I" problem? His pride contributed to his fall. Lucifer's beauty and power went to his head. Lucifer desired to usurp God's power. He was envious of Jesus. He wanted to be like the Most High God, his creator. *He wanted power, praise and great authority.* He wanted to sit on God's throne. Jesus sits on the throne with His Father and the Heavenly hosts worship them. Satan wanted the worship that Jesus received from the Heavenly hosts. He wanted the worship that was due to God only. This is very important to know because much of Satan's deception has to do with true worship, His deceptions are designed to forsake the true worship of God or to distort that worship and to set up a false system of worship. He is extremely deceptive and has been very successful in his efforts to deceive even the very elect of God.

Lucifer was created with freedom of choice. He, as well as all of God's creation, is a free moral agent. The Bible states that he became corrupted by his beauty and wisdom. His pride preceded his fall. Lucifer, the highest created being, became infatuated with himself and made the choice to rebel against the all-knowing, all-wise God, his creator. He wanted the praise and adoration of the Heavenly angels so he secretly went on a campaign trail to malign God's character. He accused God of being a dictator. He had a problem with the Godhead, God the Father, God the Son and God the Holy Spirit. He envied the position Jesus had with His Father. He wanted a position he could never have. He no longer felt comfortable bowing and worshipping Jesus, his creator. Lucifer became very jealous of the position Jesus had with his father. Jesus said "I and my father are one." (John 10:30). Jesus is the Creator and He is equal with the Father. Satan became jealous of this relationship and coveted the supreme power that Jesus had. He felt that he should be part of the Godhead who created him. He then secretly went around heaven injecting the other angels with his evil venom. He no longer wanted to worship God but he was seeking the adoration and worship from as many of the other angels as he could influence. This cherished angel rebelled against the government of God. He envisioned victory and thought he would be the commander and chief of the Heavenly host. The omnipotent God was fully aware of Lucifer's rebellion and He was patient with Lucifer. Lucifer was given many opportunities to change his direction but he did not turn back from his destructive course of action. His iniquity multiplied and he was filled with violence and hatred toward God.

Lucifer misaligned God's character until war broke out in Heaven. Satan and the angels who joined him in rebellion against God lost the battle. Revelation 12 states that Satan lost the battle in Heaven and was cast out of Heaven and he came to this earth with his vast army of rebellious angels, about one-third of the angels in Heaven.

In Luke 10:18 Jesus said "I saw Satan as lightening fall from heaven." Lucifer the light bearer now becomes Satan the adversary. Satan did not arrive on Planet Earth alone. He was cast out of Heaven with a large host of the Heavenly angels. He has quite an army at his disposal. Satan left Heaven angry and has a big score to settle with God and his Law. Revelation 12:12 says "Woe to the inhabitants of the earth and the sea! For the devil is come down with great wrath, because he knows that he hath but a short time."

Satan is not a fictional cartoon character. He is a real entity. Satan is the result of Lucifer's choice. God did not create Satan. If you see a drunken man laying in the gutter, you would not say "what mother gave birth to this drunk?" He was once somebody's precious little baby but as he matured and he made choices. The Bible teaches that Jesus is the agent of creation and there was nothing made that he did not make (John 1:3). John states here that Jesus created everything. Everything includes Lucifer. Jesus on the other hand was not created. He is the eternal God, the creator. Lucifer was created with freedom of choice. He chose to disobey his Creator, the Eternal God. Jesus is the eternal part of the Godhead from everlasting to everlasting. The creator of whom Psalms 93:2 wrote, "Thy throne is established of old; Thou art from everlasting." This tells us that even before this vast universe was created there was God. There was never a time when God did not exist. It is a difficult concept for us humans to grasp because our minds can only relate to time. Jesus says in Revelation "I am Alpha and Omega, the beginning and the end, the first and the last." There was no God before Him and there will be no God after Him.

Lucifer, the highest created being questioned and rebelled against God's law. He began to undermine the character of God. God's character of love is embodied in His law. It is who God is, a God of love. His love for us is embodied in His law, which protects us from danger. The great controversy of the universe started when Lucifer a proud angel rebelled against God's law and convinced one third of the Heavenly angels to follow him. This is the origin of sin. God could not permit that to happen in Heaven. The great controversy between good and evil started when a created being in heaven rejected God's law. He came to earth and continued that rebellion sometimes overtly but mostly deceptively. We will look at some of the many ways he has caused rebellion against God's law and we will eventually show that God's law will stand forever even after this great controversy between good and evil ends.

God's eternal Law

Sin by definition is the transgression of God's law. Satan sinned in Heaven when He broke the principles of God's law. There are many who do not understand or refuse to accept that God's moral law is eternal. God's law did not originate at Mt. Sinai. It has been in existence before the creation of Planet Earth. It was lawlessness that caused Satan to be booted out of Heaven. Since he has been on Planet Earth he has been causing disobedience to God's law in one form or another. He caused Adam and Eve to disobey God's law. Adam and Eve knew God's law because it was written on their hearts. They sinned against God's law. Abel killed and violated the commandment that states "Thou shall not kill." The law was passed on to successive generations by word-of-mouth. Noah revered God's law and it was said that he found grace in the sight of God. Grace is what enables you to be in harmony with God's law. God destroyed the sinful world before the flood. After the flood, Noah preserved the knowledge of God and His law.

Abraham knew about God's law. Genesis 17:7 says, "I am the Almighty God. Walk before Me and be thou perfect. And I will make My covenant between Me and thee and thy seed after thee in their generations, for an *everlasting covenant*, to be a God unto thee, and to thy seed after thee. Genesis 26:5 states, "Abraham obeyed my voice, and kept my charge, my commandments, my statues and my laws." God's true followers will honor His law. Satan was booted out of Heaven for lawlessness. He came to Planet Earth and just as he cunningly deceived Adam and Eve, he has been busy deceiving the inhabitants of Planet Earth convincing us that God's moral law is not binding. Satan, using the Bible as his reference, came up with all manner of sophisticated reasons why God's Law cannot be kept. The government of God is controlled by His laws. God's Laws guide the universe. During the exodus in Egypt, the children of Israel under Egyptian slavery had been forced to violate God's laws, and soon subsequent generations forgot His laws. After their miraculous rescue from Egypt, it was necessary for God to remind them of His laws. Stubbornness and disobedience to God's Laws caused them to sojourn in the wilderness for forty years.

In John 15:10 Jesus says, "If you keep my commandments you shall abide in my law even as I have kept My Father's commandments, and abide in His law." Obedience to God is not legalism. Satan uses the term legalism to cover up disobedience to God. God's law is very important. God made a covenant with His people, all believers: Jews or Gentiles. The basis of this covenant is His moral law. The law is not the covenant. It is the foundation of the covenant relationship that we have with God. Amos 3:3 says, "Can two walk together unless they agree?" God reaches out to us, stretches out His hand, and we grasp it and agree to a covenant relationship with Him. We walk according to His *law, by His grace*. God's covenant and His law are bound together. Deuteronomy 4:13 says, "And the Lord declared unto you His covenant, which He commanded you to perform, even ten commandments; and He wrote them on two tablets of stone." God gave us His moral law to show us what He is like, as a person. He is a God of love. The first four commandments are about our love for God and the last six are about our love for our fellowmen. We can look around this vast creation and see what He is like as a Creator. When we enter into a covenant relationship with God, we accept God's law and we show the world to whom we belong when we live according to His law.

It is the grace of God that enables us to keep God's law. God's biddings are His enablings. We are saved by the shed blood of Jesus. Let us follow our example, Jesus, who says, "I have kept My Father's commandments and abide in His law." God's law is like a hedge around us and when we remove the hedge we are left without protection. Violating God's commandments is always detrimental to us.

There are those who preach that God made a new covenant and in the new covenant the law was made void. God, through the prophet Jeremiah, states, "Behold the days are coming when I will make a new covenant with the house of Israel and the house of Judah. Not according to the covenant that I made with their fathers in the day that I took them by the hand to bring them out of Egypt, which My covenant they broke although I was a husband unto them, Says the Lord. I will put My law in their inward parts and write in their hearts and I will be their God and they shall be My people." Israel broke the old covenant, and God renewed the covenant with spiritual Israel. There was nothing wrong with the old covenant itself. The problem was with them. (See Hebrews 8:7 and 8.).

When God says that He will make a new covenant with the house of Israel He is talking about a covenant relationship with every believer who obeys God. The new covenant is not limited to literal Israel. It never was. Even in Old Testament times non-Jews were included in the covenant. Rehab, the mixed multitude that came out of Egypt, Ruth, the daughter-in-law of Naomi Job; and Jethro, Moses' father-in-law are a few examples. The basic elements of the old and the new covenants are the same. The same God is seeking a relationship with His children. Gentiles are included in the new covenant. The Christian church today constitutes the house of Israel. The new covenant is better because the old had symbols, types and examples. The new covenant has Jesus, the Redeemer and High Priest. The shed bold of Jesus ratified the covenant. Christ's life, death and high priestly ministry are a better example than the sanctuary service of animal sacrifices. In Christ there in no bond or free, no Jew or Gentile. We are all one in Christ Jesus.

God became man and died because His law could not be changed to accommodate sin. Yet Satan has convinced most of Planet Earth that Gods law is flexible and that man or manmade or institutions can change it. God said, "I am God, I change not nor alter the things that have gone out of my mouth." Since I am all-knowing and all-wise and know the beginning from the end I do not have to make a law and then change it to accommodate sin. I am consistent and you can depend on that. Why did God give us a law? Is it for our own good? In Romans 7:7 Paul writes, "I had not known sin but by the law."

This text clearly indicates that the law points out the sin in our lives. Paul makes it clear in Romans 2:13, "For not the hearers of the law are just before God but the doers of the law shall be justified." Paul is saying that it is not the hearing of the law that matters; it is the doing of the law of God that matters most. 1 John 3:4 defines sin as the transgression of God's law. There are a lot of misconceptions about God's law. These are the deceptions of Satan who rebelled against God's law in Heaven. Some people teach that the law was nailed to the cross and they quote Colossians 4:14 which talks about blotting out the handwriting of ordinances that were against us, which were contrary to us, taking it out of the way and nailing it to His cross. One must be careful with the correct interpretation of the Bible. What is the law of ordinances? The law that was nailed to the cross was the law of ordinances, also known as the ceremonial law. There is a significant difference?

The Difference Between Ceremonial Law and God's Moral Law

The Ceremonial law was written by Moses (2 Chronicles 35:12) and given to the Jews as a result of sin. God's moral law, the Ten Commandments preceded sin. God wrote the moral law with His own fingers on tablets of stone and He gave them to Moses. The ceremonial laws were instructions regarding the sacrificial system of worship in the tabernacle services which prefigured the work of Jesus and therefore met their fulfillment at Calvary and were nailed to the cross. This is what Colossians 2:14 is saying. The moral law is God's law that exposes sin in our lives. The Ceremonial law pointed to Christ, the sin bearer, who takes away our sins. When Christ died on Calvary there was no need for animal sacrifices and the ceremonial law became null and void. The moral law stands fast forever. (See Psalms 111:7 and 8.) By confusing the ceremonial law, or Law of Moses, with the moral law of God, Satan has convinced many that God's law was abolished at Calvary. The law that was abolished was the Mosaic Law, also known as the law contained in ordinances or the Law of Moses. How could God's law be abolished when it is still a sin to steal to kill or to commit adultery? This is part of the Ten Commandment law. A careful study of the Bible reveals that the ceremonial law was a shadow of things to come. It pointed to the cross. Moses wrote it. God used that law symbolically to foreshadow the coming of Jesus, not so with the Ten Commandments. The sacrifices and ordinances of the ceremonial law ceased when the real sacrifice, Jesus, came. Exodus 31:18 states, "The Ten Commandments, the moral law was written by the finger of God on tables of stone. God did not allow man to write this law and when Moses broke the tablets that the law was written on God did not let Moses rewrite it. He again wrote it with His fingers on tablets of stone indicating its' permanency." God wrote this law with His own fingers and man cannot change it. When the scriptures are properly understood in their entirety there is no question that God's moral law has been around since before Planet Earth. Lucifer sinned against it in Heaven. Adam and Eve sinned against it in the Garden of Eden. Cain broke the sixth commandment that says, "Thou shall not kill".

o When Moses returned with the Ten Commandments he placed them in the Ark of the Covenant, in the most holy Place of the Tabernacle (Exodus 40:20). The law of ordinances, or the ceremonial law, was written by Moses and placed in the side of the Ark (Deuteronomy 31:26.) It came about as a result of sin and the perversion of the sacrificial system given to Adam. God needed to reeducate Israel about the proper use of the sacrificial system. Col 2:14 tell us that this law contained in ordinances was against us and was blotted out at Calvary. Be careful to note the difference between these two laws. The ceremonial law is different from the moral law. The moral law is not against us, it is for our good. The moral law existed before sin and was not abolished at the cross. The moral law was not destroyed by Christ. Christ came and magnified it (Isaiah 42:21, Matthew 5:17). The moral law is forever (Psalms 111:7 and 8), the law is perfect (Psalms 19:7). Romans 4:15 states, "For where there is no law there is no sin. Where there is no sin there is no need for grace to overcome sin. Where there is no need for grace there is no need for a Savior." Keeping the law does not save us; we keep the law because we are saved. The law points out sin in our lives so that we can come to Christ, our Savior, and be cleansed from our sins. Galatians 3:24 says, "Wherefore the law was our schoolmaster to bring us unto Christ, that we might be.

o The law is like a mirror, it tells us that our face is dirty and we need soap and water to cleanse it. This soap and water, in the spiritual realm, is grace and faith. When we sin against God's we need grace and faith. Romans states, "Do we make void the law through faith?" Romans 6:1 says, "Shall we continue in sin (transgressing God's law) that grace may abound?" Romans 7:5 and 6 says, "Before we accepted Jesus we were in the flesh and controlled by our sinful nature. Now that we have accepted Christ our sinful lives have been buried in Christ. We are delivered from the condemnation of the law. We serve God with a new spirit, not the old way of obeying the letter of the law." Christ's death saves us from the penalty of the law, not the jurisdiction of the law. The old way was attempting to obey the law apart from Christ. The new way is having Christ in us and having the hope of glory. We can do all things through Christ who strengthens us. We can obey God's righteous law and there is grace when we fail. He goes on to say, "Without the knowledge of the law there is no sin." Many people try to misconstrue Paul's writings to say that you do not need to obey God's law because we are under grace. Try to understand what Paul is saying in its totality and not pluck out a sentence and interpret that by itself. Read the entire chapter of Romans 7. Romans 7:12 says,

"The law is holy and the commandment holy and just and good." Here Paul clearly asserts it is possible to meet the righteous requirements of the law because of Jesus sacrifice for us. Righteousness by definition is right doing or obedience to God's law. You cannot receive justification and Christ's righteousness apart from God's moral law. In Romans 7: 22 Paul writes, "I delight in the law of the Lord." In Romans 8:4 he says, "For what the law could not do in that it was weak through the flesh, God, sending His own Son, in the likeness of sinful flesh and for sin, condemned sin in the flesh." Simply put, sinful man cannot obey God's law. Jesus came to earth and did what the law could not do and when we take on His nature we can live in harmony with God's law. We must be in harmony with God's law if we are going to be in harmony with God. The law points out our sins and leads us to Jesus, who can cleanse us from our sins.

o   Satan, the great deceiver, separates law and grace. God's plan of salvation ties them together. In Romans 6:1 and 2 Paul makes it clear that grace is no excuse for sin. Some people would tell you that you are under grace therefore you do not have to keep God's law. 1 John 2:4 states, "He that says, I know Him and keep not His commandments is a liar and the truth is not in him." Paul makes it clear in Romans 3:20 that by the law is the knowledge of sin. In other words the law is like a mirror, it points out sin; it cannot save you but it will point you to a Savior, Jesus Christ. 1 John 11:7 says that the blood of Jesus cleanses us from sin and the Bible teaches that every human being is saved by grace and grace alone. God's grace is not a license to sin. Jesus warns, "Go and sin no more." It has always been about God's grace. Grace has been available since Adam sinned. The Bible states, in Genesis 6:8, that Noah found grace in the eyes of the Lord. It is evident that grace was operant in the Old Testament times and grace is part of the plan of salvation also in Old Testament times. This whole misunderstanding of the role of grace, faith and the law is another of Satan's weapons of mass deception.

o   Without faith it is impossible to please God. The Bible states that we are saved by faith but we will be judged by our works. Do not believe Satan's lie that you are free from the law. In order to be free from the law you must live in harmony with the law. In Romans 3: 31 the apostle Paul warns "Do we make void the law through faith?" Yes we establish the law. When you break God's law and you are pardoned by His grace, go and sin no more. His grace is not a license to sin. God says, "If you love Me, keep My commandments and My commandments are not grievous." Do not let Satan deceive you with regards to the issue of God's moral law.

The Plan of Redemption

- The Bible clearly teaches that the plan of redemption of man was planned by the Godhead and a member of the Godhead took on humanity and died to restore man to God. He laid aside divinity and took on humanity to redeem sinners. Through Jesus, man and God united. Jesus voluntarily laid aside His divine power to save us. As a man, Jesus successfully overcame Satan and showed us we can follow His example and be successful in this battle against Satan. The name "Son of God" is the role He took on before the creation of this world in order to redeem man. The all-knowing God knew man would sin and the Godhead prepared for this emergency. Jesus became man. What condescension to save humanity! We see Jesus becoming the Son of Man, indicating the role He has taken on to save humanity. He is the only member of the Godhead who became visible. The plan of salvation was the work of the Godhead, the Father, Son and Holy Spirit. Jesus came to this world to reconcile sinful man to God. Hebrews 1:8 says, "But unto the son, he says, Thy throne, O God, is forever and ever. A scepter of righteousness is the scepter of Thy kingdom." The truth is the second person of the Godhead. Jesus Christ volunteered to become our Redeemer and be the Mediator between God and man. The Bible in 1 Timothy 2:5 states, "For there is one God and one Mediator between God and man, the man Christ Jesus". There is one God because the Godhead is one God in three persons. They are one in will, thought and purpose.

- The plan of redemption was planned by the Godhead before the foundation of the world. This is told to us in 1 Peter 1:20, which states that "who verily was foreordained before the foundation of the world but was manifest in these times for you." The plan of salvation was made before this world was created. The Bible indicates no inferiority between the three members of the Godhead. Satan orchestrated a campaign to deceive the world about Jesus. He refused to worship Jesus in Heaven and lost the battle against God in Heaven and he came to Earth deceiving people about Jesus. Jesus came to Earth and showed us that He is God. Jesus claimed that He is the "I Am" and He is equal with the Father (John 8:58). The Jehovah of the Old Testament is the same Jesus of the New Testament. It was Jesus who was the pillar of cloud by day and the pillar of fire by night as He led the Israelites in the Old Testament. Satan has been very successful in deceiving people about who Jesus is. He is the father of mass deception and outright lies and many of them are quite subtle on the surface but devastating in reality. One needs to be constantly on the lookout for deceptions, even when they seem insignificant.

A War of Deception

- Satan has been waging a war of mass deception for a very long time. This war of deception is responsible for the mass confusion and diversity of beliefs that exists on Planet Earth. How did we get to this level of confusion? Remember that Satan's deceptions started in Heaven when he accused God of being unfair and arbitrary and for giving a law that was unfair and impossible to keep. Satan has no respect for God, His government or His law. Satan was unrepentant in Heaven, is unrepentant on Earth and he has deceived God's people and corrupted truth. In Ezekiel 28:17 God states that He will expose him before kings so they can see the bag of goods that Satan has been selling and finally God will destroy him forever. When Satan became rebellious in Heaven God could have destroyed him instantly but the security of the universe was at stake. God wants all of His created beings to worship Him out of love, not fear. God has allowed Satan to play out his entire hand so that the universe can see clearly the horrible effects of disobedience. Since being ousted from Heaven Satan gained control of this planet by deceiving Adam and Eve by getting them to transgress God's commandments. Satan has a big score to settle with Jesus. Remember the text that states that there was a battle in Heaven and he lost and was kicked out of Heaven. He is definitely anti-Jesus. He is the original antichrist who will use people and institutions to carry out his mass plan of deception in dishonoring God.

- Deception is Satan's successful weapon in his warfare against God. Satan disguises himself. His camouflage is so good that he deceives many who do not recognize that they are deceived. Many people do not believe he exists and they are an easy target for him. Satan has all bases covered. He deceives believers and they too often do not discern his deceptions. His evil deeds are often attributed to others and often many people blame God for Satan's afflictions on mankind. We need to understand the nature of this battle since there is a lot at stake. Eternity and our very lives are at stake Satan is very crafty and deceitful and has comfortably woven himself into the body of Christ. He is responsible for all the divergent teachings that we find in Christianity today.

- We are in the midst of a dangerous cosmic war raging between God and Satan and although the battlefield is now confined to Planet Earth the entire universe is watching. In 1 Corinthians 4:9 Paul states, "We are made a spectacle unto the world and to angels and to men." What happened to Job is happening to us on one scale or another and, like Job, when we are successful in this battle we are trophies that God can show to the universe. The battle is raging for every human being. The stakes are high and the prize is man. The enemy is a formidable foe. In Ephesians 6:12 Paul warns us about this enemy.

He writes, "For we wrestle not against flesh and blood but against principalities and powers, against the rulers of the darkness of this world and against spiritual wickedness in high places." The apostle Paul is saying that we are not fighting against other human beings but against powers that are more intelligent than us. They are demonic forces in the supernatural realm. These evil spirits rule the darkness and control this planet.

- We cannot limit ourselves to what is visible. Sin has separated us from a Holy God but just because He is invisible to our naked eye does not mean that He is not with us. God is real and lives in a real place called Heaven. We should not place limitations on Him based on our limited vision. This is true in many aspects of our existence on Planet Earth In the spiritual realm we are also limited and unless the Holy Spirit opens our eyes we cannot see the spiritual world. There is ample evidence for this in the many lessons taught in the Bible. A good example is found in 2 Kings 2, beginning with verse 8. The King of Syria was at war with Israel and camped outside Samaria. The King of Israel knew what the King of Syria was up to. The king was angry and accused his officers of tipping off the enemy. One officer said, "No one is telling. There is a prophet, Elisha, in Israel who tells the King of Israel even the things you say even in your bedroom." The King of Syria sent a large army to capture God's prophet. They surrounded Dothan where the prophet was staying. Elisha's servant woke up the next morning and saw the Syrian troops with their horses and chariots surrounding Dothan. Elisha reassured his servant saying, "Fear not. We have a bigger army than they have." Elisha prayed that the Lord would open the eyes of His servant and the Lord did and he saw that the surrounding mountains were filled with horses and chariots of fire. When they attacked Elisha prayed, "Lord strike them blind" and it happened. Elisha told them they were on the wrong road, "This is not the town you are looking for" and he led them to Samaria. When they got to Samaria Elisha prayed again, "Lord open their eyes." They realized that they were in Samaria. The King of Israel asked the prophet, "Should I kill the Syrians?" The prophet admonished him, "No, feed them". The King of Israel made a great feast for them and sent them back to their king. From then on the Syrians did not invade the land of Israel.

- Sin has blinded our eyes and has given us limited vision. The visible things we see now are temporary but the invisible things of God are permanent. God is not trying to make Himself invisible to us. Our sins have done that. The invisible God is with us. His spirit lives in us. The apostle Paul, in Romans 8:38 and 39, states, "Nothing can separate us from the love of God, neither death nor life, neither angels nor demons, neither the present nor the future, neither height nor depth. There is nothing created that will separate us from the love of God, which is in Christ Jesus, our Lord." When we accept Jesus the invisible God dwells in us and we make God visible to the world by our lives. The human eye is limited in many ways. We cannot see electricity or the wind but we see the effects of it. Before sin God was visible. Blinded by sin we cannot see Him now but the evidence of His existence is everywhere. There is an invisible world all around us and we need to be aware of it because we are caught up in this war which is also being fought in the invisible realm.

o Satan has legions of evil armies engaged in a military style attack against us. God, through the apostle Paul, admonishes us that we must be prepared for this battle by putting on the whole armor of God that we may be able to withstand the evil schemes of Satan and his vast army of evil angels. God knows this enemy. The enemy is a master of camouflage. He can operate in the invisible realm. He is a master of deception. Remember, he deceived Heavenly beings with greater intellectual capacity than us.

o In the first century the apostle Paul, with the help of the Holy Spirit, wrote these admonitions for the church of Ephesus and they have been relevant down to us living in the twenty-first century. The apostle Paul, along with Aquila and Priscilla, took the gospel to the city of Ephesus and started the church there. Satan started a riot and Paul was imprisoned. While under arrest Paul was chained to a Roman soldier for two years. During this time he continued to spread the gospel in the city of Rome and wrote a series of letters to various churches. In a letter to the church at Ephesus he used the uniform of the Roman soldier to describe the nature of the battle we are engaged in. He was fully engrossed in this battle, having been chained to Roman soldiers during his arrests for the cause of Christ. He used the uniform of the Roman soldier to describe how a Christian should be dressed everyday as we fight the daily battle for our lives. He admonishes us that, just like a soldier prepared for battle; the Christian is in the battle of his life and needs to be dressed appropriately. You need to cover all vulnerable parts. We need to be vigilant and put on our fighting gear. A good soldier does not go to war without the appropriate gear. We need to be prepared. In Ephesians 6:14 Paul says. "Protect yourself spiritually."

o Paul suggested that you protect your waist with the belt of truth. A Roman soldier wore a belt to keep his robe from getting in the way lest the enemy grasp your garment and turn you around. Similarly, you need to gird up the loins of your mind, or protect your mind by guarding the things that get in, so you will not be turned around by false doctrines. We are to guard ourselves with the belt of truth. Jesus is the truth, the way and the life. Pray always that he will reveal truth to you.

o Cover your chest with the breastplate of righteousness. The soldier's breastplate protected his vital organs from injury. As a Christian we are to cover ourselves in the righteousness of Christ. A right relationship with God will protect against the fiery darts of Satan.

o Cover your feet with the preparation of the gospel of peace. Like the soldier who must have the appropriate footgear to stand firmly in battle so the Christian must be firmly grounded in the truth as it is in Jesus. Salvation through the grace of our Lord and Savior Jesus Christ is the truth on which we firmly stand.

o Take the shield of faith to quench all the fiery darts of the wicked. The soldier's shield protected him from incoming arrows and spears. Similarly, a deep abiding faith in God and His word is a protecting shield against Satan and his fiery darts of sin such as lying, stealing, cursing, swearing, jealousy and hatred.

o Cover your head with the helmet of salvation. God has given His salvation to us and it is a powerful weapon against the devil.

o Have your sword of the spirit, which is the word of God within us. It dissects truth from false teachings. Armed with the word of God you can mount an offensive attack. The word of God is a crucial part of the Christian armor. Without it you are no match for Satan. Satan knows the Bible. Satan knows that the Bible is no ordinary book. He knows the Bible is about God and His plan of salvation. That is why he tries to destroy the Bible. Your best defense against Satan is good offensive knowledge of the Bible. Like Jesus, you can confidently say to Satan and his temptations, "It is written in the Bible that man shall not live by bread alone but by every word that proceeds out of the mouth of God."

o Make no mistake about it. There is a battle going on for every human being that has ever existed. When finally, through the grace of God, we are over-comers in this battle, we would be battle torn soldiers on the verge of defeat but rescued by our leader and commander, Jesus Christ, when He comes the second time with great power and glory. We will lay our armor down and study war no more. Jesus will highly decorate us as war veterans in the Heavenly kingdom. We will no longer be prisoners of war in the enemy's camp. We will be rescued from this prison cell of sin into the palace of our Heavenly King. Then we can sing this song to its fullest meaning, "Free at last, free at last, thank God Almighty we are eternally free at last."

This battle to gain control of the human mind is being fought on physical, spiritual and emotional fronts. Although the battlefield is Planet Earth the real battlefield is fought at the level of the mind. It is here that the battle is won or lost. Every human being on this planet is a participant in this battle of good versus evil, God versus Satan. There are no spectators in this great controversy. The problem that we face is that we do not see the weapons of battle aimed at us so we do not appreciate the battle. Life here on Planet Earth has been a battle for most of us. Sometimes it seems as though we are stranded in a wilderness. We should know that we are caught up in a cosmic war and we need to know the battle plans so we can be successful. Do not fall for Satan's deceptions that we are not in a battle. He is a liar and a deceiver. He can disguise himself as an angel of light and his angels appear as ministers of righteousness. He often disguises himself in popular music or as a minister of the gospel preaching that which sounds good to the ear but is contrary doctrines to the truth of the scripture. He disguises himself in false religions. He is the master of deception. Satan is extremely clever and you are dealing with an entity that is smarter than you are and can only be overcome by the power of God. Without a sound understanding of the Bible and application of that knowledge with the help of the Holy Spirit and a desire to follow the Lord faithfully we will not overcome Satan.

o Satan is a masterful and powerful deceiver and the only force in this universe that can overcome the forces of Satan is God. We need to guard our minds everyday against Satan by diligently studying and following God's word. To be a successful over-comer of Satan it takes no less training than is required to win an Earthly marathon.

o I have had the opportunity on several occasions to be a medical volunteer at the New York City Marathon station at mile twenty-one. I like the opportunity to see the world's fastest marathon runners fly by our station. We set up our station with the necessary equipment to meet the needs of runners who stop for help. As the runners approach our station the front-runners sail by in seconds. They seem like birds flying by. There is no excess weight or baggage. They are in tip-top shape and have put in the necessary training for this race. At this point in the race they are nearing the homestretch in Central Park. They can taste victory. They do not stop for water. They do not want any help because mentally they can see the finish line and victory is within grasp. They have no time to waste. A moment's delay could cost them the race. These front-runners are well prepared, mentally and physically, and their stride reflects that as they fly by.

o About a half hour later the crowds begin to pour in, seeking help. From here on out we get those who are struggling to finish the race. Some give up close to the victory line.

One man was fifth in the race and felt he should be the frontrunner. He just sat down at our station crying. He gave up so close to the finish line. We encouraged him to keep running but you need perseverance, patience and endurance and you have to be in the race to win it. It requires a lot of practice to be a well-seasoned athlete.

- o The runners are seeking a victory. With victory comes fame, recognition as a great runner, a car, money and success. These are all perishable things. All of us are engaged in a marathon longer that the New York City or Boston marathon. It is the race of our lives. Day after day we are running this race and it requires daily training and no less commitment than these Earthly marathons. The final reward is permanent, the crown that is everlasting, life that is everlasting and a mansion in the New Jerusalem built by God.

- o Hebrews 12:1 says, "Therefore seeing that we are surrounded with so many witnesses, let us lay aside every weight and the sin that does so easily beset us. Let us run with patience the race that is set before us." Keep your eyes on the finish line where Jesus is standing with a victory flag. He is the Author and Finisher of our faith and He ran this race, enduring the shameful cross, despising the shameful death. He looked ahead in time and He suffered it to be so that we could be justified. He won the race and is now set down at the right hand of the throne of God. Jesus' victory can be ours if we keep our eyes on Him. Do not look at the crowd. Let us cast off all the unnecessary baggage of sin that is impeding our progress and run the race.

- o Some days we may be running through major obstacle courses. Sometimes we are running in the valley of the shadow of death. Sometimes we may be running by peaceful, still waters but let us keep running and victory will be ours. One day we will stand in Heaven's grandstand along with all the other successful runners waving palms of victory at our forerunner Jesus Christ. Because He won we too can win. Here is the statement of one who ran this race and was at the point of dying, "I have fought a good fight, I have finished my race and I have finished my course. Henceforth there is laid up for me a crown of righteousness which the Lord, the righteous judge, will give me at that day and not to me only but unto all them that also love His appearing." There will be many winners in this race and I pray to be one of them.

- o So why are we not more diligent in our preparation for our eternal home? Satan keeps preoccupied with the temporary things of this life. Satan dangles money, fame, and the temporary achievements of this life and does not let us see the finish line. He hides the realities of Heaven from us. The Bible states that God is going to give His faithful children eternal life and take them to Heaven where eyes have not seen, ears have not heard, neither has it entered into the mind of man the things that God has prepared for His children. Some of the most brilliant minds that exist are trapped in the temporary gains of this life. Why invest everything in this temporary life? Instead, invest in the bank of Heaven where the returns are out of this world. Your profits will last forever and you will have eternity to enjoy them. The Bible is full of examples of people who have been successful in this life's adventures and then died leaving it all behind.

o The Bible tells us that King Solomon was the wisest man who ever lived. He was extremely wealthy and powerful. Whatever his heart desired he had the means and influence to obtain. These earthly gains turned his heart away from the Lord and he lost his way. He took his eyes off Jesus and was running in the opposite direction from the finish line. King Solomon got old and, facing the grim reality of death, he repented and turned his heart back to God. God warns us, "What does it profit us if we gain this whole world and loose our soul?" It would be the biggest disappointment in history if we were to gain this whole world and lose our souls. Most of our time in this life should be spent preparing for eternity by studying God's word and preparing for the second coming of Jesus. Why spend so much of your time amassing treasures on this earth that you cannot keep? Store up your treasures in Heaven where they will last forever.

Satan Lies About God and Distorts God's Plan of Salvation

o God alone is the creator and rightful owner of everything in this universe. Psalms 24:1 says, "The Earth is the Lords and the fullness thereof, the Earth and them that live in it." We are temporary tenants and stewards entrusted with the management of God's possessions in this world. We are accountable to God for all of the things that He has entrusted to our care; this includes our time, possessions, money and actions. God did not abandon Planet Earth. He still holds the title deed. In Leviticus 23:23 God says, "The land is Mine. You cannot sell it forever. You are temporary tenants." We come into this world with nothing and no matter how much money, how many possessions or how much fame we have amassed we leave with nothing. One generation after another passes away but the Earth is the Lord's and it remains forever. The sovereign God of the universe is eternal and abides forever. He never slumbers nor sleeps. He sees every sparrow that falls. He knows everything about us. He sees and records everything that takes place on Planet Earth. Matthew 12:36 says, "Jesus said that every idle word that men speak they shall give an account for in the judgment. By thy words thou shall be justified and by thy words thou shall be condemned." God knows everything about us, even in the womb. The biblical evidence for this is in Jeremiah 1:5, "The Lord said to Jeremiah, before I formed you in the belly I knew you and before you came out of the womb I sanctified you and I ordained you a prophet unto the nations." Jesus, the good shepherd, knows His sheep and His sheep know Him. He knows our name and our address. He knows our thoughts. He knows every strand of hair of our head. In Psalms 103:13 David says, "God knows our frame and He remembers that we are dust. God created us from dust and He molded and formed us in His image." God loves us and He has not abandoned His creation.

God Is Greater Than Our Thoughts

o It is impossible for our finite minds to comprehend the infinite mind of our Creator God. Isaiah 55:8 and 9 states, "For my thoughts are not your thoughts, neither are my ways your ways, says the Lord. For as the Heavens are higher than the earth so are my ways higher than your ways and my thoughts than your thoughts."

o We cannot truly define God. He defies all human categories. He is the Holy God, the potentate of time, majestic in every way yet He is a friend that sticks closer than a brother. In 1 Kings 8:27 the wisest man who ever lived, King Solomon, at the dedication prayer of the temple, which he built for the glory of God, he prayed, "But will God indeed dwell on the earth? Behold, the Heaven and Heaven of Heavens cannot contain thee. How much less this house that I have built?"

o However you describe God it is not enough. He dwells in light unapproachable. He rules this vast universe yet He lives in our hearts. We cannot describe God in human language. He is more than any human language can describe. He is more that amazing, intelligent, miraculous, gracious, He is more than any words can describe. In the final analysis He is unexplainable.

The Truth About The Godhead

o Satan has distorted the truth about the Godhead. The Bible teaches that there is one God that exists as three distinct yet equally divine beings (Matthew 28:19). The Father, the Son and the Holy Ghost are one God (Deuteronomy 6:4). They are three co-eternal distinct beings united as one God. They are one in purpose. God the Father is the Master Designer; God the Son is the Creator and God the Holy Spirit reveals Jesus Christ to us. Genesis 1:26 says, "Let *us* make man in *our* image". This indicates that the Godhead created us. From the very beginning the Bible establishes the triune nature of our God. They are one. Hebrews 1:1–3 tells us that Jesus is the express image of the Father and in John 14:9 Jesus says, "If you have seen Me you have seen the Father." They created man and all three members of the Godhead are actively involved in the redemption of man. Genesis is the book of our beginning and in Genesis 1:1 God tells us, "In the beginning God created the Heaven and the Earth and the Earth was without form and void and at that time there was darkness on the face of the deep. God, the Holy Spirit moved upon the face of the waters."

o God, the Holy Spirit, was active at creation. God, the Holy Spirit, is part of the eternal Godhead. God, the Holy Spirit, inspired holy men to write the Bible and one of the functions of God, the Holy Spirit, is to progressively lead us to an understanding of the Bible. The entire Bible testifies about Jesus, the second person of the Godhead. Jesus describes the work of the Holy Spirit in John 16:5–16, "The Holy Spirit works with us to convict us of sin, of righteousness and judgment." All 3 members of the Godhead are working for our salvation. The Godhead is crucial to our existence.

o The triune God has no beginning and no end (John 1:1–3, Revelation 22:13). Our God lives in the past, the present and the future. When time rolls into eternity we will see that time was a mere speck on the great scope of eternity. This speck of time was important because the Creator of this vast universe stepped into time and became one of His creations to save our doomed world that went astray from His vast creation. So not only did He create us but when we went astray from His original plan for us He died to redeem us. We are twice His, by creation and redemption. Creation is not possible without a creator. Redemption is not possible without creation.

Satan Generates Evil, But God Changes Lives

o The evidence is irrefutable. All over Planet Earth are people whose lives have been changed by the knowledge and power of God in their lives. There is no other reality that has such a positive impact on the lives of humans on this planet. People are changed and what a difference God makes in their lives. We have seen hardened criminals change. Wicked men and women change and their hearts soften because God has worked a miracle in their lives. People on the brink of suicide and ruin turn their lives around under the influence of the Holy Spirit. Prison wardens will tell you it is the most effective means of preventing recidivism among the prison population. Drug addicts clean their lives up and now help to spread the glad tidings of salvation. There is now purpose, meaning and direction since God came into their lives. God is our only real hope in this otherwise temporary existence called life. The Bible gives us great hope that God will save us, forgive our sins and give us overcoming power so we can live with Him for eternity.

God's Redemptive Power

o   The enormous capacity of God to redeem, love and forgive is mind boggling and is told in those amazing Bible stories. Story after story and prophecy after prophecy in the Bible tells of a holy and faithful God and the extent He would go to redeem His lost creation. These stories are inspiring and teach us a lot about God. The Bible portrays God as operating in many dimensions. He is our Creator, Sustainer, Savior, Redeemer and soon coming King. One of the dimensions of God that is so appealing to us is His intervention in our lives to save us. These stories give us hope and reveal a loving and caring God. Let us look at some of these biblical stories.

The Story of a Man Who Satan Could Not Deceive

o   At some point Satan gets to most of us and wreaks havoc in of our lives. His deceptions are so widespread that we often do not know that we are being deceived. God placed many stories in the Bible to help us to live godly lives in this sinful mortal state. One such story is found in the book of Job. This life story encourages us and gives us an example of a godly lifestyle to aspire to. Some biblical experts think that Job is the oldest book of the Bible. The book of Job, like the book of Genesis, was written by Moses in the desert of Midian under the inspiration of the Holy Spirit (*Education*, page 159). Moses lived at about 1500 BC and Job lived at about 2000 BC Moses did not know Job. The book of Job is a revelation of God to one of His prophets.

o   Job lived in a place called Uz, believed to be located east of Palestine on the borders of the Arabian Desert, south of Damascus and probably in the vicinity of Edom (*Seventh-day Adventist Bible Dictionary*, page 579). The background of the book depicts an Arabian Desert culture. Job was a wealthy successful businessman with a large family and he extolled family values. He loved his wife and prayed for his children daily. He was a well-respected community man. His story is recorded in the Bible because of his relationship to God not because of his wealth or culture. He was well known for his moral perfection and uprightness before God. He loved and obeyed God and hated evil. The record shows that Satan hated Job because of his right relationship with God.

- The story is told in Job 1:6 that one day God had an intergalactic conference and all the sons of God, most likely other celestial beings, ambassadors or representatives of other planets, attended the conference. It appears from this account that when Satan was initially kicked out of Heaven he was not totally confined to Planet Earth because he showed up at this intergalactic conference. How did he know that there was a conference? God called His representatives from all over the universe to a conference and Satan came to represent his interest on Planet Earth. He apparently had access to Heaven until Jesus walked out of the tomb triumphant and went back to glory. Jesus won the decisive victory that day and went back to glory and Satan was permanently barred from Heaven.

- Revelation 12:10 states, "And I heard a loud voice saying in Heaven, 'Now is salvation and strength and the kingdom of our God and the power of His Christ. For the accuser of our brethren is cast down which accused them before our God day and night.'" In Zechariah 3:1 we see Joshua the high priest standing before the Lord and Satan is standing at his right hand accusing him of sin. Satan, the accuser of the brethren, shows up and accuses God for forgiving us of our sins.

- The book of Job reveals that Satan, our accuser, showed up at this conference. Adam, the son of God, should have been the one to represent Planet Earth at this universal assembly but he lost control to Satan. Instead the uninvited Satan came to the conference to represent Planet Earth. God asks Satan, "Where did you come from?" He answers, "From Planet Earth, from going to and fro in the Earth and from walking up and down in it."

- We learn from this story that since the fall of man, which we will get into later, Satan has had control over most of the inhabitants of Planet Earth and he has been roaming up and down the earth like a lion seeking whom he may devour. He causes the suffering on Earth but God, in His mercy, often overrules him. We learn from this story that there was a man on Planet Earth named Job who respected and obeyed God and Satan did not have control of him. Job was a man who deeply loved and obeyed God.

- The Bible describes Job as perfect and upright in the sight of God. God told Satan that he did not have full control of *all* the inhabitants of Planet Earth. After all, there was a man named Job who obeyed God and Satan did not control him. Satan asserted that Job only served God because of all the things that God had given to him. Satan accused God of catering to Job and placing a hedge around Job so that he could not get to Job. He challenged God that if He would remove His protection from around Job that Job would curse God. God took Satan's challenge and, with the exception of taking Job's life, Satan was permitted to use his power against Job.

- In one day Satan brought tremendous tragedy to Job. Satan used the Sabeans and the Chaldeans to steal Job's livestock and kill his workers. He sent a tornado from the wilderness and destroyed the eldest son's house, killing all of Job's children. With the exception of his wife Job lost all of his Earthly possessions in a short period of time. This deeply affected Job but his faith in God was steadfast and he did not sin against God. Job said, "Naked came I out of my mother's womb and naked will I return thither. The Lord gave and the Lord takes away. Blessed be the name of the Lord."

- Job 2 tells of another day when the sons of God came to present themselves to God and again Satan showed up to represent claiming to be the representative of Planet Earth. God reminded Satan that he did not represent everybody on Planet Earth. There was still righteous Job, despite Satan's afflictions. Job still believed and trusted God.

- Satan again asserted that a man would give anything for his life. Satan told God that if He were to touch Job's bones and flesh he would curse Him to His face. God again permitted Satan to afflict Job and Satan left the conference and did not waste any time. Satan cursed Job with painful boils from the crown of his head to the soles of his feet. So great was his affliction that his wife, who could not bear to see his suffering anymore, said to him, "Curse God and die!" Job said to her, "You speak like a foolish woman. Shall we not receive good at the hand of God and shall we not receive evil?"

- Job did not sin in the midst of this terrible affliction. Job had many concerns, his faith was severely tested and his friends came to mourn with him. These friends accused Job of self-righteousness when he proclaimed his innocence before God. His friends were sure that Job must have done something to deserve this punishment. This was the belief of the people in Job's time. Some people today believe that if misfortune takes place it was because of God's punishment.

- Why did Satan hate Job? Job feared, loved and obeyed God. The story of Job tells us that Satan inflicts diseases and is the cause of our problems and if God gave him full control he would destroy us. In Job's case Satan made the charge before the assembly that God bribed Job in serving Him by giving him so much. God proved Satan wrong by removing His protective hedge from around Job allowing Satan to inflict his damage. God has a protective hedge around all of His creation. Many times God is blamed for that which He does not prevent.

- There are some people who think that they can explain God's actions. Finite human beings cannot explain the actions of an infinite God unless He reveals them. Job's four friends who said they came to comfort Job made matters worse by trying to explain God's actions. These friends were convinced that Job's problems were God's punishment for something Job had done wrong. These friends had no idea of the cosmic struggle that was taking place over Job yet they were quick to give their opinion that Job must have done something wrong and assume that God was punishing him.

- In Ecclesiastes 5:1 the wisest man who ever lived admonished us, "Be not rash with our mouth and let not your heart be hasty to utter anything before God. God is in Heaven and we are on Earth therefore let thy words be few." This was not the case with Job's friends. They thought they knew more than they did and tried to impose their false beliefs on Job.

- Job was human after all and he became discouraged about his situation but he never gave up on God. He pleaded his case before the just God of the universe and, in Job 14:13 he pleads that God would hide him in the grave until his wrath is passed. He still believed in God and had faith. God allowed Job's situation to prove to the entire on-looking universe that Satan was wrong and was the cause of all the turmoil on Planet Earth. However, Satan made it look like God was the cause of the evil and horrible things that happened day after day.

- In the midst of this trial Job said, "If only I knew where to find Him so that could argue my cause before Him. He knows me and when He has tried me I will come forth as gold." Through it all Job came to the conclusion that God knew what He was doing. He is almighty, excellent in power and in judgment and has plenty of justice and would not afflict him.

- In the end of the book of Job, chapter 38, God, who controls the elements of nature, answers Job out of a whirlwind. Interestingly God does not begin by answering Job's question of why the wicked seemingly prosper while the righteous suffer. He does not tell Job why he is suffering but, instead, He begins to put things into perspective for Job. He begins to show Job how little man knows about God. Listen to some of the questions God asks Job and see if you have the answer. God asks Job, "Who is it that is speaking without knowledge?" God took Job to the beginning. "Where were you when I created the world? Who decided and laid the measurements of the Earth? Tell me if you understand. On what foundation does the Earth stand on? Who laid the cornerstone of the Earth while the morning stars sang together and the sons of God shouted for joy after My creation?"

- There were eyewitnesses to God's creation of this planet. They were not earthly beings. God informed Job that the sons of God, most likely celestial beings from Heaven and other existing planets, jumped for joy as He created Planet Earth. Here God tells Job of the existence of created beings before Planet Earth was formed.

- God continues with Job, "Where were you when I made the clouds to cover the earth? And where were you when I said unto the seas, 'Hitherto shall thou come and no further'? Who commands the mornings? Can you keep the 250 suns of Pleiades together, moving in unison? Can you loose the bands that keep the constellation Orion in place?" The stars of Orion are moving to different parts of the universe and the bands are loosed in the process.

- "Can you guide Arcturus with his sons?" Arcturus is one of the greatest suns of the universe. Guided by God, Arcturus and its sons, a group of stars moving with it, travels at immense speed and yet does not crash into other Heavenly bodies.

- "Do you know the laws that control the Heavens? Can you provide food for the lions and her cubs? Who provides food for the ravens and when their young ones cry out to God and wander for lack of food? Can you lift up your voice to the clouds and water come down and wet you? Who gave the peacock her wings? Do you know why the ostrich behaves the way she does? She hides her eggs in the sand; she is hard on her young ones and treats them as though they are not hers. I did not give her wisdom or understanding, yet I made her to run faster than the horse and its rider. Does the eagle soar at your command and make her nest on high places? She dwells on the lofty mountains and her eyesight is so keen she can see food afar off."

- These are a sample of the questions God asked Job. God was trying to impress on the mind of Job that if He cares for and controls everything in this immense universe, from celestial beings to the wild animals, he certainly could solve Job's problems.

- In Job 42 Job answered the Lord saying, "I know that you can do everything and know your thoughts." Job admitted to God that he spoke of things that he did not understand. He repented in dust and ashes and asked God for forgiveness and God forgave and blessed Job in all aspects of his life. God restored Job by giving him greater blessings than he had before Satan attacked him. Through this calamity Job understood the mighty power of God and His great mercy towards us. Our trials help us to understand God better. These Heavenly bodies mentioned in Job over three thousand years ago were not discovered until the twentieth century. Why would a God with such creative powers; the creator of billions of galaxies and worlds, chose to die to save lost humanity on this speck of a planet? It is mind boggling and the redeemed of this Earth will study this for eternity.

God Communicates to Us Through His Prophets

o God has always had a prophet among His people. Down through the centuries God has led His people and has communicated His will through His prophets. In Isaiah 46:9 and 10 God says, "Remember the things of old. I am God and there is no other God, there is none like me. I know the end from the beginning. I knew what would happen from ancient times. My purpose will stand and I will do all that I please."

o The amazing prophecies of the Bible are proof that God's word is true. He does indeed know everything, including future events, and He has revealed much future information to His prophets. These prophets have left very important information for us, particularly for those who live in the end of time. 1 Corinthians 10:11 states, "Now all these things happened unto them for examples and are written for our admonition upon whom the ends of the world are come," God is speaking particularly to us who are living in the end of time. He is telling us that He has given us the Bible as a guide and we should learn from the experiences recorded in the Bible, in this case, the story of the Israelites. To them was entrusted the law and the knowledge of God but disobedience to God led to their prolonged wilderness experience and their eventual destruction. God warns us not to make the same mistakes they made, particularly those of us who live so close to His second coming. We have no excuse because the mistakes they made are well documented in the Bible and we need to take heed lest we suffer the same fate. God cares for and loves us enough to forewarn us through His prophets.

What Have the Prophets Revealed to Us?

The Bible contains many prophecies. God wants us to understand these prophecies or He would not have put them in the Bible. God's revelations to us through the many prophecies of the Bible deserve our utmost attention as does the Bible. God chooses men and women of diverse backgrounds and education at specific times in history to be His messenger or prophet. He uses them to reveal His plans for us. The prophets often encourage us and warn us about unforeseen danger. These prophecies are not only relevant for the historical time in which they were given but for the end-time. God wants us to pay attention and heed these messages given to the prophets. Satan, on the other hand, does all he can to discredit prophecy in any way he can. God's true prophets expose Satan's deceptions.

God Has Always Had A Prophet Among His People

Our loving God has long been warning His children of oncoming judgments and He has been sending us warnings through His chosen prophets. The prophet Amos assures us in Amos 3:7 that surely the Lord God does nothing unless He reveals His secrets to His servants the prophets. God promises us that He will do nothing; He will not destroy us without warning us through His prophets. This is a wonderful promise that He will reveal His future plans for us through the prophets. He has always kept His word. Down through the centuries God has chosen certain individuals, both men and women, and has bestowed on them the prophetic gift. He reveals His plans for us through these chosen prophets. The prophets are God's messengers to the world. God gives us an opportunity to make the right decisions by forewarning us of His impending judgments. This pattern is consistent throughout the Bible. In ancient Israel when the people wanted to know what the Lord had to say they would go to the prophet. God, through His foreknowledge, revealed future events to His prophets. Deuteronomy 29:29 tells us that the secret things belong unto the Lord but those things which are revealed belong unto us and to our children forever that we may do all the words of this law.

God has always had a prophet among His people. God chooses men and women to be His prophets or messengers and they often carry solemn messages to His people. There are some individuals in the body of Christ who are endowed with the gift of prophecy. Prophecy is the revelation of Jesus Christ. In Revelation 19:10, through the medium of the Holy Spirit, the angel tells the prophet John that the testimony of Jesus is the spirit of prophecy, indicating that prophecy testifies about Jesus. Revelation 1:1 tells us that the prophecy that was given to John is the revelation of Jesus Christ, which God the father gave to him to show unto His servants things which must shortly come to pass. He sent and signified it by His angel unto His servant, John. So God the Father gave it to God the Son, who gave it to the angel Gabriel, who gave it to the prophet John, who gave it to the seven churches of which we are a part.

Many of the prophecies reveal to us those things that will take place in the closing scenes of this Earth's history. God gave us the gift of prophecy because of His love for us and His desire for us to avoid Satan's deceptions. We need to know the truth so we can make right decisions. We also need to know who God's true prophets are. Simply because someone proclaims to be a prophet does not make them a prophet. You must examine them and to see if what they say is consistent with the law and the testimony of the Bible. The Bible has given us guidelines on how to identify God's true prophets. Let us see how the Bible helps with the identification of God's true prophets.

God's true prophets often expose Satan and his deceptions. Satan retaliates by rising up false prophets, often with a counterfeit message, so he can deceive. From the beginning of time wherever God has a true prophet Satan raises false prophets.

How can we tell who God's true prophets are? Here are some helpful identifying features found in the Bible.

1. *The prophet must be in agreement with scripture.* Isaiah 8:20 states, "To the law and to the testimony if what they speak is not according to God's word there is no light in them. Therefore, *the prophets must agree with the Bible and their prophecy must agree with what God's other prophets have revealed.*"

Any prophet who prophesies beliefs that are contrary to the Bible is a false prophet. It is as simple as this: if a prophet says that God gave us permission to break His law he is a false prophet because they are prophesying against Gods' word. Since prophecy is from God it cannot contradict God's word. A true prophet from God will admonish us to keep all of God's commandments. If you find a prophet who is not in alignment with God's commandments they have failed the test. God would not send a prophet who contradicts His commandments.

Deuteronomy 13:1–3 says, "If someone among you claims to be a prophet and performs sign and wonders to prove that they are, even if what they say comes to pass and they tell you to go after other Gods, do not believe them because this is a violation of God's commandment that thou shall have no other God before me."

The prophets should lead people back to God and His commandments (see Deuteronomy 13:1–5). When the prophets speak you should search the scripture to see if what they say agrees with scripture. The true prophet will lead you to a deeper study and understanding of God's word.

2. *A true prophet will recognize the incarnation of Jesus Christ.* We are warned in 1 John 4:1–4, "Beloved, do not believe every spirit but try the spirits whether they are of God because many false prophets are gone out into the world. Any spirit that does not confess that Jesus came in the flesh is not of God."

Note here that the apostle is giving us admonition about how to tell false prophets from true prophets. The prophets testify of Jesus. The prophet's work exalts Jesus. Prophecy testifies about Jesus' death, life and resurrection. The prophet John, in Revelation 1:1, tells us prophecy is the testimony of Jesus.

3. *A true prophet edifies, exhorts and comforts the church spiritually* (see 1 Corinthians 14:3 and 4).

4. *A true prophet points out the sins of the people against God.* Isaiah 58:1 says, "Cry aloud, spare not, raise your voice like a trumpet and show My people their transgression and the house of Jacob their sins."

God chooses His prophets and requires that we listen to the words of the prophet (see Deuteronomy 18:18–22).

5. *The prophet's life should be Christ-like*. "By their fruits you shall know them" (Matthew 7:15–20). The prophet's life and the result of the prophet's work will be recognized as godly.

6. *A true prophet warns about coming judgments* (see Revelation 14:6 and 7). Throughout the Bible God's prophets have been warning His people about God's on-coming judgments.

7. *A true prophet does not give his or her own interpretation of prophecy.* 2 Peter 1:21 says, "For prophecy came not in old time by the will of man but holy men of God spoke as they were moved by the Holy Spirit." It is the Holy Spirit that inspires the prophets, not man.

8. *God often speaks to His prophets by visions and dreams*. God knew that Satan would imitate the prophetic gift and so He often communicates with His prophets in a supernatural way. In Numbers 12:6, 8 the Lord says, "Hear now My words: If there be a prophet among you, I, the Lord, will make Myself known to him in a vision and will speak unto him in a dream."

God communicates with His prophets primarily through dreams during sleep and visions when awake. These visions are inspired by the Holy Spirit and are often given under unusual supernatural conditions. For example, both Daniel and John had lost their natural strength. God's supernatural power sustained them during their visions. They were totally unaware of their surroundings, had no respiration but they could speak. God gives visions under supernatural conditions that cannot be duplicated by Satan.

The Bible gives us certain physical characteristics of a prophet in vision. They lose physical strength and receive supernatural strength (Daniel 10:8, 18, 19). They have no breath but they can speak (Daniel 10:16 and 17). Their eyes are open (Numbers 24:4). They are not conscious of their surroundings (Daniel 10:5–8). This is clearly a supernatural phenomenon.

9. *A true prophet will not be a diviner or fortune teller, an observer of times or an astrologer, an enchanter or a magician, a charmer or a spell caster, a consulter of familiar spirits or a spirit medium, a wizard or a psychic, a necromancer or one who consults with the dead* (Deuteronomy 18: 9–12).The Bible calls these people an abomination unto the Lord.

Miracles do not prove that a prophet is true because Satan can perform miracles. The magicians of Egypt were able to turn their rods into serpents, duplicating what Moses and Aaron did. This tells us that Satan gives power to false prophets. Healing also does not prove that you are a true prophet. The same devil that can inflict diseases can take them away when it is to his benefit.

10. *God's true prophets do not make many predictions*. True prophets reveal the future

as God shows it to them and it comes through with one hundred percent accuracy.

11. *There is one hundred percent accuracy in the fulfillment of prophecies except when the prophecies are conditional.* Jonah's prophecy about Nineveh was conditional. The inhabitants of Nineveh heeded the prophet's message and the conditions necessary for the destruction of Nineveh were not met and so Nineveh was not destroyed.

The Bible clearly reveals that God's people are blessed when the prophet is in their midst. There have been times in the history of God's people when the spiritual condition of the church was not conducive to the spirit of prophecy and the word of prophecy was scarce in the church. An example of this is seen in 1 Samuel 3:1. During the days of Eli the word of the Lord was scarce and the spirituality of Israel was low. This changed when the Lord called Samuel to the prophetic office. The Philistines were the enemies of ancient Israel and they troubled Israel but in 1 Samuel 7:13 we read that the hand of the Lord was against the Philistines all the days of the prophet Samuel. The Bible states that all the land, from Daniel to Beersheba, knew that Samuel was the prophet of the Lord.

As has been the case throughout the history of God's people, the people did not fully appreciate the gift of prophecy in their midst. Despite having the messenger of God in their midst telling them what God expected of them and despite the many blessings they enjoyed with God's prophet among them, they asked for a king to rule over them like the other nations around them. God warned them that a king would exploit them but they insisted and rejected God's leadership despite the successes they had when the prophet guided them.

Misconceptions About Prophets

The history of God's prophets is a troublesome one. In every dispensation people have been extremely critical of God's prophets and outright reject his prophets There is so much misconception and misunderstanding among God's professed people about His prophets that the people cannot get to the prophet's message because of their misconceptions. God does not choose perfect people to be His prophets. If He did there would be no prophets because there are no perfect people. It is true that when the prophet is relaying a message from God it is one hundred percent accurate. There are also times when the prophet is not speaking under the inspiration of the Holy Spirit and is giving his or her own opinion. Prophets are people too and have opinions.

1 Chronicles 17, King David wanted to build a temple for the Lord. He called the prophet Nathan and inquired of him whether he should build a temple for the Lord. Nathan, the prophet, told him to do that which is in his heart, for the Lord was with him.

That night when the Lord spoke to Nathan concerning this matter he told the prophet Nathan, "Tomorrow morning go back and tell David that he should not build the house of the Lord. His son Solomon will build the house of the Lord."

Does this make Nathan a false prophet? No, Nathan initially gave his opinion. He was not relaying a message from the Lord but when the Lord did speak to Nathan concerning the matter Nathan was able to relay the Lord's message to the king. David had no problems accepting the prophet's second admonition. The prophet was not speaking under the inspiration of God when he gave his initial opinion. One must be careful in their understanding of prophets and their roles. A prophet is God's messenger but that does not mean that every sentence they utter is a message from the Lord. The prophet tells us when the Lord has given them a message for His people.

Numbers 22 to 24 tells the story of Balaam, a prophet of God who became covetous and apostatized. He was offered great wealth and honor by Balak, the King of Moab, to curse the Israelites. One night God spoke to Balaam and told him not to go and curse Israel because they were blessed. Balaam initially listened to God. The King of Moab offered him more riches and honor. In his heart the prophet wanted to do what the King of Moab wanted and to curse Israel so he again consulted God and the Lord allowed him to follow his heart's desires. The next morning he saddled his donkey and he set out on his journey to the King of Moab. Despite hearing from Heaven, Balaam was bent on disobeying God. There are many people like that today. They are not going to follow God's will unless it is in harmony with what they want to do.

The story tells us that an angel of the Lord stood with a sword to slay Balaam. The donkey saw the angel and turned away three times. Balaam beat the donkey mercilessly until the donkey spoke like a man saying, "What have I done unto you that you smite me these three times?" If God can use a donkey to speak for Him why can he not use you?

The Lord opened Balaam's eyes and he beheld the angel and fell on his face. He realized that the donkey had saved his life by turning away from the angel three times. Balaam did meet with Balak and when he saw the Israelites encampment he was convinced that God was leading them. Balaam, seeing the encampment of the Israelites, advised Balak that the way to bring down the Israelites was through idolatry and it worked. This story has an interesting end and is very typical of the way Satan operates. Satan infiltrates the camp of God with his worldly ideas and God's people fall for it. That is how he separates them from God. The fate of this prophet was sad. He apostatized. Once a person is a prophet does not mean that they are always a prophet. Once saved does not mean always saved (see Luke 8:5–15, Matthew 24:13, 1 Corinthians 9:27, Ezekiel 18:24, and Romans 11:16–21).

It is important to study the lives of the prophets and understand their works before condemning them. If this story was not in the Bible some people would say that because

Balaam turned away from God's instructions he was not God's messenger. The Bible tells the whole truth, the good, the bad and the ugly and it is up to us to read and understand so that we can make the right decisions. Look at the lives of other biblical prophets; they have the same struggle with sin as any other human. Did Moses sin? Yes, sin prevented him from entering the Promised Land. Moses also murdered an Egyptian man but God forgave him and he became one of the greatest leaders of God's children. How about David? God told him that he could not build His temple because he had blood on his hands. David repented of his sins and God loved and forgave him and he was a prophet. God's prophets are people too and have opinions. I make these points because some people have misconceptions about prophets without a good base of knowledge about the prophets and their work. The area of prophecy is one that requires sincere thorough study. A superficial understanding can lead to wrong conclusions.

God has always had a prophet among His people and God always has a people, usually a small minority, who will heed the words of His prophets. God has never had the majority on his side.

When ancient Israel was at the crossroads of decision they turned to the prophets or the seers because the prophets see into the future as God reveals it to them. God gave the prophetic gift not only for the benefit of ancient Israel but also for His worldwide church today, which constitutes spiritual Israel, and the prophetic gift is part of God's church. Is it possible to reject God's true prophet? Yes, believers have done just that throughout history. Paul, in 1 Thessalonians 5:20, admonishes us to *"despise not prophesying*, prove all things, hold fast to that which is good."

There are many false prophets that have gone out into the land. They are sent by Satan to deceive you. This is the devil's plan of deception. He has been deceiving the lost and tempting the saints since the time of Adam. Prophecy is God's tool that Satan has perverted in too many instances.

False Prophets

Sometimes hundreds of years go by before there is a visible prophet among God's people. It seems that when God raises up a true prophet Satan raises up a false one to confuse the issue. It is not hard to see through false prophets. The best way to see through false prophets is to know the scriptures. Satan's prophets have no real biblically oriented message. Their prophecies are not Jesus centered and their messages do not follow the theme of the biblical prophets and give us insights into the future. Satan's prophets often extol the kingdom of Satan and its temporary gains. Their prophecies are more self-centered rather than Christ-centered. People are, by nature, self-seeking and are often seeking a feel-good experience so they can gratify themselves. Satan knows that people do not want to disrupt their comfortable lives to make great sacrifices to do God's will so he sends his false prophets who often prophecy smooth things to them. A common theme of false prophets is the Lord showing how you can break out and acquire more temporal worldly possessions. Contrary to popular theology today, Earthly wealth is not necessarily a sign of divine favor. This theology of greed is often masqueraded as the gospel.

A True Story

A man fell down at a church one night and busted his head on a pew as he fell. The wife of the man came to the hospital about two days after the burial asking me how to go about getting an autopsy on her husband who was buried two days ago. She was initially in shock and did not think about getting one before the burial. He attended the night service at church and the service continued up to midnight. A woman who said that she was a prophetess told him that the Lord showed her that if he would do a praise run around the church several times that he would receive a large sum of money by the end of the week. In this service the worshippers were worked up until they began to jump and shout. They believe this action to be a manifestation of the Holy Spirit.

This man was a poor man with young kids and multiple medical problems, including an underlying heart problem, and the thought of receiving money at the end of the week was no doubt attractive to him. He listened to this self-proclaimed prophetess and began to jump and run and shake his body as if in frenzy. During this exercise he fell down with a massive heart attack and died. In the process of falling, his head hit a pew and he sustained a large forehead laceration. That was why his wife wanted an autopsy. She was suspicious that someone hit him in the head at church that night. He died and left many young children with no means. His wife, who did not attend church, was suspicious of the cause of death because of the forehead laceration. She was furious at the church and demanded that they pay for his burial since she did not have the money for funeral expenses. This is an example of a poor, believing man who was led astray by a self-proclaimed false prophet. Beware of self-proclaimed prophets. Test all the spirits to see if they are of God and see if what they say lines up with scripture.

Prophecies About Wealth

Beware of those who prophesy to you that God wants you to get rich. Christians must be careful with the popular teaching that God desires us to have Earthly wealth. This is a very popular teaching that has attracted millions to some ministries. God never promised us wealth in the Bible. In Philippians 4:19 God promises to supply all of our needs, according to His riches in glory. Wealth is a want, not a need. The gospel of Christ is not one about prosperity. Jesus left the splendor of Heaven; denied Earthly wealth and lived in poverty. He did not preach a prosperity gospel. His followers gave up their wealth to follow Him and many became poor in this world's goods to follow Him. His disciples were poor men.

Nicodemus was an extremely wealthy and influential rabbi who believed that Jesus was the Messiah. When Jesus was crucified he stepped forward and boldly claimed the body of Jesus. He spent all of His wealth to support the early church and became poor in this world's possessions. How many wealthy professed Christians today will give up all their wealth to help the poor? This was the practice in the early church. In 2 Corinthians 8:5 the Apostle Paul describes the generosity of the poor Macedonian believers. Despite their poverty they gave to support the work. In Matthew 19, Mark 10 and Luke 18 the story is told of a rich young ruler who came running to Jesus and knelt before Jesus saying, "Good Master, what shall I do to inherit eternal life?" Jesus answered him saying, "You know the commandments." Jesus began naming the commandments. Take note here that Jesus taught that it is important to keep the commandments and the young man stopped Him, saying, "-All these I have kept from my youth." Jesus lovingly said to him, "One thing is still lacking. Go and sell all that you have and give to the poor and you will have treasures in Heaven." This young man had great possessions and he did not want to give them away so he walked away into eternal darkness forever. As Jesus looked on He said to His disciples, "It is hard for a rich man to enter the kingdom of Heaven.

Luke 19 tells of the story of the rich tax collector, Zacchaeus, who climbed up a Sycamore tree to see Jesus as He passed by. Tax collectors were hated people but Jesus is in the business of saving everyone. He called Zacchaeus down from the tree and went to his house. After meeting with Jesus Zacchaeus gave half of his goods to the poor and restored fourfold anything that he robbed from anyone.

Contrary to popular preaching and teaching today Jesus did not teach a prosperity gospel. He did not go around merchandizing the gospel. He did not accept money for his speaking engagements. Jesus said to His disciples, "Heal the sick, cleanse the lepers, raise the dead and cast out devils. Freely you have received, freely give. Do not provide gold, or silver or brass in your purses." The wealth of this world will cause many to lose their eternal home.

In this earthly state of affairs Jesus came and brought us the kingdom of grace. When Jesus comes the second time He will usher in the kingdom of glory with eternal life and all its eternal riches. If Earthly riches come, use them wisely. Build up God's kingdom. Invest in the kingdom of God where the riches will last forever. The Bible warns us to build up treasures in Heaven where moth and rust cannot destroy and where thieves cannot enter. Beware of a prosperity gospel! Jesus is our example in these matters. Many people pocket a lot of money donated for the Lord's cause. Some become wealthy and live extravagantly and then they say, "Look what the Lord has given me." Many people obtain wealth dishonestly but no one ever admits that their wealth may have come from Satan. Similarly, Satan causes calamities but God usually gets the blame for not preventing them. Do not assume that the Lord is responsible for the enormous wealth some have amassed and the luxurious lifestyles they exhibit while preaching the gospel.

In Mark 12:38 Jesus warns, "Beware of the scribes." One of their sins was that they devour widows' homes. The widows would donate their homes to the Lord and these Pharisees would use the money for their own personal use as opposed to enhancing the cause of God. God expects us to be faithful stewards of the possessions that He has blessed us with and use them to build up the kingdom of God.

Jesus warns in Luke 12:15, "Take heed and beware of covetousness for a man's life consists not of the abundance of things that he possesses. It is foolish to build up treasures on an Earth that is temporary. Build up treasures in a Heaven that is permanent. Moses refused the wealth of Egypt choosing instead the treasures of Heaven that are permanent. Be aware of false prophets, false teachers and healers who are getting rich in the name of the Lord and using the Bible to justify it. Jesus did not heal or teach for money. Satan is extremely clever in how he wraps up error. It comes in many deceptive forms wrapped as the gospel. Do not be fooled by Satan's deceptions such as, "God wants you to send more money into my already wealthy ministry so I can buy another expensive exclusive plane to take me around the world to preach or to build a bigger and more expensive church."

In Jesus' day there were no mega-churches with independent ministries. The disciples went abroad teaching and starting various congregations and the message was the same one they learned at the feet of Jesus. Be careful what you accept as truth. Listen to God's messengers or prophets and look at what Jesus did and what He says. Jesus is our example in all things.

God really cares about His church. He started the church and He is its protector and guide. How do you protect yourself from Satan's false teachings? A good fundamental understanding of the Bible and its many prophecies is an important tool in safeguarding against error. The prophecies were placed in the Bible for our benefit and they help to protect us from Satan's errors. 2 Peter 1:19–21 assures us that "we have also a more sure word of prophecy. Whereunto you do well to take heed as unto a light that shines in a dark place until the day dawn and the day star arise in our hearts. Knowing this first, that no prophecy of the scripture is of private interpretation. For the prophecy came, not in old time by the will of man, but by holy men of God spake as they were moved by the

Holy Ghost." God is the author of prophecy. The prophecies of the Bible serve a very important function in the life of the believer. It is very important that we study the Bible so that we can understand prophecy and identify who God's true prophets are.

Unlike the self-proclaimed prophets who say things people want to hear, God's prophets often bring news that the majority of people do not want to hear. That is why they are so often rejected. God's professed people often want to hear smooth prophesying. They do not want to hear any message that would call for a change in their belief system. Because of this they often proclaim God's prophets false and extol the teachers who say the things that they want to hear. This is true in both Old and New Testament times. Since the fall of Adam and Eve God has been sending us admonitions through His prophets. A study of some of the prophets and their messages is very important to us living at the end of time.

Prophetic Guide To The Second Coming

Throughout the course of history God has sent His prophets to guide His people. Before every major judgment that affects God's people the prophets are there to warn of impending disaster. God does not leave us to guess about the future. He knows the beginning from the end and He sends his messengers to us. The prophets tell the story of a God who so loves us and is doing everything He can to save us. God reveals His secrets to His servant's the prophets, and sends them sometimes on perilous journeys to warn us of God's judgment so that all who hear and accept His gift of salvation will be saved.

The prophets tell the story of a God who is clearly in control of everything. He created this universe and everything in it is under His control. He is in control of the events of history and has a plan to save His lost children. He has been sending us instructions so that we can be saved. God is actively involved in the shaping of the events of this world to fulfill His purposes in His great plan of salvation.

God's prophets are often called to do an unpopular work, to carry the message of God's impending judgments to a world that has gone astray from His sovereign will. These prophets are often sent to carry out God's messages to people who do not want to hear. The people are comfortable in their beliefs and God's prophets are often ridiculed, discredited, persecuted and killed. Down through the centuries Satan has incited his followers, including professed godly people, to discredit God's prophets. Professed godly people often inflict the worst damage to God's prophets. They do not like the messages that threaten their status quo so they try to discredit God's prophets. Throughout the course of history God has sent us warnings through His prophets. These warnings reveal a God intimately involved with His creation and very active in the salvation process.

God's Prophetic Warnings To The World

Surely the Lord God does nothing unless He reveals His secret to His servants the prophets. God has manifested the prophetic gift among His people since the fall of Adam and Eve. From the entrance of sin God has been communicating His plan of salvation for us through His prophets. These prophets have played a pivotal role throughout the history of God's people. The plan of redemption was revealed to Adam and Eve. In Genesis 3:15 God gave them the promise that Satan's power would be crushed. Jude 14 and 15 tells us that Enoch, the seventh generation from Adam, prophesied to his generation about the second coming of Jesus. Let us review some of the amazing prophecies of the Bible that God wants us to know.

Noah The Prophet

God looked down and saw that the wickedness of man was great in the Earth. Evil thought and action was continuous and violence filled the land. Wickedness was at its maximum and the world was about to self-destruct. God could not allow such evil to continue indefinitely. He had to save them from themselves. He pronounced judgment on the Earth and decided to destroy the Earth that He created.

Amid the disobedience upon the Earth there was a man who obeyed God. His name was Noah. Noah found grace in the sight of God and He chose Noah to be His messenger to that doomed world. He told Noah that He could no longer tolerate the wickedness in the world and He would destroy everything on the Earth with a flood (see Genesis 6:17) except for Noah and his family. God told Noah to build an ark.

Noah was not a builder but he had great faith in God. God designed the ark and gave the blue print to Noah. By faith, Noah believed God and for 120 years he built an ark and prophesied to the people. He told the people about God's impending judgment but people laughed and ridiculed Noah calling him a religious fanatic. Building an ark seemed like a foolish idea to the people of Noah's day, just as the second coming of Jesus seems foolish to some people today. They refuse to believe God's messenger.

The people refused to believe God and thought that the idea of a flood was ridiculous. It could never happen and would never happen. The Earth was watered from a mist that came out of the earth (Genesis 2:5 and 6). They had never seen rain and they thought a flood was out of harmony with known scientific knowledge.

Noah had developed a personal relationship with God. He believed and trusted God and made the choice to follow God's instructions. Noah was steadfast in his appointed task to warn the world. The world had never seen rain and the great philosophers and scientists of the day thought it was ludicrous and unscientific to think there would be a flood.

Noah invested all of his money and time into building this ark and warning the people. When the ark was completed the clean animals went into the ark by sevens and the unclean animals by two. Even the animals sensed the danger and went into the ark for safety. The people saw the animals going into the ark for safety and still did not believe God's messenger. They probably called for the animal and weather experts to explain the strange behavior of the animals. People today are still debating the minor stuff such as how certain animals got into the ark. They are missing the big picture of God's destruction of the Earth with a worldwide flood.

For 120 years Noah endured the ridicule and at the appointed time God instructed Noah and his family to go into the ark. God then shut the door. For seven days nothing happened but on the eighth day it began to rain. Soon water came from everywhere. Every living creature, except those in the ark, was destroyed. The entire world except for Noah and his family and the animals were destroyed. Noah's investment in the ark paid big dividends. Everything else was destroyed. Similarly, in the end of time when this Earth is destroyed the only lasting possessions would be that which is invested in the kingdom of Heaven.

Noah's flood is not fiction. Jesus believed it and, in Luke 17:26 and 27 and in Matthew 24:38 and 39, Jesus warns, "As in the days that were before the flood they were eating and drinking, marrying and giving in marriage, until the day that Noah entered the ark and knew not until the flood came and took them all away. So shall also the coming of the Son of Man be."

Jesus warns that the people of Noah's day did not take the warning of the flood seriously and they were all killed except for eight people. A similar situation will occur at the end of time. Of the billions of people on Planet Earth only a comparatively few will heed the message and be saved.

Apart from the Bible there is much scientific evidence for a sudden great catastrophic flood occurring about 4,300years ago. The impressive collection of well-preserved fossils with teeth, skin and scales speaks for a rapid burial. The condition of the fossils in many instances can only be explained by a sudden event. Some fossils show that the animal was in the birthing process when they were fossilized. Some were eating and still have grass in their mouth. We know that organic matter decays rapidly but there are well preserved fossils of soft tissue fish such as jellyfish and sponges that should have disintegrated over the postulated millions of years that evolutionists claim. These fossils can also be found on the highest mountains all over Planet Earth. Evolutionary scientists cannot show any life on Planet Earth that predates the flood 4,300 years ago. There are also fossils of great dinosaurs found clustered together in the great dinosaur graveyard in Utah. The cluster of dinosaur tracks in the coal mines of Utah can be explained as the dinosaurs tried to escape this great flood and left their heavy imprint in soil which later became coal.

These animals were all buried in that great catastrophic worldwide flood. The vast coal mines in the Earth's crust are easily explained by the flood. It does not take billions of years to form coal. Given the right conditions you can produce coal in a scientific lab. These conditions came together in the great flood and the cataclysmic volcanic activity that accompanied it. The scientific method of radiometric dating to explain the age of the Earth is fraught with assumptions such as the constant decay rate. We should not be so quick to believe these scientific assumptions. I do not want to get into the scientific debate about the existence of the flood. It would require too much time and space. I will accept, by faith, what the Bible says. It has not been wrong on anything yet.

For 120 years Noah warned the world of God's judgment and only eight people from Noah's family went into the ark of safety. Jesus warns that as it was in the day of Noah so shall it be in His second coming. The same conditions that existed then will again prevail and the people will reject God's messenger who is warning them and giving them vital information so they could be prepared for His second coming.

God has foreknowledge and He knew just how many people would be saved. He instructed Noah to build the ark accordingly. It was God's desire that everyone should be saved and that is why He sent His messenger to warn them for 120 years. Similarly, in the end of time God knows who will be saved. In Revelation we are told the dimensions of the New Jerusalem, the Holy City that God has prepared for the saved. This city of God, called the New Jerusalem, will descend from Heaven at the end of the millennium. God, with His foreknowledge of who will accept and follow His instruction and be saved, has made provisions for them.

God is not bound by the dimensions of time. He can separate the past, present and future. He gives us free choice and calls us all to repentance. He will save those who respond. He sends us many warnings through His prophets. *Surely the Lord God does nothing unless He reveals His secrets to His servants the prophets.*

After the flood Noah and his family got out of the ark to an entirely different world devastated by the flood. Noah immediately erected an altar and worshipped God. God promised Noah that He would never again destroy the world with a flood. He instructed Noah and his descendants to be fruitful, to multiply and populate the Earth (Genesis 9:1).

One would think that after such devastation man would obey God. It was not long after the flood that disobedience to God resurfaced. In Genesis 10, Noah's great grandson Nimrod (Noah-Ham-Cush-Nimrod), whose name means rebel, was a mighty man and a mighty hunter and he decided to build a city called Babel on the banks of the river Euphrates. They started to build a city and erect a tower, called the Tower of Babel, so high that it could reach into Heaven. They did not want to be scattered over the Earth. This was in direct rebellion to God's command, in Genesis 9:1, to populate the Earth. Genesis 11:1 says that at that time the inhabitants of Planet Earth spoke one language. God came down to see the city and the tower and confused their languages so that they could not understand each other and could not continue with the building of the tower. This is the origin of languages. The Lord scattered them abroad throughout the Earth and those who spoke the same languages eventually settled together. The name of the place was called Babel because the Lord confounded the language and scattered them abroad.

Babel was later named Babylon, which represents rebellion against God. Nimrod built many cities, including Nineveh (Genesis 10:11). From Babylon came false worship, false religions and rebellion against God. When Nimrod died his followers believed that his spirit took possession of the sun and he became the sun god. Sun worship originated here. Nimrod's wife Semiramis was believed to have become pregnant by Nimrods spirit and the child called Tammuz who was born on December twenty-fifth.

In Ezekiel 8:14 God showed the prophet the gate of the Lord's house and there sat a woman weeping for Tammuz. God showed the prophet a greater abomination. There were twenty-five men in the temple of the Lord worshipping the sun. This is important because we see how Satan began these pagan beliefs in Babylon and he will disguise these rebellious beliefs down through all generations until they are destroyed by the second coming of Jesus.

The Prophet Abraham

God chose Abraham as His prophet (see Genesis 20:7) and revealed His future plans to Abraham. About 2000 BC the patriarch Abraham, a descendant of Noah's son Shem, was born into a well-to-do family living in Ur of the Chaldees. This is an ancient city of Mesopotamia in Southern Iraq (Acts 7:2). The world around Abraham had again forsaken God and the worship of many Gods was prevalent. Such was the case even in His household. His father Terah made idols. Abram, before his name was changed to Abraham, believed in one God and God found Abraham to be faithful and so God chose him and revealed to him His law. God always has someone to preserve truth and to carry on with His plan of Salvation. God revealed His law and his salvation plan to Abraham. God called Abraham out of Babylon. He told him to leave his people and home in Ur of the Chaldees and go to an unknown land that He would show him.

Genesis 11:31 states that Terah took Abram his son and his grandson Lot, the son of Haran, and Sarai, Abram wife, and went forth from Ur of the Chaldees, in Iraq, toward

Canaan. When they got to a place called Haran they stayed for a while. Abraham's father Terah died and the Lord told Abraham to proceed on. Abraham followed God and went out, not knowing where he was going. Abraham and his family lived in tents and wherever he pitched his tent he set up an altar to the only one true God. Abraham, his wife Sarah, his nephew Lot and some members of his household followed God's leadings and eventually reached the land of Canaan. Abraham was shown the Promised Land and was told that his descendants would occupy the land of Canaan. From the seed of Abraham came the Arabs and the Jewish nation. Abraham is the biological father of the Jews and Arabs.

The Christian church today is the spiritual descendent of Abraham. Galatians 3:29 states, "And if we are in Christ then we are Abraham's seed and heirs according to the promise." Abraham himself did not possess the land of Canaan. Hebrews 11:9 and 10 states, "By faith he sojourned in the Land of Promise as in a strange country, dwelling in tabernacles with Isaac and Jacob, the heirs with him of the same promise. He looked for a city which hath foundations whose builder and maker is God." Verse 13 says, "They all died in the faith, not having received the promises but having seen them afar off and were persuaded of them and embraced them and confessed that they were strangers and pilgrims on the Earth."

Do not miss the larger view point here. Although Abraham's seed did occupy Earthly Canaan God had the big picture in mind and gave Abraham a view of the Heavenly Canaan, our eternal home. Galatians 3:28 and 29 says that in Christ there is neither Jew nor Greek, there is neither male nor female for we are all one in Christ Jesus. And if we are Christ's then we are the seed of Abraham and heirs according to the promise. The promise that God made to Abraham is being fulfilled through Christ.

In Matthew 8:11 and 12 Jesus warns, "Many will come from the east and west and shall sit down with Abraham and Isaac and Jacob in the kingdom of Heaven but the children of the kingdom shall be cast out into outer darkness. There shall be weeping and gnashing of teeth." The true children of Abraham will look for the same city that Abraham longed for, the city whose maker and builder is God. It is the eternal city of God and not an earthly domain.

God promised Abraham that he would have a son but he grew old and his wife could no longer have children. They grew impatient and thought they would help God out. Sarah, Abraham's wife, gave her handmaiden, an Egyptian woman named Hagar, to Abraham to be his wife and she conceived and bore a son name Ishmael whose descendants are now the Arabs. Abraham thought that he was the heir of the promise but Ishmael was not. It appears that it was the culture in those days to give your handmaiden to the husband and we see this happening in subsequent generations with Jacob, Abraham grandson. This created all kinds of problems in these marriages.

Some 4,000 years ago Abraham and Sarah did not wait for God and created significant problems in their marriage. Abraham, at the ripe old age of 100, and post-menopausal Sarah, at age ninety, conceived and bore the son of the promise, Isaac, whose descendants are now the Jews.

God can make a post-menopausal woman conceive if He wants her to. He is the Creator. The story of Abraham is an important part of the plan of Salvation. In this story God reveals to Abraham His plan of salvation, to give His only begotten Son on Calvary to save this world. The Bible states that Abraham obeyed God's laws (Genesis 26:5).

When Abraham was 120 years old God told him to take his son Isaac and offer him on Mt. Moriah as a burnt offering. Abraham obeyed God and as he lifted the knife kill his beloved son God stepped in and said to him, "Lay not your hand upon the lad, neither do thou anything unto him for now I know that thou fear God, seeing that thou hast not withheld thy son, your only son, from me."

God revealed His plan of salvation to Abraham. God the Father had promised His only Son to die to redeem this fallen world. Let us continue to follow the story of our redemption as we read about Sodom and Gomorrah.

God's Warnings To Sodom And Gomorrah

Abraham's nephew, Lot, chose to live in the Jordan valley and pitched his tent toward the wicked city of Sodom. Sodom and Gomorrah were wicked cities in the plains of Jordan. The wickedness of these two cities was exceedingly great and God pronounced judgment on Sodom and Gomorrah. The Lord told Abraham his plans to destroy Sodom and Gomorrah. Abraham intervened and begged God to spare the city if there were fifty righteous people. In that entire city God could not find fifty righteous people and so Abraham bargained with God to spare the city if there were ten righteous people. Sadly, they could only find one man who did not partake of the sins of Sodom and that was Abraham's nephew Lot.

The angels warned Lot and his family to flee for their lives and not to look back because they would die. Lot could not tear himself away from the city and he lingered. The angels literally had to drag Lot out of Sodom by the hand. The heart of Lot's wife was in Sodom and she looked back at her beloved city and became a pillar of salt. For many centuries people dismissed many of these biblical stories as myths but the stones are crying out and many of the biblical cities and peoples are being discovered and these discoveries are mounting every day.

The cities of the plains, which include Sodom and Gomorrah, have been discovered. The Hittites are frequently mentioned in the Bible and for many centuries historians doubted the Hittites existed. The finding of the Rosetta stone has changed this. This stone unlocked the mystery of the hieroglyphics and now a record has been found outside the Bible to substantiate the biblical mention of the Hittites and their numerous battles against Israel. Hattusa, the capital of the Hittites, was found in Turkey. Archeology today, more than ever, is supporting the biblical stories. Recent excavations have revealed David's kingdom in Israel. Jericho has been excavated and more recently the tomb of King Herod has been found. The Bible is an accurate historical record and the stones are crying out and telling mankind that God's word is true. The Bible is leading these excavations. The absence of non-biblical evidence for the places mentioned is not evidence of the absence of these places and peoples mentioned in the Bible.

These biblical stories reveal that God is intimately involved in our lives and He can miraculously use sinful lives that have been turned over to Him and can work out His plan of salvation in our lives. Let us continue to follow the historical record of our redemption and how God choose a nation through whom the Messiah would come. From Abraham came Ishmael, the father of the Arabs, and Isaac, the child of the promise. From the generations of Isaac the promised Messiah would come. From Isaac came Esau and Jacob.

About 100 years after the covenant with Abraham we come to the patriarch Jacob. He had twelve sons who became the twelve tribes of Israel. God changed Jacob's name to Israel. This is the origin of the Jewish nation. God also renewed the promises to Jacob that he made to Abraham and his son Isaac. It is through this chosen nation that God would reestablish His law and His covenant. Through this nation the Messiah would come and die to redeem lost humanity. This nation was chosen by God to introduce the Messiah to the world.

As we fast forward down the time line of history, somewhere around 1706 BC the Jews are living in Egypt. Joseph, the son of Jacob, was sold into slavery in Egypt by his brothers. God blessed Joseph and through a series of miraculous events he became ruler of Egypt and eventually Jacob, his father, and the rest of his brothers moved to Egypt. After many years in Egypt, and long after the death of Jacob and Joseph, the Jews were made slaves in Egypt.

Moses was born in Egypt during the time of the 18th dynasty. His adopted mother was Hatshepsut, the daughter of Thutmose I and co-ruler with Thutmose III. Moses was heir to the pharaoh's throne when he killed an Egyptian and fled from Thutmose III. He spent forty years in the Midian desert near the Sinai Peninsula before returning to Egypt to free his people.

The great Exodus from Egypt took place under the leadership of Moses at about 1447 BC The Egyptian army drowned in the great flood and most likely Thutmose III as well. Having successfully led the children of Israel out of Egypt God again reestablished

His law that was lost during the Exodus.

Around 1010 BC the children of Israel rebelled against God's theocracy and demanded a king. Saul was Israel's first king, from 1050–1010 BC David reigned from 1010–970 BC and Solomon reigned from 970–930 BC.

1 Kings 11 tells how King Solomon, the wisest man who ever lived, turned his back on God. He had 700 wives and 300 concubines and his wives turned his heart away from the true God to their pagan gods. This is one of the reasons why God does not permit his people to marry outside the faith. 1 Kings 11:5 says that Solomon worshipped Ashtoreth, the goddess of the Zidonians. She is also Semiramis, the wife of Nimrod, the Babylonian goddess. Pagan culture was now widespread. Solomon did evil in the sight of God, sacrificing children to these pagan Gods. He did not heed God's instructions and the kingdom was eventually divided under the poor leadership of his son Rehoboam. The Kingdom of Israel was divided into the Northern Kingdom, consisting of ten tribes: Asher, Dan, Ephraim, Gad, Issachar, Manasseh, Naphtali, Reuben, Simeon and Zebulun. The Southern Kingdom of Israel was divided into the two tribes of Judah and Benjamin. God had a great purpose for Israel because through them the Messiah of the world would come to redeem us.

Throughout the history of Planet Earth Satan has been deceiving God's creation. God intervenes time and again and puts his plan of salvation back on track. Let us continue to see how God is leading His people and how His plan of salvation is being executed from beginning to end.

The nation of Israel was called forth for a grand and lofty purpose. God chose Israel to be His people and to be the keeper of His law in all the Earth. Through them, His saving plan of salvation will be carried to all the inhabitants of the Earth. There is no greater job or any loftier purpose in this present world. Despite widespread apostasy from God down through the centuries in every dispensation God has always had a faithful few to carry out His plan of redemption and He always had a prophet among His people to lead them back to His will for them.

Let us continue to look briefly at God's leading through His prophets and see how kingdoms fall because they fail to listen to God's prophets and repent of their sins. Satan is constantly trying to deceive God's people and destroy God's plan of salvation. Time after time he causes God's church to go astray. Time after time God sends His prophets to get His people back on track. Often the church refuses to listen to God's prophets. God warns us that He does nothing unless He reveals His secrets to His prophets. That is a promise we can count on. He has done just that and will continue to do so until time runs out. Before its' demise God sent numerous prophets to the northern kingdoms. Let us look at some of these messages.

God's Warnings Through The Prophet Elijah (850 BC)

This story is told in 1 Kings 17. The time is about 850 BC and sitting on the throne of Israel is one of the most wicked king with his foreign wife Jezebel. During his reign from 871–853 BC Israel grew steep in apostasy and idolatry. Ahab did not marry according to God's will. He married a non-believer, Jezebel. The Queen of Israel was an idol worshipper. Her father was a worshipper of Baal and she brought all of her idol worship and strange beliefs with her.

The spirituality of Israel under the leadership of Ahab and Jezebel had reached an unprecedented low. They did not obey God and had completely forgotten how God had led and protected Israel in the past. They refused to turn from evil despite warnings and they blatantly rejected the commandments of God and did evil in the sight of the Lord.

The Lord called a God fearing-man living in the mountains of Gilead, east of Jordan. The Lord bestowed on him the prophetic gift and sent him with warnings of punishment for Israel because they refused to obey Him. God's true prophets usually do not bring a feel-good message. God sends these messages to His people who erred from His word but God's professed people rejected these messages as undesirable and called God's prophet false.

At this time in history God sent a true prophet to His people. God chose a prophet by the name of Elijah. The name Elijah means Yahweh is God. Elijah left his home in the mountains and went to Ahab's palace in Samaria. He gained entrance to the king and stood before him boldly delivering God's message of judgment on Israel. "As long as the Lord God of Israel lives, before whom I stand, there shall not be dew nor rain these years, but according to my word." He then disappeared as abruptly as he appeared.

God then told Elijah to hide by the brook Cherith, which is before Jordan. God commanded the ravens to feed him and they obeyed. Instead of accepting God's judgment and repenting of their sins, King Ahab and Queen Jezebel blamed the prophet for the drought and they looked for him to kill him. The Lord protected His prophet and hid him. They searched high and low for the prophet Elijah. Jezebel refused to accept God's punishment and repent and was determined to kill Elijah. Unable to find him, the wicked Queen Jezebel, angry that she could not find Elijah, proceeded to kill all of God's true prophets.

Obadiah, the head of the king's household, was a faithful follower of God and hid 100 prophets in a cave. As a result of the drought in the land the brook Cherith, where Elijah was hiding, dried up and God sent him to a Phoenician widow living in the city of Zarephath in Zidon, Jezebel's hometown. God hid Elijah right in Jezebel's hometown. The widow generously shared her last meal with him and as a result the Lord blessed her and preserved her life during the drought. This woman was not an Israelite but she served God to the best of her knowledge and God rewarded and blessed her. God has always included everyone in His plan of salvation. He has no favorites. He used Israel as His chosen instrument to share His salvation plan to all nations.

After the three years of drought in the land the Lord said to Elijah, "Go show yourself to Ahab and tell him that I am ready to send rain upon the earth."

On his way to the King's palace in Samaria he ran into Obadiah, who was sent by the king to look for grass and water so the animals would not all die. Elijah told Obadiah to tell the king that Elijah was here. Obadiah could not believe that he was actually seeing Elijah and was afraid to tell the king, fearing Elijah would disappear again and the king would kill him, but Elijah assured him that he would not disappear.

Obadiah told the king and the king went out to meet Elijah. Finally they met. In those days a king would have his soldiers just execute Elijah but Ahab was mindful of what had happened to his country and so he fearfully asked Elijah "Are you he that troubles Israel?" The prophet Elijah was forthright with his message and replied that the problem was not with the prophet but with Israel. Israel had forsaken the commandments of God and had fallen into idolatry.

Elijah told Ahab to gather all of Israel on Mt Carmel and bring 450 prophets of Baal, the god of rain, and 400 other false prophets that ate at Jezebel's table. "Let us go up to the mountain top and meet God on the mountain and decide what Israel is going to do."

Ahab gathered all of Israel on Mt. Carmel that day. The false prophets outnumbered God's prophet 850 to one. A lone prophet stood up for God against Satan's army that day. That day God's true prophet warned Israel to stop halting between two opinions. Do not say you are serving God while you are worshipping according to the dictates of Baal. If you are serving God, do what he says. Do not mix truth with error. You cannot serve God and Baal at the same time.

Elijah told them to choose two bullocks, one for them and one for him, and to cut their bullock and put wood, but no fire, under it. They were to call on their God to send fire to consume it. Elijah gave them plenty of time to call on Baal. All day long the people screamed and beat themselves up for their false god but to no avail. Elijah, told them, "Cry louder, maybe he is talking or pursuing or in a journey or sleeping." Baal never answered because there was no Baal to answer.

It was Elijah's turn to pray and he uttered a simple prayer to God with no fanfare. As soon as Elijah concluded his prayer God send down fire and consumed Elijah's sacrifice. The fire works on Mt. Carmel dazzled the people and they repented and acknowledged Elijah's God as the true God who controlled all of nature. The people repented and were spared destruction but the false prophets who led them into idolatry were destroyed that day lest they lead the people back into idolatry.

Elijah told King Ahab to prepare for rain and as King Ahab left Mt. Carmel it began to rain. It rained so hard that Elijah had to run in front of King Ahab's chariot to guide him home. Ahab did not invite the prophet into his palace. He left him out in the rain. When King Ahab got back to the palace and told his wife Jezebel what had happened at Mt. Carmel that day and that Jehovah had prevailed and the false prophets were slain she was infuriated. She refused to acknowledge God and ordered the killing of Elijah.

After that vivid demonstration of God's power on Mt. Carmel Elijah did not expect Queen Jezebel to react this way. He thought the nation of Israel would have been converted back to God. Elijah was disappointed and discouraged and thought to himself, "What use is that demonstration by God at Mt. Carmel? If it did not change them nothing will."

Instead of looking to God for his next move he fled into the wilderness and found himself alone under a Juniper tree. There he prayed to die but God knew where His prophet was and sent an angel to Elijah. God asked Elijah, "What are you doing here? Who sent you here?" God told Elijah to stand at the opening of the cave and He would pass by. As Elijah stood there a powerful wind blew but God was not in the wind. Then came an earthquake and God was not in the earthquake. Then came fire and God was not in the fire. Then came a still small voice. It was the voice of the Lord in a person to person conversation with Elijah asking him, "What are you doing here?" Elijah replied, "I have been jealous for the Lord God of hosts, for the children of Israel have forsaken thy covenant, thrown down thine altars, and slain thy prophets with the sword; and I, even I only, am left and they seek my life to take it away."

The Lord told Elijah to return to Israel through Damascus and to anoint Hazael as King of Syria and Jehu as King of Israel and Elisha as his replacement. Hazael will attack Israel soon and Jehu will kill everyone from King Ahab's house who escapes from Hazael. The Lord assured him that there were 7,000 people in Israel who were faithful followers of Jehovah and had not bowed their knees to Baal. In every dispensation and now, at the time of the end, God always has a faithful few. Only God knows who they are. It is not our duty to number them but to pray that we are among them.

History happened as the Lord had revealed it to Elijah. After the death of King Ahab his son, King Ahaziah, did not heed the message and worshipped Baal and it displeased the Lord. One day he fell in his house and injured himself. He sent his servants to inquire of Baalzebub, the god of flies, whether or not he would recover. On their way they ran into Elijah who asked them to ask the king, "Is there no God in Israel that you will inquire of Baalzebub, the God of Ekron (the god of flies). Go back and tell the king that because of this he will die."

When the servants returned with the message the king inquired who the man was. They answered, "He was a hairy man and girt with a girdle of leather about his loins."

The king exclaimed, "Oh no, not again. That must be Elijah the Tishbite. I know all about him from the days of my father."

The prophet was right again and the king died from his injuries.

At the end of Elijah's prophetic life God told Elijah to anoint another to be prophet in his stead. Guided by God he chose Elisha, a man from a God-fearing family. Elijah passed by the field and saw Elisha plowing with twelve yoke of oxen before him. Elijah passed by him and cast his mantle upon him and he left his oxen and followed Elijah. Elijah trained Elisha and one day, as they were together, Elijah was taken to Heaven in a chariot of fire representing those who will be redeemed without dying first.

Even Prophets Can Be Disobedient

It is an awesome responsibility to be a prophet. It is dangerous not to follow the instructions given by the Lord. 1 Kings 13 tells the story of a prophet from Judah who was warned by God not to eat bread nor drink water or return the same way he came. The prophet did not follow God's instructions and he was killed by a lion because of his disobedience. God requires strict obedience to His commands.

From 787–745 BC God sent warnings through the prophet Jonah. Some prophets initially rejected the call to be God's messenger. The story of Jonah is a good example of one called to the prophetic office who initially rejected the call to prophetic ministry. God called Jonah and told him to leave his hometown of Gath-hepher in northern Israel (2 Kings 14:25) and go to Nineveh, some 500 miles away.

This story takes place during the reign of Jeroboam II (787–745 BC). Nineveh was a large city, the capital of the Assyrian Empire. According to Jonah 3:3, it was an exceedingly great city of three days journey. The city of Nineveh was founded on the banks of the Tigress River by Nimrod, the great grandson of Noah (Genesis 10:11). It became a budding metropolis filled with crime and lawlessness. God decided to destroy Nineveh because of their wickedness. The Ninevites were a heathen people. They did not have the true knowledge of God. God did not give up on Nineveh. He made the decision to warn them about the destruction. He knew that there were people in Nineveh who, if they knew the truth about Him, would accept Him and change their wicked ways.

God had a relationship with Jonah and he sent the prophet to Nineveh, which is close to the modern day city of Mosul in northern Iraq, 250 miles north of Baghdad. This is the lofty purpose for which the Jewish nation was chosen by God. God had chosen the Jewish nation and equipped them with the necessary information to tell the world about him.

According to Jonah 1:1 and 2, "The word of the Lord came unto Jonah, the son of Amittai, saying, 'Arise, go to Nineveh, that great city, and cry against it for their wickedness is come up before me.'" Jonah was sent by God hundreds of miles away to a city on the banks of the Tigris River to warn the heathen people of Nineveh that their city would be destroyed because of their sins. Jonah was called to leave his hometown and go to the great metropolitan city of Nineveh and tell the city folks that they needed to repent from their sins or their city would be destroyed. God is patient with us and slow to anger and before He pronounces judgment and punishes the crime He sends His prophets to warn us. When we respond by accepting His pardoning grace and turning away from our sins He has pity and forgives us. *Surely the Lord God does nothing unless He reveals it to His servants the prophets.*

Can you imagine God sending Jonah to Assyria, a nation that had invaded Jonah's country of northern Israel? God has no favorites. He cares deeply and wants to save *everyone* so He sent a Hebrew prophet to warn a heathen nation. I hope that you are appreciating God's plan of salvation and why He chose the Jewish nation at that time and deposited His laws so that the world would know about God and His plans for lost humanity.

That is the wonderful thing about God, He wants to save everybody and will do everything to save one soul. Every soul is precious to Him. It does not matter how steeped you are in sin and unbelief, God can lead you to salvation. Some of the greatest Christian leaders were once atheists. The decision is yours to make. Since the fall of Adam God has been in the business of saving humanity. The story of the salvation of these heathen Ninevites is a demonstration that God cares for all and He often sends His prophets to warn all. God uses people to reach people. That is why it is so important for us to share God's saving message with everyone.

To Jonah this was mission impossible and he was scared to go to Nineveh. He did not appreciate the fact that the God who called for such a daunting mission was able carry him through. Jonah did not want to go so he took a cargo ship going in the opposite direction to Tarshish, a distant place believed to be thousands of miles away. Jonah could not see the benefit of taking God's message to that wicked pagan city and so he decided to run away from God. It is not possible to run from God. He knows everything, even your thoughts. In Psalms 139:7 David writes, "Whither shall I go from thy spirit? Or whither shall I flee from thy presence? If I ascend up into Heaven thou art there, if I make my bed in hell, behold, thou art there. If I take the wings of the morning and dwell in the uttermost parts of the sea even there thy right hand shall hold me."

Instead of heeding these words, Jonah decided to run away with strangers, people who did not believe in the only true and living God. The ship had not gone very far when God sent a mighty tempest and the ship seemed that it would be torn apart.

The sailors were afraid and they began praying to their heathen Gods. They emptied the ship of their precious cargo but Jonah, the only one on that ship who knew the only true and living God, was fast asleep down in the ship. The captains had to wake Jonah up saying, "Get up and pray to your God."

The storm was so ferocious that the sailors believed that their Gods were angry with them and sent the storm so they cast lots to see who caused this major storm and the lot fell on Jonah. The men asked Jonah who he was and Jonah told them that he was a Hebrew and he feared the Lord, the God of Heaven, who hath made the sea and the dry land. Jonah told the men that it was his fault and that he was running away from God and begged the men to throw him overboard. The men were reluctant. They did not want Jonah to die. They tried to bring the ship back to land but the storm continued to rage and when their very lives were endangered they reluctantly threw him overboard into the angry Mediterranean Sea and the storm ceased.

These men had an opportunity to learn about the only true God from this experience. Jonah 1:16 says, "Then the men feared the Lord exceedingly and offered a sacrifice unto the Lord and made vows." Then God the Creator sent a large fish to swallow Jonah. God, who has the might and power to do whatever he chooses to do, miraculously preserved Jonah in the belly of that fish. This is an incredible story that tells us that God who created this vast universe and who hangs innumerable numbers of stars in space can do a lot of things that you and I cannot understand. After three days and three nights in the belly of this large fish Jonah cried earnestly unto God who heard him in the depths of the sea and God spoke to the fish and the fish vomited Jonah onto dry land.

God did not give up on Jonah. After the fish vomited onto dry land God called to him a second time, saying, "Arise, go to Nineveh, that great city, and preach unto it the preaching that I bid thee." This time Jonah found his way to Nineveh and, as fast as he could, he delivered God's warning. As soon as Jonah entered the city he began to cry out, "In forty days the city of Nineveh will be destroyed." Jonah did come to them with smooth prophesying. No, it was a gloom and doom message about God's judgment on Nineveh.

Now what would you do if a stranger came running into your city crying loudly, "Repent for in forty days your city will be destroyed!" Your beautiful home, your automobiles, all of your earthly possessions would be destroyed in forty days. How many people today would listen and heed this warning of repentance from a stranger? Led by their king the non-believing inhabitants of Nineveh listened to Jonah and believed God. The king and all the inhabitants, from the greatest to the least, covered themselves with sackcloth. The men of Nineveh ceased their violence and cried mightily unto the Lord. The Lord heard them and forgave them and Nineveh was spared from destruction.

After such a successful evangelistic effort one would expect that the prophet Jonah would be happy with the result. The record says he became angry because God was merciful towards the Ninevites and did not destroy them. Jonah 4:1 and 2 says, "But it displeased Jonah exceedingly and he was very angry. He prayed unto the Lord and said, 'I pray thee. I knew this would happen even before I left home that is why I fled to Tarsish because I knew that you are a gracious God and merciful, slow to anger and of great compassion, eager to forgive.'"

Jonah felt that he carried this message of destruction but because God did not destroy the city he would be considered a false prophet. Prophets cannot afford to worry about their critics. Jonah was angry that God did not destroy this great city with hundreds of thousand inhabitants who repented of their sinfulness and were spared the wrath of God. God saw the whole picture that Jonah did not see. Jonah was so annoyed that he prayed to die but God is wise, merciful and slow to anger and did not grant Jonah his wish. God had to work with His angry prophet.

God is long suffering and does not destroy us when we sometimes fall into sin. The problem lies when we languish in sin. Jonah left and went outside the city and built a booth and waited to see what would happen to Nineveh. Jonah was exposed to the hot sun so God prepared shade for Jonah by growing a gourd vine and providing an east wind. Jonah was happy for that. Then God sent a worm which destroyed the gourd. Jonah fainted from the heat and again wished to die. God told Jonah, "You had pity on the gourd which you did not work or make grow. Why should I not spare the great city of Nineveh, among its inhabitants are more than 120,000 people who did not know right from wrong."

God knows the minutest details about us. A loving God does not destroy people who did not know right from wrong. He lovingly sends repeated warnings to us. *Surely the Lord God does nothing unless He reveals His secrets to His servants the prophets.* God had to teach Jonah that He is a God of forgiveness to all, even to heathen nations.

The truth is, God cares about everyone and does all He can to save us. There is a place in God's heart for every one of His children, both believers and unbelievers, and just like a father hurts over his erring children, God does too. God wants to do more for us than we want to do for our children. The inhabitants of Nineveh heeded Jonah's message and turned to the true God. This is a powerful story that shows, among other things, that God wants to save everyone and all of nature is under God's control and command. At God's command the storm arose, the fish appeared to swallow Jonah, God preserved Jonah in the belly of a fish and the fish spat Jonah out at God's command. At the end of the story an east wind appeared, the gourd vine appeared as well and then the worm came at God's command. Nature obeys its creator but the chosen prophet, Jonah, ran in the opposite direction. How about you? Are you running in the opposite direction from God's will?

God's message is for all people. He may use a particular group to send His message but that does not mean God is partial to any one group. He is not and His invitation is for everyone. Today God is still sending His warnings to all nations, kindred, tongue and people. Modern-day spiritual Israel is the Christian church that is taking the gospel to all the nations of the world. God is still in the saving business and His plan of salvation is still fully intact. The Christian church today constitutes the spiritual Israel that is carrying God's salvation message to Earth's most remote areas before the second coming of Jesus which seems to be very soon.

Centuries later Jesus talks about Jonah and the city of Nineveh in Matthew 12:39–41. He warns the scribes and pharisees who rejected Him that the people of Nineveh repented when they heard Jonah. He also told them that the Queen of Sheba believed Solomon and was impressed with his wisdom. God Himself, who is greater than Jonah and Solomon, was present with them in the form of Jesus Christ and they believed Him not. The people of Nineveh and the Queen of Sheba will condemn them in the judgment. This is a powerful waning from Jesus.

The ancient city of Nineveh, the Capital of Assyria, sunk back into idolatry and was eventually destroyed around 612 BC. As the kingdom of Assyria was disintegrating at the hands of the Babylonians, Assyria finally fell to Babylon in 610 BC,. Archeological excavations of the 19th century have unearthed this ancient city of Nineveh and its ruins are located near Mosul in Iraq. *Surely the Lord God does nothing unless He reveals His secrets to His servants the prophets.*

God Warning Through The Prophet Amos (767 BC)

God did not permit the destruction of the northern kingdom of Israel without first repeatedly warning them. He sent many prophets with warnings. About 767 BC God sent the prophet Amos, a herdsman from Techoa, a small town five miles south of Bethlehem, to warn Israel of His judgment. He was a herdsman and a gatherer of Sycamore fruit when God sent him from the southern kingdom of Judah to prophesy unto the northern kingdom. God took a poor uneducated country boy away from taking care of animals and picking sycamore figs and sent him to the nation's capital to warn Israel that, although this was a time of great economic prosperity, the nation was spiritually far from God.

In Amos 1:1 the King of Israel at this time was Jeroboam II (787–747 BC) and the King of Judah was Uzziah (787–736 BC). This prophecy was given two years before the earthquake; mentioned in Zechariah 14:5.

The nation of Israel was a very prosperous nation and many had luxurious lifestyles. Amos 3:15 said they had winter homes and summer homes and houses made of ivory (see 2 Kings 22:39). In Amos 4 the poor were oppressed, the needy crushed and the high society women of Samaria consumed liquor. Israel had strayed far from the high ideals God had for them. They were affluent, proud and self-sufficient. They worshipped calves and idols and worldly possessions.

Remember, He chose this nation and brought them out of bondage in Egypt around 1445 BC and reintroduced His law. At Mt. Sinai He established a covenant relationship with them and they agreed saying, "All that the Lord hath said we will do."

He gave them His law and in Deuteronomy 4 He charged them to be obedient to His commandments, statutes and judgments. Moses called upon Heaven and Earth to be a witness. He warned them that if they forgot God they would be scattered among the heathen nations. God preserving them as a nation was contingent on their obedience to His commands. He wanted them to be an example to the world, to teach the world about the true God. He taught them right from wrong but time after time they slid into sin and became like the unbelieving nations around them.

At this point in their history, about 760 BC, they were prosperous and forgot about God commandments. Their material prosperity led to their spiritual decline and they did not perceive their fallen state. Israel, who God brought out of the land of Egypt, out of the house of bondage in such a miraculous way, forgot their history, broke their covenant with God and followed the other nations into idolatry.

God does not give up on us easily so into this sophisticated, wealthy Capitol Hill, Wall Street-like environment God sent the poorest of the poor, the prophet Amos, to speak for Him and warn them about the judgments that would befall them for their disobedience to His law. This has been the story since the fall of Adam. Generation after generation has violated God's command and prophet after prophet has been rejected and killed.

God revealed to the prophet Amos the many sins of Israel and admonished them in Amos 5:6, "Seek ye Me and ye shall live". Now just imagine that you are a wealthy, successful and influential person. Why would you listen to a poor unknown man who states that he has a message from God? You can just imagine what happened when Amos arrived in the capital city of Samaria. It was a far different society from his own. Amos brought a solemn message to the people of the northern kingdom that because of their stubbornness and lack of repentance they were about to be captured by the powerful nation of Assyria.

In addition to Samaria, Amos prophesied at Bethel but the priest of Bethel, Amaziah, sent word to the king that Amos was conspiring against him by saying that he would die by the sword and Israel would be taken captive. The greatest enemies of God's truth are often professed godly people. They lead the fight against God's prophets.

Amaziah, the priest of Bethel, did not like the message Amos brought and told Amos to go back home to Judah and prophesy there and leave Israel alone. Amos held his ground informing Amaziah that he was sent by God to warn Israel of its sins against God. Amos describes his call for the job in Amos 7:14 and 15. I was no prophet, neither was I a prophet's son. I was a herdsman, a gatherer of sycamore fruit and the Lord took me as I followed the flock and the Lord said unto me, "Go, prophesy unto my people Israel." I am just a poor lowly man whom the Lord chose to send to warn you about impending danger.

The prophet Amos fearlessly discharged his duties and gave God's warning to Israel but they rejected him. God's prophets have been rejected in every dispensation even up to the end of time. The words of a poor country prophet were not appealing to them. He did not say what they wanted to hear. They were set in their belief system and not even God's true prophet could change their minds. In their belief system he did not fit their profile of a prophet from God. After all, why would God send them warnings through someone of such lowly estate in life? They did not respond like the Ninevites and the results were sad.

Two years later there was a devastating earthquake and about forty years later, around 721 BC the northern kingdom fell to Assyria and they lost everything. The ten tribes of the northern kingdom were gradually scattered throughout the Assyrian kingdom. God send prophet after prophet to warn Israel of His impending judgments but they continued in their rebellious ways so they lost their kingdom and were scattered in the heathen land of Assyria. God sent His prophets to warn them but they rejected the prophets. It is up to us, with the help of the Holy Spirit, to know who God's true prophets are so that we can heed their warnings. These examples are written in the Bible for us who live in the very end of time so that we do not make the same mistakes. The prophet Amos tells us, *"Surely the Lord God does nothing unless He reveals His secrets to His servants the prophets"*.

750 BC: God's Warnings Through The Prophet Hosea

Hosea was called to the prophetic ministry during the reign of several kings—Uzziah, Jotham, Ahaz, Hezekiah and Jeroboam II. The Bible does not tell us where he is from but states that his father's name was Berri. We do not have much biographical information about this prophet. His literary style suggests that he was an educated man with impressive literary and poetic skills and that he probably lived in the northern kingdom.

Hosea was given a tough assignment. He was the last prophet sent to prophesy to the northern kingdom before it fell. His prophecies came in the form of messages as opposed to dreams. His messages reveal the infinite love of God and the passionate appeals of God for His wayward people to return to Him. During the time of Hosea's ministry Israel was a prosperous but spiritually adulterous nation that had hit rock bottom in apostasy. They were headed for annihilation but God loved them and tried desperately to get their attention and prevent their destruction. This extreme state of apostasy required extreme measures to correct it. This critical situation required God to take extreme measures and make a most unusual recommendation to demonstrate their fallen state. How did God do this? God asked Hosea to demonstrate in his personal life what was happening in the northern kingdom.

God told the prophet Hosea to marry a wife of whoredom because the people had committed great whoredom by departing from the Lord. Hosea chose a woman named Gomer, the daughter of Diblaim. I could only imagine the gossip around town that Hosea the prophet had married a prostitute. How many would doubt Hosea's prophetic gift because of this decision to marry a prostitute?

Hosea married Gomer and they had three children. The names of the children reflect the fallen state of Israel. God told Hosea to name their firstborn son Jezreel meaning God will soon scatter and punish the house of Jehu. At the massacre at Jezreel He will put an end to the kingdom of Israel and in the valley of Jezreel He will destroy Israel's military power.

Under the leadership of Jeroboam II Israel relied on their military power and not on God. They only needed God when they were in trouble. God, who sustained Israel although she had forsaken him, would allow her to scatter so he could gather her up again.

Despite Hosea's godliness, faithfulness and goodness to her Gomer went after other lovers. The story seems to suggest that the last two children were probably not Hosea's and, as good as he was to her, she deserted him and left him with the children and went out prostituting. The second child was a girl and God told Hosea to name her Lo-Rahamath for I will no longer show mercy to the house of Israel that I should at all forgive them. The Lord said since she went out and had a daughter with someone else that He would have no pity.

Gomer had another son and the Lord told Hosea to call him Lo-Ammi meaning you are not My people and I am not your God. The names of the children should have started Israel thinking that about the messages God was trying to send them. The names of the children reflect the three last messages sent to Israel: I am going to scatter you, I am not going to have mercy on you and you are not My people. God again gave three last messages to His apostate end-time people in Revelation 14:6–12.

Here in Hosea we have the picture of a faithful husband and an unfaithful wife. Israel is unfaithful to God. What have her lovers given her? Maybe some gave her strong drink to make her stay longer. God gave her corn and wine and oil and multiplied her silver and gold. Everything came from her faithful husband yet Israel went out whoring after strange Gods such as Baal and Ashtoreth.

One day word came to Hosea that Gomer had fallen on hard times and she was down on the auction block ready to be sold as a slave. The Lord told Hosea to go down to the slave market and retrieve her. She had fallen so low that the bid was half the cost of a slave. Hosea outbid the others and bought her back for fifteen pieces of silver and a bushel and a half of barley. He bought her back and redeemed her.

God wants us back in the same way Hosea wanted Gomer back. She was married to him. She should have appreciated her status as the wife of the prophet of Israel. We should appreciate our position as children of the King of the universe. Hosea's life with Gomer was very symbolic of the state of affairs with God's people in Israel. The wife of the prophet of Israel was behaving like a desperate housewife and ran off prostituting again. God abhors her behavior but still loves her and commanded Hosea to go find her and love her just as God loves the children of Israel and forgives and takes them back.

Hosea acted on the principle of love and trusted God and he did what God wanted him to do. Hosea can only do this because of his relationship with God. How else can you love a prostitute who keeps running away from you and having children for strange lovers? Gomer is symbolic for Israel. She is unfaithful to Hosea as Israel is unfaithful to God, going after other God's. God spoke through Hosea, "You must love her just as I love the people of Israel. I would rather have love than burnt offerings. My people are doomed for lack of knowledge. Everything they do from morning to night is useless and destructive. I took My people up in My arms but they did not acknowledge Me."

In Hosea, chapter 11, the Lord continues to express His love for His people and how far He has brought them. From Egypt as children and now they refused to obey him. Assyria was ready to destroy them and the Lord would not protect them this time. This was a tough decision for God. Listen to what he said, "How can I give you up, Israel, My heart cannot abandon you. My love for you is too strong.

God is crying for His erring people. "The people are stubborn as mules. How can I feed them like lambs in a meadow? They are stubborn as mules let them go."

Despite his pleas and warnings through His prophet Hosea, God finally had to let them go. "I have done all I could for you. I cannot force you. I have to let you go."

Hosea demonstrates that in his relationship to Gomer. He can force her no more than God can force us. Gomer goes out prostituting and Hosea takes her back time and again and loves her. Despite God's great love for them, they insisted on having extra-marital affairs.

In chapter 4 Hosea lays out the controversy God had with Israel. There was no truth, no mercy nor knowledge of God in the land. They broke the commandments by swearing, lying, killing, stealing, committing adultery and breaking the Sabbath and there was violence in the land. Despite Hosea's warnings the people fell deeper and deeper into apostasy. Not even the illustration of an unfaithful wife and a bad marriage could get Israel to repent. They did not listen to the prophet and the northern kingdom fell in 722 BC. They were captured by the powerful nation of Assyria.

Hosea appears to have been the last prophet sent to warn the northern kingdom. God sent prophet after prophet to warn the northern kingdom about the consequences of disobedience to God's law and for centuries they rejected and killed these prophets. The northern kingdom of Israel eventually self-destructed around 722 BC.

We may not identify with Gomer but our relationship to God is no different from Gomer and Hosea. We constantly sin and repent and He forgives us and takes us back again and again. We call on God's name and use God and His goodness to us but our lives reveal that we are going after other loves.

In Hosea 2:13 God states that He will punish Israel for the days she burned incense to Baal, for decking herself with rings and jewelry, for going after her lovers and acting as if God did not exist.

When things are going well with us we do our own thing. When things are bad we run back to God. Maybe that is why we often see more jailhouse and deathbed confessions than at other times. We are not true to Him sometimes because we do not have the right picture of Him. The northern kingdom of Israel did not listen to God's true prophet and they were scattered among the nations of Assyria. History has proven that the majority of Earth's inhabitants have not learned from the history of previous generations and they continue to make the same mistakes over and over again. They refuse to acknowledge their apostate ways and expect God to fall in line with what they do. Instead of being obedient to God they continue to think that whatever they do, God will accept. God loves us dearly but He will not bend the rules to accommodate our disobedience.

God Warned The Southern Kingdom
God's Warnings Through The Prophet Isaiah (736 BC)

About 736 BC another prophet Isaiah, whose name means Yahweh is salvation, was called by God. His prophetic ministry lasted about sixty years through the reign of several kings. His prophetic ministry was to the southern kingdom of Judah. During Isaiah's prophetic time the nation of Judah was prosperous, sinful and rebellious. The rich were getting richer and the poor were getting poorer, much like today. Isaiah 5:8 states that they built house on house and lay field to field. The king during this period of material prosperity was Uzziah and it was at the end of King Uzziah's reign that Isaiah was called by God to warn this nation. God sent him to warn His people who had strayed away from the true worship of God. Vain formalism characterized the worship of many. God wanted to warn His people and remind them to whom they belong and what was required of them.

Isaiah knew that his people were not going to abandon their idolatry and heed God's message. He was reluctant to carry out this daunting mission. Isaiah pondered these things as he was worshipping in the temple one day and he was shown a vision of the Most Holy Place in Heaven and he saw God sitting high and lifted upon on His throne and His train of glory filled the temple. He saw the seraphim, each one had six wings and one cried to another, "Holy, holy, holy is the Lord of hosts! The whole Earth is full of His glory!"

Isaiah cried, "Woe is me! For I am undone because I am a man of unclean lips and I dwell in the midst of a people of unclean lips for mine eyes have seen the King, the Lord of hosts."

Then a Heavenly seraphim flew to Isaiah with a live coal from the altar. He laid it on Isaiah's lips saying, "This has touched your lips and your sins are taken away and purged."

Isaiah heard the voice of the Lord saying, "Whom shall I send and who will go for us?" Then Isaiah said, "Here am I, Lord, send me." The Lord said, "Go and tell this people, 'Hear ye indeed but understand not and see ye indeed but perceive not." In other words, their hearts were closed to the truth because they did not want to accept truth.

Isaiah wanted to know how long the people would continue in their sins. The answer was that they would continue for a long time, until their cities were laid waste and houses uninhabited and the land desolate. Isaiah warned the people of Judah for sixty years. His prophetic ministry foretold the coming of the Messiah and the Earth made new.

Today we appreciate and we are awe struck about the messianic prophecies of Isaiah. This was not the case then. The nation of Judah, like most nations, did not heed the prophet's warnings. Instead they sunk further into idolatry, especially under the rule of King Ahaz. Despite the prophets warnings the people continued in their rebellious ways and the nation fell as will every nation that does not heed the word of the Lord. It is just as dangerous not to recognize God's prophetic warnings as it is to ignore them. *Surely the Lord God does nothing unless He reveals His secrets to His servants, the prophets.*

Faithfulness Pays

After destroying the northern kingdom, the kingdom of Assyria continued on its expansion and set its sight on the southern kingdom of Judah. One of the greatest kings to rule Assyria was King Sennacherib (704–681). Modern archeology has just caught up with the biblical record and confirmed his existence. During the time of King Hezekiah, King Sennacherib set his sights on conquering the southern kingdom of Judah. In 701 BC Sennacherib and his army ravaged all of Judah except for one city, the crown jewel of Judah called Jerusalem. King Hezekiah was a God fearing king who turned to the Lord for help and the Lord came through in an amazing way.

Here is what the prophet Isaiah records. About 701 BC Assyria ruled the world and the King of Assyria, Sennacherib, declared himself to be the king of this universe. This amazing story is told in Isaiah 36 and 37. The Assyrian King Sennacherib called himself the great king, the king of the universe and we see what happened when he came up against the real King of the universe.

Wicked King Ahaz is dead and his son Hezekiah is now on the throne of Judah. Unlike his father Ahaz, Hezekiah is a God-fearing king and worked diligently to bring his people back to the true worship of God. Hezekiah inherited many problems from his father. King Ahaz had made a deal with the Assyrians to protect him against the alliance of Syria and northern Israel. The nation of Judah was forced to pay protection money in the form of tribute to Assyria.

Assyria is now the most powerful nation of the ancient world. She is cruel and ruthless, conquering and besieging nations. She had dispersed the remnants of the northern kingdom among the provinces of Assyria and had captured Samaria. Assyria decided that she would not only take the money from Judah but she would capture the whole nation of Judah. Let us pick up the accounts in 2 Kings 18 and Isaiah 36:1.

"Now it came to pass, in the fourteenth year of King Hezekiah, that Sennacherib, King of Assyria, came up against all the defended cities of Judah and captured them."

This is bad news for Judah. Even the fortified cities were taken and now the Assyrians were heading for the crown jewel of Judah, the city of Jerusalem. Sennacherib had captured all the fortified cities of Judah and the capture of Jerusalem would complete his conquest. King Hezekiah, realizing the Assyrian threat, sent ambassadors to the King of Assyria and offered to pay whatever tribute money he asked for. The King of Assyria took the money and still decided to capture Jerusalem. The King of Assyria went off to war with Ethiopia and Egypt but sent his generals to capture Jerusalem. When King Hezekiah realized that Sennacherib intended to take the capital city of Jerusalem he met with his cabinet and made extensive preparations for war (2 Chronicles 32: 5, 6, 7, 8, and 30).

- He cut off the water supply outside the city of Jerusalem so the Assyrians would not have water and he secured the supply of water inside Jerusalem.

- He strengthened his fortifications by repairing broken walls and building up new and higher ones.

- He further equipped his army by making darts and shields in abundance.

- He organized them militarily by setting captains of war over the people

More important than military and organizational leadership, Hezekiah provided spiritual leadership as he encouraged his people to be strong and courageous, "Do not be afraid of the King of Assyria and his great army because they are depending on the arm of flesh to win but Judah will trust in the Lord our God for victory."

When you read the prophecies you know in advance what will happen and Hezekiah knew from the prophecies of Isaiah 14:24–28 that the Assyrian kingdom would be broken in the land of Judah and so he prepared with confidence in the Lord that this was the appointed time. As the Assyrian army marched towards Jerusalem, King Sennacherib sent Rabshekeh, his chief of staff, with a mighty infantry down to Jerusalem. The Assyrian field commander Rabshekeh stopped in the upper pool, just outside the gates, and asked for a meeting with the representatives of Jerusalem. The Assyrians, confident of victory, asked the representatives of Jerusalem to surrender. Why take the city of Jerusalem by force if you can convince the people to surrender voluntarily?

The Assyrian commanders stopped at the upper pool and three Judean officials, King Hezekiah's envoys, came out to meet them. The Assyrian's started a propaganda campaign. They made insinuations that Hezekiah had sinned against God when he destroyed the worship places of the false Gods (Isaiah 36:7 "But if thou say to me, 'we trust in the Lord our God', is it not He, whose high places and whose altars Hezekiah hath taken away and said to Judah and to Jerusalem, 'Ye shall worship before this altar'?")

Hezekiah was a great reformation king and after destroying the high places of false worship he told the people to bring their sacrifices only to one altar in Jerusalem where the true God was worshipped.

Due to ignorance of truth the Assyrians were confused and they thought that removing the high places was a rebuke to the true God. In fact Hezekiah was destroying the places of worship of the false Gods. See how the devil works? King Hezekiah was a great reformation king but the devil was putting a false spin on his actions. That is the deceptive genius of Satan.

Satan paints the false pictures and he tells the people, "Why would God help Hezekiah when your king has destroyed the popular places of worship?" The king of Assyria sent mixed messages of truths, half-truths and lies to the people of Judah. What were some of the half-truths that the Assyrians told the people of Jerusalem?

- They could not rely on Egypt to help because she was weak and unreliable. The King of Ethiopia, Pharaoh Tirhakah, came to Hezekiah's assistance (2 Kings 19:9 and 10). He was defeated and returned home.

- That Hezekiah could not save them.

- That the Lord could no more save Jerusalem than could any of the other gods of the other countries conquered by Assyria.

- If the siege took place they would have nothing to eat or drink.

It is just like the old devil to take truth and destroy it. Do not be fooled by the devil's spin on the truth. The devil is a dangerous deceptive liar and he knows that if he tells an obvious lie you would recognize it so he mixes truth and error. That is how he gets his victims.

The Assyrians tried to convince the people that the Lord was on the side of Assyria and the Lord told King Sennacherib to destroy Judah. In Isaiah 36:8 and 9, the King of Assyria mocks Hezekiah by offering to give him horses. King Hezekiah could not muster enough soldiers even if he were given the horses. What were some of the truths in Rabshakeh's, the chief of staff, story?

- They had destroyed the northern kingdom.

- They had just destroyed the heavily fortified city Lachish, thirty miles south west of Jerusalem. The prophet Micah, in Micah 1:13, foretold the fate of Lachish. This city was a Canaanite city captured by Joshua (Joshua 10:31 and 32). King Rehoboam, the son of King Solomon, rebuilt it.

- Hezekiah had destroyed various places of sacrifice in order to centralize worship at Jerusalem.

In Isaiah 36:10, Rabshekeh, the Assyrian chief of staff, addresses the representatives of Judah. "I have not come to attack you just for the fun of it. It was your God who said we should come up against Israel and destroy it, so here we are."

This exchange took place outside the city gates and the three representatives of Israel asked the men to speak in the Syrian language and not the Jewish language so that the rest of the people of Judah who overheard the conversation would not understand what they were saying. Rabshekeh said, "I was not just sent here to speak to you and your king, but also to the people." He shouted loudly in Hebrew, "Listen people, hear the words of the great King of Assyria. This is what the great King says. Do not let Hezekiah deceive you! He cannot save you. Do not let him tell you that your God can stop the Assyrian army from conquering your city when he has not done it for any of your other well-defended cities. Do not listen to Hezekiah. The King of Assyria is asking you to come out and surrender. He promises that every one of you will eat from his own vine and fig tree and drink water from his own well until the king can resettle you in a land much like your own with vineyards for wine and rich wheat for making bread. Has any God been able to deliver his people from the hand of the King of Assyria and from the hand of our God? Then what makes you think that your God can deliver Jerusalem?"

The people who sat on the wall listening were silent as Hezekiah told them to be.

The three representatives of Jerusalem tore their robes in grief and went and told Hezekiah. King Hezekiah was shaken to the core and was mourning in distress. He tore off his robe and put on sackcloth and went to the temple to pray. *God had a prophet in the midst of his people* and so Hezekiah sent three representatives to the prophet Isaiah. They said to the prophet, "This is what the king wants you to know. Today is a day of distress and shame. Judah is like a woman who is having a baby but is just too weak to deliver it."

Hezekiah humbly sought the intersession of the prophet Isaiah. The very prophet whose counsel his father had ignored. Ahaz, his father, turned to other people but Hezekiah, the son, turned to God. Read Hezekiah's prayer in Isaiah 37:15–20. He appealed to God to demonstrate who He was so that all the kingdoms of the Earth would know that He alone was the true Lord. God took the whole situation in His hands and sent a message to Hezekiah through the prophet Isaiah, saying, "I have heard your prayer concerning Sennacherib, King of Assyria. Go tell the king this is what the Lord, the God of Jacob, says, 'Do not be afraid of the Assyrians or be troubled at the words of their commander. Do not listen to his threats and believe that the Lord cannot save you. The King of Assyria has publicly challenged me and I will respond. I will cause him to hear of a plot back home to take his throne. He will return to his home and there he will die by the sword.'"

The Assyrian representatives then spoke with their King Sennacherib who was with another division of the army fighting at the city of Libnah trying to cut off any help to Judah from Egypt. His commanders briefed him about the pending attack on Jerusalem. The King of Assyria then sent a letter to Hezekiah saying, "Do not let your God fool you into believing that He will deliver Jerusalem. I am sure that you have heard what the Assyrians have done to all the other fortified cities like Gozan, Haran and Rezeph and the children of Eden which were in Telassar. Where is the King of Hammath, Arphad, the king of the city of Sephardivaim, Hena, and Ivah? (Isaiah 37:13). The gods of those other lands have not delivered their people out of my hand, why do you think your God will deliver you?"

When Hezekiah received the letter he took it to the temple and laid it before the Lord in earnest prayer. King Hezekiah acknowledged before the Lord that Assyria had indeed destroyed all those lands but those people called upon a nonexistent god of their own making. He now call on the only true God of this universe.

The Lord heard Hezekiah's prayer and sent the prophet Isaiah to Hezekiah, saying, "Because you have prayed to Me and asked Me for help this is My response to the King of Assyria. 'I know what you have done, where you are camped and what your plans are. I know your rage against the city of Jerusalem and against Me. I have heard your insults and your arrogance has not gone unnoticed. Because your rage against Me and thy tumult is come up into Mine ears therefore will I put My hook in your nose and My bridle in your lips and I will turn you back the way you came. (2 Kings 19:20–28) I will accept your challenge. Jerusalem will survive and *in Judah a remnant will be left.*

The King of Assyria will not enter this city nor will he shoot one arrow against it. He and his troops will return the same way they came. I will defend this city and save it for My sake and for the sake of My servant David.'" (Read the rest of what the Lord says about Assyria in 2 Kings 19:32.)

God miraculously defended Jerusalem by sending one angel into the Assyrian camp and that *one* angel killed 185,000 soldiers. When the people of Judah woke up that morning and looked over the wall of Jerusalem the Assyrian soldiers lay dead. When the news of the disaster reached Sennacherib he was afraid and had no choice but to go home. And it came to pass that sometime after his return home Sennacherib was worshipping in the temple of his god when his two sons came in and killed him with their swords. He was assassinated in the presence of his own god, a god of his own making. God answered Hezekiah's prayer and defended Jerusalem.

In 701 BC the kingdom of Assyria was about to destroy the southern kingdom of Israel but King Hezekiah was a God-fearing king who listened to the prophet Isaiah and Jerusalem was spared. God's judgments are conditional and God heard the prayers of this God-fearing king. God destroyed Assyria. This is true for all nations or people who array themselves against God, not only in ancient times but today as well.

Sennacherib was succeeded by his son Esarhaddon (Isaiah 37:38). Esarhaddon was succeeded by his son Ashurbanipal, the last Assyrian king. Babylonian and Persian forces defeated the Assyrian forces in 626 BC After the death of King Ashurbanipal in 626 BC the Assyrian Empire began to disintegrate. Subsequently Assyria became a weakened power and its capital city Nineveh fell in 612 BC fulfilling the prophecy of Zephaniah 2:13. While Assyria was disintegrating the Egyptian power tried to control western Asia and was defeated at the Battle of Carchemish in 611 BC About 610 BC Assyria had completely fallen to Babylon and so ended the great Assyrian kingdom that ruled the world for centuries.

After Assyria, Babylon became the next world ruling power and the prophet Isaiah revealed to King Hezekiah the time when Babylon would become a great nation and would besiege Jerusalem and take all of the treasures of Jerusalem to Babylon. God, through His foreknowledge revealed the future to us through His prophets. Only God knows the future of this world and He has revealed a lot of information to us through His prophets. This is important information to know. *Surely the Lord God will do nothing unless He reveals His secrets to His servants the prophets.*

History Repeats Itself

The fall of the southern kingdom was also foretold in 2 Kings 23:27 "And the Lord said I will remove Judah also out of My sight as I have removed the northern kingdom of Israel and will cast off this city Jerusalem which I have chosen and the house of which I said My name shall be there."

After sparing Jerusalem from destruction by Assyria subsequent kings of Judah did evil in the sight of the Lord and God continued to send warnings.

God's Warnings Through The Prophet Jeremiah (626 BC)

One hundred years after the fall of the northern kingdom of Israel the people of the southern kingdom had not learned from the error of the northern kingdom. They continued in their rebellion and sinfulness before God. Jerusalem was about to fall into the hands of Babylon if the people did not repent and amend their sinful ways. God did not want this to happen and so He sent another a prophet to warn them.

In every dispensation of history God has sent a prophet to warn His people. This will continue to the end of time. About 626 BC God called Jeremiah to the prophetic office at a youthful age. Jeremiah came from the Levitical priesthood background and was brought up in the ways of the Lord. Jeremiah was the last prophet called to prophesy to Judah before the Babylonian captivity. He also prophesied to the remnant left in Jerusalem after the captivity. When he was called the Lord said that before he was formed in the belly He knew him and before he came out of the womb He sanctified him and ordained him to be a prophet to the nations. To which Jeremiah responded, "Ah, Lord God, behold I cannot speak for I am a child." The Lord said to him, "Do not say that you are a child for you will go to all whom I send you and you will say what I tell you to say."

The Lord assured His prophet that He would be with him to deliver him. The Lord advised Jeremiah in Jeremiah 16:2 that he should not marry and have children because all of this was about to end. Jeremiah was sent from Anathoh, his hometown and the hometown of the priests) to go to Jerusalem and cry out to the people. When he arrived in Jerusalem he saw the sinfulness of the people. The people had apostatized and were following after Baal (Jeremiah 2:23). The people had no desire for the things of the Lord. Jeremiah 5 describes a scenario similar to Sodom. God told him to run to and fro through the streets of Jerusalem and see if he could find a man that executed judgment and seek the truth and He would pardon Jerusalem. The group of people he found refused to receive correction and refused to return to the Lord so he thought that surely they must be the poor and foolish because they did not know the way of the Lord or the judgment of the Lord. He then sought out the great men or those educated in the law of the Lord to speak to them but to his surprise they were no better. The inhabitants were not ashamed of their sins and were unrepentant therefore God could not save Jerusalem.

God chose the Jewish nation and enlightened them. He gave them His law so that they could be a light to the world. They failed miserably and He sent numerous prophets to warn them. Jeremiah faithfully and fearlessly warned Judah of her sins against God. He pleaded with the people to return to the Lord but the people did not respond. The people in Jerusalem did not accept Jeremiah and in so doing rejected God.

Word got back to the priests in his hometown and they were ashamed of him and plotted to kill him but God revealed the plot to him. The people did not like Jeremiah's message because they preferred the smooth prophesying of the false prophets. Most of God's prophets have had similar experience. In Jeremiah 17 God told Jeremiah to go and stand in the gates of Jerusalem and say unto all the inhabitants of Jerusalem that pass by that they should take heed and remember the Sabbath day to keep it holy and do no work. In Jeremiah 25 God revealed to Jeremiah that Nebuchadnezzar of Babylon would take Jerusalem captive and the Jews would serve the King of Babylon for seventy years before they would return to Jerusalem.

Satan rose up a false prophet named Hananiah who prophesied smooth messages to the people telling them that the captivity would only last for two years. He was lying but the people would rather hear nice pleasantries than the truth. The Lord was displeased with the false prophet Hananiah and in Jeremiah 28:17 and 18 the Lord revealed to the prophet Jeremiah that the false prophet Hananiah would die that year and he did.

The prophet Jeremiah was called a false prophet. He was hated, persecuted, rejected, jailed, mocked and ridiculed. All manner of evil things were said about him because the prophetic messages that he brought to Israel were not smooth. Nonetheless the prophet delivered God's solemn warnings to the inhabitants of Jerusalem. The people would rather hear smooth sayings about their good life now than what God really wanted them to hear.

Jeremiah further warned them that if they did not listen that the palaces of Jerusalem would be devoured by fire. When the people heard these things the priests and the false prophets gathered together against Jeremiah in the house of the Lord. They said to the princes of Judah and to the people that God's prophet should die because he prophesied against the house of Judah and the city of Jerusalem. God rose up certain elders of the land who came to Jeremiah's defense and his life was spared.

In Chapter 36 the Lord instructed Jeremiah to take a roll of a book and write all the prophecies that he had spoken against Israel, Judah and all the nations from the days of Josiah (626 BC) to Jeremiah's day. Jeremiah asked Baruch, a scribe, to write down the prophecies. Jeremiah was not free to go to the temple so he asked Baruch to read the roll before the people gathered at the temple on the day of fasting. The scroll was later read to King Jehoiakim as he sat by the fire in his winter house. The king did not like the message and cut up the scroll and threw it into the fire. The king ordered the arrest of the prophet Jeremiah and the scribe Baruch but the Lord hid them.

The Lord told Jeremiah to write it all down again on another scroll and tell King Jehoiakim that the King of Babylon would destroy his country and no one would sit on the throne of David. His dead body would be cast out in the day to the heat and in the night to the frost. He did not heed Jeremiah's message and because they ridiculed the prophet the results were disastrous.

Babylon destroyed Jerusalem and the seventy year captivity began when the first set of captives were taken in 605 BC The second set of captives were taken in 597 BC and the third in 586 BC The city and the 400 year old temple were destroyed during the invasion of 586 BC In the book of Lamentations, written during the early exilic period, the prophet Jeremiah laments about the fall of Jerusalem.

In every dispensation God has sent His prophets or messengers to warn people that we must obey His law. Instead of listening to God's messengers the people, often led by their appointed religious leaders, have mocked, ridiculed, criticized and tried to prove God's prophets false. The prophets have done their appointed tasks and it is up to us to recognize and heed their warnings.

God's warnings through His prophets have disastrous consequences if they are not heeded. This is true for Old Testament times and again at the end of time. There are many who think they know more than God's appointed prophets and tell people that God's prophets are false. Proverbs 14:12 says, "There is a way that seems right unto a man but the end thereof are the ways of death." Proverbs 3:5 says, "Trust in the Lord with all your heart and lean not to your own understanding."

Satan has cleverly designed plans to lead God's children away from the proper understanding of God's word so in every dispensation God has sent His prophets to help us in our understanding of His divine will for us. *Surely the Lord God does nothing unless He reveals His secrets to His servants the prophets. God never destroys without ample warning.*

Prophets During The Seventy Year Exile

Despite their rebelliousness God was not through with His people. He still had great plans for them to spread the truth about Him to the world and through them the Messiah of the world would be born. The Lord had not forgotten His people during their seventy years of captivity. God still had a remnant during this captivity and He rose up prophets during the captivity such as Ezekiel, Daniel and Haggai.

The Exiled Prophets

The prophet Ezekiel was born in Jerusalem about 627 BC His father, Buzi, was a priest. Around 597 BC he was taken to Babylon as a captive. He was among the elite that King Nebuchadnezzar took to Babylon during the second round of captivity. Among this group was King Jehoicahin who was only on the throne for three months.

Ezekiel lived in Judah during the reign of King Josiah, Jehoahaz, Jehoiakim and Jehoiachin. Only one king ruled Judah after Ezekiel's captivity. He was King Zedekiah who ruled for eleven years before the final round of captivity by Nebuchadnezzar in 586 BC While captive in a foreign land Ezekiel was called by God to be a prophet to a people still rebellious in exile. One would think that after the demise of the northern kingdom, and now the southern kingdom, that God's people would have learned their lesson. God's people refused to accept His sovereign leadership and worship according to His command.

In Ezekiel 2:2 God sent His prophet to a rebellious nation. Verse 5 says, "Whether they listen or not they will know that a prophet has been among them. Do not be afraid of their words or looks." The God of this universe spoke through this man and gave him messages for His people but the people rejected these messages.

It is 2,600 years later and we are still studying these messages given to Ezekiel and applying them to our spiritual condition. God's word will never fail, even when the contemporary generation rejects God's instructions. That is the story of all of God's prophets from the beginning to the end of this world. Great would have been the peace of Jerusalem and Israel would have been a powerful nation had she followed God's leadings.

The prophet Ezekiel's life was filled with disappointment and tragedy but his life is exemplary of one whom, through tremendous personal tragedy such as the loss of his homeland, his family, his friends, his career, and his wife, lived a victorious life for God.

God's Warnings Through The Prophet Zechariah (520 BC)

Zechariah was born during the captivity of the Jews in Babylon. The name Zechariah means "God remembers". He was a Levite and his grandfather, Iddo, was a priest and a prophet (see Zechariah 1 and Nehemiah 12:16). Around the year 520 BC, during the reign of Darius, the second ruler of Babylon after Cyrus, God called this young manto the prophetic ministry. Before the captivity, God, in is mercy, had sent messages to His people that, if they had been heeded, would have prevented the captivity. During the captivity God remembered His people and sent prophets to them.

The messages He gave to them have profound implications for us living at the end of time. We will go into great detail about the messages He gave to Daniel, a prophet called during the captivity. God remembered His people in exile and sent a series of visions to the prophet Zechariah urging the Jews to return home and rebuild Jerusalem. The Lord sent messages of encouragement to the small remnant who returned to Jerusalem to rebuild the temple. Zechariah returned from the captivity and the Lord told him to tell the people that He was very disappointed with their forefathers and warned them not to be like them.

"Return unto Me and I will return unto you," the Lord said to them. Numerous times the Lord begged them, through the prophets, to stop sinning and turn from their evil ways. The Lord asked the question, "Where are your forefathers now?" They were dead in Babylon. Did the prophets live forever? No, they do not, but the word of God lives on forever. The lesson here is that God's people should follow the words of the Lord. The word of the Lord is the only thing that will live forever. Do not get excited about your favorite teacher or the latest popular Christian book. Get excited about God's truth that will last forever.

Through Zechariah the Lord encouraged His people to rebuild Jerusalem and the temple. The Lord also promised the people that He would return unto them and would dwell in the midst of them and Jerusalem would be called a city of truth (Zechariah 8:3, 7, 8). These promises made to Israel were conditional on their obedience to God. In 2 Chronicles 24, starting at verse 19, we read, "The Lord sent prophets to them to bring them again unto the Lord and they testified against the prophets and would not listen."

In verses 20 and 21 the prophet Zechariah warns the people, "Why transgress the commandments of the Lord so that you cannot prosper? Because you have forsaken the Lord He has forsaken you." It was not the message that the people wanted to hear and at the command of the king the people stoned the prophet Zechariah to death in the court of the house of Lord. Jesus, just before His crucifixion by the very people whose ancestors crucified the prophets, commented on Zechariah's death in Matthew 23:35–39. Jesus spoke about the treatment of His prophets by saying, "Behold I send you prophets and wise men and scribes and some of them you shall kill in your synagogues and persecute them from city to city. O Jerusalem, Jerusalem, you who kill the prophets and stone those that are sent to thee, how often would I have gathered thy children together as a hen gathers her chicks under her wings and you would not?"

John 12:37 states that the people among whom Jesus had performed so much miracles refused to believe in Him and in verse 38 John quotes the prophet Isaiah who predicted this in Isaiah 6:10. "He hath blinded their eyes and deadened their hearts so they can neither see with their eyes nor understand with their hearts."

Before the seventy year Babylonian exile God sent numerous prophet to warn them. Obadiah, Joel, Jonah, Amos, Hosea, Isaiah, Micah, Nahum, Zephaniah, Habakkuk,

Jeremiah, Ezra, and Nehemiah are among them. What more could God have done to save them? The last Old Testament prophet was Malachi and then there was a 400 year gap between prophets.

God sent numerous prophets down through the centuries to warn His people of impending doom. He sent Noah before the flood, Moses before the Exodus, Elijah to ancient Israel, and numerous prophets before, during, and after the captivity. Before His first coming He sent the greatest prophet, John the Baptist, to warn His people. John the Baptist did not write a single book in the Bible yet Jesus called him the greatest prophet born of a woman. John the Baptist prepared the way for the first coming of Christ.

The second coming of Jesus is the most important event in the history of our lives. Are your curious who God sent to prepare us for that event? Stay tuned. *Surely the Lord God will do nothing unless He reveals it to His servants the prophets.*

I hope that you are appreciating God's plan of salvation and how He has chosen people at different times in history to warn His people and save them from the natural consequences of sin, which is destruction. All of these events are pointing to the second coming of Jesus when sin and suffering will be over. The greatest event in history is about to take place and with so many in the body of Christ teaching such divergent doctrines, each claiming correct biblical interpretation. It would seem quite consistent that God would send His people a prophet, or prophets, to set the final movements of the body of Christ in one accord so they could prepare the body of Christ for the second coming of Jesus. There is overwhelming evidence that He has but, like our forefathers, we have rejected the prophets, criticized them, and continue with our own plans and call them God's plans. Throughout the history of this world Satan has obscured God's true prophets and has extolled his messengers. The people of God would rather hear the smooth messages than God's true message so the prophetic word has been rejected in most churches today.

God is long suffering and really cares about us. God has sent numerous prophets to warn the worlds' inhabitants of impending disaster. The Bible is filled with God's messages to us through these prophets. Many of God's prophets, such as Abraham, Enoch, Noah, Gad, Deborah, Elijah, Elisha, Miriam, and John the Baptist, did not write a book in the Bible. The fact that they have not written a book in the Bible does not mean they did not have a significant message. Some of these messages were for local people.

Of the many prophets that God has sent to warn his people there are two prophets whose messages to us, living in end times, require diligent study to understand God's messages through these prophets. These 2 prophets are Daniel an Old Testament prophet and John, a New Testament prophet. The books of Daniel and Revelation are called apocalyptic prophecies. Apocalyptic means a Revelation. These prophecies are Revelation about the future particularly the end of time. God wants us to know how it would all end and so he used these prophecies filled with symbolism to reveal the future to us. These prophecies reveal that God is and has always been in control of human destiny. They clearly reveal that God knows the future and cares enough about us to reveal the future to us through these amazing prophesies. God gave these prophecies for our benefit and so they are really worth studying in detail. I am not going to tell you that I have the perfect understanding of Daniel but as we study together we will discover a lot of information that God has revealed to us. With the help of God's Holy Spirit, I will put a handle on things and you can then study and grab hold of it for yourself.

God warnings and Revelation through the prophet Daniel

The prophecy to Daniel was given during the 70 year captivity of the Jews in Babylon. These prophecies foretold the history of this world from the time of captivity to the very end of time. Prophecy is history before it happens and history confirms prophecy. They go hand in hand. Almost all of the events foretold by these prophecies have already taken place with 100% accuracy. In these prophecies, God shows the outline of the history of this world and his plans for us. These prophecies help us to understand where we are in the stream of time. Every Bible believing Christian that has the capability of understanding should know these prophecies. God gives us these prophecies to prepare us for his coming.

God has given his blessing to whosoever reads, and hears the words of his prophecy. Rev 1:3 reads, "Blessed is he that reads and they that hear the words of this prophecy, and keep those things that are written therein, for the time is at hand." In 2 Peter 1:19; The Apostle Peter tells us that "we have a more sure word of prophecy, whereunto ye do well that ye take heed, as unto a light that shines unto a dark place, until the day dawn, and the day star arises in your hearts." In verse 20 and 21 Peter tells us that prophecy is not for private interpretation; the same Holy Spirit, which inspired the prophets to write, is still available to reveal to us the correct interpretation. God has given us the assurance through the Apostle Peter that if there is anything you can be sure about, it is the sure word of prophecy. There are about one thousand prophecies in the Bible and well over ninety percent of them have been fulfilled exactly as the Bible states. The fact that these prophecies were written and foretold thousands of years before they happened, tells us that God is real, dependable, reliable and truthful. God has foreknowledge; he controls this world's history and he has revealed the future to us. It assures that we can trust the Bible and we can trust the God of Prophecy. Many of the prophecies that God has sent to us have dual application; they were for the people to whom they were sent as well as for us living at the very end of time. When people do not want to obey God they say that the prophecies were written for that time in history. The Bible states in 2 Timothy 3:16–17 that all scripture is given by the inspiration of God and is profitable for doctrine, for report, for correction, for instruction in righteousness that the man of God may be perfect thoroughly furnished for good works. God's people need to know these prophecies. The prophecies of Daniel have important relevance for the end of time. These prophecies give us important information about the history of the world from the 6th century BC to the end of the world.

There are many types of prophecies in the Bible. Some prophecies like Isaiah are referred to as classical prophecies. Some prophecies are messianic prophecies foretelling Jesus 1st advent and death. The books of Daniel and the Revelation are referred to as apocalyptic prophecies or a Revelation of the end time. There are other books that contain apocalyptic prophecies like Matthew 24 and Mark 14, etc. Much of the books of Daniel and the Revelation are written in symbols, and so it is necessary to decode these symbols to get the right understanding. Why did God encode the messages of Daniel and the Revelation in symbols? I do not have all the answers but I know one thing for sure; God has infinite wisdom and does things for our good. Is it possible that he is trying to get God our attention? Does he want us to diligently study for understanding? Or is it possible that this is one of God's methods of protecting and conveying truth. The freedom to write and express oneself freely was not always available. There are places and times in history when you can be killed for having a Bible. It is also possible that the world powers that these prophecies talk about would have destroyed these prophecies if they could have understood them. Thank God for these prophecies and today thousands of believers are finding their way to God's truth through the understanding of these prophecies. Let the Holy Spirit guide you into the correct interpretation of these prophecies. It matters how prophecy is interpreted. 2 Peter 2:20 tells that no prophecy is of private interpretation. Let the Bible interpret itself. The Bible decodes itself when you do an in-depth study.

It is important to ask the Holy Spirit for clear understanding. There are many false interpretations of these prophecies. Satan has wrapped up much of these prophecies in attractive paper that sells to people who refuse to search the scriptures diligently for themselves. Satan does not cease in his attempts to destroy truth especially the truth about God. The book of Daniel is one prophetic book that the Devil has tried hard to suppress and distort and the reason should be clear to the reader. This book exposes Satan and his deceptive ways and so he has made an all-out effort to destroy it. In order to understand the book of Daniel and its crucial application to everyone a detailed analysis is necessary so that the reader will not be deceived. Satan has discredited many of the institutions that God has set up and he has been successful in doing so. The books of

Daniel and Revelation have exposed Satan and his many deceptions. The information is so important that it is worth a detailed study.

Overview of Daniel

The prophet Daniel is a role model for all ages. He was highly esteemed by God and to him was given great Revelation of the future of this world. He was born in Palestine about 622 BC seemingly of Royal heritage. He came from the household of King Hezekiah. He was taught at an early age how to live according to God's commandments and this training stuck with him all of his life. Daniel grew up in the southern kingdom of Judah. He lived at a time when the last of the kings ruled Judah. A study of the books of Kings and Chronicles gives interesting insights about the kings that ruled Israel. All of the kings of the Northern Kingdom did evil in the sight of the Lord. Some of the kings in the Southern kingdom did good in the sight of the Lord but most of them did not. It was not God's will that his people should have a king but they insisted. 1st Samuel 8 tells us that when the prophet Samuel grew old the elders of Israel came to the prophet Samuel and asked for a king. The surrounding nations had a king and God's people wanted to be like the rest of the world and have a king to judge them. Despite having God's true prophet in their midst God's people wanted to do things their way, instead of the way God was leading them. This is true today Satan is constantly trying to insert his ways of doing things among God's people. The prophet Samuel was displeased at their request and sought the Lord in prayer and through Samuel the Lord warned them the exploitation that comes from having a king but the people insisted that they wanted a king to rule over them. The Lord told the prophet Samuel to listen to the people and make them a king; so Saul was anointed Israel's first king and as the Lord warned Israel, king after king exploited them.

Some of the kings started out well but became corrupted; it seems that corruption comes easily with wealth and power. Such was the case with King Solomon, he began as a great king but he strayed from the Lord and during his reign the moral fabric of the nation of Israel began to disintegrate. His son Rehoboam took over and did evil in the sight of the Lord. He did worse than his father, taxing the people heavily and oppressing them. The nation of Israel fell apart splitting into the Northern Kingdom and the Southern Kingdom. King after King in the Northern Kingdom did evil in the sight of the Lord and the Lord sent prophet after prophet to warn them. They ignore the messages and often killed God's prophets and the Northern Kingdom met its final doom in 722 BC

The Southern Kingdom also rejected God's warnings through his prophets and the Southern Kingdom lasted about 136 years later until the king of Babylon besieged

Jerusalem. God did all he could to protect his people but they would not listen to his prophets. He permitted the captivity hoping that the lessons that they refuse to learn in freedom they would learn in captivity. God did not abandon them during the captivity, the captivity was allowed so that they could return to God. These were the circumstances from which Daniel came. Daniel was a teenager living in the Southern Kingdom when Babylon's King Nebuchadnezzar besieged Jerusalem and took him and other princes of royal blood captive to Babylon during the first round of captivity about 605 BC Nebuchadnezzar made several expeditions; the last round of captivity lasted from 588–586 BC when Jerusalem was destroyed.

We are not told how Daniel got to Babylon. The journey from his homeland of Judah to Babylon was about 1000 miles and he could have walked all the way there after he was captured by the Babylonian army. When he arrived in Babylon, Nebuchadnezzar ordered that Daniel should be trained for service in the Babylonian government. He was placed in training to become a royal officer of the king; he was trained in the language of the Chaldeans so that he would become an advisor to the king. In order to make the grade, he was given the best of Babylonian food, the king's meat and wine. As a child he was instructed in the ways of the Lord and it stuck. At a youthful age he purposed in his heart to obey God and that included eating the right food. He did not defile himself with the king's food; instead he requested a simple diet consisting of water and vegetables. At the end of 10 days he looked healthier than all the other children that ate the king's food. God honored him and gave him skill in all learning and wisdom and he had understanding in all visions and dreams. Daniel was true to God and stood firm for what he believed even under adverse circumstances. It is always more important to obey God than man.

God blessed Daniel and he became a high official in the Babylonian Government, and at one time he became the Prime Minister of Babylon. Most important, God honored him by making him a prophet of the Most High God. Through his messenger Daniel, a leading representative of the pagan world King Nebuchadnezzar, king of the greatest kingdom in the world, came to acknowledge God as the God of the universe and declared that Daniel's God was the true and living God. During the captivity the knowledge of Daniel's God was spread to this heathen nation. Despite this knowledge, Nebuchadnezzar's descendants did not walk after Daniel's God and so his nation fell, as do all nations that do not follow after God. One important point to note here; the righteous sometimes suffers with the wicked. God had faithful people living among the rebellious children of Israel, men who would stand for him even though the Heavens fall. Many of these faithful godly people were taken as captives e.g. Daniel and his three companions. In captivity God used them to be a light to the heathen nation of Babylon. It was God's intention that Nebuchadnezzar should make Daniel's God, his God. God loved and honored Daniel but God did not prevent the captivity of Daniel; he was right there with Daniel, helping him to deal with the circumstances that life brought him.

The book of Daniel is both historical and prophetic. The first half of the book is historical and mostly written in Aramaic, the official language of the Babylonian and Persian Empires. The latter half of the book is prophetic and written in Hebrew which is Daniel's native language. As we study the book we see that many of the prophecies are classical and were sent for the rulers of Babylon at that time; others were apocalyptic and are for people living at the end of time. The theme of this important book is not Daniel but God, a God who loves this world so much that he reveals to us through history and prophecy his ultimate plan of salvation for us. He tells us what to expect in history and how to prepare for the second coming of our Lord and savior Jesus Christ which brings an end to this present world. What good is history and prophecy if it doesn't point us to a God who is our only fire escape from this doomed planet? As we study the book of Daniel you will be impressed with the detailed information that God has given to us and this information should be studied diligently and be understood by God's people. Let the prophecies of Daniel and Revelation inspire you into greater love for the study of God's word not only the prophecies but all of it. An in-depth study of these prophecies will help you to discern truth from error. God want us to know these prophecies and he has given us the understanding. When you study and understand these prophecies right you will not be tossed about by false doctrines and misinterpretations of these important prophecies. Also an in-depth study of these prophecies authenticates Daniel as the writer and that he indeed lived during these times. In order to deny the significance of the book of Daniel and to make void the prophecies of Daniel, Satan has cast doubt the existence of Daniel or the time that Daniel lived and the authorship of the book of Daniel.

The proof of the pudding in the eating and an in-depth study of Daniel will reveal the truth. We will do an in-depth study of Daniel to show how God has outlined the history of this world in great detail. This book is just one example of how Gods has revealed the future to us. Beginning in Genesis 3:15 we are promised the Messiah. Throughout the Old Testament we are given great details of his coming so we will not miss his first coming. The Bible tells us of the great empires that ruled this world. In every age all of the nations that did not honor God and his moral law and make God's law their law have fallen. The great dynasties of Egypt once ruled the world and they fell. The prophet Ezekiel 29:15 said of Egypt "It shall be the basest of kingdoms; neither shall it exalt itself any more above the nations: for I will diminish them that they shall no more rule over the nations. Subsequently Egypt came under foreign domination and has not regained its' former glory. After Egypt Assyria ruled the world. Assyria was founded before 2000 BC.

About 1300 BC it ruled as a great nation then it declined and then regained power and from about 1100 BC it ruled as a great world empire. It was the Assyrian kingdom that carried the Northern Kingdom of Israel into captivity and eventually brought it to its doom. 11 Kings 15:19–20 tells of King Tiglath-Puleser (745–727 BC) also known as Pul came in against the Northern Kingdom and the king of Israel. King Menahem of Israel gave Pul 1000 talents of Silver and was allowed to remain on the throne as a vassal of Assyria. The great Kingdom of Assyria fell and Babylon came to power. The prophet Daniel will take us from the Babylonian rule to the end of this world.

God reveals to Daniel the rise and fall of Nations

The book of Daniel is important to study in detail for many reasons. It reveals a God with foreknowledge of the history of this world and he has chosen to reveal it to us in this book. It reveals that God is in control of this world he sets up rulers and he takes them down. This gives us more confidence and bolsters our faith in the God of this universe. It is an important book in understanding Bible prophecy. It reveals to us the exact date of the coming of the messiah to earth. You cannot truly understand Revelation without the understanding of Daniel.

Daniel wrote the book of Daniel about 2500 years ago in the 6th century BC and only someone with intimate knowledge of Kingdom of Babylon could write the information that Daniel gives to us during the 6th century BC Archeological discoveries during the last century have supported this information. While in captivity for over 70 years Daniel wrote the book of Daniel and he tells you so in Daniel 7:1 where he vividly describes a dream that God gave him and he wrote it down. This happened during the reign of Nebuchadnezzar's great grandson Belshazzar and as you read throughout the book of Daniel, he vividly describes the history of Babylon and his experiences there during those years of captivity. God sent many prophets to the Jewish nation before the captivity, during the captivity and after the captivity. The detailed description in Daniel is obviously from the prophet in captivity and we know that the captivity was from 605 BC to about 535 BC

Jesus authenticated the prophecies of Daniel in Matthew 24:15; here Jesus is referring to prophecies written by the prophet Daniel thus confirming that Daniel is God's prophet and he recorded these prophecies given to him by God. Jesus here is telling his disciples to pay attention to the prophecies of Daniel they are relevant to the end of time. God said Daniel was a prophet and he wrote the book and I believe it and that's good enough for me. The prophet Ezekiel was a contemporary of Daniel. Both belong to the aristocratic society in Jerusalem and both taken captive By Nebuchadnezzar. Ezekiel was exiled to Babylon in 597 BC and both were chosen by God as prophets during the exile.

Ezekiel 28:1–3 the word of the Lord came to Ezekiel and told him to say to the Prince of Tyrus "Behold, thou art wiser than Daniel; there is no secret that they can hide from thee." Daniel is also mentioned in Ezekiel 14:19, 20. I mention this because Satan has left no stone unturned and he has attacked the book of Daniel on many fronts including questioning its authenticity and misleading others to misinterpret this book so that the prophecies could be misinterpreted to fit his deceptions. The book of Daniel is an amazing and very informative prophetic book. As we study the book of Daniel we will see that this book describe events from 605 BC until the second coming of Jesus at the end of the world and you will be so enlightened that you will not be tossed about by Satan's deceptions to obscure the true Revelation of Daniel.

Although the book of Daniel gives us great insight into Babylonian life in the 6th century BC, the book of Daniel is given to us not for its historical account, but God is showing us that he is God, he exists in the past, the present and the future and therefore he can foretell the future with 100% accuracy. The book of Daniel gives us insight to future events from the time of Daniel to the second coming of Jesus. The book of Daniel holds the key to understanding the book of Revelation. The book of Daniel is one of the most fascinating book of the Bible and an extremely important to understand.

The book of Daniel begins with a siege. The year is about 605 BC and the Southern Kingdom of Judah is under siege. The siege was permitted to happen because God's chosen people were unfaithful to him. Time after time they were disobedient and repeatedly rejected God's prophetic warnings. They were engaged in numerous wars. They knew what was right but did wrong. For 208 years during the reign of 20 kings Israel continued to rebel against God. God in his mercy sent prophet after prophet to warn them, but they won't listen. God, with numerous warnings, tried to save them. They continually rejected God's mercies; in 2 Kings 17:13 God said to them "Turn ye from your evil ways, and keep my commandments and my statutes, according to all the law which I commanded your fathers, and which I sent you by my servants the prophets". Despite recurrent prophetic warnings, Israel continued to frustrate the purposes of God, ignoring his commandments, worshipping idols, and mixing pagan worship with the worship of God etc. They refused to follow God's instructions and so their captivity was permitted; maybe in the land of captivity they would seek after God.

Daniel chapter 1 verse 2 states that the Lord gave Jehoiakim, king of Judah into the hand of Nebuchadnezzar, the Babylonian king. God who had so miraculously on numerous occasions delivered Israel from her enemies and permitted her to settle in the Promised Land now permits Nebuchadnezzar to capture Jerusalem. It wasn't Nebuchadnezzar's ability to capture his prey that caused this, it is clear that God permitted the natural consequence of sin to take its course. God does not act precipitously. He gives us plenty of time to repent. God chose the Jewish nation to be a light to the world, so the world would come to know him. They clearly were not fulfilling his purposes instead they joined the pagans in disobeying God. When you read the story of the Kings of Israel you will see how power, money, pedigree corrupted them, even the wisest man who ever lived, king Solomon, became corrupted by wealth, power and worldly women etc. In Jeremiah 17:24–27 God makes it clear that had Israel been faithful to God the city of Jerusalem would remain forever.

Babylon

Israel did not hearken to the voice of God and Jerusalem fell to Nebuchadnezzar the king of Babylon. Babylon as described in the Bible is an interesting word that has both spiritual and physical connotations. In Geneses 10:10 Babylon is an ancient city founded by Nimrod, Noah's Grandson. About 100 years after the great flood that destroyed the earth, the descendants of Noah founded the city of Babylon. After the flood you would think that the people would seek God's diligently and living according to his plan, instead of spreading out in different places as God instructed them they were defiant and they began to build a tower high enough to reach Heaven so they can escape another flood. While they were building it God confounded their language (hence the origin of the different languages) and there was much confusion and God scattered them abroad. Babylon, both physically and spiritually speaking, is known for its rebellion against God. Out of Babylon came many nations. Babylon represents confusion, rebellion against God, self-exaltation, and salvation by works. Spiritual Babylon that is mentioned in the book of Revelation represents a false power, false system of worship and a false message. Spiritually speaking, Babylon is Satan's Capital City.

The physical kingdom of Babylon became a world power after the fall of the Assyrian kingdom. The kingdom of Babylon was rebuilt centuries later by King Nebuchadnezzar and it was his headquarters. Babylon was located on the river Euphrates 60 miles south of modern Baghdad. It was 10 miles in circumference and was the center of idol worship. It had numerous temples dedicated to different gods. The chief god was Marduk and his temple was enormous with an altar made of gold. Nebuchadnezzar built the famous hanging gardens of Babylon for his wife who came from Lebanon. It was one of the wonders of the ancient world. The kingdom of Babylon ruled the world and Nebuchadnezzar wanted Babylon to rule forever. It was powerful and hostile to God's people. The Lord permitted Babylon to destroy the surrounding nations because of their wickedness (See Jeremiah 51:7). He also foretold the destruction of Babylon in Jeremiah 21:3, 10, and in Isaiah 13:17–22. Many years before the Medo-Persian King Cyrus captured Babylon,

God revealed this capture to his prophet Isaiah. *In Isaiah 45:1 God called Cyrus by name 150 years before he was born, and states what he would capture Babylon.* This prophecy was fulfilled 150 years later when Cyrus (580–529 BC) captured Babylon. This should leave no doubt as to who is in control of history. God is the ruler of this universe and he controls the affairs of men. He has a plan to redeem man and he is working out his plan of redemption and the nations of this world rule for only a time until he establishes his eternal kingdom. In the meantime he is working out his plan of redemption and he reveals his plans to the prophets. *Surely the Lord God does nothing unless he reveals his secrets to his servants the prophets.*

Because of continuing disobedience to God, the King of Babylon was permitted to capture the Southern Kingdom of Judah. God had not forgotten his people even in captivity. Numerous prophets were sent to them while still in captivity. The prophet Daniel is one of them. While still a teenager Daniel was captured from the land of Judah and was taken captive to the great metropolis of Babylon. While in captivity the great creator of this universe looked down at this faithful captive servant and bestowed on him the prophetic gift in a tremendous way and in visions and dreams God revealed the history of the world to him from 6th century BC to the second coming of Jesus. We will study the prophetic messages of Daniel in great detail because the messages God gave to Daniel is for us who live at the very end of time so we need to study it carefully. It is preferable that you read the Bible and study it as you read the explanations given here. Here is a verse-by-verse analysis that should help in understanding these prophecies.

Chapter One
606 BC
DANIEL

1. In the 3rd year of the reign of Jehoiakim king of Jerusalem, the Babylonian army of King Nebuchadnezzar came to Jerusalem and besieged it.

Daniel is the author and he is using the Babylonian method of counting a King's reign. The 3rd year of Jehoiakim's reign was from 606 to 605 BC The first year of a king's reign was his ascension year; the following year was considered his first year. So the third year of king's reign in Babylon would be reckoned as the fourth year in Israel (see Jeremiah 25:1). The book of Daniel begins with the first of Nebuchadnezzar's several attacks on Jerusalem, the Capital of the Southern Kingdom of Judah. In the first two years of his reign, King Nebuchadnezzar ruled simultaneously with his father King Nebopolassar. Daniel places his first assault on Jerusalem about 605 BC. Remember the powerful Assyrian nation finally fell to Babylon about 612 BC. Babylon was now the world-ruling empire. Egypt was concerned about the expanding Babylonian Empire to the north and formed an alliance with Assyria. Remnants of the Assyrian army were pushed west of the Euphrates. At Carchemish (now Iraq) some Assyrians revolted against Babylonian rule of King Nabopolassar. The King, who was too old to fight, sent his son Nebuchadnezzar to take care of the revolt.

Pharaoh Necho II of Egypt decided to assist the Assyrian forces at Carchemish. In order to get to Carchemish he had to pass through the land of Judah. As he passed through Judah, King Josiah despite warnings sent by God not to attack him, did so and was killed in the battle in the valley of Megiddo about 609 BC (2 Kings 23:29). King Josiah was one of the five good kings of the Southern Kingdom in its 350-year existence.

He tried to establish godly reforms in his country but his untimely death ended Judah's religious reformation. King Josiah's son Jehoahaz (age 23) then became King of Judah (2 Chronicles 35 and 36). From 609 BC to 605 BC The nation of Judah came under the control of Egypt and according to 2 Kings 23:33 after a 3-month reign Pharaoh Necho captured King Jehoahaz put him in chains and took him to Egypt where he died. According to 2 Kings 24 Egypt now control Judah. Pharaoh Necho replaced Jehoahaz with his brother Eliakim and changed his name to Jehoiakim (age 25). Both Jehoahaz and Jehoiakim did evil in the sight of the Lord. King Jehoiakim rejected God's prophet and cut up the prophecies of Jeremiah and threw them in the fire. He ordered the prophet Jeremiah arrested. His reign as king lasted from 609–598 BC.

Daniel 1:1 tells us that in the 3rd reign of King Jehoiakim about 605 BC came Nebuchadnezzar and besieged Jerusalem. Nebuchadnezzar's forces put down the Assyrian revolt and defeated Egypt at the battle of Carchemish near the Euphrates River (Jeremiah 46:2). After defeating the Egyptian forces Nebuchadnezzar's forces attacked Jerusalem. Suddenly Nebuchadnezzar received news that his father died in Babylon. He hastily returned home by a shorter route through the Arabian Desert to replace his father as king. He left orders for his commanders to bring the Hebrew captives back. Daniel and his three companions were taken captive during Nebuchadnezzar's first attack on Judah in 605 BC. Daniel and many Jewish captives were escorted to Babylon by Nebuchadnezzar's troops.

King Jehoiakim rebelled against Babylon and died untimely. When Jehoiakim died his son Jehoiachin began to reign at age 18. He also did evil in the sight of the Lord. According to 2 Kings 24:1 Jehoiachin reigned only three months when Nebuchadnezzar besieged Jerusalem and took Jehoiachin, his mother, his servants, his princes and officers to Babylon about 598 BC. The prophet Ezekiel was also taken to Babylon. Nebuchadnezzar raided the temple in Jerusalem and the palace in Jerusalem and took their contents to his country. He took thousands of captives leaving the poorest people behind. Nebuchadnezzar made Jehoiachin's uncle, Mettaniah, king at age 23. He changed his name to Zedekiah. Zedekiah, the brother of Jehoiachin's father, became the last king to rule Judah from 598–586 BC. He did not learn from the experiences of the previous kings. He too ignored the prophets and did evil in the sight of the Lord.

King Zedekiah rebelled against Nebuchadnezzar. In 2 Kings 25 we read that Nebuchadnezzar invaded Jerusalem for the 3rd time in 588 BC. He built forts around the city and besieged it for two years until the 11th year of the reign of Zedekiah. Zedekiah and his entourage tried to escape but were captured. Nebuchadnezzar ordered the execution of his sons in front of him. They put out Zedekiah eyes and he was taken to Babylon in brass chains. Nebuchadnezzar burned down the city of Jerusalem. He destroyed the temple that Solomon built about 970 BC and took the valuables to Babylon. Jerusalem was destroyed and most people were taken to Babylon except the poorest of the poor who were left to work on the vineyards and fields. Some captives escaped to Egypt, among them was the prophet Jeremiah. So a hundred and thirty six years after the Northern Kingdom fell the curtain also fell on the Southern Kingdom of Judah. The 400-year reign of kings on the throne of David came to an end. Daniel continues to tell us the story.

Verse 2. And the Lord gave Jehoiakim King of Judah into the hand of King Nebuchadnezzar, the King of Babylon. Nebuchadnezzar took some of the holy vessels that were in the temple in Jerusalem and carried them off to Babylon. The holy vessels were taken to the land of Shinar and placed in the treasure house of his Babylonian God Marduk.

This is a fulfillment of a prophecy given to King Hezekiah by the prophet Isaiah 100 years earlier in Isaiah 39:6 and in 2 Kings 20:14–18. Here the Lord revealed to his prophet Isaiah 100 years before that the Babylonians would do this. God has foreknowledge. Surely the Lord God will do nothing unless he reveals it to his servants the prophets.

3. Nebuchadnezzar told Ashpenez, one of his chiefs of staff, to take the young men of royal descent from the king's house as well as the first families of Judah, back to Babylon.

Daniel now gives details only someone with such intimate knowledge can give.

4. He chose the best; children with no blemish, handsome, well mannered, knowledgeable, understand science, and well educated and with keen intellect, easily teachable who can learn the literature and the language of the Chaldeans.

5. They were treated royally and were given a daily portion of the same food the King ate, the same wine that the king drank, so that by the end of 3 years they would be fit for the king's service.

6. Now among the many captives of Judah were 4 notable young men, Daniel, Hannaniah, Mishael, and Azariah. Many were taken captives during this invasion of Jerusalem but these four stood out because of their stand for God.

7. Ashpenez, who was in charge of these men, gave them Babylonian names. He gave unto Daniel the name of Belteshazzar; and to Hannaniah the name Shadrach, and to Mishael the name of Meshach and to Azariah the name Abednego.

These young men had their Hebrew names changed to names that indicate that they were now subjects of the Babylonian Gods. Daniel's name in Hebrew means God is my Judge. Belteshazzar means the Babylonian God Bel Provides. Hannaniah means the Lord is Gracious, while Shadrach means exalt Murduk or Aku, the Babylonian God. Mischael means who is what the Lord is, while Meshach means who is what Murduk or Aku is. Azariah means the Lord is My Helper, while Abednego means the servant of Nebo, a Babylonian God. If they could get them to forget their names, they would forget their God, their heritage, and their identity.

8. But Daniel purposed in his heart to live in harmony with God's law so that he would not defile himself with the portion of the king's meat, nor with the wine which he drank: therefore he requested of the prince of the eunuchs that he should be given a diet consistent with his beliefs so that he might not defile himself.

Their names were changed in honor of Babylonian gods. They were offered the best of Babylonian life but they remembered the lessons taught to them at home and they decided come what may they were not going to eat the king's meat or drink his wine. The king's food was offered up to idols and they could not dishonor God by partaking of that food.

9. God honors those who honor him and so God had brought Daniel into favor and tender love with Ashpenez, the prince of the eunuchs. Daniel's exemplary behavior gained the love and respect of Asphenez.

10. And Ashpenez said unto Daniel, I am afraid because the king chose your food and if he sees that you are not as robust as the others he will cut off my head.

11. Then said Daniel to Melzar, whom Ashpenez, the prince of the eunuchs had put in charge over Daniel, Hananiah, Mishael, and Azariah.

12. Daniel pleaded with Melzar who was in charge of them to give them 10 days on the simple diet and see what happens. "Prove thy servants, I beseech you, for ten days give us a simple diet of vegetables and plain water to drink."

13. "Then examine us after 10 days and compare us to the other children that eat of the portion of the king's meat: then decide based on your evaluation how you should deal with us in this matter."

14. So Meltzar gave in to their request, and gave them 10 days to prove themselves.

15. And at the end of ten days when Meltzar examined them, and the result of the healthier diet was evident. They appeared to be much healthier than all the children, which did eat the portion of the king's meat.

16. Thus Melzar took away the portion of their meat, and the wine that they should drink; and gave them their simple diet of vegetables and water.

17. As for these four children, God gave them knowledge and skill in all learning and wisdom: and Daniel had understanding in all visions and dreams. They did their part in obeying God and they were successful because God gave them his grace to obey his will and God rewarded them for their obedience. They were obedient to the Babylonian king request and accepted the Babylonian training and way of life so long as it did not interfere with the commandments of God.

18. Now the three years of training came to an end and it was time for the king to examine them; then the prince of the eunuchs Ashpenez brought them in before King Nebuchadnezzar.

19. And the king examined them; he was most impressed by these four Hebrew young men, among the captives he found none like Daniel, Hananiah, Mishael, and Azariah: therefore he chose them to work in the Royal Court and to serve before the king.

20. And in all matters of wisdom and understanding, that the king enquired of them, he found them 10 times better than all the magicians and astrologers that were in all his realm. You cannot beat God's giving; when you surrender your will to Him He can work wonders in your life.

21. And Daniel continued even unto the first year of King Cyrus (605 BC–539 BC).

Commentary: This is truly an amazing story; Daniel has got to be one of the most inspiring real life heroes of all times. He is one of my favorite Bible characters. He was born into a royal family, probably relatives of King Zedekiah. He was captured from his homeland as a teenager and taken thousands of miles away to a pagan country. Yet he was faithful to God; he never forgot his God. He was faithful throughout his life. Exiled in a foreign land he had no one to turn to but God and that was enough. He was faithful to God and prayed to God three times a day. Daniel honored God and God honored Daniel with wisdom, knowledge, integrity, honesty and success even in a foreign land. This young man was taught of the Lord and it stuck. He had a purpose in life to serve God and he stood firm, even though he was alone in the foreign land of Babylon. He did not make any excuses. He did not complain about his circumstances and become rebellious. He followed God's leading. That should encourage us.

Chapter Two
603 BC

Through the prophet Daniel God reveals to us the rise and fall of many nations. In chapter 11 Daniel lays out the prophetic history of the world from the 6th century BC until the end of time on Planet Earth. We are privileged to know this information. Daniel, the prophet, to whom this information was given, could not have understood it all. Today we have a much better understanding as these prophecies unfold with time. History books confirms that these prophecies has been fulfilled with amazing accuracy.

Verse 1 – In the 2nd year of the reign of King Nebuchadnezzar (about 603 BC according to the Chaldean method of counting 606–605 as his inaugural year, 605–604 his 1st year). In Nebuchadnezzar's second year and Daniel's 3rd year of captivity (603 BC), God gave an impressive dream to Nebuchadnezzar, king of Babylon. The dream was so disturbing to him that he could not sleep. When the king awoke he could not remember the details of the dream, but it left a fearful impression on his mind and he was troubled.

Verse 2 – The king then commanded that the magicians, and astrologers and sorcerers, and the Chaldeans come and tell him the dream. Dreams were important to Babylonian life. This dream revealed the future and it was very important that the king understand his dream, so he called on these professional dream interpreters. They came before the king.

Verse 3 – The king told them that he had a dream and his spirit was troubled to know the dream.

Verse 4 – The Chaldeans speaking in Aramaic assured the king that if he told them the dream, they would interpret it for him.

Verse 5 – The king then told them that he couldn't remember the dream and if they could not tell him the dream and the interpretation of the dream that heads were going to roll. He would cut them up into pieces and destroy their houses. This king was ruthless and meant what he said.

Verse 6 – If however, they showed him the dream and its interpretation, they will receive gifts, rewards and great honor.

Verse 7 – They again ask the king to tell them the dream and they will interpret it for him.

Verse 8 – The king told them that they would take their time because they saw that the king had forgotten the dream.

Verse 9 – But if they would not tell him the dream, there is one decree for them; the king felt that the longer they took to tell him the dream, the more time they had to come up with a lie. He insisted on them telling him the dream so that he could believe in their interpretation.

Verse 10 – The Chaldeans told the king that there was no one on earth who could comply with the king's request and that no king, Lord or ruler had asked this of any magician, astrologer or Chaldean.

Verse 11 – The king's request was unusual and no one on earth could tell the king what he dreamt, except the gods who do not live on this earth. They now admit to the king that they cannot do what they claimed they could do and that is to interpret dreams.

Verse 12 – This made the king very angry, and he threatened to kill all the wise men of Babylon that could not interpret the dream.

Verse 13 – As the death decree went forth to kill the wise men, Daniel and his friends were sought out to be killed with the wise men of Babylon.

Verse 14 – Arioch the captain of the King's guard had gone forth with the decree to kill the wise men of Babylon and when he got to Daniel, Daniel answered with counsel and wisdom, saying

Verse 15 – Why is the king issuing such a decree so hastily? So Arioch explained the situation to Daniel.

Verse 16 – Daniel then went in to see the king and asked the king for time and promised the king that he would show him the interpretation.

Verse 17 – Daniel went home and told his fellow companions Hananiah, Mishael and Azariah what had taken place.

Verse 18 – Daniel then asked his companions to pray that the God of Heaven would be merciful to them concerning this matter, so that they won't perish with the rest of the wise men of Babylon.

It appears that God did not allow Nebuchadnezzar to remember the dream because the so-called wise men would get together and come up with a lying explanation to satisfy the king. Daniel had a peace that passes all human understanding. He relied on God and placed the whole matter in God's hands. Daniel had a prayer meeting and sought the answer from the only true source of knowledge God. Sorcerers and psychics are mere mortal and they truly do not know the supernatural.

Verse 19: God revealed this secret dream to Daniel in a night vision and Daniel blessed the God of Heaven.

Verse 20: Daniel answered and said "Blessed be the name of God forever and ever, for wisdom and might is his".

Verse 21: God controls the times and the seasons. He removes kings and sets up kings. He gives wisdom to the wise and knowledge to those that have understanding.

Verse 22: God reveals the deep and secret things, and he sees the things that are hidden to man. Light dwells with him.

Verse 23: Daniel again praises God for giving him wisdom and might and for revealing the king's dream to him. He utters I thank thee, and praise thee, O thou God of my fathers, who hast given me wisdom and might, and hast made known unto me now what we desired of thee: for you have revealed to me the king's dream and its interpretation.

Verse 24: Daniel then went to see Arioch, the one in charge of the destruction of the wise men, and asked him not to destroy the wise men of Babylon. "Take me to see the king and I will reveal to the king the dream and its interpretation."

Verse 25: Then Arioch hurriedly brought Daniel in to see the king and told the king that he found a man, one of the Jewish captives, who would tell him the interpretation of the dream.

Verse 26: The king then said to Daniel who was given the Babylonian name of Belteshazzar, "Are you able to tell me the dream that I had and the interpretation of?"

Verse 27: Daniel answered the king; ...no wise man, astrologer, magician, soothsayer can reveal the dream or its interpretation, but—

Verse 28: ...there is a God of Heaven, who can reveal all secrets and he also has revealed to the king the events of the latter days or the time of the end. Here is the dream and vision that you had. Daniel gives credit to God. Only Daniel God can reveal secrets. He is the only true God.

Verse 29: Daniel informs the king that as he lay in bed his thoughts were centered on the future of his kingdom and God who is the revealer of secrets was revealing to him future events.

Verse 30: Daniel told the king that God revealed the interpretation to him not because Daniel had more wisdom than anyone else. It was given so that he could make known the interpretation to the king, so that the king may know the thoughts of his heart that he had dreamt about.

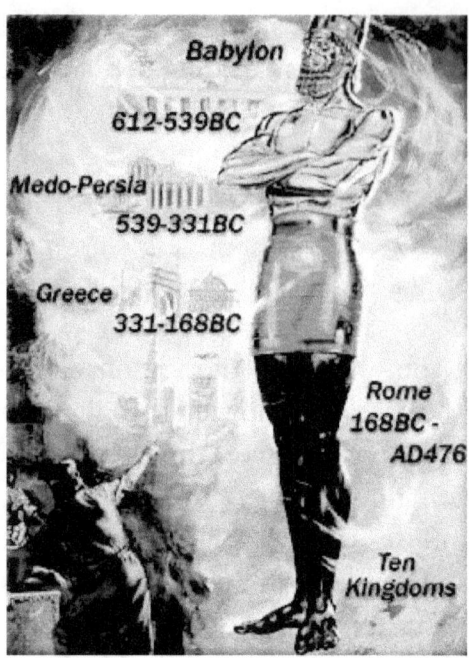

The king was concerned about the future of his Babylonian Empire. Nebuchadnezzar worshipped many false gods. He believed that these gods communicated through dreams. He went to bed one night wondering if this great kingdom that he had established would last forever. God who knows the history of this world, gave him the answer in a dream that he could relate to.

Verse 31: Daniel reveals the dream, "Thou O king saw this great awesome image. It shone brilliantly and it looked terrible."

Verse 32: The head of this image was made of fine gold, the chest and arms of silver, the belly and thighs of brass.

Verse 33: The legs of iron, and the feet partly of iron and partly of clay.

Verse 34: In that very dream as the king beheld the image, a stone not made by human hand was carved out and it smote the image on the feet of iron and clay and broke it into pieces.

Verse 35: Then this image made of iron, the clay, the brass, the silver, and the gold were broken up into pieces until the whole statue was ground like fine residue of a summers' threshing floor and the wind came and blew away the dust, and nothing was left, except the stone that destroyed the image became a great mountain and filled the whole earth.

Verse 36: This is what you dreamt. Now we will tell you the interpretation.

Verse 37: You are a king of kings and it is the God of Heaven who has given to you the kingdom of Babylon and power and strength and glory. Babylon having overthrown Assyria was now the greatest nation on earth and its' king was Nebuchadnezzar. King

Nebuchadnezzar was not a believer in the God of Heaven and hence did not recognize God as the giver of his kingdom, wealth and power; this was Daniel's opportunity to acquaint him with God. God is the ruler of earth and sets up kings and brings down kings.

Verse 38: Wherever men, as well as the animals and birds dwell, God has given you control over them and made you ruler over them. You are the head of Gold. Babylon was known as the Golden Kingdom. God told him what the future held. This is very important as God revealed from a biblical standpoint the history of the human race from Nebuchadnezzar rule of Babylon to the second coming of Jesus. God used various illustrations or symbols to help us to understand. Here he used the metals on the image.

Verse 39: But another kingdom will come after Babylon– inferior to Babylon, as silver is inferior to Gold. Babylon fell to Medo-Persia in 539 BC The Medo-Persian Empire was inferior to the Babylonian Empire in culture and science. Yet, another kingdom will replace the silver; this kingdom is represented by brass. The Macedonian Empire of Alexander was inferior in wealth and opulence but it ruled over a larger area. The 3rd kingdom on the image is the belly and thighs of brass representing Greece (331–168 BC). The Greeks often traded with brass. In 331 BC Alexander the great, founder of the Macedonian Greek Empire, conquered Medo-Persia.

Verse 40: And the fourth kingdom will be as strong as iron: for as much as iron break into pieces and subdues all things: and as iron that break all these, will it break in pieces and bruise. The legs of iron on the image represents the iron monarchy of Rome, the world ruling empire which is the fourth kingdom on the image, will be as strong as iron; and as iron break into pieces and destroy all things so will this kingdom break and bruise. This Kingdom was Pagan Rome. Note the decreasing value of the metals but it seems that the subsequent kingdoms are very powerful.

Verse 41: And whereas you see the feet and toes, part of potters' clay, and part of iron, the kingdom will be divided; but there will be in it of the strength of the iron, for as much as you saw the iron mixed with miry clay. Next on this image are the feet and toes, made partly of potters clay and part of iron. The feet of iron and of clay represent the ten divisions of the Roman Empire. This kingdom was broken up into 10 kingdoms as depicted by the ten toes of the image. Some kingdoms will be strong and some weak as depicted by the mixing of iron and miry clay. Centuries before the Roman Empire was broken up into the ten kingdoms, God showed it to Daniel in a vision.

I hope that you are following how God is showing us through the prophecies of Daniel, an outline of the kingdoms that will rule this world until the second coming of Jesus.

Verse 42: And as the toes of the feet were part of iron, and part of clay, so the kingdom will be partly strong and partly broken. A mixture of iron and clay represents partly strong and partly weak kingdoms.

Verse 43: And whereas you saw iron mixed with miry clay, they shall mingle themselves with the seed of men: but they shall not cleave one to another, even as iron is not mixed with clay. Because of this mixture of iron and clay some of these powers will be strong, and others will be weak. They would try to unite but they would not unite into a world power, even as iron doesn't mix with clay.

God showed Daniel here that whereas he saw iron mixed with miry clay, representing the 10 divisions of the nations of Western Europe that resulted from the breakup of Rome. They shall mingle themselves with the seed of men but *they shall not cleave one to another,* even as iron is not mixed with clay. You can believe God's prophecies. This is 1500 years after the fall of the Roman Empire and the nations of Western Europe are still divided. God said they would not cleave, so far they have not and they are not going to. Numerous attempts have been made to unite Europe through various methods e.g. the intermarrying of various nobilities, the European common market, and the Euro currency. Numerous leaders have tried to unite Europe e.g. Charles V of Spain, Charlemagne, Napoleon, Kaiser Wilhelm 11, Louis X1V, Lenin, Adolph Hitler, Mussolini. It is not for the lack of trying that Europe is still not united. In this prophecy, God said they would not and they are not going to.

Verse 44: And in the days of these kings, the God of Heaven will set up his kingdom that will replace the other kingdoms, and it will stand forever.

In other words the second coming of Jesus to set up his everlasting kingdom will occur while these kingdoms of Western Europe are still in existence. This information is revealed to the prophet Daniel about 603 BC

Verse 45: Forasmuch as you were shown in your dream that the stone that was cut out of the mountain by superhuman power and broke into pieces the entire image of iron, brass, clay, silver, and the gold. God is showing you the future of the world. The dream is certain and the interpretation is sure.

God said that stone cut out without hands (of divine origin), this represents the kingdom of Jesus that will come and would strike the image, not in the head, belly, thigh or legs but in the feet of iron and clay. We are now over 2600 years after this prophecy was shown to Daniel. The stone cut out without hands, which represent the Messianic coming kingdom of Jesus, did not come during the head of gold, or the breast and arms of silver or the belly of brass or the legs of iron because God said it would not. The stone has not struck yet but it will, during the era of history represented by the feet of iron and of clay. The prophecy is sure. We have been living in the feet of iron and of clay. We can trust God's word, it will happen, and when it happen let us pray that we are ready for that momentous of all events.

Verse 46 Then King Nebuchadnezzar fell on his face and worshipped Daniel, and commanded that offered praise and sweet incense be offered unto him.

Verse 47: The King then said to Daniel it is true that your God is the God of all Gods and the Lord of kings and a revealer of secrets because you were able to reveal my dream.

Verse 48: Then the King made Daniel a great man; gave him many great gifts and put Daniel in charge of the whole province of Babylon and chief of the Governors over the wise men of Babylon.

Verse 49: Daniel then requested of the king that his 3 companions should be put in charge of the affairs of the province while Daniel stayed at the gate of the king.

In Daniel 2 God revealed to Daniel the kingdoms that would rule the world. He revealed Babylon, then Medo-Persia, then Greece, then Rome dividing into the 10 nations of Western Europe. Note that the other metals completely disappeared but the iron persisted although mixed with clay. The iron and clay mixture of kingdoms will last until the end of time until God sets up his everlasting kingdom.

The prophecy of Daniel 2 has been fulfilled with amazing accuracy. Babylon, the kingdom represented by gold, ruled the world from 605–539 BC. Medo-Persia, the kingdom represented by silver, ruled from 539 BC to 331 BC. Greece, represented by brass, ruled the world from 331 BC to 168 BC. Rome, represented as the iron kingdom, ruled the world from 168 BC until it became divided and began disintegrating into the 10 nations that eventually became Western Europe. Rome ruled the world for over 500 years. Daniel was shown that in the days of the rulers of Western Europe Jesus will come and set up his everlasting kingdom. This is the only part of the vision of Daniel 2 that has not been fulfilled. The prophecies of Daniel revealed that God has foreknowledge and he reveals the future to us.

Chapter Three

1. After receiving an impressive dream from God and the interpretation by the prophet of God, King Nebuchadnezzar slipped back into idolatry. He did not accept the prophecy as told to him. He envisioned Babylon as lasting forever despite what God had revealed to him. He was not satisfied with being the head of Gold on the image as he was shown in the dream. He was determined to make void that which God had revealed to him in his dream, and so with his vast resources he made an image sixty cubic tall (100 feet) and 6 cubits (10 feet) wide. The entire image was made of gold, from head to toe, representing his kingdom. He wanted his kingdom to last forever. He then placed this magnificent stature in the plain of Dura, in the province of Babylon.

Then king Nebuchadnezzar gathered together the princes, the governors, the captains, the judges, the treasurers, the counselors, the sheriffs, and all the rulers of the provinces, to come to the dedication of the image that he had set up.

They all came for the dedication and stood before the image that King Nebuchadnezzar had set up.

Then a king's herald cried loudly and gave the king's command "To you it is commanded, O people, nations, and languages.

When you hear the sound of the cornet, the flute, harp, sackbut, psaltery, dulcimer, and all kinds of music that you should fall down and worship the golden image that king Nebuchadnezzar had set up and whosoever do not fall down and worship this image will in that very hour be cast in the midst of a burning fiery furnace."

And when all the people heard the sound of the cornet, flute, harp, sackbut, psaltery, and all kinds of music all the people, the nations, and the languages, fell down and worshipped the golden image that King Nebuchadnezzar had set up.

Everyone fell down and worship except for three Hebrew captives who decided to honor God's law which commands, "Thou shall not bow down to any graven image". Only three people in that vast throng did not bow down and stood firm and obeyed God's commandments. Folks this has been the story of redemption, only the minority will follow God's instructions.

Some of the Chaldeans took notice and they accused these Jewish men of failing to obey the king's command. They went to the king saying "O king, live forever."

They reminded the king that he had made a decree that every man that hear the sound of the cornet, flute, harp, sackbut, psaltery, and dulcimer, and all kinds of music, shall fall down and worship the golden image.

And the consequences of disobeying were that those who did not fall down and worship the golden image would be cast in the midst of a burning fiery furnace.

They told the king that there were certain Jews, namely Shadrach, Meshach and Abednego, that he placed in high positions over the affairs of the province of Babylon who did not obey the king's command. They do not serve the king's gods, nor worship the golden image which the king set up.

King Nebuchadnezzar became furious and outraged and commanded that these men be brought in to him and they were brought before the angry king.

The king asked of them, is it true that you do not serve my gods or bow before the image that I have set up?

Listen up, I am going to give you another chance and when you hear the sound of the cornet, flute, harp, sackbut, psaltery, and dulcimer and all king of musical instruments, fall down and worship the image which I have made; if you do not you will be cast in the midst of a burning fiery furnace, who is that God that can deliver you out of my hands?

The Jewish boys Shadrach, Meshach, and Abednego responded, "O Nebuchadnezzar, our minds are made up and we are not careful to answer thee in this matter. If this is what you have decided, our God whom we serve is able to deliver us from the burning fiery furnace, and he will deliver us out of your hand, O king. But if not, be it known unto thee, O king that we will not serve thy gods, nor worship the golden image, which thou hast set up."

Nebuchadnezzar became furious and his face changed against Shadrach, Meshach, and Abednego. He ordered the fire to be heated up seven times hotter than was planned. He commanded the strongest men in his army to bind these three Hebrew men and cast them into the midst of the burning fiery furnace.

They were bound in all their clothes—their coats, hose, hats, and other garments and cast in the midst of the burning fiery furnace.

Because of the urgent command of the king and the exceedingly hot furnace the men who cast them in were killed by the flame.

These three bound men fell down bound in the midst of this burning inferno.

When the king looked into the fiery furnace he was astonished and he hastily got up and said to his counselors, "did we not cast three men bound into the midst of the fiery furnace?" They replied "true, O King."

The king said "I see four men lose, walking in the midst of the fire apparently unharmed. I recognize the fourth man as Jesus, the Son of God." Now flesh and blood did not reveal this to King Nebuchadnezzar.

The king forgot about his golden image and he came near the furnace and spoke to the three Hebrew boys, Shadrach, Meshach, and Abednego saying, "you servants of the Most High God come out and they came out of the midst of that fire."

The princes, governors, and captains, and the king's counselors saw these men on whom the fire had no effect, not even their hair singed, they did not even smell of fire.

Then the king said blessed be the God of Shadrach, Meshach, and Abednego, who sent his angel and delivered his servants who trusted in him who would rather die than worship any god, except their own God.

Then the King made a decree that anyone who spoke against the God of these Jewish boys would be killed and their houses destroyed because there is no other God that can deliver like this.

Then he promoted the three Hebrews boys, in the province of Babylon.

Chapter Four

This chapter written in the first person is a first person account given by Nebuchadnezzar. He is the writer and he states the dream that God gave him:

"From Nebuchadnezzar to all peoples, nations and languages that dwell on the earth, peace be multiplied unto you.

I thought it a good idea to share with you the signs and wonders that the high God has done for me.

How great are his signs and how mighty are his wonders, his kingdom is an everlasting kingdom and his dominion is from generation to generation.

I was at sleeping in my house and I was flourishing in my palace

I saw a dream that made me afraid. I was troubled by my thoughts and the visions.

Therefore I made a decree that all the wise men of Babylon be brought before me so they could interpret the dream for me.

The magicians, the astrologers, the Chaldeans, and the soothsayers all came but they could not tell me the dream or its interpretation.

At last Daniel came in before me, whose name is Belteshazzar, after the name of my god, in him dwells the spirit of the Holy God. I told him the dream, saying,

Oh Belteshazzar, master of all the magicians, because I know that the spirit of the Holy God is in you, and no secret trouble you, tell me what I dreamt and also the interpretation.

This is the vision I had while in bed. I saw a tree in the midst of the earth. It was very tall.

The tree grew, and became strong and it grew so tall that it reached unto Heaven, and it can be seen at the ends of the earth.

The leaves were lovely, and it had plenty of fruit, and it was food for all. The beast of the field found shade under it, the birds of the Heaven dwelt in the branches and all flesh was fed from it.

I saw in my vision that a watcher a holy one come down from Heaven

And he cried loudly, saying cut down this tree, and cut off his branches, shake off his leaves and scatter his fruit: Let the beasts get away from under it and the birds fly away from its branches.

But leave the stump of his roots in the earth, even with a band of iron and brass, let it be in the tender grass of the field, and let the dew of the Heaven wet him, and let him dwell with the beasts in the grass of the earth.

Let his heart be changed to that of a beast for seven years.

This decree is from the Holy one of Heaven and his intent is that people would know that God rules in the Kingdom of men and gives it to whomever he will, and sets up over it the lowest of men.

This is the dream that I king Nebuchadnezzar have seen. Now O Belteshazzar, tell me the meaning. The wise men of Babylon cannot tell me the meaning but you can because the spirit of the Holy God is in you.

Then Daniel, whose name was Belteshazzar, was astonished for one hour, and he was troubled by the dream. The king said to him do not let the dream or its interpretation trouble you. Daniel answered, my Lord, the dream be to them that hate you and the interpretation thereof to for your enemies.

The tree which you saw, which grew strong and which grew to Heaven and was seen by all the earth

Whose leaves were fair, and it bore much fruit, and on it was food for all, under which the beast of the field dwell, and upon whose branches the birds of Heaven find their habitat.

It is you, O King that has grown and become strong, and your greatness reaches to Heaven and your dominion reaches to the end of the earth.

The watcher and the holy one that you saw coming down from Heaven, who said cut down the tree down and destroy it, but leave the stump of the roots in the ground, surrounded with a band of iron and brass, in the tender grass of the field and let it be wet with the dew of Heaven, and let his dwelling be with the beasts of the field for seven years.

This is the interpretation, O king; this is the decree of the Most High God, of things, which is to happen to you, my Lord the King.

You will be driven from men and shall live with the beasts of the field, and eat grass as oxen and the dew of Heaven will wet you for seven years until you recognize that the Most High God rules in the kingdom of men and can give your kingdom to whosoever he wills.

And whereas they commanded that the stump of the tree be left in place; this means that your kingdom will be given back to you after you acknowledge that God rules this entire universe.

Wherefore, O King accept my counsel and break off your sins by doing what is right, show mercy to the poor, maybe it would lengthen your tranquility.

All this happened to King Nebuchadnezzar. He was given a chance to repent of his sins, do the right thing show mercy to the poor and submit and acknowledge the God of the universe. He did not and twelve months later, as King Nebuchadnezzar was walking in the palace of his kingdom of Babylon when he boastfully began to speak, "is not this great Babylon that I have built for the house of the kingdom, by the might of my power, and for the honor of my majesty?" Daniel's account here is corroborated by history which reveals that Babylon was indeed a great city and its famous hanging gardens was one of the Seven Wonders of the World.

While he was still speaking, there came a voice from Heaven saying "O King Nebuchadnezzar, to you it is spoken; your kingdom has been taken from you.

And you shall be driven from men and you will dwell with the beasts of the field and you will eat grass like an oxen for seven years until you acknowledge that the Most High rules in the kingdom of man and gives it to whomever he will."

That same hour God's word came to pass and the king was driven from men and did eat grass as oxen, and his body was wet with the dew of Heaven, till his hairs were grown like eagles' feathers, and his nails like birds' claws.

At the end of the seven years, Nebuchadnezzar lifted up his eyes to Heaven, and his understanding returned and he blessed the most High and praised and honored him that lives for ever and ever, whose dominion is an everlasting dominion, and whose kingdom is from generation to generation.

35. All the inhabitants of this earth are reputed as nothing, he does according to his will in the armies of Heaven and among the inhabitants of this earth and no one can prevent him or say unto him what are you doing.

36. At the same time the Kings reasoning returned, his counselors and Lords came looking for him, his kingdom was restored and excellent majesty was added to him.

37. Now I Nebuchadnezzar praise and extol and honor the King of Heaven, all whose works are truth, his judgments fair and those who walk in pride he is able to abase. Nebuchadnezzar became a convert to the God of Heaven, Daniel's God. This once great powerful ruthless ruler conqueror is now a humble believer in God. This is the last we hear of King Nebuchadnezzar.

Chapter Five

Historically, the events described in chapter 5 take place after chapter 7 and chapter 8.

In this chapter God sends a prophecy to King Belshazzar. Nebuchadnezzar ruled for 43 years and died in 562 BC Nebuchadnezzar's son Evil-Merodach ruled next (562–560 BC), Evil-Merodach was assassinated by his sister's husband or Nebuchadnezzar's son-in-law Neriglissar (560–556 BC), Neriglissar died and his young son Labosordacus ruled for 9 months (556–556 BC), then Nabonidus (556–539 BC) ruled simultaneously with his son Belshazzar (553–539 BC). Critics of the book of Daniel claimed that the historical records showed that the last king of the Babylonian Empire was Nabonidus not Belshazzar. Excavations in the late 1800s and the publishing of the *Nabonidus Chronicle* proved that the eyewitness Daniel was correct. The following account took place in the king's palace in Babylon. On that fateful night King Nabonidus was away and his co-regent and son Belshazzar was the presiding king of Babylon that night.

The year was 539 BC, Nebuchadnezzar was dead and his descendant Belshazzar was king of Babylon. Daniel had been living in Babylon for about 64 years and he was about to see a change in world power. Cyrus, the King of Persia, surrounded Babylon with his army. Babylon had huge walls that were impregnable and so Cyrus and his army camped outside waiting for the opportune time to invade. The Babylonians were so confident that these walls would protect them that they were not concerned about the enemy encamped outside so the leadership planned a party.

Verse 1. King Belshazzar, now king of Babylon, organized a great feast with thousands of guests including the Babylonian dignitaries- his Lords, his wives, his concubines.

2. Belshazzar while drinking alcohol, commanded that the golden and silver vessels,

which his great grandfather took out of the temple in Jerusalem, should be brought to the party so that the king, his princes, his wives, his concubines might drink liquor from these vessels that were captured from the temple in Jerusalem. He had no respect for holy things and challenged the God of the universe.

3. Then they brought the golden vessels that were taken out of the temple of the house of God in Jerusalem, and the king and his princes, his wives, his concubines, drank in them. They were wining and dining with the holy vessels taken from Jerusalem.

4. As they drank wine, they praised their gods of gold, silver, brass, iron, wood and stone.

5. The festivities continued and they partied on, totally ignoring the Persian Army outside their secure wall. That night while Nebuchadnezzar's grandson, Belshazzar, was drinking wine in the holy utensils that were captured from the temple in Jerusalem, and while he was partying with thousands of his men and their concubines, and celebrating to his pagan gods, suddenly in the midst of their revelry, part of a hand appeared through the sleeve of darkness and a handwriting, with an inscription in Aramaic, appeared on the wall. The king saw the part of the hand that wrote, suddenly the music stopped, the laughter, the singing, the noise died down, a whisper could be heard, instantly drunken men became sober enough to realize that something ominous had just been written on that wall.

6. Although they did not know that it meant, Daniel states that King Belshazzar color changed, his thoughts scared him, his limbs gave out and his knees knocked together.

7. Suddenly this powerful monarch began to cry for help. He had not learned from his grandfather's experience and he cried aloud to bring in his astrologers, Chaldeans, and enchanters, the soothsayers and promised them that whosoever can interpret the handwriting on the wall shall be clothed with scarlet, have a chain of gold around their neck, and they shall be the third ruler of the kingdom. (The first ruler was his father King Nabonidus. Belshazzar was the 2nd ruler or co-regent.)

8. Then the king's wise men came in but they could not read or interpret what was written on the wall.

9. Then King was greatly troubled, and his countenance was changed and his Lords were astonished.

10. The King who was panicking, was a member of the younger generation and although he knew of the history of his grandfather Nebuchadnezzar's experience with Daniel, he chose to call the soothsayers of Babylon over Daniel; they failed to interpret the dream, however the queen mother (probably his mother hears the commotion and comes to the banquet hall. She says to Belshazzar "let not your heart be troubled nor let your countenance be changed." (It maybe that the Babylonian custom is to call

ancestors father or mother so our grandfather could be referred to as father, another explanation is the word for father and grandfather is the same in Aramaic.)

11. She reminded him that there lives in the Kingdom of Babylon a man in whom the spirit of the Holy God dwells and in the days of his grandfather light and understanding and wisdom like the wisdom of the gods was found in him, and his grandfather made him master of the magicians, astrologers, Chaldeans, and soothsayers.

12. He has an excellent spirit, and knowledge, and understanding, interpreting dreams and unravels mysteries and dissolves doubts. King Nebuchadnezzar named him Belteshazzar. She advised her son to call him in and he will show you the interpretation.

13. Then Daniel was brought before the king and the King asks are you that Daniel whom my grandfather Nebuchadnezzar brought captive from Jerusalem to Babylon during the Jewish captivity?

14. I have even heard of you that the spirit of the gods dwells in you and that light and understanding and excellent wisdom is found in you.

15. The wise men, the astrologers, have been brought in before me but they could not read or interpret the writing.

16. I have heard of you that you can make interpretations, and dissolve doubts, and for the interpretation of the handwriting, he offered Daniel a scarlet robe, a chain of gold about his neck, and the position of third ruler of the kingdom of Babylon.

17. Then Daniel answered and said to the king, keep your gifts and give your rewards to someone else; however I will tell you what is written and the interpretation thereof.

18. Just before he gives him the interpretation of the handwriting on the wall, Daniel gives the king a brief history lesson, he reminded him that God gave his grandfather Nebuchadnezzar a kingdom, majesty, glory and honor.

19. He had such majesty that all people, nations, languages, trembled and feared him. He killed whom he wanted to, set up or put down people as he wished.

20. But when his heart was lifted up and his mind hardened in pride, he was deposed from his kingly throne and his glory was taken from him.

21. His kingdom was taken from him for seven years and his heart was made like the beasts and his dwelling was with the wild asses: they fed him with grass like oxen and his body was wet with the dew of Heaven until he recognized the God of Heaven as the supreme ruler of men and sets up who he wants.

22. He goes on to warn the king that even though King Belshazzar knew this, he did not humble his heart.

23. But instead lifted up himself against the God of Heaven, and drank alcohol from the vessels of the house of God. You and your Lords, your wives, your concubines had drunk wine in them, praising their gods of silver and gold and bronze, iron, wood and

stone. These Gods were of their own making, they do not see, nor hear, nor know, but the God who gives you breath from second to second and who knows everything about you, have not been glorified.

24. So God, who controls the kingdom of men, has written the following on your wall.

25. "MENE, MENE, TEKEL, UPHARSIN." Again the wise men of Babylon cannot interpret what was written on the wall.

26. Daniel then gives the interpretation MENE "God has numbered your days and the days of your kingdom and have brought it to an end.

27. TEKEL: You have been weighed in the balances and found wanting."

28. PERES: Your kingdom is divided and given to the Medes and the Persians.

29. Then King Belshazzar commanded that Daniel be clothed with scarlet, and a gold chain be put on his neck, and he should be the third ruler of the kingdom. Daniel was then made the third ruler in the kingdom of Babylon.

30. That very night Cyrus and his armies diverted the River Euphrates as it entered Babylon. They created a riverbed shallow enough for his army to enter Babylon. They broke through the gates and entered Babylon and found the leadership still shocked and intoxicated. They could not defend the city and save themselves and that fateful night Babylon fell to a weaker nation Medo-Persia. Belshazzar was slain and so ended the great world ruling power, the golden kingdom of Babylon.

Daniel is an accurate prophet and historian. For one thing he told us that the King Belshazzar was the king presiding over a feast in the palace that night. His critics called him a false prophet because as far as historical records go Nabonidus was the last king of Babylon. The stones has cried out again in favor of God's word and the Nabonidus Chronicle shows that Belshazzar was in fact the presiding king. His father Nabonidus who was also king was away with part of the Babylonian army out on the Tigris River trying to stop the Medo-Persian attack. Daniel, the eyewitness, had it right.

That fateful night in 539 BC the kingdom of Babylon fell. It was the head of gold on the image shown to Nebuchadnezzar and revealed to Daniel about 603 BC, some 69 years earlier. Part of the prophecy of Daniel 2 was now fulfilled. The Lord God does nothing unless he reveals his secrets to his servants the prophets (Amos 3:7). About 150 years before the fall of Babylon, God revealed to the prophet Isaiah in Isaiah 13 verses 19 and 20 that the kingdom of Babylon will be overthrown like God overthrew Sodom & Gomorrah, and Babylon will never be inhabited again. The prophet Jeremiah in 597 BC prophesied about the fall and subsequent desolation of Babylon in Jeremiah 51 specifically verses 37 and 62. Today 2600 years after the prophecies of Isaiah and Jeremiah, the ancient site of the city of Babylon lay desolate. Babylon is still in ruins. Saddam Hussein tried twice to rebuild it and he was stopped by the first gulf war, and his second attempt was halted by the second war that led to his death. He knew that God said it would not be rebuilt or inhabited but he challenged the God of Heaven. The word of God is sure and true. When God say it is over, it is over. God is in control of history and reveals it to his prophets. *Surely the Lord does nothing unless he reveal his secrets to his servants the prophets, Joel 3:7.*

God revealed to the prophet Isaiah in Isaiah 44 starting at verse 27, the drying up of the river Euphrates and goes on to mention the person that God would use to accomplish these things. God called Cyrus by name 150 years before he was born. The prophecy predicted that Cyrus would capture Babylon and free the Jews and Jerusalem will be rebuilt. This was done and recorded in 2 Chronicles 36:22–23 and Ezra 1:1–4. Isaiah 45:1 describes with remarkable accuracy that God would hold up Cyrus right hand, he would subdue the nations and God would loose the loins of kings to open the gates. Daniel 5:6 describes how King Belshazzar's loins were loosed as he saw the handwriting on the wall and the inner gates of Babylon were left open on that fateful night when Babylon fell.

God is in charge of history and an inferior kingdom Medo-Persia conquered Babylon in 539 BC in a very dramatic way. This kingdom was inferior to Babylon in magnificence, in wealth. Belshazzar, King of Babylon was overthrown by Cyrus, the Persian king, and the Jews were later liberated. Similarly the spiritual kingdom of Babylon, that exists until the end of time, will be destroyed by the second coming of Jesus and Jesus will liberate his people, spiritual Israel. We will elaborate on this later.

31. Darius, the King of the Medes took over the kingdom at age 62. This new world power is a combination of two powers; the older kingdom of the Medes, who were conquered by the Persians and Persia, which is now Iran. We now have the establishment of a single power called Medo-Persian Empire. Cyrus the Persian King installed Darius, the Mede, as king of this Babylonian part of the Persian Empire.

Chapter Six
539 BC

1. Darius the Mede was now king of the Medo-Persia and he set up his government. He sets over the kingdom 120 princes to govern the whole kingdom.

2. He set three presidents over the princes and made Daniel one of his three presidents. The princes would report to the presidents so that there would be no loss of revenue.

3. Daniel was preferred over the other presidents and princes because of the excellent spirit of God in him, and the king set him over the entire kingdom.

4. This did not sit well with the two other presidents and 120 princes and they were determined to destroy Daniel, but they could find no fault with Daniel. He was faithful and they could find no error or fault in him.

5. Then the men said we cannot find any fault with him except that he keeps the law of God, so they went after his relationship with God.

6. Then the other 2 governors and the 120 princes went to the king saying "O King live forever."(standard greeting for a king)

7. They knew that Daniel openly prayed three times a day to his God, so they came up with an outrageous decree that for the next 30 days, if any one should make a petition to any God or man except for the king Darius, they will be cast in a lion's den. They told the king that all the presidents of the kingdom, the governors, the princes, the counselors, the captains have consulted together to establish this royal stature and to make it a firm decree. King Darius did not realize that they were setting up Daniel, and he signed this decree into law.

8. "Now O king" they said, "establish the decree and sign the writing according to the law of the Medes and Persians that cannot be changed.

9. The King signed the writing and the decree, and it became law.

10. They laid wait for Daniel and when Daniel knew that the decree was signed, he did not change his daily routine. He went to his house. The windows in his chamber was open to Jerusalem and he prayed and give thanks to God as was his custom. He prayed three times a day. When the laws of man conflict with the Laws of God, the Laws of God must be obeyed. Daniel is exemplary on this issue.

11. These men were watching Daniel and found Daniel praying and making supplication to God.

12. They went to the king saying have you not signed a decree that every man that shall ask a petition of any God or man within 30 days except of you O king, shall be cast in the den of lions. The King says that the thing is true according to the law of the Medes and the Persians, which cannot be changed.

13. Then they told the King that Daniel, one of the children of the captivity of Judah does not regard the king or the decree that he signed and openly defies the king by praying three times a day.

14. The king realized that he was set up. He was displeased with himself, and from sun up to sun down he tried to save Daniel but could not, these men were skilled lawyers and had written an airtight decree.

15. Then these men assembled before the king and said to him "know, O King that the law of the Medes and Persians is that no decree or statute that the king established can be changed."

16. Then the king gave the command and Daniel should be thrown into a den of ravenous lions. The King told Daniel the God whom he serves continually will deliver him.

17. They brought a stone and covered the mouth of the den and the king sealed the stone with his own signet and with the signet of his Lords so that the purpose concerning Daniel could not be changed.

18. Then the king went to his palace and spent a restless sleepless night fasting. No instruments of music could be played.

19. Very early the next morning, the king hastened to the den of lions.

20. And when he came to the den, he called Daniel with a lamentable voice, "O Daniel servant of the living God, is thy God whom thou serve continually able to deliver thee from the lions?"

21. Daniel answered "O king, live forever.

22. My God has sent his angel and shut the lion's mouths that they have not hurt me, God knows that I am innocent and I have done you no harm."

23. The king was exceedingly happy for Daniel and the king commanded that Daniel be taken out and he was totally unharmed because he believed in God.

24. The king commanded that these men who accused him and their families should be thrown into the lion's den. The lions ate them all up before they could hit the ground.

25. King Darius wrote to all people, nations, and languages that dwell in the earth. Peace be multiplied unto you.

26. And he made a decree that in every dominion of his kingdom men should tremble and fear the God of Daniel for he is the living God and steadfast forever, and his kingdom that shall not be destroyed, and his dominion shall be even unto the end. As a result of Daniels steadfastness another pagan monarch comes to acknowledge the true God of Heaven.

27. He delivers and rescues and he works signs and wonders in the Heaven and in earth and hath delivered Daniel from the power of lions.

28. So Daniel prospered under Darius the Mede and Cyrus the Persian.

Commentary: During the Medo-Persian rule the Jews who were captured from their homeland during the domination of Babylon were restored to their homeland. Daniel was an old man at this time and did not return home. Daniel outlived his captors and saw their sons and grandsons come to power and lost power. Daniel was steadfastly fervent in his belief and worship of God and he looked forward to that final kingdom that will be set up by Jesus, that everlasting kingdom that he was shown in the vision of Daniel 2.

God is in control of history and he has revealed it to his servants the prophets. God is telling us that all earthly power is temporary. Nebuchadnezzar and all world leaders before and after him enjoyed power for a while but this earthly power is temporary. God word is true. God showed us in Daniel 2 that there would be four ruling empires and there were four. The prophecy is sure. God said the 4th kingdom would be divided into ten kingdoms and that happened as foretold. So you can be sure that the Bible and prophecy is sure. History has shown that most of Daniel's prophecies have come true except for the second coming of Jesus that is imminent. If 99% of these prophecies have been fulfilled with precision, why not the final 1% that indicates Jesus will set up the everlasting final kingdom. We cannot deny the history of the world confirming that these kingdoms followed in succession as was shown to Daniel. We will continue to show how God unfolds the future to Daniel.

Chapter Seven
DANIEL 7

Let's move on to the prophecies of *Daniel 7*. This is a very important and most impressive chapter. Here again God revealed to Daniel the kingdoms that will rule this world from Daniel's time to the end of this world, when God sets up his everlasting kingdom. God reveals a lot of information to Daniel in chapter 7. Who would not want to know the prophetic history of this world as revealed by God? The first six chapters of Daniel were historical in nature. The last six chapters are prophetic in nature. In Daniel 2 God gives a dream to King Nebuchadnezzar and Daniel interprets the dream. Daniel has been living in Babylon for about 50 years now. Here in Daniel 7 a dream is given to Daniel and God repeats, expands and enlarges on the prophecies of Daniel 2. In Daniel 2 God used a metallic image to show the progression of history. In this chapter God used different symbols to portray the same four world empires. The chapters of Daniel are not written sequentially for example Daniel 6 revealed the death of King Belshazzar and the fall of Babylon fell and chapter seven took us back to events before this happened.

Daniel 7:1

It is now 53 years later and the year is about 553 BC when Daniel receives this important vision. Daniel is about seventy years old and Nebuchadnezzar is no longer king of Babylon, as foretold in the prophecy of Daniel 2. One of his descendants, his grandson King Belshazzar, is now in the his first year reign as king of Babylon. Belshazzar is reigning simultaneously with his father. The father is ruling from a new capital in Tema,

Northern Arabia while the son is ruling as king of Babylon. The events of Chapter 7 take place between the events of chapter 4 when Nebuchadnezzar became insane and 5 when Belshazzar gave his feast and Babylon fell. Daniel is still in captivity when God gives him another vision with important information for us living at the end of time, and he wrote down the important details for us.

Daniel 7:2 Daniel spoke and said, "I saw in my vision by night, and behold the four winds of the Heaven strove upon the great sea."

In a dream Daniel was shown that the four winds of the Heaven strove upon the great sea. What does this mean? The Bible explains itself. In Jeremiah 49:36, 37 and Jeremiah 25:31, 32 we see that winds represent war, strife and commotion. The Bible is very consistent and interprets itself; a similar vision is again shown to the prophet John some 600 years later in Revelation 17:15. In Rev 17:15 we learn that water represents peoples, nations and tongues. Using the Bible to explain itself, we see that the four winds represent political activity from the corners of the earth, striving upon the great sea of humanity.

Verse 3: As a result of the four winds striving upon the sea, four beasts come up out of the sea, different from each other. As a result of war and strife, four kingdoms arise in succession, each with a king. Remember, the beasts represent kingdoms. The sea represents people. In Daniel 2 these kingdoms were represented as body parts on the metallic image shown by God to Nebuchadnezzar. Here in Daniel 7 God showed these kingdoms as beasts. The Bible is its own interpreter and the interpretation of beast is given in Daniel 8:20. Here God uses a beast to represent a nation. This should be familiar to us because this concept is still used today; an eagle represents the USA, a lion represent England, a bear the Soviet Union, a dragon Japan, and the rooster France and so on. Biblical prophecy is centered around the kingdoms that affect God's people. It is therefore not surprising that these kingdoms arise from the sea of people located around the Mediterranean Sea.

Verse 4: The first beast was like a lion. It had eagles' wings. This first beast represented the kingdom of Babylon (605–539 BC). In 605 BC Babylon overthrew the Assyrian kingdom. This winged lion is often seen on Babylonian art. Statues of lions with eagle's wings are found in the excavations of the ruins of Babylon. The lion with eagle's wings depicted Babylon's strength and power, and the rapidity with which it obtained power. Babylon became the dominant world power in 610 BC by overthrowing the great kingdom of Assyria. The lion is the king of the beasts and the eagle the king of birds. Daniel is shown that this animal's wings would be plucked. No longer can it fly and destroy its enemies. It lifted up from the earth and stood like a man, indicating that it had lost its lion-like qualities. A man's heart was also given to it. What does this mean? Nebuchadnezzar was the king of Babylon when Babylon had captured the world. This wealthy Babylonian Empire became weak and lost its strength after Nebuchadnezzar's successive generations basked in the wealth and luxury of Babylon and did not spend time in guarding the defenses of the kingdom. This is suggested by the saying "a man's heart was given to it."

Remember this power is the same power that Daniel describes in Daniel 2 as the Head of Gold on the metallic image.

Verse 5: "And behold another beast, a second, like to a bear, and it raised up itself on one side, and it had three ribs in the mouth of it between the teeth of it: and they said thus unto it, arise, devour much flesh."

Out of the sea of peoples and tongues and nations Daniel is shown the second beast power. This beast is depicted as a voracious bear and it raised itself up one side. It represents the kingdom of Medo-Persia (539–331 BC). The Medo-Persian forces with Darius the Mede and Cyrus the Persian together overthrew Babylon in 539 BC; Persia became the dominant power and ruled over the Medes as suggested by the beast raising itself up on one side. This animal is biting down on 3 ribs in its mouth. These 3 ribs in the mouth represent the three great powers that Medo-Persia conquered. These kingdoms (Lydia, Egypt and Babylon) came under Cyrus leadership. This animal devoured much flesh meaning it conquered many kingdoms on its ascent to power and it occupied more territory than Babylon. In 549 BC Cyrus overthrew his grandfather Astyages with the help of Median forces. About 547 BC, Cyrus, the Persian conquered Lydia to the North, Babylon to the west in 539 BC, and Egypt to the South in 538 BC The descendants of the Medes are the Kurds and the Persians descendants are the Iranians.

This is the same kingdom that Daniel was shown in chapter 2 as represented by the Breast and arms of Silver on the metallic image and in chapter 8 as the ram. God is repeating and giving us more information as he prophetically reveals the history of the world to us through the prophet Daniel.

Verse 6: "And after this I beheld, and lo another, like a leopard, which had upon the back of it four wings of a fowl; the beast also had four heads; and dominion was given to it."

God shows Daniel a third beast, which looked like a leopard. Which had upon the back of it for wings of a fowl: the beast also had four heads; and dominion was given to it. Daniel 8:21 tells us that this beast represented the kingdom of Greece (331–168 BC). On its back was four wings like a fowl, representing the rapidity with which this kingdom expanded. Dan 8:5, 21 states that this power had a notable horn between its eyes. This notable horn on the head of the goat represented Alexander the great, its first King. The power that followed Medo-Persia was Greece. In 336 BC Alexander took over the throne and in 331 BC, he overthrew King Darius of Medo-Persia in a battle in the plains of Arbela. He rapidly became a mighty conqueror.

In 331 BC he discovered Alexandria, Egypt. In less than 10 years his empire had expanded greatly as depicted by the wings on the back of the leopard beast.

Alexander the Great had conquered all he could when in June 323 BC, at the height of power, he died suddenly leaving no successors in control of his vast conquest. The leopard had four heads. This represented the four divisions of the Grecian Empire after Alexander the Great died. His generals fought for control and eventually in 301 BC the Greek Kingdom was divided into his four strongest generals, Cassandra, Lysimachus, Ptolemy, and Seleucus. This beast power was the same power represented by the belly and thighs of bronze on the metallic image of Daniel 2. Here in Daniel 7 God gives us more information about the same power.

Verse 7: "After this I saw in the night visions, and behold a fourth beast, dreadful and terrible, and strong exceedingly; and it had great iron teeth: it devoured and break into pieces, and stamped the residue with the feet of it: and it was diverse from all the beasts that were before it; and it had ten horns."

The prophet Daniel is still in vision and out of the sea of humanity God shows him the fourth beast. The fourth beast represented the fourth kingdom that followed. Although the prophet Daniel does not say the fourth beast would be the Roman Empire there is plenty of biblical and historical evidence to support Rome as the fourth beast. The Bible and history is quite clear that the power that followed Greece was Rome, and this is the only power that can possibly fit this beast power. This fourth beast Rome did not become a world ruling power until 168 BC when it overthrew Greece at the battle of Pydnia. Rome took a long time to overthrow Greece. It also conquered Macedonia, which later became a Roman province. Rome's rule lasted longer than any other Kingdom from 168 BC to 476 AD Rome was ruling at the time when Jesus was born. There is clear biblical evidence to support this. It was the decree of Caesar Augustus that sent Mary and Joseph to Bethlehem to pay taxes. Pilate tried Jesus in a Roman court. When Jesus ascended to Heaven Rome was still in power. In Matthew 24:14 and 15 Jesus prophesied the destruction of the temple in Jerusalem by the Roman armies.

This fourth beast is a very interesting beast. There is a lot written about the fourth beast, more so than the other beasts. It is a non-descript beast and there is no beast in the natural world that represents it. The Prophet Daniel describes it as dreadful and terrible. It is powerful and scary. It is exceedingly strong, and its great iron teeth, tore its prey to pieces and devoured them. It stamped the residue of its prey under its feet. The legs of iron in Daniel 2 and the teeth of iron in Daniel 7 represent the same iron monarchy of Rome. This beast is different from all the beasts before it. It has no representative in nature, so there is no beast to liken it to. This is representative of the Roman Empire's attitude. It was a great and terrible power with very little regard for human lives and a great many people lost their lives. It tore up its victims with its iron teeth and devoured them. The exploits of the Roman Empire are well recorded in history.

This very interesting beast with an important characteristic—it had ten *horns*.

DRAW BEAST WITH TEN HORNS
What are the 10 horns on this beast?

Daniel 7:24 give the answer. The ten horns are ten kings. The 10 horns represent nations. These 10 horns are the same nations depicted on the metallic image of Daniel 2 as the ten toes on the image. These ten nations represented the ten kingdoms that ruled the Western Roman Empire during the fifth century. The decline of the Roman Empire was a long process. In 330 AD Emperor Constantinople moved the seat of Government from Rome to Constantinople (renamed Istanbul). The Empire was essentially divided into western and eastern sections. A process of decline started in the western half of the empire and eventually various Germanic and North African tribes settled in the Western part of the Roman Empire.

The breakup of the mighty Roman Empire did not result in a single nation. It divided into ten smaller nations as indicated in Daniel 2 and Daniel 7:24. By the end of the fifth century the great Roman Empire had disintegrated, and gave way to these ten nations that occupied the center of what was once the great Roman Empire. These tribal nations eventually led to the nations of Europe today. They are roughly as follows:

1. The Visigoths who moved into the Roman Empire about 376 AD became Catholic and Settled in Spain by the 6th century.

2. The Franks entered Rome about 358 AD. They occupied French.

3. The Alemanni became Germany. They came under Catholic control in the 7th century AD

4. The Burgundians entered Rome about 412 AD and eventually became the Swiss.

5. The Lombards entered Rome about 568 AD. They settled in Italy.

6. The Anglo-Saxons settled in Britain

7. The Suevi entered Roman Territory about 411 BC. They settled in Portugal.

8. The Heruli occupied Rome about 476 AD. They were destroyed about 493 AD

9. The Vandals entered Roman Territory about 409 AD and were destroyed in 534 AD

10. The Ostrogoths entered Rome about 456 AD Belisarius drove them out of Rome in 538 AD and they were finally destroyed by 553 AD

The Heruli, Vandals, Ostrogoths were an obstacle to Roman Church becoming a political force. They were uprooted by the Catholic emperors in the Eastern part of Rome. Zeno, the eastern Roman Emperor, ordered Theodoric, King of the Ostrogoths to destroy the Heruli. This took place in 493 AD In 527 AD Justinian became the Eastern Roman Emperor. About 530 AD he waged war against the Vandals and the Ostrogoths. His general was Belisarius. The vandals were destroyed in 534 AD and the Ostrogoths in 538 AD These 3 uprooted powers became extinct (see Daniel 7:8). The other seven eventually came under the control of Rome and were converted to Catholicism. They are part of the European nations today. The history is too detailed and complicated to discuss in any detail. I'm just touching on the areas that the prophecy of Daniel shows us.

Verse 8: "I considered the horns, and, behold, there came up among them another little horn, before whom there were three of the first horns plucked by the roots: and, behold in this horn were eyes like the eyes of man, and a mouth speaking great things. Daniel was fascinated; and as he looked at the horns on this fourth beast, he saw that a little horn came up among the ten horns."

Daniel's little Horn

It is very important to identify this little horn correctly. This requires much prayer and the guidance of the Holy Spirit. God revealed to Daniel an outline of the succession of the world empires. In Daniel 2 he starts with Babylon, Media-Persia, Greece, Rome, and the divisions of the Roman Empire; now in Daniel 7 he introduces a new power—The Little Horn Power. Daniel was shown that this Little Horn Power will arise among the ten nations of Western Europe and it will becomes a powerful entity. The little horn arose after various tribes divided Rome into the ten kingdoms of Western Europe. It came out of the fourth kingdom or the Roman Empire. Daniel 7:8 states that this fascinating little Horn power came up among these kingdoms.

Before this little Horn would become a power, three of the ten horns would be plucked up by the roots leaving no trace behind. The three Kingdoms are the Heruli, the Vandals and the Ostrogoths. They are no longer in existence because the little horn kingdom plucked them up. Therefore the little horn which came up among the 10 kingdoms, which arose from the ruins of the Roman Empire, has been in existence for a long time now. It came up among the ten nations of Western Europe not the Middle East-not Jerusalem, not Israel, not America, not Africa. The Bible clearly states that it came up among them, meaning it came up among the ten kingdoms of Western Europe which came from the fourth beast which was the Roman Empire. This is very clear from this text.

As Daniel looked at this little horn, it was unusual. A characteristic of this little horn is that it has the eyes of a man denoting intelligence. It had a mouth speaking great things, so this horn will become a great power and speak great things.

This nation has the eyes of a man or a man as its leader and this nation speaks great things against God. Some people misinterpret this power because it is described as having the eyes of a man and a mouth speaking great things. Do not be fooled by this, just like all the other horns, this little horn is not a man but a kingdom. Many have tried to make this horn a person but God is showing Daniel the kingdoms that will rule the world. Pay much attention here because Satan has a vested interest in disguising the little horn and has put great effort in doing so. These beasts represent nations. Let us proceed carefully.

Verse 9: "I beheld till the thrones were cast down, and the Ancient of days did sit, whose garment was white as snow, and the hair of his head like the pure wool: his throne was like the fiery flame, and his wheels as burning fire."

The scene changes dramatically from the little horn power to a Heavenly scene. Daniel saw thrones being set up and he saw the ancient of Days, God sitting on the throne. He is shown that his garment is white as snow, hair of his head pure wool, his throne is like fiery flame and it had wheels of burning fire.

Verse 10: "A fiery flame was issued and came out of the throne and thousand thousands of Heavenly beings ministered unto him, and ten thousand times ten thousand stood before him and the judgment was set, and the books were opened."

This is very important area of study; here God introduces to us the beginning of the final judgment. These prophecies are taking us from Daniel's time down to the end of time. This is such crucial information that much prayer and study is needed here for understanding. The judgment involves every human who has ever lived. Daniel is shown the Heavenly judgment scene and he sees that God's judgment had begun and the record contained in these books were being reviewed and there were thousand times ten thousands beings in attendance at the judgment.

Verse 11: I beheld then because of the great words which the horn spoke: I beheld even till the beast was slain, and his body destroyed, and given to the burning flame." Daniel states that he beheld or he saw this phase of the judgment taking place in Heaven prior to the return of Christ. He sees that the little horn power is present on earth during this phase of the judgment. He sees the little horn power speaking great words. He is eventually shown the conclusion of the judgment of this little horn power. He sees that because of the great words which this power spoke that it is was eventually destroyed and along with the beast. This little horn power is thrown into the burning flames at the second coming of Christ, thus ending the powerful earthly system depicted by the little horn.

Do not miss the point here, this little horn power rose up among the ten nations of Western Europe after the Roman Empire disintegrated. Daniel sees this little horn speaking great words until it is destroyed by the second coming of Jesus. This little horn power has grown into such a powerful system that only when God sets us his everlasting kingdom will this power be destroyed. This is clearly not a man living this long, it has to be a ruling power.

Verse 12: "As concerning the previous beasts they had their dominion taken away, yet their characteristics were prolonged for a season and a time." This is a difficult verse to interpret, it suggests that although these kingdoms lost power they still existed as a place and their characteristics continued on. When Babylon fell it still existed as a place until the physical city was in ruins centuries later.

Verse 13: "I saw in the night visions, and, behold, one like the Son of man came with the clouds of Heaven, and came to the Ancient of days, and they brought him near before him." God shows Daniel a most impressive scene in this night vision. Daniel sees Jesus as he was brought near the father. The text states one like the son of man approaches the Ancient of Days. This is obviously a Heavenly scene taking place at the end of Christ's mediatory work for us; at this time the judgment is finished in Heaven and Jesus is borne on clouds of Heavenly angels and they bring him near the Ancient of Days, God the Father.

Verse 14: "And there was given him dominion, and glory, and a kingdom, that all people, nations, and languages, should serve him: his dominion is an everlasting dominion, which shall not pass away, and his kingdom that which shall not be destroyed."

God the father in an ordination ceremony fit for the true king of the universe bestows on Jesus dominion, glory and a kingdom that all people, nations, and languages should serve him. His dominion is an everlasting dominion, which shall not pass away, and his kingdom shall not be destroyed. Pay attention here, Jesus' work as intercessor is over. He changes from his priestly garment in his kingly garments and on his vesture is written king of kings and Lord of Lords. He is now ready to return to Planet Earth for the second time to reap the great harvest of saints. The judgment that Jesus has been presiding over is finished. Jesus says in John 5:22 and 23 that "the father judges no man but hath committed all judgment unto the son: that all men should honor the son even as they honor the father. He that honors not the son honors not the father, which has sent him."

Verse 15: "I Daniel was grieved in my spirit in the midst of my body, and the visions of my head troubled me." Daniel was distressed and mentally disturbed by this vision. His vision continues.

Verse 16: "I came near unto one of them that stood by, and asked him the truth of all this. So he told me, and made me know the interpretation of the things." Daniel came close to a Heavenly being, an angel that was close by him and he asked the angel to interpret the vision for him and the angel did.

Verse 17: These great beasts, which are four, are four kings, which shall arise out of the earth. I told you before that the Bible explains itself; Let us read what the angel had to say. The four great beasts that you were shown represent four kingdoms that came up out of the earth. They are earthly kingdoms.

Verse 18: "But the saints of the most High shall take the kingdom, and possess the kingdom for ever, even for ever and ever."

One day all earthly rulers and kingdoms will pass away and this world will again be in the hands of God's saints. The kingdom of God saints would last forever and forever. Blessed assurance, God will be the ruler of all.

Verse 19: "Then I would know the truth of the fourth beast, which was diverse from all the others, exceeding dreadful, whose teeth were of iron, and his nails of brass; which devoured, brake in pieces, and stamped the residue with is feet."

Daniel wanted to know the truth about this fourth beast, which was so different from the others, exceedingly dreadful, teeth of iron, nails of brass and which devoured, break into pieces and trampled the residue under its feet.

Verse 20: "And of the ten horns that were in his head, and of the other which came up, and before whom three fell; even of that horn that had eyes, and a mouth that spoke very great things, whose look was more stout that his fellows."

Daniel asked the angel about the ten horns that were in the beast's head, the little horn that came up after the three kingdoms were destroyed. He even asked about the horn's eyes of a man, and the mouth speaking great things, and the little horn which outgrew and became more powerful than the other horns on this beast.

Verse 21: "I beheld, and the same horn made war with the saints, and prevailed against them."

Daniel was shown this little horn that made war with the saints and overcame them; in other words, she persecuted Gods saints and prevailed against them for quite some time.

Verse 22: "Until the ancient of days came, and judgment was given to the saints of the most High; and the time came that the saints possessed the kingdom."

This power was successful against God's saints until the outcome of the judgment scene in Heaven which resulted in judgment in favor of the saints of God and the time had come for the saints to possess the kingdom.

Verse 23: The angel gives Daniel the answer. "The fourth beast shall be the fourth kingdom on the earth and it will be different from all the other kingdoms, it will destroy the whole earth, and shall tread it down and break it into pieces. This fourth kingdom was the Great Roman Empire.

Verses 24: "And the ten horns out of this kingdom are ten kings that shall arise: and another shall arise after them; and he shall be diverse from the first, and he shall subdue three kings." The ten horns that arise out of the fourth beast kingdom are the ten kingdoms that after the demise of the powerful Roman Empire. After these ten kingdoms shall arise another kingdom, the Little Horn kingdom, shall arise and this kingdom shall be different and destroy three kingdoms. The angel tells Daniel about the eventual division of Imperial Rome into ten kingdoms and then the Little Horn Kingdom.

Verse 25: The angel continues to give Daniel the identifying features of this little horn power. "And he shall speak great or pompous words against the Most High, wear out the saints of the most High, think to change times and laws: and they shall be given into his hand until time, time, and the dividing of time."

The angel gives Daniel some identifying features of this Little Horn Power and this identity is linked to what it does religiously. The Little Horn Power has major interaction with God's people and hence the Bible has much to say about it. The identifying marks of this Little Horn Power are given in verses 24 and 25. Let us discuss them in some detail before we get back to verse 26. It is important that we discuss these characteristics at length because Satan has done quite a lot of work and has been very successful in disguising this little horn power. First Satan hid the Bible and now that there is avid interest in the Bible, he chooses his next move and that is distortion of its' contents. Here he has been very successful in disguising the true identity of the little horn power. He portrays the little horn power as a man. No man can fit *all* of these characteristics shown to Daniel in these verses.

Verse 24 states that the ten horns that shall arise out of this fourth kingdom are ten kings. Note that Kings and kingdoms are used interchangeably. The text states that ten smaller kingdoms replace the fourth kingdom; and *another kingdom arose among the 10 kingdoms, which displace three kingdoms*. It is clear that God is talking about kingdoms here. Don't be led astray here. The reason for the confusion that sometimes arises here is the work of a supernatural mind, Satan. He doesn't want you to know who the little horn is. It is to Satan's benefit to disguise it because he is an artful deceiver who is operating behind the little horn power. Satan is the ultimate antichrist and he is the master of camouflage and disguise. Remember Satan modus operandi is through deception and he works behind the scenes to oppose God. He has to disguise himself or he will be seen for who he really is. This deception has worked successfully for him. He is extremely clever. In the spiritual realm, he is not going to come out as a violent opposer of Christ, he would not be as successful; instead he is going to pose as a *subtle* impostor. It works well for him. Keep in mind that there is a major controversy going on between Christ and Satan for every soul on Planet Earth. Satan is like a roaring lion seeking whom he can devour and he is going down fighting. He is the greatest deceiver with much more experience and intelligence that humans. Read and pray and the Holy Spirit will enlighten you as you study diligently for yourself.

Sadly, the majority of Christian believers today believe that the little Horn power is man. This exactly what Satan wants. Satan is the ultimate antichrist and he operates behind many powers and people and he is operating behind the little horn power. The Apostle Paul warned the early church in 2 Thessalonians 2:3 and 4 that the second coming of Christ will not come until a there is an apostasy from truth and the man of sin or *lawlessness* be revealed, in other words that day would not come until there is a falling away first from truth meaning the deception will occur in the body of Christ. Paul states that this antichrist will oppose and exalt himself over everything that is called God or is worshipped, and even sets himself up in God's temple, proclaiming himself to be God. This reveals that the antichrist is a silent impostor; he sets himself up in God's church and speaks as though he were God. He opposes the true worship of God. He opposes truth. 11Thessalonians 2:7 that this man of lawlessness, the mystery of iniquity is already at work in the church. This antichrist is not a future entity but is already at work and will continue until he is destroyed shortly before the 2nd coming of Jesus or at the close of the Heavenly judgment. 2 Thessalonians 2: 9 further describes this antichrist as him, whose coming is after the working of Satan, in other words he is a front for the real antichrist who is Satan, who really wants to take the place of God or speak for God and he is deceiving many aided by the working of miracles (signs and lying wonders).

So let us continue with the identifying characteristics of this Little Horn Power that God has given to us by the Prophet Daniel.

In Daniel 7 we are given several identifying points

The ten horns are ten kingdoms that arose from the fourth beast and the Little Horn came up among the ten kingdoms and before the little horn came to power three kingdoms were displaced.

1. *Different from the other ten kingdoms* (Verse 24).
It was more than a political power, this was both political and religious.
2. *Subdue three kings as it rose to power* (Verses 8, 20, and 24). This happens early in its history. It is a historical fact that three Arian nations were destroyed as this nation rose to power. By 476 AD the Roman Empire had lost its power and disintegrated into ten smaller nations. This little horn power began to rise to prominence and three nations

were destroyed. The last nation, the Ostrogoths, was destroyed in 538 AD and this began the middle Ages when this power began to rule supremely.

3. After the three horns fell, this power became greater than the other horns (Verse 20).

4. *Eyes like the eyes of a man* - Dan.7: 8 and 20 – Suggesting that there is a man at the head of this power.

5. *It had a mouth speaking great things.* This power claims to have great religious and political authority. It spoke great words against the most high. The head of this power claims great authority and speak great words. In 1894 pope Leo XIII said we hold upon this earth the place of God on earth. We are not to use the name Holy Father for any man. Jesus in Matt 23:9 tells us call no man your father upon the earth: for one is your father, which is in Heaven. We must follow God's sovereign will if he is our leader.

6. Makes war with the saints and prevails. (Verse 25)

7. Thinks to change times and God's laws. (Verse 25)

8. Saints given into his hand for time, times and dividing of time. It rule for 1260 years and persecutes God's people for 1260 years. (Verse 25)

Using these identifying points described in Daniel 7:25 and 26, can we identity of this little horn? Let see how scripture and history help us identify this little horn. Let us review the powers that Daniel was shown.

- He is shown the lion with wings; this is the same nation as the head of Gold in Daniel 2 – *It is Babylon*.

- Then he is shown *Animal #2* – A bear with three ribs in the mouth, the same nation as the breast and silver on the image – *It is Medo-Persia*.

- Then animal #3 – A leopard with 4 wings –same nation as the belly and thighs of brass on the image – *It is Greece*.

- Then animal # 4 –Dragon like beast with no counterpart in nature, it had iron teeth and ten horns — *It is The Roman Empire*.

Daniel is told that these beasts represent nations and he is specifically told what some of these nations are. Here is the interesting part, we are given the name of some of the powers and others we are left to identify them based on certain characteristics given in the Bible and with the aid of history. Here is where Satan has been very deceptive. Biblical scholars during the early Protestant Reformation correctly identified this Little Horn Power as Papal Rome. Many modern scholars have failed to correctly identify the little horn power.

Let us look at some of the identifying points of the little horn power in more detail because there is so much false information among the body Christ believers.

Identifying point #1: Daniel is shown the division of the fourth beast into ten kingdoms (10 horns represent 10 kings) and he is shown the little horn as it displaces three kingdoms. We identified the fourth beast as the Roman Empire and we knew 10 kingdoms replaced it. The little horn power came up among the 10 kingdoms that replaced the fourth beast. It rose to power after the ten kingdoms replaced the old Roman Empire. Daniel 7: 8 states that it came up among them. Verse 24 states that another horn shall arise after the ten horns. It came up after the division of the Roman Empire into ten parts. This power did not arise in the days of the lion (Babylon), the bear (Medo-Persia) or the leopard (Greece). It rose to power after the breakup of the Roman Empire into 10 nations.

The fourth beast, the Roman Empire was not overthrown like the other kingdoms; a slow process of decline occurred and this power or the fourth beast shown to Daniel eventually disintegrated into the 10 nations of Western Europe. From about 330 AD, the Roman Emperor Constantine moved the seat of Government from Rome to Constantinople. Barbaric tribes slowly divided up the Western half of the empire into 10 nations. The little horn power came up *among* these 10 nations in Western Europe. *The geographical location of this little horn beast is Western Europe.* It would be incorrect to look for it elsewhere in Palestine, Jerusalem or anywhere else in the world. The prophecy states that the little horn power came up among the ten nations of Western Europe. The little horn came to power <u>after</u> the declining Roman Empire had been split up into ten kingdoms and the last of the Western Roman Emperor Romulus Augustulus was deposed in AD 476. Therefore, it had to come up after 476 AD when the fourth beast or the Roman Empire fell. It came out of the ruins of the old Roman Empire.

Identifying Point #2: Daniel 7:24 He shall be diverse from the other ten and shall subdue three kings.

Why is it diverse or different? There is now union of church and state; that's why Daniel says it is different. It is now a religious-political power. The previous powers were political but this new power is a religious-political power. What power arose after the demise of the Roman Empire that was different because it had political and religious power? There is only one kingdom that arose at this time that fits this description. From History book The Rise of the Mediaeval Church written by Alexander Flick, we read, "Out of the ruins of political Rome, arose the great moral empire in the giant form of the Roman Church". Biblical scholars from the period of the Reformation and before have identified this little horn power as Papal Rome. It followed Imperial Rome and history bears this out. Many attempts have been made to make the Little Horn power a man but God is talking about powers. We have so far located the geography and the time of arrival of this power.

Identifying Point #3: He shall subdue three kings. It is a historical fact that Rome destroyed three Arian Nations. Various tribes finally destroyed the Western Roman Empire and as a result ten kingdoms were established. Many of these tribes taught Arianism. Arianism denied the divinity of Jesus and taught that Jesus was a good person but was not divine. These three kingdoms, the Heruli, the vandals and the Ostrogoths were Arian kingdoms opposed the doctrines of Roman Catholicism, and stood in the way of the papal Rome obtaining full religious political power in Rome. The Heruli were destroyed in 492 AD The Roman Emperor Justinian with the help of the Roman Church waged war against the Vandals and the Ostrogoths. His general, Belsarius, conquered the Vandals about 534 AD. The Ostrogoths were conquered about 538 AD. The city of Rome was finally freed of Arian power when the Ostrogoths were driven from Rome in 538 AD. After the defeat of the Ostrogoths, Emperor Justinian and his general, Belsarius, banished the Bishop of Rome. Emperor Justinian sets up Virgilius in the seat of the Bishop thereby giving the Bishop of Rome authority over Rome. So Virgilius ascended to the papal chair in 538 AD under the military protection of General Belsarius. This was the beginning of the Papal Reign; this religious political power replaced the Caesar who controlled the Roman Empire. (Reference – The Hx of the Christian Church. Virgilius was then declared the head of all churches.)

Seven kingdoms of the original the divisions of the Roman Empire can be found in Europe today. The little horn completely uprooted the three kingdoms that stood in its way, the Heruli, the Vandals, and the Ostrogoths, they cannot be found today; *therefore, the little horn has already arisen in Western Europe and we have just pinpointed the time it came to power is 538 AD.*

The origin of the false teachings about the Little Horn

How and why did the Christian world determine that the Little Horn Power was a man that ruled about 176–164 BC? During the great Protestant Reformation, Martin Luther and many other reformers using the historicist view of apocalyptic prophecies rightly understood from studying the prophecies of Daniel and the Revelation and from the sequence of history, that the little horn was the Papal Rome. Matter of fact the early reformers identified this little horn beast as Papal Rome. This is a very disturbing finding and truth is sometimes difficult to tell. The interpretation that the Little Horn Power is Papal Rome has been around for centuries. The early Protestant reformers having studied the Books of Daniel and Revelation understood that the Little Horn with its anti-Christ activities could be no other power than Papal Rome. This understanding was widely believed during the reformation. This interpretation did not sit well with the Church of Rome so the council of

Trent met they decided to come up with a counter-reformation strategy. They first turned to a scholarly priest, Alcazar, he studied the prophecies of Daniel and Revelation for four years and came up with the theory that most of Daniel and the Revelation was in the past. This is known as the Preterit view. The council rejected that. A few people call themselves preterits still hold on to that interpretation today. The council then turned to another brilliant scholarly priest, Francisca Ribera from Spain. He took 18 years to develop his theory and it was a more acceptable one to the council. After much study, he accepted Antiochus Epiphanes as Daniel's Little Horn and Revelation's beast. He assigned everything from Rev. 4 and onward as having yet to be fulfilled in the future just before Jesus comes. This was the beginning of the modern futuristic theory that is embraced and preached by modern Christians today. He argued that the Roman Church could not be the anti-Christ because the anti-Christ is a figure whose arrival is in the future and in the midst of the seven years of tribulation. He studied the prophecies of Daniel 8 and 9 particularly the 70-week prophecy and he broke off the 70th week from the 69th week. He came up with the rapture of the church and the left behind concept. He then interjected that the temple would be rebuild in Jerusalem and after three and a half years the antichrist would begin the temple sacrifices again and three and a half years later Jesus would come back. He moved much of the time line of the prophecy of Daniel 7 into the future. There is no biblical explanation for this. These are man-made theories, which began in the 16th century by a Jesuit priest Francisco Ribera; it was further developed in the 19th century and many today use it as the basis for interpreting Daniel and the Revelation.

As we develop these identifying marks given to us by the prophet Daniel in Daniel chapters 7 to 11 we will see why Antiochus Epiphanes does not fit the Little Horn Power. Satan uses both of these counter theories to deceive people. He used it to derail the beliefs held by the early Protestant reformers and it is working for him well now. The sad reality is that truth does not sell as well as fiction. Millions are deceived by these false interpretations.

Identifying point #4: The papacy outgrew those powers that it subdued and became a dominant world power (Daniel 7:20).

Vatican City sits on 109 acres of land it may be small in territory but it became a powerful kingdom and it is wealthy thereby outgrowing the three nations it subdued. It dominated the world for 1260 years and it has regained power since its deadly would was healed in 1929. It is the most dominant religious force today. This is a remarkable fulfillment of this prophecy. This power spans across a long historical period.

Identifying point #5: It has the eyes of a man denoting its leadership by a man. There has always been and there will always be a man at the head of this power.

Identifying Point #6: A mouth speaking great things.

This little horn power brought into the church many teachings that are not found in the scripture. Many of the beliefs and practice of this power are not supported and are contrary to scripture. We will discuss them later but as far as this identifying point is concerned lets start with blasphemy. Blasphemy is when a man claims to be God. See the Bible explanation of blasphemy in John 10:31 to 33. It is also blasphemy when man claim to have power to forgive sins (see Mark 2:5 to7).

The papacy claims 2 things that belong only to God.

- It claims to be able to forgive sins.

- Takes confessions

Let us look at some of their claims. In A Complete Catechism of Catholic Beliefs, Page 279

Q: Does the priest truly forgive sins or does he declare that they are remitted?
A: The Priest really and truly forgives sins by virtue of the power given to him by Jesus Christ.

Scripture teaches that only God can forgive sins. We should confess our sins to God alone. No man can dare claim to forgive sins. That is a godly prerogative. God alone is able to forgive our sins and cleanse us from all unrighteousness. He earned that right at Calvary. When we pray Jesus takes our prayers and presents it to the father in a way only Jesus can. Jude 24 tells us now unto him that is able to keep you from falling and to present you faultless before the presence of his glory with exceeding joy. Jesus is our great high priest in the Heavenly sanctuary and no earthly priestly system should obscure his all-important work for us.

Quote from Leo XIII —We hold upon this earth the place of God almighty.

Catholic National in July 1895: The pope is not only the representative of Jesus Christ but he is Jesus Christ himself hidden under the veil of flesh.

The pope wears a triple crown indicating that he is king of Heaven, earth and the lower regions. Listen to how people refer to the pope. They refer to terms and your Most Holy or Holy Father. These are terms that the Bible reserves only for God. Jesus in Matthew 23: 9 states call no man your father upon the earth: for one is your father, which is in Heaven.

Identifying point #7: This power shall wear out, make war or persecute the saints of the most high.

The history of the persecution of people has been chronicled in the history books and well documented in the books of Heaven. The little horn power has worn out many of

God saints, waged war against them and is a persecuting power. This religious political power was intolerant of people religious practices and millions of people died for their faith during the dark ages. I can refer you to the history of the Massacre of St. Bartholomew, The Spanish Inquisition, the martyrdom of millions of professed Christians, the Albigenses, the Waldensians to name a few. As difficult as it is to accept today, it is a historical fact that confirms the prophecy. For centuries the church distanced itself from these atrocities, lately they have apologized, but they are part of the church history and an identifying feature of this power, and is a fulfillment of the prophecies that were shown to the prophet Daniel.

In the book the History of the Rise and influence of Rationalism in Europe, W.E.H. Lechy writes, "That the Church of Rome has shed more innocent blood than any other institution that has ever existed among mankind, this will be questioned by no Protestant who has a competent knowledge of history."

The church has fulfilled this identifying point. History reveals that dissenters from the faith were punished with death.

Identifying point #8. This power will think to change time and laws.

Daniel is shown that there is an earthly power that will attempt to change the laws of God. *Which power has attempted to change the law of God?*

Taken from the Catechism of the Catholic Church – "The pope has the power to change times, abrogate laws and dispense with all things even the precepts of Christ."

The papacy eliminated the second commandment, which forbids the worshipping of image.

It shortened the 4th commandment from 94 words to 8 words – this is the only commandment that deals with time and the church changed the observance of Sabbath from the seventh day to the first day of the week.

The Papacy has divided the tenth commandment into two commandments.

Let us review God's commandments and the changes made by the Papacy.

The Ten Commandments as written by hand of God (Exodus 20:3–17)

I
Thou shall have no other gods before me.

II
Thou shall make unto thee any given image, or any likeness of any thing that is in Heaven above, or that is in the earth beneath, or that is in the water under the earth: thou shall not bow down thyself to them, nor serve them: for I the Lord thy God am a jealous God, visiting the iniquity of the fathers upon the children unto the third and

fourth generation of them that hate me; and showing mercy unto thousands of them that love me, and keep my commandments.

III
Thou shall not take the name of the Lord thy God in vain; for the Lord will not hold him guiltless that takes his name in vain.

IV
Remember the Sabbath day, to keep it holy. Six days shall thou labor, and do all thy work: but the 7th day is the Sabbath of the Lord thy God: in it thou shall not do any work, thou, nor thy son, nor thy daughter, thy manservant, nor thy maidservant, nor thy cattle, nor thy stranger that is within thy gates: for in 6 days the Lord made Heaven and earth, the sea, and all that in them is, and rested on the seventh day: wherefore the Lord blessed the Sabbath day and hallowed it.

V
Honor thy father and thy mother:
that thy day may be long upon the land which the Lord thy God gives thee.

VI
Thou shall not kill.

VII
Thou shall not commit adultery.

VIII
Thou shall not steal.

IX
Thou shall not bear false witness against thy neighbor.

X
Thou shall not covet thy neighbor's house; thou shall not covet thy neighbor's wife, nor his manservant, nor his maidservant, nor his ox, nor his ass, nor anything that is thy neighbor's.

Here is the change!

The Ten Commandments as recorded in the Roman Catholic Catechisms

I
I am the Lord thy God. Thou shall not have strange Gods before me.

II
Thou shall not take the name of the Lord thy God in vain.

III
Remember that thou keep holy the Sabbath day.
IV
Honor thy father and thy mother.
V
Thou shall not kill.
VI
Thou shall not commit adultery.
VII
Thou shall not steal.
VIII
Thou shall not bear false witness against thy neighbor.
IX
Thou shall not covet thy neighbor's wife.
X
Thou shall not covet thy neighbor's goods.

The papacy has changed God's Ten Commandments omitting the 2nd and dividing the 10th into two to keep it at 10. So they have attempted to change God's moral law. God wrote the Ten Commandments in stone with his own fingers. God's law cannot be changed. Daniel was shown in Daniel 7:25 that a power would arise that would think to change times and laws. The language used in Daniel 7:25 is interesting it did not say that this power will change God's law. It said that it will think to change times and laws. This is significant because only God can change his law and even if the whole world follow this power that does not make it right and acceptable to God. In the final analysis it will be noted by all, some too late, that man cannot change God's law. God says "I am God I change not nor do I alter the things that have gone out of my mouth."

Does it matter to you that an earthly power changed God's law and the world follow suit? The only commandment dealing with time is the fourth commandment. This power in attempting to change God's fourth commandment has changed time too. God did not leave us in ignorance about this change. The prophecy of Daniel 7:25 predicts that this power will attempt to change the moral law of God. History has confirmed the change. The Church boldly acknowledges her act of changing God's law. In Genesis, we learn that God established the weekly cycle. God specifies the seventh-day as the Sabbath. God established the Sabbath at the creation of our world. Genesis 2 verse 2 tells us that on the 7th day of the week God stopped all His work and blessed the 7th day and *set it apart for holy use and as a memorial of his creative power.* God took a block of time and call it holy. No matter who we are or where we are on Planet Earth, once a week God Sabbath rolls around and we are commanded by God to keep it holy. God created a weekly permanent memorial to remind us that He is the creator.

Satan has been waging a smear campaign against God. It started in heaven against the law of God and has continued on Planet earth for more than 6000 years now. He has convinced many that God's Sabbath is for Jews. The Sabbath is not a Jewish institution; it was given to Adam and Eve about 2300 years before the Jewish nation came into existence. Every human being can trace his or her roots back to creation. We have one common ancestor Adam and Eve who were created by God. The Sabbath was given to the human race at creation. In the beginning God ordained that man should keep his Sabbath, after his work of creation he rested on the Sabbath and Adam and Eve were taught to rest on the seventh day Sabbath. Thus the Sabbath ended the creation week. The Sabbath is that bridge that takes us back every week to creation and our creator. Once a week, God calls us to remember our roots. God commands us all to rest on the Sabbath. God's true followers Adam, Abel, Abraham, Jacob, the patriarchs of old, the disciples, Jesus, Paul, God's church of the first two centuries kept the Sabbath.

When the Israelites went into captivity in Egypt, they were forced to work on the Sabbath and lost the knowledge of the Sabbath. It is clear from scripture that God's seventh day Sabbath existed and was kept long centuries before there was a Jew in this world. In Exodus 16:4 before the law was given to Moses at Mt. Sinai the children of Israel kept the Sabbath. In Exodus 31:13–17 the Lord spoke to Moses saying speak unto the children of Israel to keep the Sabbath holy and it is a sign between God and the children of Israel *forever*: for in six days the Lord made Heaven and earth, and on the seventh day he rested, and was refreshed. The sovereign God, the creator of this universe called Moses up to Mt. Sinai and with his own fingers he wrote his commandments on two tablets of stone. The Lord wrote Remember the Sabbath day to keep it holy. Remember indicates the Sabbath has been in existence and it has been since creation week. God gave his law to the Jewish nation so that they can share it with the world around them. The Sabbath is not a legalistic requirement or a Jewish institution it preceded the Jews and dates back to creation. It will be here after the second coming and when the earth is made new, this is supported in scripture in Isaiah 66:22 which states "For as the new Heavens and the new earth which I will make…and it shall come to pass that from one new moon to another and from one Sabbath to another shall all flesh come to worship before me says the Lord. It is a perpetual memorial of God's creative and redemptive power.

How is the Sabbath a memorial of redemption too?

Exodus 20:12 "Moreover I give them my Sabbaths, to be a sign between me and them, that they might know that I am the Lord that sanctify them." Verse 20 "And hallow my Sabbaths and they shall be a sign between me and you that you may know that I am the Lord your God."

Deuteronomy 5:15 "And remember that thou was a servant in the land of Egypt, and that the Lord thy God brought thee out thence with a mighty hand and by a stretched out arm: Therefore the Lord thy God commanded thee to keep the Sabbath day."

In Hebrews 4:4, we read that God did rest from all his works on the seventh day. In verse 8, "for if Jesus had given them rest, then would he not afterwards have spoken of another day, therefore there remaineth a rest to the people of God. Let us labor therefore to enter into that rest, lest any man fall after the same example of *unbelief.*" Every Sabbath God wants us to enter into this rest; rest from our work and all our man-made efforts and act as though our work were done in him. Since creation week God has designated a day, specifically the seventh day when he commands all of his creation to rest from their labor and worship him. Simply put if God had changed his commandment and given us another day he would have told us. He would not be silent on this very important command. He did not request that we keep the Sabbath holy; he commands us to keep the Sabbath holy. We are not saved by keeping the Sabbath holy or obeying any other commandment; we obey all of God's commandments because we are saved.

The Sabbath the object of Satan's attack

The all-knowing God knew that Satan would again attack his law and destroy man's worship of the true creator. The Sabbath is more than a day it stands as a memorial to God's creative and redemptive powers. A wise all-knowing God knew that Satan would try to destroy his commandments and so he put in his moral law recorded in Exodus 20:8–10 "Remember the Sabbath day to keep it holy. Six days shall you labor and do all your work, but the seventh day is the Sabbath of the Lord your God. In it you shall do no work. God makes it very plain here. If man had kept the Sabbath from creation as God intended there would be no confusion regarding the creation of this world. Four thousand years after the creation of the Sabbath at the end of the creation week, the creator came to earth and observed the Sabbath of his creation. In Matthew 24:20, Jesus warns Pray that your flight be not in the winter nor on the Sabbath day. In Luke 4:16 Jesus warns and he came to Nazareth where he had been brought up and as his custom was he went to the synagogue on the Sabbath day and stood up for to read. Jesus is our example in all things. Jesus the creator of the Sabbath kept the Sabbath. Satan is the enemy who is trying to tear down all of the institutions that the Lord has erected. If Satan could get man to disobey God and forsake his commandments, he can get man to doubt and forsake his creator.

Satan has launched an all-out attack on God's law particularly the Sabbath commandment. Satan he has been extremely successful in this endeavor. As he deceived Adam and Eve in the Garden of Eden he has been successful in sabotaging God's Holy Day. The Bible in Exodus 20:8–10 describes the Sabbath day as the Sabbath of the Lord, that is the Lord's Day. Let us fast forward to the New Testament, in Mark 2:28 Jesus says that the son of man is Lord also of the Sabbath, so both in Geneses and Mark the Lords day is described as the Sabbath. If the Lord's Day is the 7th day Sabbath of creation in Exodus and Mark, it has to be the 7th day in Revelation 1:10 when the prophet John says he was in the spirit on the Lord's Day. The Bible does not contradict itself. The seventh day is the Sabbath of the Bible and the Lord's Day; any other day that is called the Sabbath day or the Lord's Day has its origin in tradition.

The change of the Sabbath Day

How and when did the change of the Sabbath occur? It was a gradual change that happened over many centuries. There is a church today that claims the responsibility of changing God's law, thus setting itself above God. The church simply states that she has the power to make the change and did so and all the world has followed this power. This may seem subtle to many, but this is a deliberate attack on the law of God by the subtle impostor Satan. If God's law can be easily changed and set aside why cannot the other commandments be changed too?

The Bible gives no indication of any change in the day of worship. There is no mention in the old or New Testament about a change in God's holy day. The patriarchs of the Old Testament never kept Sunday, the disciples never kept Sunday and most importantly Jesus never kept Sunday and remember Jesus is our perfect example in all things. The New Testament gospels show that it was his custom to go to church (the synagogue) on the Sabbath day. In Mark, Jesus calls himself the Lord of the Sabbath or the Lord who made the Sabbath; if he changed it he would have told us. The gospels reveal many conflicts between Jesus and the Jews regarding the way the Sabbath was kept. The controversy was not whether the Sabbath should be kept but how it should be kept. Jesus found that the Jews had made the Sabbath a burden. It was riddled with legalistic regulations and traditions. These traditions began after the Jews returned from Babylonian captivity.

Two of the reasons cited why the nation of Israel fell into Babylonian captivity were their worship of idolatry and Sabbath breaking. After the captivity, a very strict sect called the Pharisees determined not to make the same mistakes, came up with severe burdensome regulations on how to keep the Sabbath. You could not kindle or put out a fire, you could not travel far from home, you could not heal the sick, you could not spit on the ground lest a blade of grass should grow, you could not carry a handkerchief unless it was attached to your clothes. The Sabbath that was supposed to be a delight became a burden with no meaning. This continued until Jesus came to magnify and restore his law. The issue that Jesus faced was not which day was the Sabbath, or if the Sabbath should be kept. The controversy was about the way it was kept. Jesus saw that Satan had distorted the Sabbath and he proceeded to teach men how to keep the Sabbath. He was met with fierce opposition from the Jewish leaders. They followed him to find fault with him. In Mark 2:23–28 Jesus and his disciples walked through the cornfields on the Sabbath day; his disciples were hungry and plucked the ears of corn to eat. The Pharisees accused him saying, why do your disciples do that which is unlawful on the Sabbath day? Jesus showed them by example how to keep the Sabbath as the old patriarchs did. He cited the fact that when David and his men, caught up in a desperate situation, hiding from King Saul faced a situation when they were very hungry. They went into the synagogue and ate the consecrated left over bread that only the priest should eat. He reminded them that the Sabbath was made for man and not man for the Sabbath. Man was created on the 6th day and the Sabbath was created on the 7th day. Jesus is the Lord who created the Sabbath. If it was ok for David to eat the shewbread on the Sabbath when he was hungry, certainly one that is greater than David is here. Jesus was teaching that work that is necessary in the saving of souls is good to do on the Sabbath.

Another Sabbath Jesus was in the synagogue and saw a man with a withered hand, and he asked the man to come forth. Jesus could have healed that man hand quietly on another day but he used the opportunity to teach. Jesus asked his accusers, is it lawful to do good on the Sabbath days or to evil or to save life or to kill? They could not answer him, the Bible states that Jesus was grieved because of the hardness of their heart and Jesus, the creator asked the man to stretch forth his hand and he restored the man hand. Instead of rejoicing that this man was healed they accused Jesus of Sabbath breaking. Henceforth the Pharisees plotted to kill him. So here they are accusing him of Sabbath breaking while they are plotting to kill him. Do not miss the point here the issue was not whether the Sabbath should be kept but how it should be kept. So you want to know how to keep the Sabbath do what Jesus did. Jesus went to the synagogue every Sabbath and read the scriptures, and then he visited the sick and healed them. Jesus saw the distortion of the Sabbath and he did not go along with it. Jesus never taught that the Sabbath was abolished or changed, instead he magnified it; he said think not that I come to destroy the law or the prophets; I am not come to destroy but to magnify the significance of the Sabbath. If there were a change in the Sabbath of the Ten Commandments Jesus would have said so. Take note that there is no change in the Sabbath during Jesus time. The changing of God's law should be a matter of great concern to his followers and one that deserves much attention.

The change of the Sabbath was a gradual process which took firm hold during the second and third centuries of the Christian Church. We can find no change in the Old Testament Adam, Moses, David, Daniel, Isaiah, Jeremiah, Jacob and all of God's people in Old Testament times kept the Sabbath on the 7th day. In New Testament times, we see that the 7th day Sabbath is still in existence and still kept by the Jews. The first Christians kept the 7th day Sabbath. The apostles kept the Sabbath. Mathew, Mark, Luke, Paul and John were all Sabbath keepers. You are in good company when you keep God's 7th day Sabbath. Our greatest example Jesus, the author of the Sabbath, honored the Sabbath commandment and even in death he rested on the Sabbath. No one can find one text in the Bible that God has approved any change in his law and no one can change God's law.

So when did the change from Saturday to Sunday, the 1st day of the week, began? The book of Acts chronicles the 1st 30 years of the Christian church and there is no change recorded. The book of Mark written about 55 AD records no change; Matthew and Luke recorded between 60–80 AD records no change. We come to the end of the first century and John wrote the book of Revelation, still no change recorded. There is nothing recorded in the Bible about the change in the Sabbath from the 7th to the 1st day. In the first century Jews still worshipped on the 7th day, and the newly formed Christian church also worshipped on the 7th day. Jesus did not change the day of worship, and so the new Christian believers in Christ both Jews and gentiles worshipped on the 7th day. In the first century, the Christian church worshipped on Saturday while pagans worshipped on Sunday.

How did Sunday become the Christian Sabbath?

From the beginning it was not so. Adam and Eve kept the 7th day Sabbath. Noah kept the 7th day Sabbath. Noah had three sons Shem, Ham and Japheth. Shem had a son name Canaan and his descendants were the Canaanites. They practiced open rebellion against God. The descendants of Noah's grandson Canaan became the Canaanites and they were rebellious against God and worshipped the sun rather than the creator of the sun, God. Ham had son named Cush and he had a son name Nimrod, the founder of the Babylon. The Babylonians worshipped many different gods. When Nimrod died he was worshipped as a God. He was also known as Baal the god of rain. The worship of the sun can be traced back to the descendants of Ham. The sun God was the highest and most glorious of the Gods worshipped by pagans. The pagans had a day for each of their Gods and the day on which they worship their highest God was Sunday. On Sunday they worshipped the sun God, Monday the moon god, Tuesday Tiw day, Wednesday sodden day, Thursday thor day, Friday Friga day, Saturday Saturn day. These names were derived from paganism. God named the days of the week from one to seven.

How does God feel about Paganism? In Leviticus 18:1–3 The Lord warned the children of Israel not to follow the practices of the Egyptians where they left nor the Canaanites where they were going. In Ezekiel 8:14 describes conditions about 593 BC when God took the exiled prophet Ezekiel in vision back to his temple in Jerusalem and showed him the condition of his people and the condition of the temple and the abominable things that were going on in his temple. The worship of the Lord was strange and abominable to him. The Lord expressed how offended he was that blatant Paganism was practiced in his temple. The people worshipped the sun; at this time the southern kingdom of Judah had fallen and was taken into captivity and the Lord's temple was desecrated. He showed the prophet 25 men, probably priests because they were standing in the inner court restricted to the priests with their backs turned toward the temple of the Lord and their faces toward the east, worshipping the sun. They turned their backs on the creator God to worship the sun, a created object. In verse 17 the Lord told Ezekiel that it was an abomination. Sun worship which started in Babylon, spread to many cultures, Medo-Persian, and Egyptian pagan culture, had now crept into God's holy temple. There were worshippers kneeling in the temple of the Lord and they turned their faces to the sun and worshipped it. Sunday was sacred to the Pagans and God called this worship of the sun an abomination. In Deuteronomy 12, God warned Israel that when they entered Canaan they were not to even inquire about the gods, and they were not to worship God the way these nations do because their worship was an abomination.

When the children of Israel were in the wilderness for 40 years, God did not reigned manna on the Sabbath for 40 years. He sent manna twice on Friday for 40 years and those who went out on the Sabbath to get manna were killed. The Sabbath is not a Jewish institution but is for all people. Isaiah 56:1–6 God states "blessed is the man who keep from polluting my Sabbath; also the sons of the stranger, that join themselves to the Lord to serve him, and to love the name of the Lord, to be his servants, every one that keep the Sabbath from polluting it, and take hold of my covenant. Even them will I bring to my holy mountain and make them joyful in my house of prayer: their burnt offerings and their sacrifices shall be accepted upon mine altar, for mine house shall be called a house of prayer for all people." One should not get the opinion that the Sabbath is only for Jews; the Sabbath is part of the moral law in existence long before there was a Jew. At the end of creation week when God had finished all his work he created the Sabbath and rested on it; he commanded man whom he had just created on the 6th day of creation to rest on the Sabbath day. God created the weekly cycle. Unlike the daily, monthly or yearly cycle that is dependent on celestial movements, the weekly cycle revolves around God. The Sabbath of the moral law is here for eternity. In the earth made new when all the redeemed are gathered home the Sabbath will be kept. In Isaiah 66:22 and 23 "For as the new Heavens and the new earth, which I will make, shall remain before me, says the Lord, so shall your seed and your name remain. And it shall come to pass that from one new moon to another, and from one Sabbath to another shall all flesh come before me, says the Lord. Hollow my Sabbath for it will be a sign between you and me forever. In Nehemiah 13 starting with verse 15 Jeremiah warned his people about the desecration of the Sabbath. They were working on their vineyards, loading their donkeys, buying and selling on the Sabbath. He reminded them that their forefathers went into Babylonian captivity for profaning the Sabbath.

Sunday keeping has long been a part of pagan tradition; nowhere in the Old Testament did God accept it. When did Sunday worship begin in the Christian era? We begin to see the change in the first century. About 120 AD Christians in Alexandria, Egypt first began to worship on Sunday. At that time, Alexandria, Egypt was noted for its library, philosophy and culture. Since the Bible does not record a change in the day of worship, the earliest writings that could be found justifying Sunday worship was found in the writings of a new convert to Christianity named Justin Martyr who wrote "But Sunday is the day on which we hold our common assembly because it is the first day on which God having wrought a change in the darkness and matter made the world and Jesus Christ our savior on the same day rose from the dead." This is one of the earliest documented evidence of the change of Sabbath and it is not Biblical.

The change in the day of worship was gradual and Satan operated on many fronts to effect this change. He created many reasons why Sunday became an attractive replacement for the seventh day Sabbath of the Lord our God. One of the first reasons for the acceptance of Sunday was a strong anti-Jewish feeling that permeated the church in the early centuries. Jews wanted a Jewish nation and many Jewish revolts plague the Roman Empire. In AD 132–135 there was a major Jewish revolt and many Romans and Greeks were killed in the process. After this revolt, the Roman Emperor Hadrian drove the Jews from Jerusalem. There was a strong anti-Jewish sentiment. Since Christians and Jews worshipped on the same Sabbath, Christian believers were often mistaken for Jews. Many Christians were persecuted with the Jews so Christians did not want to be associated with Jews for fear of persecution.

These conditions in Rome in the second century created an environment that made Sabbath keeping difficult. There was great persecution of Jews and Christians. Christians in order to distance themselves from the persecuted Jews began avoiding practices that associated them with Jews. This included Sabbath keeping. Roman Emperor Hadrian was very repressive and he persecuted Jews and Christians. He banned the Jewish religion and the Sabbath could not be kept. This led the Christian church was doing everything possible to be separate from the Jews. Anti-Jewish writers, such as Justin Martyr, first wrote against the Sabbath. Their argument was that Christians should not keep the Sabbath because the Sabbath was Jewish, and if they kept the Sabbath they would be considered Jews. The keeping of the seventh-day Sabbath fell into disfavor in Rome.

During the second Christians were the minority in Rome. The worship of Mithra, the Persian sun God, had spread to the Roman Empire. Interesting, the chief festival days of Mithra was Christmas and Easter, December 25th was the celebrated birthday of Mithra or Tammuz to the Babylonians. How did it become the birthday of Jesus? Here is an interesting quote. "The observance of Sunday as the Lord's day is apparently derived from Mithraism. The argument that has sometimes been used against this claim, namely, that Sunday was chosen because of the resurrection on that day, is not well supported." Gordon J. Laing, *Survivals of Roman Religion,* 1931.

The emergence of Sunday as the day of worship appeared in the second century when conditions in the Roman Empire created an atmosphere conducive to the change. The disciples did not know about this change and hence nothing is written in the gospel or the Bible about this change in God's commandments. There is no biblical authority for the change. Satan used the circumstances in Rome to cause this great apostasy from biblical truth. The day on which pagans worshipped the sun was chosen as the day of worship by the Christian church. The Sunday movement picked up momentum and by the 4th century Sunday was now fully established in the Christian church. This was written about AD 337: "Christians shall not Judaize and be idle on Saturday, but shall work on that day, but the Lord's day (Sunday was now being referred to as the Lord's day) they shall especially honor, and being as Christians, shall, if possible do no work on that day, if however, they are found judaizing they shall be shut out from Christ." *The History of the Councils of the Church,* Hefele.

During the fourth century, the Roman influence on the Christian church was strong. The Roman Emperor Constantine, a sun worshipper, became a convert to Christianity on account of a vision he had. He was going into a battle when he dreamt he saw a flaming cross. He interpreted this to be a sign of victory from God and this prompted his conversion to Christianity. The conversion of Constantine was a turning point in the Christian church. Constantine and many of his soldiers got baptized. His conversion gave him political advantage and he merged Paganism and Christianity.

It has been said that as a result of this merger that Rome conquered Christianity. The Pagans worshipped the sun on the first day of the week. Constantine got the pagans to embrace Christianity and he their day of worship the Lord's Day. In 321 AD, Constantine signed into law the following first Sunday law. The law states "let all the judges and town people and the occupation of all trades rest on the venerable day of the sun. But in the country husbandmen may freely and lawfully apply to the business of agriculture; since it often happens that the sowing of corn and the planting of vines cannot be so advantageously performed on any other day". The Christian church apostatized from the truth and transferred the solemnity of the Sabbath to Sunday, which they now call the Lord's Day. Constantine on his conversion to Christianity, legalize Sunday as the Lord's Day; with no regard for the law of Jehovah.

As a result of the merger of Paganism and Christianity many other elements of paganism crept into the Christian church. The Pagans worshipped Baal or Tammuz. They had of time of weeping for Tammuz. This crept into the Christian church and is now known as lent, Easter, the Easter egg, the Easter bunny, hot cross buns, they were all part of pagan tradition.

The change of God's Holy day occurred gradually and there was considerable discussion in the church over the substitution of Sunday for the Sabbath of the Bible during the second, third and fourth centuries. Here are some of the documentation on the change of the day.

"The people of Constantinople, and almost everywhere assemble together on the Sabbath as well as on the first day of the week, which is never observed at Rome or Alexandria. Sozomen, 440 AD). So as late as 400 years after Christ historian tells us that almost all Christian churches in the world were still keeping the Sabbath, but Rome was now keeping Sunday only. On Saturday the Gospels and certain portions of the scripture shall be read aloud" *Council of Laodicea* (343–381 AD)

"Although almost all churches throughout the world celebrate the sacred mysteries of the Sabbath of every week, yet the Christians of Alexandria and Rome on account of some ancient tradition have ceased to do this." Socrates Scholasticus, *Ecclesiastical History,* 5th century.

The keeping of Sunday started at Rome. The practice of downgrading the Sabbath and uplifting Sunday also started at Rome. As Rome spread and began to exercise jurisdiction over other churches, Sunday worship spread with it. In the book the rise of the Medieval Church written by Alexander Flick in 1909, he notes some of the issues that came up when the Roman church attempted to take over the Celtic Church around 600 AD. The two churches differed on the Sabbath issue. The Celts permitted their priests to marry, the Romans forbid it. The Celts held their own councils and enacted their own laws independent of Rome. The Celts used a Latin Bible unlike the Vulgate, and kept the day Saturday as a day of Rest with special religious services on Sunday.

Sabbath keeping was deeply rooted in the early New Testament church, that in spite of the attempts of the Roman Church to suppress it and exalt Sunday in its stead, true

Sabbath keeping remained in the church for over 600 years after the coming of Christ. It was only after the Roman Church attained full control of Christendom during the Middle Ages that the Sabbath was lost sight of, but God always had a witness or a group no matter how small who observed his law.

By the 6th century the papacy was fully established and during this time Christians were not reading the Bible and the tradition of the fathers flourished. Many of the early Christian writers refer to the fact that in the third and fourth centuries AD the church kept both Saturday and Sunday. It was the Roman Church who proposed the keeping of a special Sunday named Easter Sunday in honor of the resurrection. Many Christians wished to keep Easter on the same date each year, but Rome insisted that it be on Sunday, and Rome won. Pope Victor I in 189–199 AD was credited with instituting the Roman practice of celebrating Easter on Sunday. Christians in Rome, who came from the province of Asia, observed Easter on the 14th day of the moon, whichever day of the week that fell on. The institution of Easter is a papal tradition; the Bible is silent on that tradition. Jesus gave specific instructions as how his death burial and resurrection should be celebrated. He instituted the communion service and said as often as you eat this bread and drink this wine this do ye in remembrance of me.

The Roman Catholic Church declares that the change of the Sabbath from Saturday to Sunday was her prerogative and boldly states that the church has the power to change laws. Individual Christians should ponder these issues and decide for themselves what is right. It is up to the individual Christians to seek after truth and practice it. There are sincere Christian believers in every church. God has many of his dear saints in these churches.

The changing of the Sabbath to Sunday is apostasy from biblical truth. The Apostle Paul warned us about this apostasy that will arise within the body of Christ. The Prophet John wrote about this great apostasy in his letter to the seven churches of Revelation. The church of Ephesus depicts the first 100 years of the Christian church. This was the era of the apostles. Shortly after Jesus ascension to Heaven, he told his disciples to wait in Jerusalem and he would send them the Holy Spirit. As they waited and prayed the Holy Spirit descended on them and they were able to speak in tongues, which simply mean that they were given the ability to speak foreign languages and spread the Gospel of Jesus to people from many different lands that were gathered in Jerusalem at the time of Pentecost. This was the early rain that set the early church on fire and the gospel spread like wild fire so that the Apostle Paul in Colossians 1:23 could say that the gospel had been preached to every creature under the Heaven. At this point in history the doctrines of the church were uncorrupted, these believers held on to the pure doctrines as taught by Jesus. Persecution was also hurled at the church from the Jewish leaders (Acts 13:45 and Acts 14:2). Jesus commended this church for their patience, hard labor, he however warned them that they had left their first love and had fallen and he warned them to repent and do the first works (see Rev 2:4). Even in this early church there were false teachers in the church and Jesus commended this church for rejecting the error of these teachers. Jesus also commended this church for hating the deeds of Nicolaitans, a Gnostic sect that infiltrated the early church. This Gnostic group did not accept the divinity of Jesus nor his crucifixion. They frankly taught false doctrines about Jesus and taught doctrines that were contrary to the pure doctrines Jesus taught. They practiced polygamy and fornication, they felt that whatever you did in the flesh had nothing to do with salvation. God said he also hated their deeds and commended this church for rejecting their deeds. Beware of Gnostic teachings the Bible states that God hates them. The early church was not swayed by these false teachers because they held on to the pure doctrines of Jesus. The church today has since strayed from the pure doctrines and today is powerless to convince the world about God's truth because she does not practice it.

The church of Smyrna AD 100–AD 313 the church went through great persecution and martyrdom as the Roman Emperors notably Decius, Valerian and worst Diocletian, a devoted sun god worshipper, tried to wipe out Christianity. This was one of the worst times in history to be a Christian. Roman officials permitted the killing of professed Christians. Millions were arrested, maimed, decapitated, fed to lions, burned at the stake and killed. It was bloody era for the Christian Church. This church rejected the error around then and stayed so close to Christ that he had no reproof for them (see Rev 2:10.) He admonished them "Fear none of these things, which thou shall suffer, be thou faithful unto death and I will give thee a crown of life."

The period of the church from 313 AD to 538 AD was the church of Pergamos, also known as the era of compromise. This is when the church erred and strayed away from truth, and Satan, unable to destroy the church during the first two apostolic eras, now established himself firmly within the Christian church. Satan took his seat as head of the Christian church. The Roman Emperor at this time was Constantine, a pagan, who became a Christian and the persecution of the church relaxed. Bad things happened to the church during this period; Constantine united his Pagan teachings and beliefs with Christianity. Some of these Pagan teachings are the immortality of the soul and spirits live on and come back, an everlasting burning hell, Sunday was a sacred day, Christmas, the birthday of the pagan God, was now the birthday of Jesus, Easter, Good Friday, Easter egg, Easter bunny, hot cross buns, infant baptism, purgatory, burning of incense, the veneration of saints etc, etc. all became part of the Christian church. The pure simple doctrines of the church as instituted by Jesus now became laden pagan idolatrous doctrines that soon became human traditions. Paganism and Christianity clasped hands.

Jesus told the church of Pergamos that Satan dwelt in that church. In Revelation 2: 13

he told them, "I know thy works and where thou dwelleth, even where Satan seat is". Jesus reprimanded them for teaching false doctrines. They called on the name of the Lord while teaching false doctrines. He told them to repent and forsake these false doctrines or else he will come unto them quickly and fight against them with the sword of his mouth.

Satan, unsuccessful in his attempt to destroy Christians, now turned his attention to distorting the doctrines of the church. These pagan doctrines that are not found in the Holy Scriptures are still practiced and defended by Christian leaders in many churches today.

During this time, during the period of the church era of Pergamos, Rome was disintegrating as a nation and the Papacy was being established. When the Papacy became the political and religious leader of the Western Europe. The Catholic Church then enforced Sunday observation on all Christians. This occurs the era of compromise. Satan unable to destroy the church during the church eras of Ephesus and Smyrna proceeded to corrupt the church during the Pergamos period.

The next apostolic era was from 538 AD to 1400 AD Tis apostolic period of the church of Thyatira or the era of apostasy. This is the longest period of the Christian church and during these dark ages, darkness abounded because the word of God was hidden. The word of God was not read and followed. If you wanted to know what God's word said, you had to ask the priest. In Revelation 2:21, Jesus rebuked this church for her fornication with false teachings. In every dispensation, God have a faithful few and there were some in Thyatira who opposed these false doctrines.

The church era of Sardis was from the 1500–1700 AD This is the era of reformation when men like Luther, Wycliffe, Huss, Calvin, Knox, Wesley and others challenged the established church and started new denominations. The church era of Philadelphia was the era of revival. Jesus said that he set before them an open door that no man can shut because they had little strength and kept the word. The door was now opened for the study of God's word and various Bible societies started and the great evangelical movement or the Protestant reformation took hold.

We are now living in the final dispensation of the Christian church, the church of Laodicea from 1800's AD to Jesus return. This church is described as lukewarm, neither hot nor cold, know it all, rich and have need of nothing and have eyes that are blinded to their nakedness. Jesus says that he will constantly stand at the door and knock; if anyone chose to hear him and open the door and he will come in.

In addition to the seven letters about the church era; John in Revelation 5 was shown a book perfectly sealed with seven seals. No one in Heaven or earth or anywhere was able to open the book or to loose the seals except Jesus, the lion of the tribe of Judah; the lamb slain from the foundation of the world. What is written in this book is of interest. This book apparently contains details of the historic periods of the Christian church. Everything is documented. Jesus keeps accurate records of everything. The history of Salvation is well chronicled. Jesus took the book sealed perfectly with seven seals, and when he opened the first seal a white horse appeared with a bow and a crown. White denotes the purity of the church in the first century and the bow the rapidity of the spread of the gospel in that era. Under the second seal was a red horse the church had lost its purity and this corresponds to the church of Smyrna. When he opened the third seal the horse was black you cannot recognize the church anymore, its' doctrines were corrupt the unbiblical doctrines of indulgences, purgatory were taught. Under the fourth seal 538–1500 AD the horse was pale no light in the church, a fearful time for the church, the church faced death during the dark ages and millions were killed. Under the fifth seal 1517–1755 AD Terrible persecutions occurred, and there were many martyrs. During this time Martin Luther translated the Bible.

The sixth seal is characterized by the great Lisbon earthquake 1755; the sun becoming black on May 19, 1780 at 10 am, and the stars fell in 1833. This was noticed by Frederick Douglas and Abe Lincoln. Time is running out we are now between the sixth and last or seventh seal. The second coming of Jesus takes place under the seventh seal.

Paul, a first century Christian and a Sabbath keeper, foresaw the great apostasy of the church from the law of God and warned the church in 2Thessalonians 2:1–7 about the mystery of iniquity or lawlessness that would invade the church or the man of sin that opposes and exalts himself against all that is called God and sits in the temple of God setting himself up as God. The mystery of iniquity is a man calling himself God; the mystery of Godliness is God becoming man. Almost 700 years before Paul warned the church about this apostasy from truth, the prophet Daniel was shown this attempted change of God's law in Daniel 7:25.

Did God want us to worship on Sunday in honor of his resurrection? No! How did Christ instruct us to honor his resurrection? Christ in 1 Corinthians 11:26 left us with instructions regarding the celebration of his resurrection. He said "as often you eat this bread and drink this wine ye show the Lords death until he comes. This do ye in remembrance of me." This is how you celebrate the Lord's resurrection, not by a day of worship. We have to follow God's instructions explicitly. We cannot follow the commandments of men even when they seem like a good thing to do. There is a way that seems right but the end thereof is destruction.

The Catholic Church does not deny the change of God's day and readily admits it in her literature. This is what the Catholic Church says about itself.

The following is taken from the convert's catechism of catholic doctrine, 2nd edition, 1910 *The Catholic's new convert's catechism*.

Q. "What is the third commandment?
A. The third commandment is: Remember that thou keep holy the Sabbath day.

Q. Which is the Sabbath day?
A. Saturday is the Sabbath day.

Q. Why do we observe Sunday instead of Saturday?
A. We observe Sunday instead of Saturday because the Catholic Church transferred the solemnity from Saturday to Sunday. Peter Geierman, *The Convert's Catechism of Catholic Doctrine*, 1951.

Q. What does the 3rd commandment command?
A. The third commandment commands us to sanctify Sunday as the Lord's Day. Page 50–51 of the catechism.

Q. How prove you that the Church hath power to command feasts and holy days?
A. "By the very act of changing the Sabbath into Sunday which Protestants allow of; and therefore fondly contradict themselves, by keeping Sunday strictly, and breaking most other feasts commanded by the same church" Henry Tuberville, *An Abridgment of the Christian Doctrines*, 1833, p.58.

Q. Why did the Catholic Church substituted Sunday for Saturday?
A. The church substituted Sunday for Saturday because Christ rose from the dead on Sunday and the Holy Ghost descended upon the apostles on a Sunday.

Q. By what power the church substituted Sunday for Saturday?
A. The church substituted Sunday for Saturday by the plentitude of that divine power which Jesus Christ bestowed upon her.

Question on page 99 "In keeping Sunday non-Catholics are simply following the practice of the catholic church for 1800 years a tradition and not a Bible ordinance."

Dr. Edward Hiscox, author of the *Baptist Manual*, Nov 13, 1803 "What a pity it (Sunday) comes branded with the mark of paganism, and christened with the name of the sun-god, and then adopted and sanctioned by the papal authority, and bequeathed as a sacred legacy to Christendom."

The Catholic Encyclopedia, volume 4, page153 "The church after changing the day of rest from the Jewish Sabbath of the seventh day of the week to the first day made the third commandment as the day to be kept holy as the Lord's day."

Catholic Record, September 1, 1923 "Sunday is our mark of authority…The church is above the Bible, and thus transference of Sabbath observance is proof of that fact." The church claims the change of the Sabbath as a mark of her authority.

In the book *Catholicism and Fundamentalism,* page 38, Karl Keating writes "Fundamentalist meet for worship on Sunday, yet there is no evidence in the Bible that corporate worship was to be made on Sundays. The Jewish Sabbath, or day of rest, was of course Saturday. It was the Catholic Church that decided Sunday should be the day of worship for Christians, in honor of the resurrection."

Saint Catherine Catholic Church Sentinel, May 21st, 1995 "Perhaps the boldest thing, the most revolutionary change the church ever did happened in the first century. The holy Sabbath day was changed from Saturday to Sunday… not from any directions noted in the scripture, but from the church's sense of its own power… people who think that the scripture should be the sole authority should logically become Seventh-day Adventist (SDA) and keep Saturday holy."

In the book *Faith of our Fathers*, Page 561, Cardinal James Gibbons writes "You may read the Bible from Genesis to Revelation and you will not find a single line authorizing the sanctification of Sunday. The scriptures enforce the religious observance of Saturday."

American Catholic Quarterly review January 1883

"Protestants in discarding the authority of the church has no good reason for its Sunday theory and ought to logically keep Saturday with the Jews. In other words if they are not going to regard the authority of the Catholic church and say the Bible is their only guide, the observation of Sunday is a Catholic institution."

During the early Protestant Reformation Martin Luther declared that the Bible and Bible only was our guide. The church argument against Luther is found in *Cannon and Tradition*, page 263 "The authority of the church could therefore not be bound by the authority of the scriptures because the church had changed the Sabbath into Sunday, not by a command of Christ but by its own authority."

There are many who do not see the issue clearly. The issue is one of obedience to God. God has placed his seal on his law. Isaiah 8:16 says, "Bind up the testimony, seal the law among my disciples." A seal authenticates. Gods seal and mark is in the fourth commandment. There are 3 essential elements to a seal the name, the title and the territory. e.g. Abraham Lincoln, the president of the United States; or the seventh day is the Sabbath of the Lord thy God, creator of Heaven and earth. Satan would like to erase the authority of God from this planet and so he attacked the fourth commandment, which contains the seal of God.

If God desires us to change from the seventh day of the week to the first day he should say so. There is no evidence in the Bible for a change. There are eight texts in the New Testament that some use to justify Sunday worship but they do not support this change.

#1. Luke 24:1 - "Now upon the *1st day of the week*, very early in the morning, they came unto the sepulchre, bringing the spices that they had prepared on Friday the preparation day, and certain others came with then." The Sabbath of the commandment was kept by Jesus followers in AD 33. Luke states that they prepared the spices on the preparation day for the body of Jesus. They rested on the Sabbath and on Sunday they returned with the spices for the body of Jesus. Note here how careful the disciples were about the Sabbath, how many people today would not take care of the body of Jesus on the Sabbath. In Luke 24 Dr. Luke gives us a fascinating story of two believers who were in Jerusalem for the Passover, they were intensely discussing the events that took place in Jerusalem that weekend. It was Sunday and they were walking home to Emmaus about 7 miles from Jerusalem, the resurrected Jesus joined them. They did not recognize him. He inquired of them what conversation made them so sad. They were surprised at the question because everybody in Jerusalem was talking about the crucifixion of Jesus. Where are you from? Are you a stranger here? These disciples did not fully understand his mission and so were greatly disappointed. They went on to tell this stranger about the death of Jesus and how they had hoped that he was the one to deliver Israel from the Roman bondage. He knew that they had totally misunderstood his mission. In verse 25 he said to them "Oh fools and slow of heart to believe all that the prophets have spoken." He went back to the Old Testament reminding them that Moses and all the prophets had prophesied about Jesus and finally it had come to pass. Here Jesus took the time to explain to these two disappointed disciples what the scripture said about him. He started with the prophets and the prophecies. Had they believed the prophets they would know what was happening. Jesus is the fulfillment of the prophecy of Isaiah 53 that foretold his rejection and crucifixion centuries before crucifixion was invented. The Old Testament prophecy of Micah 5:2 foretold that he who existed from eternity would be born in Bethlehem. There are many Old Testament messianic prophecies that should have provided the necessary information that these disciples needed. But they missed it. It is possible to be reading the scriptures, teaching and preaching the scriptures and miss essential truth. Jesus enlightened these two disciples and when they got to Emmaus, he pretended that he was going further but the two disciples were so excited, their hope in the Messiah had been revived and so they invited him in. He came in and as they sat to eat dinner he stretched out his hands to bless the meal and as they recognized him and he vanished. Forthwith they returned to Jerusalem in the dark and finding the eleven disciples in the upper room hiding from the Jews they told them of their encounter with the risen Lord. Jesus then appeared to these disciples. These disciples were not gathered here to worship on the first day of the week; they were gathered for fear of the Jews (John 20:9). They did not believe Jesus was resurrected at this point and so they certainly were not meeting to celebrate his resurrection on the first day of the week.

Dr. Luke, writing 30 years after Christ ascended, states that when Jesus was buried the women having prepared the spices on the resurrection day rested on the seventh day Sabbath according to the commandment. Dr. Luke makes it clear that Friday was the preparation day, Saturday was the Sabbath that God rested on even in death and Sunday was the resurrection day.

Text #2

Mark 16:1 and 2 "And when the Sabbath was passed Mary Magdalene and Mary the mother of James, and Salome had bought sweet spices that they might come and anoint him. And very early in the morning the first day of the week, they came unto the sepulcher at the rising of the sun."

This is crystal clear evidence that Sunday is not the Sabbath. They kept the Sabbath and when it was over the next day Sunday they came to the tomb. Mark 16:2 says very early in the morning *the first day of the week* they came unto the sepulcher at the rising of the sun. This place the resurrection on the first day of the week after the Sabbath was passed. Clearly the change in the Sabbath had not occurred yet. We are still in the era of the pure church.

Text #3

Matthew 28:1 "in the end of the Sabbath as it began to dawn toward *the first day of the week*, came Mary Magdalene and the mother Mary to the sepulcher." Obviously no change of the Sabbath is mentioned, nor is there mention of the keeping of Sunday as the resurrection day.

Text #4

1Cor 16:1 and 2 "Now concerning the collection for the saints, as I have given order to the churches of Galatia even so do ye. Upon *the first day of the week* let every one of you lay by him in store, as God hath prospered him, that there be no gatherings when I come."

Some say that Paul is sanctioning worship on the first day of the week. The truth is that there was a famine in Jerusalem (read about it in Acts 11:27–30 and Romans 15:26.) Paul was simply telling the Corinthian Christians who were Sabbath keepers that when they balance their checkbooks on Sunday, after they had observed the Sabbath, they should set aside some money for the famine in Jerusalem. In Romans 15:26 we see that the churches of Achaia and Macedonia had already done this. He is requesting that this be done before he returns that there be no gatherings (collections) when he comes. There is nothing here to suggest that Paul sanctioned the keeping of the first day. Paul was a Sabbath keeper.

Text #5

Revelation 1:10 'I was in the spirit on *the Lord's Day*." This is one of the most used texts to support Sunday observance. There is no biblical reference to support Sunday as the Lords day. The Lords day is the 7th day Sabbath (see Exodus 20:10, Mark 2:28, Isaiah 58:13.) John was a Sabbath keeper who along with the other disciples, was banished to the isle of Patmos for the truth, He was keeping the Sabbath and praying when the vision came to him. The text said that he was in the spirit on the Lord's Day. Nowhere does the Bible say that the Lord's Day is Sunday. Many of the biblical texts used to support Sunday are misunderstood by many. Satan's aim is to discredit God and obtain worship for himself and he does it in the most deceptive and clever way, distorting God's word.

Text #6

Acts 20:7 "*And upon the first day of the week*, when the disciples came together to break bread, Paul preached unto them ready to depart on the morrow and continued his speech until midnight."

The Apostle Paul was making his farewell trip among the churches. Realizing that this was the last time that he would see them, He called the leaders of the church of Ephesus and preached his farewell sermon warning the church that after his departure grievous wolves would enter the church not sparing the flock. In addition, within the church will men arise teaching false doctrines and drawing people away. He saw the contamination of the pure church with false doctrines. In Acts 20:25 Paul says "and now behold I know that you all, among whom I have gone preaching the kingdom of God shall see my face no more." On this occasion they broke bread. Act 2:46 states that the apostles broke bread from house to house every day, so the breaking of bread doesn't make Sunday the new day of worship.

Text #7

Colossians 2:14–17 "Blotting out the handwriting of ordinances that was against us, which was contrary to us, and took it out the way, nailing it to the cross. And having spoiled principalities and powers, he made a show of them openly; triumphing over them in it, let no man judge you in meat or drink or in respect of a holy day or of the new moon or of the Sabbath days."

This biblical reference is often used by many to say that Christ abolish the Sabbath. What is the handwriting of ordinances? Christ abolished the handwriting of ordinances at the cross. Ephesians 2:15 "Having abolished in his flesh the enmity, even the law of commandments contained in ordinances for to make in himself of twain one new man, so making peace." Hebrews 9:10 also describe the law contained in ordinances. It points out that the meat and drink offerings and the ordinances were temporary pointing to the real thing, the true redeemer.

The ceremonial law is also called the law of ordinances. The ceremonial law pointed to Christ the remedy for sin while the purpose of the moral law is to reveal sin. The ceremonial law or the law of ordinances was written by Moses (2 Chronicles 35:12 and Deuteronomy 31:24–26). It was placed in the side of the ark (Deut 31:24–26). The moral law was placed in the ark (Exodus 40:20, Deuteronomy 10:1–5 and 1 Kings 8:9). The moral law was not destroyed by Christ, He magnified it (see Matthew 5:17). The moral law is eternal (see Psalms 111:7 and 8, Matt 5:18, Romans 3:31. The ceremonial law on the other hand was temporary it was written after sin (Hebrews 5:1 and 8:4) and was abolished at the cross, when the veil of temple rend an end to the ceremonial services (Colossians 2:14 and Matt 27:51).

The Moral law of God is our compass and guide and must be revered by all mankind. Many would say we that we are no longer under law but under grace. The obvious truth is that we are indeed saved by Grace but Grace does not mean that you are exempted from the law. When Christ pardons you that is no license to continue to sin. If you want to be free from the law your life must be in harmony with the law. Matter of fact the moral law of God is called the law of liberty (see James 2:8–12). You are free from the law as long as you live in harmony with its claims. You and I are not imprisoned today because we live in harmony with the law. The ceremonial law is clearly a different entity. When the Jewish legal system ended so did the ceremonial law. The meat and the drink system were also part of the Jewish law. They met their fulfillment in Christ. This is not to be confused with the eating of unclean meats which precedes the ceremonial law (see Genesis 7:2). The law of ordinances or the ceremonial law contained many holy days e.g. the Passover, the feast of unleavened bread, Pentecost, the day of atonement, the feast of the tabernacles (see Leviticus 23), the new moon, and the first day of each month celebration (Num 10:10, 28:11). The Sabbath days that Paul is referring to are the ceremonial rest days mentioned in Leviticus 23. The ceremonial law also contained seven annual Sabbaths and the new Jewish converts to Christianity still wanted to esteem these days. Paul admonishes the church in Colossians 2:16 and 17 "Therefore let no man judge you by what you eat or drink, or with regard to a religious festival, a New Moon celebration or a Sabbath Day." In the early Christian church Paul had to contend with Judaizing false teachers. These converts wanted a continuation of the ceremonial law. Paul is letting them know that this law pointed to Jesus and therefore met its fulfillment at Calvary.

Jesus foreknew the destruction of Jerusalem in AD 70 and told his disciples pray that your flight be not in the winter or the Sabbath day. Why would Jesus give this admonition if the Sabbath were changed? The Bible evidence supports the continuation of the Sabbath of creation. Genesis 2:1–3 Thus the Heavens and the earth were finished and all the host of them. And on the 7th day God ended his work, which he had made and rested on the 7th day from all his work, which he had done. And God blessed the 7th day and sanctified it because that in it he had rested from all his work, which God created and made. God did bless any day he blessed the 7th day. Exodus 16:26 and 30 states that when God brought the children of Israel out of Egypt he fed them manna in the Wilderness He said Six days ye shall gather it but on the 7th day which is the Sabbath in it there shall be none. And it came to pass that there went out some of the people on the 7th day for to gather and they found none. Then the Lord said "how long refuse ye to keep my commandments and my laws? See for the Lord hath given you the Sabbath therefore he giveth you on the 6th day the bread of two days abide ye every man in his place let no man go out of his place on the 7th day. So the people rested on the 7th day." For 40 consecutive years on every 7th day no manna fell because it was the Sabbath. God is particular about his Sabbath and in Ezekiel 20:20 He says "Hallow my Sabbaths and they shall be a sign between you and me that ye may know that I am the Lord your God." God is particular about which day is the Sabbath Day. When Jesus came to earth and lived among men the Bible states that he went to the synagogue on the 7th day the Sabbath and that was his custom. Jesus did not change the Sabbath. The writer to the Hebrews in Heb.4:9–11 states "There remains therefore a rest to the people of God. For he that entered into his rest, he also hath ceased from his own works, as God did from his. Let us labor therefore to enter into that rest, lest any man fall after the same example of unbelief." The Sabbath is not only the sign of God creation but of redemption and sanctification. In Exodus 31:13 God said to Moses "speak to the children of Israel saying "Verify my Sabbaths for it is a sign between me and you throughout your generations: that ye may know that I am the Lord that doth sanctify you." The promises that God to literal Israel are also for spiritual Israel too. In Isaiah 58:13 and 14 God says "If you will keep your feet from breaking the Sabbath and from doing as you please on my Holy Day, if you call the Sabbath a delight and the Lord's Holy Day honorable, as if you honor it by not going your own way and not doing as you please or speaking idle words, then you will find your joy in the Lord, and I will cause you to ride on the heights of the land and to feast on the inheritance of your father Jacob." God has placed a blessing on his holy day. After a lengthy discussion on the change of God's Sabbath, let us return to the study of Daniel and specifically the 9th identifying mark of the beast power.

Identifying #9. Then the saints shall be given her for a time, times and dividing of time.

We are now told the time that this beast power would rule over people. It will rule for time, times and dividing of time. This is a prophetic time period lasting 1260 years. How did we get 1260 years? This is an important area to understand, the correct interpretation of these prophecies is contingent on the proper understanding of the day to year concept that is necessary in interpreting some biblical time prophecies, including this one. The following texts support this interpretation of a day equal a year.

- Ezekiel 4:6 I have appointed thee each day for a year.

- Numbers 14:34 After the number of the days in which ye searched the land, even forty days, each day for a year, shall ye bear your iniquities even forty years and ye shall know my breach of promise we know that they wondered in the wilderness for forty years not days.

A prophetic year has 360 days. There are 360 days in a year in the biblical Jewish calendar (12months x 30 days each).

Time   = 1 year   = 360 days = 360 years
Times   = 2 years = 720 days = 720 years
Half a time = ½ year   = 180 days = 180 years
                         1260 days = 1260 years

In many of the Bible prophecies one prophetic day equals one literal year. The prophecy of Daniel states that this beast power would rule over men for 1260 days and it did so for 1260 years. The papal power came into existence in 538 AD and ruled for 1260 years until 1798. It ruled for 1260 years just as the prophecy predicted. This church held political power in Europe for 1260 years during the middle ages. The prophet John is also given the time period for the rule of this power in several different places in the book of Revelation, chapter 12:14 and Revelation 12:6.

So far Daniel chapter 7:24–26 given us enough information to identify this power but to be sure no one misinterprets who this power is more information is given in Daniel 8,9,10,11 and the book of Revelation. God has given us these identifying points because he loves us. He wants everyone to know the truth and he has many of his dear children in this church and many of them are the kindest, sincerest God-fearing Christians who love the Lord and are loved by the Lord. It is not our business to sit in judgment of anyone. God is the only righteous judge and in the final analysis only God determines who of us will be saved. Our responsibility is to share truth and pray for each other. We really do not know what the final roster of the saved will look like.

Verse 26: "But the judgment shall sit, and they shall take away his dominion, to consume and to destroy it unto the end."

The little horn came to power in 538 AD and it dominated until 1798 when the French armies of Napoleon abducted the pope, took Vatican City thus temporarily wounding the papacy. It recovered from that near fatal wound in 1929 and it will continue on until the end of time when judgment will be given to the saints and its power will be taken away and it will be destroyed forever.

Verse 27: "And the kingdom and dominion, and the greatness of the kingdom under the whole Heaven, shall be given to the people of the saints of the most high, whose kingdom is an everlasting kingdom, and all dominions shall serve and obey him."

Christ will come and will give the kingdom to the saints of the most high. It is important to note that as a result of the judgment mentioned in the previous verse that this power, the little horn power, is defeated and judgment is decided in favor of God's saints, many of whom were martyred for holding on to truth. In the final analysis only God's everlasting kingdom will last forever; all other earthly power whether secular or religious will come under the judgment of God and will be judged accordingly.

Verse 28: "Hitherto is the end of the matter. As for me Daniel, my cognitions much troubled me, and my countenance changed in me: but I kept the matter in my heart." The vision ended, however Daniel continued to be greatly disturbed and saddened by it but he kept it to himself.

Addendum to Chapter 7: There are some interpreters of Bible Prophecy who claim that the little horn is the Syrian King Antiochus 1V Epiphanes 175–164 BC who in 168 BC plundered Jerusalem, massacred thousands of Jews, desecrated the temple at Jerusalem, and took the temple treasures. This interpretation has been around since the first century. Josephus, a first century Jewish historian, believed this and it was a common belief among the Jews at that time. The Jews felt that he was the abomination of desolation spoken of by the prophet Daniel. Despite these horrible crimes by Antiochus, he clearly does not fit the prophecy for the many reasons stated in the prophecy; Antiochus was a minor Seleucid king, a footnote in history, in light of the issues of the great controversy that is taking place in these prophecies. He clearly does not fit the power described in these prophecies. He was before the time of Jesus and Jesus clearly states that the abomination that causes desolate was in the future. It is clear that God is speaking of world powers not a man. When did this little horn power arise? Daniel 7:24—this little horn power came up among the 10 horns that is after the division of the 4th kingdom or the Roman Empire and it plucked up 3 horns before it. It plucked up the last horn about 538 AD. How long will it have power for? 1260 years. When will it end?—Until the judgment (see Daniel 7:8, 9, 26). The timing of Antiochus clearly does not fit the prophecy, he came to power before the fourth beast or Roman Empire. This man Antiochus lived over 500 years before the breakup of the Roman Empire and did not uproot 3 kings/kingdoms. He does not fit the time period alluded to in these prophecies. He was a Seleucid king at a time 175–164 BC After the death of Alexander the great four kingdoms arose and the Seleucid kingdom was one of them. Antiochus was the eight Seleucid king there were 21 kings after him. For three years, he defiled the temple in Jerusalem. In 164 BC his Seleucid forces were beaten back during the Maccabean revolt and Jerusalem was liberated. Daniel 8 verse 4 states that the Medo-Persian ram became great; verse 8 the Grecian goat became very great and verse 9 states that the little horn waxed exceedingly great or greater that the others. This eliminates Antiochus. Antiochus did not grow greater that Medo-Persia or Greece the kingdoms that preceded him. Antiochus is dead and this power continues on today and will continue until the end of the judgment (Daniel 7:11). Daniel 8:25 states that this power will stand up against the Prince of Princes or Christ and be broken without hand. This occurs when Jesus comes to set up his everlasting kingdom. Antiochus is clearly not the Little Horn Power. He is a mere distraction created by Satan.

Chapter Eight

In Chapter 8 God expands on the prophecies of Daniel 7

Verse 1. Daniel has another vision about 2 years after the vision of Daniel 7 that we have just studied. This one was given to him 551 BC during the third year of the reign of King Belshazzar. This vision is given toward the end of the Babylonian Empire's rule. It would soon be overthrown by Medo-Persia. It's over 50 years since his captivity in Babylon and the Babylon Empire is losing power to Medo-Persia.

    Verse 2: The setting for this vision is at the Palace of Sushan, in the province of Elam. Sushan was the winter palace of the Persian Kings. Daniel was standing by the Ulai River.

    Verse 3: As he looked up he saw a ram standing at the river. The ram had two horns, one horn was higher than the other, and the highest horn came up last.

    Babylon is not included in this prophecy because it is declining and a new world power is rising. What power is this? In verse 20 the angel explains to Daniel that the horns represent the kings of Media and Persia. The new world power is the Medo-Persian Empire and the ram with two horns symbolizes it. Persia became the dominant power as indicated by the higher horn. Media is the older empire and Cyrus the Persian King captured it in 550 BC It grew to prominence and controlled more territory than Babylon. In the days of king Ahasuerus it controlled territory from India to Ethiopia.

    Verse 4: He sees the ram pushing westward conquering Babylon in 547 BC and northward conquering Lydia in 539 BC pushing southward conquering Egypt and Ethiopia in 525 BC No other beast power could stop it nor deliver anyone from his power. It did whatever it wanted and it became a *great* nation.

Verse 5: As I was considering, behold, a he goat came from the west on the face of the whole earth, and touched not the ground: and the goat had a notable horn between his eyes. As Daniel was thinking about what he had seen, a male goat suddenly approached from the west, it moved so fast that it did not have time to touch the ground. This goat had a prominent horn between his eyes. In verse 21 the angel explained to Daniel that the goat represent Greece. Greece is located to the west of the Persian Empire. The prominent horn on this goat is its first King, Alexander the Great. His conquest was swift.

Verse 6: As the goat came to the ram with the two horns that was standing by the river; it attacked the ram with fury.

Verse 7: The goat came close to the ram and attacked the ram with great fury and smote the ram breaking its two horns. The ram had no power to withstand this attack and the goat cast him to the ground and stamped on him and there was no one was able to rescue the ram. The Medo-Persian Empire was no match for Alexander the Great.

Verse 8: Then the he goat waxed great or became a powerful nation. At the height of power the prominent horn broke off and four notable horns replaced it, each one pointing in the direction of the 4 winds of the earth. About 334 BC Alexander the great began his powerful conquest. He was a powerful leader whose accomplishment in 12 years still marvels the modern world. At the height of his power in June 323 BC he died suddenly at age 32. This vast empire was left without a leader and it began to disintegrate. His 4 generals fought for power. Finally his empire was divided into four separate Macedonian or Hellenistic kingdoms. General Cassander ruled Macedonia, Ptolemy ruled Egypt and Palestine, Lysimachus ruled Trace and parts of Asia Minor, Seleucus ruled Syria and Babylon.

Verse 9: This is a direct continuation of the previous verse. Out of one of them most likely the 4 winds of Heaven described at the end of verse 8 and also in Dan. 7:2 or from the 4 points of the compass not directly from the 4 notable horns would come a little horn power. It began small but it became an *exceedingly* great power, it extended to the south. Rome controlled Egypt for a long time before Egypt became a Roman province in 30 BC, Rome extended towards the East, Syria became a Roman Province about 65 BC, and towards a pleasant land and Palestine became part of the Roman Empire in 63 BC The angel does not give Daniel the name of this Little Horn Power but gives its characteristics. The angel says that this power became exceedingly greater than the previous powers. Here in chapter 8 God again expands on the identity of this Little Horn Power.

Verse 10: It became a great nation even to the host of Heaven and it cast down some of the host and of the stars to the ground and trampled upon them. The prophet is shown Rome in its two forms pagan and papal. The Little Horn power arose from the Great Roman Empire. Both have persecuted and trampled on God's people who dare not agree with her beliefs. It makes a spiritual attack against God.

Verse 11. Yea, he magnified himself even to the prince of the host, and by him the daily "sacrifice" was taken away, and the place of his sanctuary was cast down."

Gabriel now gives more information about the little Horn Power. Rome magnified itself, even to the prince of the host. The Prince of the host is Jesus. In Daniel 9:25 The Messiah is called the Prince. In Joshua 5:14 Jesus refers to himself as the Captain of the host of the Lord. In Daniel 12:1 Christ is referred to as Michael the great prince. How does Rome magnify itself to the prince? In its Pagan Phase, the Roman Governor Pontius Pilate sentenced Christ to die, Roman soldiers nailed him to a cross, and pierced his side and spat in his face, put a crown of thorns on his head and gambled for the only earthly possession he had, his garment.

The angel now describes Rome's activities in its Papal phase and these activities are spiritual in nature. Daniel is shown that this power takes away the daily. What is the daily? The Lord gave us the earthly sanctuary as a model of the Heavenly. The Priest in the earthly sanctuary had daily ministrations. In the Holy place of the earthly sanctuary were the daily shewbread, the daily burnt offerings, the perpetual altar of incense, and the perpetual burning candlesticks. The daily represented the day-to-day operation of the sanctuary services. These were earthly shadows of the Heavenly reality. In the Heavenly sanctuary the daily is Christ continual daily ministry as High Priest in the Heavenly sanctuary. This earthly power has obscured Christ continual ministry for us in the Heavenly sanctuary. The earthly sanctuary services have met their fulfillment and have been null and void since Calvary, when the veil of the temple was torn asunder separating the holy from the Most Holy Place. The sanctuary operation moved to the Heavenly sanctuary. The actual earthly sanctuary was later destroyed in AD 70, so this attack by the Little Horn is on the Heavenly sanctuary.

How did the little Horn obscure Christ's mediatory work in Heaven? The little horn power has obscured this all-important ministry of Christ in the Heavenly sanctuary by casting it down and setting up an earthly religious system, through which Christ dispenses salvation. Clearly, this power is a religious power that is attacking these spiritual institutions set up by God. Christ is our High Priest interceding for us in the Heavenly sanctuary, and he is our only mediator between God and man. We are to come boldly to his throne of grace.

The Little Horn Power has magnified itself as equal to God and has eclipsed the work of Christ in the Heavenly sanctuary by instituting earthly services that is not set up by God. The little horn has instituted the confessional, the Little Horn Power sacrifices Christ in each mass and his intercessory work in the Heavenly sanctuary is obscured. Jesus is our mediator in the Heavenly courts; there is no need to confess to an earthly system. Sinners should be guided to Jesus directly not through a mediator, the Bible states that there is one mediator between God and man and that is Jesus. The death of Christ on Calvary and the tearing asunder of the veil of the temple brought an end to the earthly priesthood in AD 31. The little horn power cast down the place of the sanctuary and sets up intermediaries like saints, Popes, Mary, priests, the confessional, the mass thereby obscuring Jesus' rightful place in the Heavenly sanctuary as mediator between God the father and sinful man. We are admonished by the writer to the Hebrews to come boldly to the throne of Grace; we do not need an earthly system, we have a great high priest in the Heavenly sanctuary; he alone has earned the right to be our mediator. The names that the head of the power is called are named that are attributed only to God e.g. Most Holy Father. Jesus in Matthew 23:9 says "and call no man your father upon the earth: for one is your father, which is in Heaven." So this power has magnified itself to the status of God. The sanctuary services all point to Jesus, and Satan has successfully distorted its significance and meaning and has set up an elaborate earthly system, which comes between Jesus and the believer. Christ established his church and he did not institute this system. Daniel was shown that Heaven does not approve of this system and warns us that this power has taken away the daily sacrifice and the minds of people are taken away from Christ ministry in Heaven.

Daniel is shown that the little horn power has cast down the place of the Heavenly sanctuary. The truth about God's Heavenly sanctuary is not taught in most churches today. Professed Christians today reject this vital truth. God has a plan to deal with sin, this plan is centered in the Heavenly sanctuary. Here Christ pleads his blood for sinful man, and can you understand why this aspect of the prophecy has been fulfilled, most Christians today do not acknowledge or teach about Christ ministry in the Heavenly sanctuary. Satan doesn't want us to focus on this important phase of Christ work on behalf of sinful man.

The angel mentions the Little Horn attack on the daily but not on the yearly sacrifice because the yearly sacrifice in the second apartment of the sanctuary did not start until the end of the 2300 years. If you can get people to disbelieve the daily they will also disbelieve the yearly service in the sanctuary.

Verse 12: And an host was given him against the daily sacrifice by reason of transgression, and it cast down the truth to the ground; and it practiced, and prospered.

This power corrupted the truth cast it to the ground and trampled on it and despite her errors she prospers. How do you cast truth to the ground? Do you kill everybody who believes truth? Satan tried that down through the centuries and it did not work. Satan's best weapon against truth now is to distort it or cast it to the ground. Daniel is shown that the little horn will cast truth to the ground and will prosper. Christ is our great high Priest in the Heavenly sanctuary presiding over the judgment. Satan cannot railroad the plan of salvation; it is fully operational and will soon conclude.

Verse 13: Then I heard one saint speaking, and another saint said unto that certain saint who spoke, how long shall be the vision concerning the daily sacrifice, and the transgression of desolation, to give both the sanctuary and the host to be trodden under foot? Then Daniel heard a Heavenly being speaking, and one saint said to the other, how long will be the vision concerning the taking away of the daily sacrifice, the transgression of the truth, and trotting under foot of both the sanctuary and the host of people.

Daniel hears two Heavenly beings discussing the time period involved in the vision. They are discussing the question how long will all these things last? How long will this power be able to carry on these anti-Christ activities?

Verse 14: *The saint answered and said unto Daniel unto 2,300 days, and then shall the sanctuary be cleansed.*

In other words at the end of the 2300 days/years, the cleansing of the Heavenly sanctuary and the simultaneous work of judgment will begin.

Verse 15: And it came to pass, when I, even I Daniel, had seen the vision, and sought for the meaning, then, behold, there stood before me as the appearance of a man. Daniel did not understand what he had seen. He was perplexed and sought an explanation. He could not understand the relationship between the seventy years of captivity as prophesied by Jeremiah and the 2300 years that would occur before the cleansing of the sanctuary. He prayed for an explanation and behold, a being in the appearance of a man stood before him.

Verse 16: Then he heard a man's voice between the banks of the river Ulai; saying to the angel Gabriel, make Daniel understand the vision.

Verse 17: Then Gabriel came over to where Daniel stood, Daniel was so afraid that he fell down, the Gabriel said to him, "understand, O son of man that the vision extends to the time of the end." Gabriel is the angel, which stands in the presence of God, the place where Lucifer, now Satan, once stood.

Verse 18: As Gabriel was speaking with Daniel; Daniel was in a deep sleep with his face to the ground. Gabriel touched Daniel and stood him up.

Verse 19: Gabriel said to Daniel, Behold, I will let you know what will happen in the last end of the indignation: for at the time appointed the end shall be. The vision is not for Daniel's time is for the time of the end. Next Gabriel gives Daniel the names of some of these kingdoms.

Verse 20: The ram that you saw with the two horns represents the kingdom of Medo-Persia.

Verse 21: The rough goat is the kingdom of Greece, the great horn its first king. Alexander the great was the first king of Greece. Alexander defeated Cyrus the Persian at the battle of Arbela in 331 BC

Verse 22: When the power of its first king was broken or at the death of Alexander, four kingdoms arose, but not with the same power. The angel Gabriel tells Daniel that these powers would not be as strong as Alexander's kingdom. The angel Gabriel interpreted the vision for Daniel except for the 2300-year vision.

Verse 23: "In the latter stage of these kingdoms when the transgressors are come to the full, a kingdom of fierce countenance and understanding dark sentences shall arise." Gabriel does not reveal the name of this kingdom to Daniel but most likely the power is Rome in its Pagan and Papal phases.

Verse 24: This power will be mighty, but not by its own power it will be helped probably by the state; he will be very destructive, and he will be prosperous and will destroy God's people.

Verse 25: His policy will be successful, and cause deceit to prosper, people won't recognize its deceit, it will magnify himself, will destroy many; he will stand up against the Prince of Princes, Jesus. Jesus was killed under Roman Authority. He shall be broken without hand meaning divine power, Jesus himself at his second coming will put an end to this power, and this is a power that will last until the end of time. This vision goes way into the future to the end of time. This is obviously a world power that last for a long time.

Verse 26: The angel tells Daniel that the vision of the 2300 days/years *is true*. For now shut thou up the vision, it will come to pass in the distant future.

Verse 27: After that awesome vision, Daniel fainted and was sick for many days, then he went back to work on the king's business; but he still astonished by the vision and did not understand the vision about the 2300 days/years. He understood some of it because the angel told him who the ram and goat was. Daniel sees this Little Horn waging a long and successful battle against God.

Sequence of kingdoms in Daniel 8 – Media-Persia-Greece-Rome-Papal Rome

Major events were introduced in Daniel 8— The cleansing of the Heavenly sanctuary and the work of judgment are simultaneous events.

Chapter Nine

539 BC
DANIEL 9

Verse 1. In 539 BC the first year of the reign of Darius, the son of Ahasuerus, of the seed of the Medes, who became the king of the realm of the Chaldeans or Babylon. Having deposed Belshazzar the last ruling king of Babylon, Media-Persia was the ruling power and Daniel and his people were still captives.

2. In the first year of Darius reign (539 BC), some 14 years after Gabriel explained the vision of chapter 8 and Daniel fainted. Daniel still does not understand the vision of the 2300 years. Daniel was studying the word of God as recorded by the prophet Jeremiah hoping that he could to understand the 2300 days/years vision that Gabriel told him about in Daniel 8:14. He began by praying and studying the seventy year prophecy of Jeremiah. The Lord said in Jeremiah 29:10 that when the seventy years were finished at Babylon the Jews can return to Jerusalem. Daniel knew that the seventy years of captivity, which began in 605 BC, was coming to an end in about four years. He knew that God still had plans for his people after the captivity.

Verse 3: Daniel sought the Lord's help and he began to pray and plead with the Lord with fasting, sackcloth and ashes. Daniel again prayed to God for help in understanding the vision.

Verse 4: Daniel prayed earnestly and confessed his sins and said, "Oh Lord, the great and dreadful God," he acknowledges God as a covenant keeping God, who loves and show mercy to those who love him and keep his commandments.

Verse 5. Daniel acknowledges his sins and the sins of his people. We have sinned, and have committed iniquity, and have done wickedly, and have rebelled, even by departing from thy precepts and from thy judgments.

6. Neither have we hearkened unto *thy servants the prophets*, which spoke in thy name to our kings, our princes, and our fathers, and to all the people of the land. God's professed people then and now have not listened to his prophets.

7. Oh Lord, righteousness belongs unto thee, but unto us confusion of faces, as at this day; to men of Judah, and to the inhabitants of Jerusalem, and unto all Israel, that are near, and that are far off, through all the countries where you have driven us, because of the sins that we have committed against you.

8. Oh Lord, to us belong shame on our faces, because all of us, our kings, our princes, our fathers have sinned against you.

9. But you, oh Lord our God are merciful and forgiving, though we have sinned against you.

10. Neither have we obeyed the voice of our God, to obey his commandments, which he told to us through his servants the prophets.

11. Yea, all Israel have broken your law and have departed that they would not obey your voice, therefore the curse is poured upon us, and the oath that is written in the law of Moses that would happen to those who disobey God's law. (Read Leviticus 26.)

12. And he hath confirmed his words, which he spoke against our judges that judged us, by bringing upon us a great evil: for under the whole Heaven hath not been done as hath been done upon Jerusalem. In other words the words of Moses, which he spoke against us and our judges have come true, a great evil has been brought upon the inhabitants of Jerusalem. Such great evil hath not been done anywhere under the Heaven.

13. As it is written in the Law of Moses, all this evil is come upon us and yet we have not prayed to the Lord and turn from our evil ways and understand your truth.

14. Therefore, the Lord sees all the evil, and permitted it to happen to us: because the Lord our God is righteous in all that he does: because we have not obeyed his word.

15. And now O Lord who have delivered us out of the land of Egypt in a mighty way, and you were renowned for this miracle; and at this day we have sinned and have done wickedly.

Verse 16. O Lord, according to all your righteousness, Daniel now beseeches or pleads with the Lord to turn his fury and his wrath away from Jerusalem, the holy mountain because of their sins and their father's sins. Jerusalem and thy people have become a reproach to all nations around us.

Verse 17. Now therefore O our God, hear my prayer and my supplications and let your face shine upon the sanctuary that is desolate, for the Lord's sake. He is pleading for the restoration of the sanctuary and the end of the captivity.

Verse 18: O my God, incline your ear and hear our prayer and open thine eyes and look at our desolation; look at the desolation of the city that is called by your name; we do not present this prayer for our own righteousness but because of your great mercies.

Verse 19: O Lord, hear; O Lord, forgive; O Lord, hearken and do, do not defer your promise of restoring Jerusalem for your own sake, O my God: for the city and people that are called by your name.

Verse 20: While Daniel was speaking and praying and confessing his sins and the sins of his people, and presenting his supplication before the Lord for the holy mountain of the Lord.

Verse 21: And while he was still speaking and praying and confessing his sin and the sin of his people Israel, and presenting his supplication to the Lord, the angel Gabriel, who had already explained part of the vision to him in chapter 8, reappeared unto him about the time of the evening worship and touched Daniel.

Verse 22: About 14 years after the last vision Gabriel appears to Daniel and tells Daniel I am now come forth to give you skill and understanding regarding the 2300 years. Daniel understood the seventy years of captivity was close to an end but he did not understand the 2300 years vision given in the vision of Dan 8:14 and he feared that the captivity would now extend to 2300 years. It is possible that Gabriel did not explain to Daniel the meaning of the 2300 days/years because at the end of Daniel 8 while Gabriel was explaining the vision Daniel fainted and was sick several days after he saw the vision. In the beginning of Chapter 9, Daniel then searched the scriptures, the prophecy of Jeremiah for more understanding. He realized that the seventy years of captivity was close to an end, it is now 66 years since Daniel was in captivity, and the prophecy of Jeremiah said that after 70 years God would again restore Israel but he feared that his sins and the sins of his people would extend the captivity. In Daniel 8 he was shown that the sanctuary and the host would be trodden under foot for 2300 years. He did not understand this; he probably thought this meant that since his people were still so disobedient to God that the captivity would continue for 2300 years instead of the 70 years, so he prayed earnestly for the answers. God sends Gabriel to explain the 2300 day/year vision. What an honor! God felt it was important to send Gabriel to explain to Daniel the meaning of the 2300 day/year vision. This explanation is not only for Daniel but also for God's people down through the centuries.

Verse 23: At the beginning of Daniel's prayer, Gabriel reappears to Daniel. He informs Daniel that at the beginning of his prayer, the command came forth from God that Gabriel should come and reveal these things to Daniel for he was greatly beloved by God. Therefore understand the message and consider the vision, says Gabriel. Gabriel now gives Daniel an explanation of the vision of Chapter 8 verse 14 and he expands and elaborates on it. *This is extremely important stuff.*

Verse 24 Gabriel tells Daniel more about this extremely important time prophecy; he tells Daniel that seventy prophetic weeks or 490 years using the day is one year principle) are determined (or cut off from the 2300 year prophecy) to thy people and upon the holy city, to finish the transgression, to make an end to sins, to make reconciliation for iniquity, and to bring in everlasting righteousness, and to seal up the vision and prophecy and to anoint the Most Holy or the Messiah. The Messiah here refers to Christ, the anointed one, who was promised in the beginning when man sinned. Gabriel explains to Daniel that the seventy weeks are cut off. The question is from what period of time is the 70 weeks cut off. The only other time prophecy mentioned by angel Gabriel is the 2300 prophetic days or 2300 years in Daniel 8:14. Here Gabriel makes it clear to Daniel.

That seventy prophetic weeks or 490 years of this longer time prophecy was allotted to the Jewish nation. God had a great work for them to do after their release from captivity. At the time Daniel was given this vision the Jewish people were still in captivity but the captivity was soon to end and God was giving them 490 years to make things right with him. God reveals through the prophet Daniel that the first 490 years of the 2300 years longer time prophecy was allotted to the Jewish nation. The 2300 year prophecy was not only about the Jewish nation but it had implications for the future and gave *the time of the Messiah's coming and the beginning of the judgment and the cleansing of the Heavenly sanctuary. God's church must understand and teach this message. It has major implications for the church particularly at the end of time.* Gabriel informs Daniel some specific things that should be accomplished in the seventy prophetic weeks or 490-year period. These things are related to the role of the Coming Messiah. Prophecy is all about Jesus and these time prophecies centers around his great plan of redemption. During the first seventy weeks of this prophecy the Jewish nation has important work to accomplish after their release from captivity. It is an important Messianic prophecy that was given to Daniel 500 years before it happened. There is simply no excuse for not knowing the time of the Messiah's coming, the beginning of the judgment and the cleansing of the Heavenly sanctuary. God gave this information to Gabriel to give to Daniel who wrote it down for us. What are these things that the Jewish nation is expected to accomplish by the end of the seventy weeks. Gabriel makes the vision clear to Daniel?

1. **To finish the transgression** – God gave the Jewish people seventy weeks or 490 years to put an end to sin and choose whom they will serve; their sin separated them from God and Jesus came to restore this relationship with God.

2. **To make an end to sins** – Through the blood of Jesus and his vicarious death on Calvary Jesus took on our sins thus bringing them to an end. When we accept Jesus, the blood of Jesus cleanses us of our sins.

3. **To make reconciliation for iniquity** – Jesus took on the sins of the whole world and just like the high priest in the earthly sanctuary, he makes atonement for our sins and the father sees Jesus and not our sins.

4. **To bring in everlasting righteousness** – When the plan process of redemption is complete, God will establish his everlasting kingdom of righteousness. This can only be accomplished through Jesus death on the cross.

5. **To seal up the vision and the prophecy** – the coming of *Jesus*, the Messiah is a fulfillment of this biblical prophecy. History confirms this. We have seen the fulfillment of the seventy week prophecy and the 2300 day/year prophecy and this gives us the reassurance that all of these prophecies will be fulfilled. These prophecies deal with the all-important work that Jesus is performing in the plan of salvation. Our faith is buttressed by these realities.

6. **To anoint the most holy** – After his crucifixion *Jesus* was inaugurated as our high priest in the Heavenly sanctuary initiating the work of the cleansing of the Heavenly sanctuary. At his Baptism Jesus was anointed with the Holy Spirit.

I hope you are appreciating the focal point of prophecy, Jesus and his all-important work in the salvation of mankind.

In the seventy weeks prophecy, God reveals to Daniel that he was giving the Jewish nation seventy prophetic weeks or 490 years (70 weeks x 7 -the number of days in a week = 490 days, one prophetic day = 1 year, hence the 490 years). The seventy prophetic weeks or 490 years were to be cut off (the Hebrew word used is chatak which means to cut off) from the larger period 2300 years. Here we see that the seventy weeks are symbolic, you cannot cut off 70 weeks (or 490 years) from 2300 days, it has be 2300 years. The day equal a year principle is validated here because 70 weeks is just over one year, this cannot take us down to the rebuilding of the temple and coming of the Messiah but using the day equal year principle it fits perfectly. The beginning of the 70th week (490 years) and the beginning of the 2300 days/years is the same time. At the beginning of the 70th week God moved the Medo-Persian king to help the Jews to rebuild the temple at Jerusalem and paved the way for the exiled Jews to return home. The coming of the Messiah was foretold in this prophecy, the Jews waited for his return but as the prophet Isaiah prophesied in Isaiah 53:2 they discerned in him no beauty that they should desire of him. And so he came to his own and they rejected him. The seventy prophetic weeks or 490 years were fulfilled as foretold; the Jewish nation did not accept the Messiah and they did not accomplish the great work for which century after century they were preserved and chosen.

They lost their status as God's chosen nation; and in AD 34, the seventy prophetic week culminated at the time of the stoning of the early Christian martyr Stephen. The gospel went out to the gentile and every born again true follower of Jesus is a seed of Abraham and heir according to the promises. *The Christian church now constitutes Spiritual Israel who now has the responsibility of taking the great commission of Jesus to every kindred, tongue and people.* There are many Christians who do not believe this and are looking for a revived Jewish nation and a third temple in Jerusalem. This is a deception of Satan and it is contrary to scripture and does not reflect a true understanding of these prophecies. I pray that the body of Christ the Christian church would grasp and teach these truths.

Verse 25: Know therefore and understand, that from the going forth of the commandment to restore and to build Jerusalem unto the Messiah the prince shall be seven weeks, and three score and two weeks: the street shall be built again, and the wall, even in troublous times. This prophecy is divided into three time periods: seven weeks, then 62 weeks, and then one week making it seventy continuous weeks. This verse tells us when the seventy prophetic week/490 year prophecy begins. Know therefore and understand that from the time the commandment went forth to restore and rebuild the city of Jerusalem until the Messiah comes shall be seven prophetic weeks (7x7) or 49 years later using the day to year principle) Jerusalem will be rebuilt even amid trouble so this first period of seven prophetic weeks or 49 years was allotted to the rebuilding of Jerusalem, so from 457 BC to 408 BC the walls, the street and the temple in Jerusalem were rebuilt. The command to restore the temple and rebuild and rebuild Jerusalem was the decree set forth by King Artaxerxes in the seventh month of his reign in 457 BC (see Ezra7: 27; 4:7–23; 7:12–26). There were previous decrees given to rebuild the temple of Jerusalem; one in 537 BC by Cyrus (see Ezra 1: 1–4), and by Darius in 519 BC, these are not the ones that fit the prophecy because they did not rebuild the city. The third and final decree in 457 BC was the only one that made provision for the restoration of the city of Jerusalem thus restoring Israel's civil and religious government. The book of Ezra 7 tells that this decree was given in the seventh year of the reign of King Artaxerxes. Artaxerxes became king in 464 BC He is the son of King Ahasuerus who married Esther. Ezra was a priest, a prophet and a scribe who returned with Jerusalem to help with the rebuilding and restoration. After the long years of captivity the Jews were scattered throughout the Medo-Persian Empire. The captivity of the Jews to Babylon occurred over different periods of time similarly the return to Jerusalem occurs in groups over different times. Many Jews chose to return to Jerusalem while others stayed in Medo-Persia. Many had to be pleaded with to return to Jerusalem. Ezra and Nehemiah returned at different times. Nehemiah was a cupbearer and trusted confidante of King Artaxerxes. Nehemiah lived in the palace of Sushan (Nehemiah 1:1). The king assisted Nehemiah to return to Jerusalem and rebuild the walls and restore the worship of God. The second time period given in the prophecy is 62 prophetic weeks after Jerusalem is rebuilt or 434 years later (again a day equal one year principle) later the Messiah will come and he did in AD 27. This again validates the day to year principle necessary for the correct interpretation of these prophecies. This prophecy tells us that in 69 prophetic weeks or 483 years the anointed one or the promised Messiah would come.

Verse 26. After threescore and two weeks shall Messiah be cut off but not for himself: and the people of the prince that shall come shall destroy the city and the sanctuary; and the end thereof shall be with a flood, and unto the end of the war desolations are determined. After 62 weeks the Messiah shall be cut off or killed, but not for his sins but for the sins of the people. After (7+62) 69 prophetic weeks or 483 years the Messiah came (Read Mark 1:9). In AD 27 the promised Messiah came right on time (Read Luke chapter 3) History tells us that the fifteenth year of Tiberius Caesar was AD 27. Luke 3 tells that Jesus was baptized in the fifteenth year of Tiberius Caesar. Jesus was baptized in the fall of 27 AD He was anointed by God the father and became the Messiah. The baptism of Jesus began the seventh week or 483rd year of this prophecy. These apocalyptic time prophecies given to Daniel covers thousands of years and the day equal one-year principle that is necessary to correctly interpret apocalyptic prophecy must be applied. When applied here this prophecy takes us from the Medo-Persian Empire at 457 BC to the appearance of the Messiah in 27 AD The prophecy foretells the rejection of the Messiah and the subsequent destruction of Jerusalem and the temple in AD 70 by the Roman armies led by Titus. Shortly before his crucifixion in AD 31 Jesus spoke about this abomination that causes desolation. It happened in AD 70.

Verse 27: And He shall confirm the covenant with many for one week, but in the midst of that seventieth week He shall cause the sacrifice and ablation to cease, and for the overspreading of the abominations He shall make it desolate, even until the consummation, and that determined shall be poured upon the desolate.

The third part of the seventy-week prophecy covers a span of seven years from AD 27 to AD 34. The correct interpretation of the above text is important. Pay strict attention here the angel Gabriel tells the prophet Daniel that He (or the Messiah of the preceding verse) shall confirm the covenant with many for one prophetic week. The only He in the Bible who made a covenant with His people is God. God had a covenant relationship with national Israel. Jesus confirmed the covenant with the Jews for one prophetic week or seven literal years. For the first three and a half years, from His baptism in AD 27 until His death in AD 31, Jesus ministered unto them personally and some accepted Jesus as the Messiah. For the next three and a half years (AD 31 to AD 34) His disciples ministered to the Jews. The covenant that was made to the Jews was confirmed; the 490 years allotted to them in Daniel 9:24 to make an end to sins and to anoint the Most Holy Jesus ended in AD 34.

The prophecy continues by saying that in the midst of the seventieth week, He (The Messiah) shall cause the sacrifice and ablation to cease. This was fulfilled when Jesus was crucified. Jesus appeared in the fall of AD 27 and 3 1/2 years later in the middle of the 70th week (or the spring of AD 31), the Messiah was crucified. When he died on the cross the veil of the temple separating the holy from the most holy place where the high priest was officiating was torn asunder from top to bottom indicating that the hand of God did it, thereby bringing an end to the 4000-year-old sacrificial system. It was no longer necessary. (See Matt 27:51, Mark 15:37 and Hebrews 10:8–10). There was clearly no need for the ceremonial system of animal sacrifices; this symbol met its reality in the death of Jesus. This is how Jesus caused the sacrifice and ablation to cease. Contrary to popular theology today the antichrist had nothing to do with causing the sacrifice and ablation to cease. This is another deception of Satan. Christ was the Passover lamb sacrificed for us (see 1Corinthians 5:7). There was no more need for the earthly sanctuary services and the whole economy switched from the earthly sacrifice of lambs to the Lamb of God slain from the foundation of the world. A change in the priesthood occurred and Christ priesthood in the Heavenly ministry was about to begin. He ascended back to Heaven in AD 31, having completed the sacrificial phase of his ministry. He entered the holy place of the Heavenly sanctuary and was inaugurated as High Priest.

In Acts chapters 7 and 8 Stephen the first Christian martyr was tried for blasphemy before the Sanhedrin council the highest religious body in Jerusalem. He defended himself by going over the history of God's chosen people. God had a covenant with his people and here at the end Stephen gives a review of the history of Israel. He begins with Abraham and connects the prophecies to Jesus the Messiah. In verse 51 Stephen says you stiff-necked and uncircumcised in heart and ears; you do always resist the Holy Ghost as your fathers did. Which of the prophets have not your father's persecuted? Who foretold the coming of the Messiah and you have betrayed and murdered him. In verse 56 Stephen saw the Heavens open and Jesus standing at the right hand of God. This confirms that Stephen was telling the truth. At this point they stopped their ears and they rushed and killed him. As they stoned him they laid their coats at the feet of a young man named Saul.

In AD 34, an important year, Stephen was stoned to death, Saul was converted and received his commission from Christ and Peter received the vision to spread the gospel to the Gentiles. So we see that the gospel went out to the gentiles. A new covenant relationship was established to include the Gentiles (see Romans 11:17–21) and the Christian church now consist of Jews and Gentiles working to spread this everlasting gospel.

Through the Jewish nation, the way was to be prepared for the entrance of the Messiah, the savior of the world. God chose this nation for this important mission. As a nation, they failed on this important mission, the seventy week or 490 years ended in AD 34 and they rejected Christ and killed his disciples. After the death of Stephen at the hands of the Sanhedrin in AD 34, the seventy prophetic weeks prophecy had ended, the message went out to the Gentiles; the persecuted disciples went everywhere and preached the gospel. *Events of major spiritual significance were accomplished during these 490 years – the release of the Jewish nation from Babylonian captivity and the restoration of Jerusalem, the coming of the promised Messiah, and his vicarious death on the cross.* Jesus is the cornerstone and all the prophecies are about Jesus. These prophecies are a testament of God's great love for us and what he is doing to affect our salvation.

The time periods given in these apocalyptic prophesies cover long periods of time. When these time periods are taken literally they do not fit the historical periods when the actual events happen.

```
------------70 weeks (Dan 9:24)------------
   AD 34-457 BC        408 BC


----7 weeks------------69weeks------------1week----
  1810-1844    2300yrs (Dan. 8:14)   2300yrs
```

When the day equal a year principle is applied the fit perfectly into the historical periods. We know that the angel Gabriel told Daniel that the seventy week prophecy would begin with the decree to rebuild Jerusalem. In 457 BC using the Jewish fall to fall calendar the command was given to rebuild the city. The rebuilding was completed in 408 BC The prophecy tells us that in the sixty-ninth week the Messiah would come. Four hundred and eighty three years later or in sixty-nine prophetic weeks Jesus Christ was anointed the Messiah just as the prophecy predicted. The prophecy also states that in the midst of the seventieth week Jesus would die thus bringing the sacrifices and ablation to cease. Three and a half years later in AD 31, the midst of the 70th week Christ was crucified. Christ sacrificial death put an end to the sanctuary services, no more animal sacrifice, no earthly priests, no more earthly sanctuary. The real sacrifice that ended all symbolic sacrifices came to an end at Calvary. That precious blood spilled at Calvary was the only currency acceptable to make our redemption possible. All of the animal sacrifices merely pointed to Jesus and now that the real sacrifice took place on Calvary it brought an end to the symbolic sacrifices of animal blood. The religious rulers of Israel who rejected the Messiah continued with the animal sacrifices until the temple was destroyed in AD70. This 4000 year practice of the shedding of animal blood for sins has not been practices for almost 2000 years now, thus confirming that Heaven no longer approves the shedding of animal blood because the Messiah came and died and caused the sacrifice and oblation to cease. This happened when the best that Heaven had to offer in the person of Jesus Christ put an end to that practice which he instituted in the beginning when Adam sinned. He came to earth and shed his own blood for sinners on Calvary in AD31.

Prophecy is all about Jesus and since Satan is very much antichrist. It should not surprise that the subtle impostor Satan will try to distort the true understanding of these prophecies. Thus the last part of the prophecy as with so much of the Bible has been the target of Satan's lies and hence there are erroneous interpretations of this prophecy. Many people teach that the he who will confirm the covenant is the antichrist. If you read the prophecy starting with Daniel 9:26 the subject is the Messiah that will be cut off and it continues in verse 27 with the Messiah that will confirm the covenant with many for 1 week. Some sincere Christians insert the antichrist as the one confirming the covenant and causing the sacrifices and ablation to cease. This is Satan's deception and clearly a misinterpretation of these prophecies and the Bible. The antichrist made no covenant in the scriptures. It was Christ who made and confirmed the covenant, Romans 15:8 reads "Now I say that Jesus Christ was a minister of the circumstances for the truth of God, to confirm the promises made unto the fathers." Jesus is a covenant keeping God. Jesus clearly says think not that I am come to destroy the law or the prophets; I am come not to destroy but to fulfill." To fulfill does not mean to destroy. Jesus said to John the Baptist at his baptism by immersion, "suffer it to be so to fulfill all righteousness." Speaking of the antichrist, popular teaching in some churches today and in some bestselling books is the antichrist is coming in the future and would sit in the rebuilt temple in Jerusalem and reestablish the animal sacrifices. This is unscriptural. The antichrist is not a future entity. 1 John 4:3 was written about 100 years after Jesus birth, and John states clearly that the spirit of the antichrist was already in the world; so there is clearly a misunderstanding in the Christian world of who and what the antichrist really is.

At the end of sixty nine and a half weeks the Messiah ascended back to Heaven. What happened to the other prophetic ½ week or 3 ½ years literal years? Remember that the angel Gabriel told Daniel that 70 weeks are cut off from the 2300 years for thy people to put an end to sins and reign in everlasting righteousness. The seventy weeks are continuous. It started in 457 BC during the Persian Empire rule and ended in AD 34 during the reign of Imperial Rome. The seventy week must follow the sixty ninth week or for obvious reasons it cannot be called the seventy week. It is illogical to move the seventieth week to the end of time and call it the seven years of tribulation. The Bible says nothing about a seven year tribulation period, nor does it say that the temple that was destroyed in AD70 will be rebuilt. This is a misinterpretation of scripture. The 490 years was a period of grace for the Jewish nation, and then the gospel would go to the gentiles. This 490-year period ended in

AD 34. In AD 34 Stephen was martyred and from thence the gospel went out to the gentile world. *Galatians 3:28,29 teaches that there is neither Jew nor Greek, male or female for ye are all one in Christ Jesus, and now are ye Abraham's seed and heirs according to the promise.*

The last week of the seventieth week or 490 year prophecy has clearly been tampered with. Many sincere Christian teachers and believers move this last week to the future, thus separating the sixty ninth week from the seventieth week. They then separate the sixty ninth and the seventieth week by 1000 years, Watch out for Satan, he is clever and his deceptions are woven with some truth, that's why his deceptions are so effective. There is no biblical reason for this dissection of this prophecy.

From the dissection of this prophecy came the concept of the secret rapture and many use biblical texts to support this theory. One such text is found in 2 Peter 3:10 "But the day of the Lord will come as a thief in the night; in which the Heavens shall pass away with fervent heat, the earth also and the works that are therein shall be burned up." Many use this text to say that Jesus is going to rapture the church or to say that the rapture will occur because Christ will come as a thief in the night, but they ignore the rest of the text which say that the coming of Christ is anything but secretive or silent because the Heavens will pass away and the elements will melt with fervent heat. This is certainly the most catastrophic event in history. There is no biblical evidence for the secret rapture theory so prevalent in many churches today.

Since so many Christians believe the concept of a secret rapture today, it is worthwhile exploring it a little. If you ask the average believer where did the rapture theory come from? They cannot tell you. They simply do not know. Many heard it from their pastor who read it in a book that is not the Bible. A word of caution be careful about beliefs that are not centered in the Bible. Here is the origin of the rapture theory. Fifteenth century reformers like Martin Luther, John Hus, John Calvin and others studied the prophecies of Daniel and Revelation and came to the conclusion that the little horn was Papal Rome. This was obviously disturbing to the Church of Rome. The church decided to address these serious reformation charges. The Church of Rome convened the famous Council of Trent and the Church called on the Jesuits society of priests to come up with a counter-reformation theory. The Council of Trent met from 1545–1563. Among the Jesuits was a brilliant priest Francisco Ribera (1537–1591) and he was called on to come out with a theory to counteract this Protestant reformation theory. He took many years of research to come up with his theory. As early as 130–202 AD Irenaeus, the bishop of Lyons wrote that the antichrist is a person of Jewish origin who would come about 3½ before the return of Christ. This theory was further developed by Francisco Ribera after his many years of research. He came up with the futurist theory applying most of Revelation to the future. He theorized that the antichrist as future evil person. The council of Trent accepted Ribera version. Ribera's version remained in the Catholic Church for centuries. In the late 1820's the rapture theory was introduced by the Catholic Apostolic Church and this theory spread to the Protestant Churches when John Nelson Darby, an Anglican preacher one of the leaders of the Plymouth Brethren in England, popularized this teaching and he introduced the rapture theory that Jesus would return secretly and rapture his true followers leaving the rest behind. The antichrist will then rule the world and there will be a seven year period of tribulation. In America Cyrus Scofield a Kansas lawyer and author of the Scofield Reference Bible popularized this theory and it was further accepted by Protestant seminaries in this country. This erroneous interpretation has been accepted as truth and has been the subject of best sellers and blockbuster movies. People would rather believe fiction than truth. The truth is the prophecies of Daniel and Revelation does not teach that the antichrist or the little horn power is a person. These prophecies are revealing powers, nations, and systems of worship that expands over hundreds sometimes thousands of years. Popular teachers today say that the antichrist will appear and make a covenant with the Jews and revive the temple services and offer animal sacrifices. He would then suddenly change and for three and a half years will cause Armageddon in Palestine. This is not a correct interpretation of the Bible and it just does not fit the prophecy or make sense. This was also not the belief of the early reformers.

Let us conclude and reemphasize some of the important truths introduced in Chapter 9. The seventy week/year and the 2300 days/year are prophetic periods, which represent actual years. It cannot be taken literally; the vision is symbolic. The 2300 days/years vision began with Media-Persia and continued with Greece and Rome until the end of time when according to Daniel 9:25 the beast power will be broken by a power without hand, God's power. It is obvious that this vision covers a greater period of time than 2300 days. The correct interpretation of this prophecy requires the application of the day for year principle similarly used in Ezekiel 4:6 and Numbers 14:36.

Daniel prayed for the answer to this 2300-year prophecy and the answer was given to him in Daniel 9. He wanted to know when this prophetic time began. The angel Gabriel returned and gave him the answer in Daniel 9:25, "Seventy weeks are determined (or cut off) upon thy people to finish the transgression and to make an end to sins and to make reconciliation for iniquity and to bring in everlasting righteousness and to seal up the vision and prophecy." Daniel needed to know from what period of time the seventy weeks were cut off? When did the seventy weeks begin? Verse 25 Daniel was told the beginning of the seventy weeks and he was told that this time period was cut off from the larger time period and 70 weeks or 490 years was allotted to the Jewish people. Daniel was told what the Jewish nation were required to do in this time period. History confirms that the actual decree that led to the total restoration and rebuilding again began in 457 BC This was the decree that allowed the Jews to return home from captivity; two previous decrees failed to accomplish this. God has a timetable set up for the events of Planet Earth and with the help of these prophecies that he has sent to us we are privilege to know the times that he has revealed to us.

These events are centered on Jesus work to redeem man. The reason why these prophecies are not understood and taught in all churches because Satan in his battle against Jesus has clouded the minds of men and has distorted and misinterpreted these prophecies. He often criticizes those who try to understand these prophecies but God always has a people amid this vast throng of humanity who would not bow to popular opinion or tradition and would rightly divide the word of God. Jesus in the center of these prophecies so be careful when you in any way lessen the significance of these prophecies. We need to uplift Jesus in every way we can. The entire 2300-year prophecy centers on Christ work to redeem man. The first part of it his earthly work ending the work of the earthly sanctuary and his final work in the Heavenly sanctuary for the salvation of mankind.

Daniel is told that the cleansing of the sanctuary occurs at the end of the 2300 years. Which sanctuary does this refer to? Is it the earthly or Heavenly? In Hebrews 9 Paul describes both sanctuaries earthly and Heavenly. The earthly sanctuary services were only a type of the reality in Heaven. It was done unto the example and shadow of Heavenly things. We know that at the end of 2300 years nothing happened to the earthly sanctuary because there was no earthly sanctuary, the temple in Jerusalem was destroyed in AD 70. The cleansing of the sanctuary could not be the earthly sanctuary that was cleansed once a year, not in 2300 years. Remember the 2300 years is the longest prophecy and the seventy prophetic weeks or (490) years were cutoff from that longer prophetic time period. It is logical to think that since the seventy year prophecy was cut off from the 2300 year prophecy that the starting point of this prophecy is also 457 BC this would then bring us to 1844 AD which gives us the starting point for the cleansing of the Heavenly sanctuary. If we use the day to year principle to the seventy week prophecy, we must also apply it to the 2300-day prophecy especially since the 70-week was cut off from the 2300-year prophecy.

So if the seventy weeks or 490 years ended in AD 34 then the rest of the 2300 years must extend beyond that time. Daniel 9:25 gave us the beginning of this longer prophetic time period as 457 BC, if you add 2300 years that takes us to 1844. You go from 1 BC to 1 AD because there is no 0 year on the calendar. Adding 2300 years to 457 BC takes us to 1844 and not 1843.

The cleansing of the sanctuary as foretold in Daniel 8 and the work of judgment or the pre-advent judgment described in Daniel 7:10 are linked; they are the same event. God instructed Moses to build the earthly sanctuary after the pattern of the Heavenly sanctuary. The model of the earthly sanctuary that God showed Moses helps us to understand the reality that is taking place in Heaven. In the earthly model, on the Day of Atonement the priest went into the Most holy Place once a year called Yom Kippur. On that most solemn day the sanctuary was cleansed from the sins of the people that had defiled it all year by the daily services. Similarly in the Heavenly sanctuary at the end of this 2300 years Christ stepped into the Most Holy Place or the second apartment of the sanctuary in Heaven and began cleansing the Heavenly sanctuary of our sins.

The work of judgment and the cleansing of the Heavenly sanctuary are simultaneous events that are clearly depicted in Daniel 7 and Daniel 8 and we studied this in great detail in those chapters. The interpretation of the prophecy given by the angel Gabriel clearly takes this prophecy to the time of the time of the end. Daniel 7:26 tell us that as a result of the judgment that begins at the end of the 2300 years and ends shortly before Jesus returns, the saints will inherit the kingdom and judgment will be against the little horn power. This puts the cleansing of the sanctuary and the 2300days/years an end time event just before the second coming of Jesus. We learned that the 2300 years began in 457 BC when the decree went forth to restore Jerusalem. If you add 2300 years to that, you arrive at the year 1844. What happened in the year 1844 has been the study of Bible scholars and prophetic interpreters. In 1844 Christ entered the Most Holy Place and the work of judgment and the cleansing of the Heavenly sanctuary from the sins of people since Adam began. Christ work of judgment began *in the Most Holy place began in 1844* and it coincided with the first angel of Revelation 14:7 which cries with a loud voice "Fear God and give glory to him for *the hour of his judgment is come."*

While Christ is doing this all important work of judgment in the Most Holy Place he is still interceding for our sins, just like in the earthly sanctuary the daily service did not cease on the day of atonement (see Numbers 28:3 and 4). In the earthly sanctuary, which was a shadow of the Heavenly sanctuary, the sanctuary was cleansed on Yom Kippur, the Day of Atonement. That was judgment day and the only day when the sanctuary was cleansed. In the earthly and the Heavenly sanctuaries the cleansing of the sanctuary and the judgment are simultaneous events. A study of sanctuary and the judgment will help in understanding these time prophecies about Jesus and his redemptive plan for us.

The Sanctuary

Let us look at the concept of the sanctuary, a study of the sanctuary is very important; this is another neglected and misunderstood area of study. Why did Satan obscure this important study? The sanctuary services play a key role in God's plan for our salvation, so pay close attention. In this great controversy between Christ and Satan, Satan does not want you to know what is going on in the sanctuary, it is detrimental to him, so He has successfully cast down and obscure the place of the sanctuary in the minds of God's people. The sanctuary is where God dwells and here is where he has chosen to deal with the sin problem. The sanctuary is where the final decisions involving the great controversy between God and Satan will be dealt with. The sanctuary reveals God's plan of Salvation. The eradication of sin and the plan of Salvation are very important issues to us; therefore, a study of the sanctuary is very important. The sanctuary is not a mere structure for worship it has deep significance. It is God's classroom from where the lessons of the plan of redemption is taught. As you understand the sanctuary services a lot of biblical concepts like high priestly work, atonement, sacrifice, redemption would be better appreciated. After Jesus' sacrificial death on Calvary, he ascended to Heaven and he assumed the position of high priest in the Heavenly sanctuary. This high priestly work of Christ in the Heavenly sanctuary is part of the plan of salvation and the book of Hebrews gives us good insight into Christ work in the Heavenly Sanctuary.

The Apostle Paul, who wrote the book of Hebrews was very familiar with the sanctuary services and wrote to Hebrew Christians who were familiar with these services. Here he encouraged these Christians and used the concept of the sanctuary services to show them God's entire plan of Salvation. The letter to the Hebrews fills in some of the information we know about the sanctuary services. The earthly sanctuary is a copy of the Heavenly sanctuary. Therefore the study of this sanctuary gives us this awesome unbelievable opportunity to study the sanctuary in Heaven. Many of the Bible writers have been shown the Heavenly sanctuary. In Hebrews 8 and 9 Paul describes this real sanctuary where Jesus is ministering as our high priest. John describes it in Rev 11:19 "And the *temple* of God was opened in Heaven, and there was seen in the temple the ark of his testament: and there were lightening, and voices, and thundering, and an earthquake, and great hail". Rev 15:5 "After that I looked, and behold the temple of the tabernacle of the testimony in Heaven was opened." Satan the arch deceiver and enemy of God have been successful in obscuring Jesus and his role in the Heavenly sanctuary.

Since what is taking place in the Heavenly sanctuary is part of God's salvation plan for us, it is important that we study the sanctuary. The events that are taking place in the Heavenly sanctuary can best be understood when the earthly sanctuary is studied and understood. The Sanctuary concept was introduced in the Old Testament, after enslavement in Egypt the children of Israel had forgotten the true worship of God; after their miraculous deliverance from Egypt, they encamped about Mt. Sinai. Here God called Moses up to the mountain and gave him an earthly pattern of the Heavenly sanctuary.

Heaven has a real sanctuary where God dwells. It is here that Jesus; our High Priest pleads his blood on our behalf before the father. God instructed Moses to build an earthly sanctuary that was patterned after the sanctuary in Heaven. The services in the earthly sanctuary were a visible example of the plan of salvation that is occurring in the Heavenly sanctuary. God was demonstrating to us the great plan of salvation that is being conducted in the Heavenly sanctuary. In Exodus 25:8 "He said let them build me a sanctuary that I may dwell among them." It's unimaginable that this infinite God, creator of this unending universe, would meet us in an earthly man-made sanctuary. What condescension to save us. Soon after their miraculous escape from Egypt when they were in the wilderness God gave Moses a pattern of the sanctuary, it was a portable structure made of cloth. Later Solomon built a permanent structure. 1 Kings 8:17 says that it was in the heart of King David to build a house for the Lord God of Israel. The Lord chose his son King Solomon to build the temple instead. In the dedication prayer of the tabernacle Solomon stretching his hands towards Heaven said "but will God indeed dwell on the earth? Behold the Heaven of Heavens cannot contain thee much less this house that I have built.

Let us first look at the earthly the sanctuary services; they are part of the covenant laws described in Exodus 25–31. The institution of the sanctuary services, the sacrificial system, and the earthly priesthood are part of these covenant laws. This specific system was abolished at Jesus death. The writer to the Hebrews in Heb 7:12 says if that system could have made us perfect before God, what need was there for a change in the priesthood. Since that system changed it was necessary to change the ceremonial laws that created that system since a new superior system is in place. The Sanctuary services are now carried on in Heaven by our high priest, Jesus Christ.

What lessons does God want us to learn from the sanctuary?

In Hebrews 8:5 the writer states that God admonished Moses to build him a sanctuary, and Moses was shown a pattern of the Heavenly sanctuary and was told to build an earthly sanctuary after the pattern of the Heavenly one. This earthly sanctuary was but a mere shadow or a type of the Heavenly sanctuary. In Exodus 25:8 God said to Moses "let them build me a sanctuary that I may dwell among them." In the subsequent verses and chapters God gave Moses specific, detailed information about the construction of this earthly sanctuary. He showed Moses a pattern of the Heavenly Sanctuary and the pattern of the furniture therein and told Moses to build him a sanctuary just like the one he showed him. In the rest of the chapter and the subsequent chapters God gave Moses detailed instructions as to the construction of the earthly sanctuary. The last verse of Exodus 25:40 God reminds Moses to be careful that he build the sanctuary and furnish it after the Heavenly pattern, which he showed him in the mountain. God is a particular God and he expects us to follow his instructions explicitly. Noah had a similar experience he was given specific instructions about the building of the ark. God showed Moses a pattern of the sanctuary in Heaven. So far, we learn that there are two sanctuaries; one in Heaven built by God and the other an earthly pattern of the Heavenly built by Moses as instructed by God. Other supporting Biblical evidence for the existence of these two sanctuaries can be found in Hebrews 8. In verse 5 we see that the earthly sanctuary is merely a shadow of the Heavenly sanctuary. In other words, the earthly sanctuary and its services mirrored the Heavenly sanctuary and its services. The earthly sanctuary services can best be appreciated and its' significance understood only because of the Heavenly sanctuary; in other words the earthly sanctuary services are meaningless without the Heavenly reality. Hebrews 9:24 say that Christ did not minister in the earthly man-made sanctuary but in the true sanctuary in Heaven.

The Jewish religion was rich in types and symbols that were a shadow of the reality to come, namely the messiah. When the messiah came he was the meaning of all those services; the earthly sanctuary services met their fulfillment in Jesus. The death of Jesus ended the earthly tabernacle services. At his death an unseen hand tore the curtain between the Holy and the Most Holy place of the earthly sanctuary. He is the substance of those shadowy services; the substance has arrived therefore it is futile to continue embracing the shadow when the substance is reality. The services of the earthly sanctuary came to an end at the death of Jesus, type met antitype. Jesus death is what the sacrificial offerings pointed to and the Jewish priesthood pointed to Jesus high priestly ministry in the sanctuary in Heaven.

Hebrews 4:15 and 16 tells us for we have not a high priest who is unable to sympathize with our weaknesses but one who in every respect has been tempted as we are, yet without sin. After his ascension, Jesus took up his high priestly position in the Heavenly sanctuary; this parallels the earthly high priestly work in the earthly sanctuary. The earthly priesthood system was merely a foreshadowing of Christ's ministry in the Heavenly sanctuary.

Hebrews 4:15 places Jesus as our high priest in the Heavenly sanctuary. Hebrews 8:1 tells us that this high priest sits at the right hand of the throne of the Majesty in the Heavens. Here he functions as the High priest. Here he bids us to come boldly before his throne to obtain mercy and secure forgiveness for our sins. Here at his throne of Grace we obtain mercy and forgiveness of sins. There is no room in God's plan of Salvation for an earthly intermediary. Jesus bids us come boldly to the throne of grace; do not let anyone or anything stand between you and me. Jesus alone lived a sinless life and hung on Calvary and bore the divine wrath of sin so that we could take advantage of this great plan of Salvation. Christ alone can atone for our sins through his shed blood on Calvary.

The Earthly sanctuary services were most important to God's people and an understanding of it is of no less importance today. God has revealed to us the significance of the sanctuary. Many do not understand fully the concept of the Heavenly sanctuary. It teaches an important lesson about how God deals with the sin problem. There is a process and the old sanctuary services help us to understand. The study of the Sanctuary and its' services has deep meaning for us. Read Exodus 25–40 for the sanctuary in the Old Testament, a study of the earthly sanctuary has a lot of meaning for us, there are deep truths to be learned in this study of both sanctuaries (Read Exodus 27 and 30).

The Sanctuary services give us a good look at the plan of Salvation. The entire sanctuary services pointed to Jesus, the way the truth and the life. Acts 4:12 tells us "neither is there salvation in any other man; for there is none other name under Heaven given among men, whereby we must be saved". Jesus is the door to the father. There is no middleman or woman. There is no alternative entrance; you must go through Jesus. Every piece of furniture in the earthly sanctuary pointed to Jesus. He is the way, the truth and the life. No one comes to the father without Jesus atoning sacrifice. Simply put, the plan of Salvation is all about Jesus and His plan to save humanity. Do not let Satan obscure or diminish Jesus in any way.

Let us see how a study of the earthly sanctuary services helps our understanding of the Heavenly sanctuary. The earthly sanctuary consisted of 3 main parts – a courtyard, and two other compartments: the holy and the most holy place. As we study further we will see how they correspond to different phases of Christ ministry and the plan of salvation.

An outer courtyard – consisting of the altar of Burnt Offerings where all the sacrifices were made. The daily temple services took place here. It is here that the daily offerings were brought. In the earthly sanctuary system when an individual sinned they brought an animal to be sacrificed. The rich brought a lamb and the poor a turtledove. The sinner entered at the eastern door of the outer court which had the brazen altar of burnt offering, made of Acacia wood and overlaid with brass. The sinner would confess their sins over the spotless lamb thus symbolically transferring of his sins to the lamb. The priest then takes the Lamb and put it on the altar of burnt offering. The sinner would kill the lamb, the sacrifice would be consumed upon the altar of burnt offering and the priest spilled the blood of the animal. The spilled blood should impress the sinner how hideous sin is and it foreshadowed the death of the spotless lamb, Jesus. The sinner having done his part by acknowledging that he broke God's law and confessing his sins. The sinner has now done what God ask him to do and he left knowing that his sins were transferred to the spotless lamb and that his sins are covered by the blood of the lamb. This is part of God's plan of salvation in symbol. This is quite symbolic because salvation in not obtained in this symbolic plan. The Bible teaches us that the blood of animals cannot take away sins, so why would God establish such an elaborate plan? He is showing us the plan of salvation and how offensive sin is. This earthly model teaches us in a more immediate way and helps us to appreciate the larger and universal plan of salvation.

Before the door of the tabernacle was the laver made of brass and filled with water so the high priest washes his hands and feet before entering the first apartment of the sanctuary.

This is a holy process and the priest must make himself clean. After cleansing himself the priest takes the blood of the lamb into the first apartment of the sanctuary. The priest therefore took the sin in the form of blood into the Holy Place of the sanctuary. Sin is now transferred into the sanctuary.

The first apartment is called the holy place had three pieces of furniture. As the priest enters the holy place, on the left was the seven-branch candlestick or Menorah. These are lamps filled with olive oil, light is a symbol of God's presence and seven is perfection. The lamp represents Jesus the light of the world; the oil is the Holy Spirit. On the North side was the table of showbread made of acacia wood and covered with gold. In Leviticus 24:5 and 6 every Sabbath the appointed priest shall put twelve loaves of flat unleavened bread in stacks of six each on the table of showbread. The loaves represent Jesus the bread of life. He is everything to us: our savior, our food, our shelter, our everything. The priest also put incense in a cup on each stack. The fragrance of incense filled the tabernacle when the burnt offering was made. In front of the veil separating the holy from the most holy place was made of acacia wood and covered with gold. Here the priests sprinkle the blood of the lamb before the veil daily thus transferring the sin into the tabernacle. The priest makes a record of the individual sin in the Holy Place. The priest burns incense every morning and evening. This represents our prayers mingled with the intercession of the Holy Spirit. The incense represents the righteousness and merits of Christ, which makes our prayers acceptable to God. His perfect life of righteousness is applied to our prayers. Every day the sins of the people were transferred to the Holy Place and so the Holy Place needed to be cleansed of the sins of the people. This cleansing was done once a year on the Day of Atonement known as Yom Kippur.

The third apartment – is called the Most Holy Place or the Holy of Holies, is separated by a veil or curtain. Here the yearly special services took place. The Day of Atonement was the most solemn day, on this day the Children of Israel would make sure that all is right with God and all sins are confessed. On the Day of Atonement the sins were removed from the sanctuary. If an individual did not acknowledge that he broke God's law and confess his sins and his sins were in the Sanctuary that individual would be cut off from the camp of Israel. This was such an important process that for ten days before Yom Kippur the trumpet was blown so that the people could get right before God. On this solemn day the High Priest would take 2 young goats, lots were cast to see which was the Lord's goat and which would be the scapegoat. After confessing his sins and the sins of his family, the High Priest then places his hands on the head of the Lord's goat and transfers all the sins of the people that had accumulated there all year. The Lord's goat is slain and High Priest takes the blood into the Most Holy Place. Once a year on, the Day of Atonement, only the earthly high priest could pass through this veil into the Most Holy place. This curtain was very important. This was the one was torn asunder at the moment Jesus died on the cross, thus giving the sinner direct access to the father through Jesus Christ our High Priest.

The Most Holy Place consists of one piece of furniture called the Ark of the Covenant. What is the covenant that is in this ark? It is sacred container for God's unchangeable holy law, the Ten Commandments. A replica of which was given to Moses on Mt. Sinai. The ten commandments is the entity over which the covenant or agreement is made between God and man. In Exodus 25:17 the cover of the ark is called the mercy seat. Here the ark illustrates God's justice and mercy blend together. The law must be kept but there is mercy for the lawbreaker. Sin is the transgression of God's law and the penalty for sin is death. Justice demands the death of the sinner; and only the mercy of God can save us from certain death so mercy is applied through the sacrificial death of Jesus at Calvary. On either end of the Mercy Seat were two cherubims or angels, and between them was the very presence of God.

What biblical evidence supports the existence of the second apartment of the sanctuary? Hebrews 9:2 describes the first apartment of the sanctuary and its furnishings and verses 3 to 5 describes the second apartment of the sanctuary called the holiest of all, verse 4 states that it also had a golden pot that had manna, Aaron's rod that budded. Aaron's rod that budded and the pot of manna later appeared in the Most Holy Place, the bowl of manna symbolized God's providence and Aaron's rod God's authority and discipline. The High Priest on this Most Solemn day would transfer the sins of the people to the Lord's goat, which was slain, and its blood taken into the holiest of all or the Most Holy Place and the blood was offered up before the mercy seat. After the High Priest has finished his work in the Most Holy Place and said "It is finished", probation closes for all of Israel once a year. The High Priest would then transfer the sins that had accumulated in the sanctuary to the live goat, which was led away from the camp of Israel thus cleansing the sanctuary and the people of sins. The High priest represented Christ, the sin offering represents Christ sacrifice at Calvary and the scapegoat represent Satan who along with the sins he has caused will eventually be removed from this universe.

I hope that you are appreciating the significance of all of the sanctuary services; it was not just a ritual. It was not just a Jewish institution; it has major significance for God's people. We mentioned before that the earthly tabernacle was a shadow of the Heavenly tabernacle. In the Bible a type is used to foreshadow the antitype. The type may be a person an event or an institution. When Jesus died on the cross his sacrificial death was the antitype of all the types that was performed in the courtyard, in other words the sacrifices of all those animals was merely foreshadowing the death of Jesus. Hebrews 10:4 tell us that it is not possible for the blood of animals to take away sins. Countless animals were slaughtered year after year for thousands of years before the real lamb came; yet the death of animals cannot remove one stain of sin. God was deeply impressing on our minds the high price of sin and yet this invaluable lesson was not understood and appreciated by the masses of society then and now. Hebrews 9:26–28 states that Christ died once to bear the sins of many. His sacrifice on the cross once was enough to bear our sins, it is therefore not necessary to sacrifice him and kill him again and again in our worship.

It is difficult for the human mind to grasp all that happened at Calvary. The events of Calvary are so amazing that they should be studied over and over by everyone. On Calvary Jesus exchanged places with us; we should therefore appreciate Calvary to our fullest extent. In Matthew 27 we read of the crucifixion of Jesus, here in AD 31 Jesus is nailed on a wooden cross between two thieves and he cries out "MY God My God why hast thou forsaken me;" an exact quotation made by David a thousand years before in the Messianic Psalm 22. He is literally quoting the prophecy to his killers and they do not see it. At the end of this horrendous ordeal, Jesus cried out with a loud voice "It is finished" and he died. It was the hour of the evening sacrifice and the priest was officiating in the temple in Jerusalem, only the High Priest was allowed to lift the veil and enter the Most Holy Place where God himself dwells; he was getting ready to slay the lamb, which represents Jesus Christ; suddenly by unseen hands, the veil of the temple between the two apartments the holy and most holy place was torn asunder exposing the most Holy Place signifying an official end to the earthly sanctuary services. The knife drops from the priest hands and the lamb escapes because Jesus the perfect lamb had just completed the great sacrificial part of the plan of redemption at Calvary. The earthly sacrifices that began with Abel in Geneses 4:4 up to the day of Christ's death on Calvary all pointed to Jesus, the Lamb of God slain from the foundation of the world, in other words this plan of redemption was made way back in the corridors of time before the existence of man on this planet. God had already made a plan of redemption in the event man sinned. Here at Calvary, the success of the plan was a reality. Jesus was now our High Priest and the only way to the father. Hebrews 9:12 states "neither by the blood of goats and calves but by his own blood he entered in once into the holy place having obtained eternal redemption for us.

The sacrificial system foreshadowed Jesus death on the cross. The sacrificial system did not begin with the Jews; it was instituted as soon as man sinned in the Garden of Eden. God instructed Cain and Abel to slay a lamb, and offer up the blood. Abel followed God's instructions explicitly but Cain did what he pleased hoping that God would be pleased with it. This sacrificial system was also foreshadowing the plan of salvation.

They all pointed to Jesus the real sacrifice. The Tabernacle services brought a clearer understanding of the plan of salvation. These services were temporary and symbolic and they played a very important role in understanding how God deals with the sin problem. The act of killing an animal to make sacrifice for sin should be so repulsive that the sinner should hate sin but this was not often the case.

Jesus death on the cross put an end to the earthly tabernacle services. Since the Jewish nation on a whole did not accept the messiah they continued the services until the physical temple was destroyed by the Romans in AD 70. The earthly tabernacle services had met their fulfillment in Jesus; it was Jesus who instructed Moses to build the earthly sanctuary. These sacrifices pointed to Jesus. After his crucifixion, the shedding of animal blood was over, the real sacrifice was here. Services in the earthly tabernacle became meaningless after Jesus death. With the termination of the earthly sanctuary services the ceremonial law ended. This law contained the various burnt offerings, peace offerings, ceremonial Sabbaths e.g. the feast of unleavened bread (Leviticus 23:6–8), the Pentecostal Sabbath (Leviticus 23: 15–21), the blowing of the trumpets, the day of atonement, the feast of the tabernacles (Lev 23:34–43) and the octave of feast of the tabernacles. In the new testament church the early converts were Jews, the apostles were mainly Jewish and so was the apostle Paul many of these new converts came into the church and wanted to continue with these ceremonial Sabbaths and so Paul in Colossians 2:16 rightly warned the Christian believers that these ceremonial feasts and special Sabbaths were met their fulfillment in the real thing, the death of Christ on Calvary. Some confuse this text and say that this includes the Sabbath of the ten commandments, which was established at creation. No, the ten commandments are part of the moral law of God, which is contained in the Ark of the Covenant in the second apartment of the sanctuary also the Holy of hollies. The great original commandment is in the Heavenly sanctuary. God copied it for Moses on Mt. Sinai but it existed long before Mt. Sinai.

There are some who teach that when Jesus died the plan of salvation was over. This is not consistent with a full understanding of the sanctuary services. When Jesus died the sacrificial aspect of the plan of salvation was full and complete. God has a more detailed and elaborate plan. You cannot say once the lamb was killed in the outer court that the sanctuary service was complete, then you would not be following God's plan. After the sacrifice in the outer court the priest had a lot of work to do. Similarly after Christ's' death on Calvary the plan of redemption continued with Christ's high priestly ministry in the Heavenly sanctuary. 1Cor 15:17–18 says "if Christ is not raised, your faith is in vain and you are yet in your sins," his death alone is only part of the redemption plan. His resurrection and high priestly ministry in Heaven is a very significant part of the plan of salvation. In Psalms 77:13 we read that God's way is in the sanctuary.

Let us review the process of worship in the earthly sanctuary and see how it reflects the order of the Heavenly sanctuary.

God instructed Moses to build him an earthly sanctuary, which was a replica of the Heavenly sanctuary. God who is infinite and transcends space and time has condescended to place himself in a sanctuary such that he can communicate with us. No human being can fully grasp this, but there are many lessons that he wants to learn from the sanctuary services. This sanctuary was a living, visible illustration of God's plan of Salvation for all mankind, from Adam to the last man on Planet Earth. Jesus death on Calvary is D-day, it is the great event in history that the service in the outer court represented. When Jesus gave up his life on the cross of Calvary this was the ultimate sacrifice, the creator of this universe died to save his lost creation. All nature moaned that day while most of humanity had no interest in this great drama.

When an individual sin, a lamb was brought to the sanctuary, the sinner places his hand over the lambs head, the sinner confesses his sins; the sinner kills the lamb himself, the lamb is slain in the courtyard and offered on the altar of burnt offering, the death of lamb alone, symbolic of Jesus death on the cross, did not bring forgiveness of sins; forgiveness never is given at the outer court. The sanctuary service did not end with the death of the animal. The sanctuary service continued with the priest taking the blood of the slain lamb to the holy place. So daily the priest took the blood of the animals into the holy place, in some cases when blood was not used the priest ate the meat of the sacrificed animal. This is the process of the atonement for sins. The priest could not enter the sanctuary with shoes on their feet (Exodus 30:19.20). They had to wash hands and feet and purify themselves before approaching the presence of God. Morning and evening the priest takes the blood into the holy place and sprinkles the blood of the lamb on the altar of burnt offering near the veil that separated holy and most holy place. This indicates that the sin is removed from the sinner to the lamb and now it is transferred to the sanctuary via the blood of the lamb. This removal of sins is removed from the sinner every day is called the daily. This work of sacrifice was performed daily until the appointed day the tenth day of the seventh month called the Day of Atonement. The purpose of the daily sacrifices was to allow the sinner to admit that they had transgressed God's law and that they had faith that the Messiah would come and take away their sins. Only a few priests could enter the holy place daily and only the high priest could enter the most holy place yearly.

The sins of the people were transferred to the holy place, this is the daily; the sins of the people accumulated there all year and once a year, the yearly or the day of atonement Yom Kippur, a special service was held so that the sins were removed from the sanctuary. The sanctuary had to be cleansed from the daily sins of the people that had accumulated there all year. On this most solemn day the congregation refrained from work and searched their souls. The earthly sanctuary had earthly priests who officiated according to the old ceremonial system.

Once a year, on Yom Kipper, this most solemn day, the high priest selected 2 goats and brought them to the sanctuary. Lots were cast, one lot for the Lord's goat and the other the scapegoat. The Lord's goat is slain as the sin offering and the blood is carried into the most holy place. In the most holy place is the most sacred piece of furniture, the mercy seat covering the Ark of the Covenant. In the Ark of the Covenant is the *unchangeable* law of God. In the most holy place God makes his will known to the high priest. Here Christ pleads his blood for sinners. Justice and mercy meet. The priest takes the blood on the Lord's goat on this the most holy day of the year, the Day of Atonement, and sprinkles the blood on and in front the mercy seat. This is the only day of the year that the priest is permitted to enter the Most Holy Place. The sanctuary is therefore cleansed from the daily sins of the people. When this atonement process is complete, the priest making atonement for the sanctuary and the sins of the people, then places the sins on the head of the scapegoat. Then a fit man takes the scapegoat into the wilderness to perish, symbolizing that the sins of the people have been forgiven and removed from the people of Israel. The banishment of this goat into the wilderness is symbolic for the removal of sin from the universe thus ending the great controversy between God and Satan.

Let us study the lesson God is revealing to us by compare the earthly and the Heavenly sanctuary, when Jesus died on the cross, he represented the lamb slain in the courtyard, that was the sacrificial part of his ministry, when he ascended to Heaven he entered the second part of his ministry the holy place. The writer to the Hebrews gave us a profound understanding of the sanctuary services and its significance. The writer in Hebrews 3:1 declares that Jesus is our High Priest. In Hebrews 4:14 we are told that our high priest Jesus has gone to Heaven and has taken up his rightful position at the right hand of the father and verse 16 declares that we can come boldly to the throne of grace that we can obtain mercy and grace. In Hebrews 7:27 and 28 we learn that Jesus, our high priest, do not have to sacrifice animals as the earthly high priests did first for their own sin then for the sins of the people. Jesus our Heavenly high priest did it once at Calvary when he offered up himself and God the father took an oath and made Jesus our high priest forevermore. Hebrews 8:1 and 2 "Now of the things which have been spoken this is the sum; we have such an high priest, who is set on the right hand of the throne of the Majesty in the Heavens; A minister of the sanctuary, and of the true tabernacle, which the Lord pitched, and not man". Clearly the passage states that Jesus is ministering in the Heavenly sanctuary. Hebrews 9:24 states "for Christ is not entered into the holy places made with hands, which are the figures of the true; but into Heaven itself, now to appear in the presence of God for us." Here he is interceding for us, when we accept him as our personal savior he pleads his blood for us and we are forgiven. The holy place represents his work of intercession for us. This is the good news of the gospel. The angel told Daniel in Daniel 8:11 that the place of the sanctuary has been cast down by the little horn power that would cast truth to the ground and prosper in the process.

Jesus is currently ministering in the Most Holy Place of the heavenly sanctuary. Christ ascended in AD 31. Hebrews was written AD 65. About AD 95 John wrote the Revelation. In Rev 1:12 and 13 the apostle John saw Jesus in the holy place of the Heavenly sanctuary. When Jesus ascended to Heaven, he began his intercessory work for sinners in the holy place. In Revelation 1:12 John sees seven golden candlesticks which is in the holy place of the sanctuary and in the midst of the candlesticks, he sees one like the son of man. We know that the seven golden candlesticks are located in the holy place; therefore Jesus is walking in the holy place, the first apartment of the sanctuary.

Compare with the earthly sanctuary we find in the first compartment or behind the first curtain of the sanctuary called the Holy Place, we find the seven branched candlestick and the table of shewbread. Each piece of furniture has its location and function in the sanctuary services (Read Hebrews 9:1–7). In the service of the earthly sanctuary after the Levites had set up the tent, and arranged the furniture in the correct places the priest would minister in the holy place. Only the High Priest alone can go behind the second curtain once a year (see Heb 9:7), and in verse 8 we learn that Jesus work as High Priest in the Heavenly sanctuary could not begin while the work in the holy place of the earthy sanctuary was taking place. There was no salvation in the services of the earthly sanctuary, it was temporary it was pointing to the real service, Jesus the redeemer and his ministration in the Heavenly sanctuary not made by hands. The shedding of his blood was the perfect sacrifice that the blood of the sacrificial animals pointed to. Jesus did not continue work in the earthly sanctuary it was rendered null and void at his death on Calvary AD31. When Jesus the Passover lamb was sacrificed on Calvary, in the temple in Jerusalem the priest was about to slay a lamb when a mighty earthquake occurred and the lamb escaped. The inner veil of the temple was torn by an unseen hand ending the purpose of the earthly tabernacle and all of its services and the religious feasts all pointed to this great event at Calvary. Shortly After his sacrifice on Calvary Hebrews 9: 24 indicates that Jesus transitioned from the sacrificial lamb to the role of our High Priest entered into the true sanctuary in Heaven appearing before the father for us.

In Rev. 11:19 John sees the ark of the testament in the temple in Heaven. This furniture is located in the Holy of Holies or the Most Holy Place. The scene changes and Jesus is now in the Most Holy Place. Let's briefly review the services in the Most Holy Place of the earthly sanctuary.

Once a year in the Earthly sanctuary, a special work was done in the Most Holy Place that work involved the cleansing of sin from the holy place and it was called the yearly. The sinner had to wait once a year for the forgiveness of sins, every day of the year the altar of burnt offering was defiled with the blood that represented the confessed sins. Once a year the high priest went into the second apartment of the sanctuary, the Most Holy Place or the Holy of Holies to cleanse both the sinner and the sanctuary, this is the Day of Atonement, the tenth day of the seventh month; all Israel searched their soul. The high priest had a work of preparation to do before this solemn service, he entered into the presence of God and he had to confess his sins and the sins of the people. Sin is then transferred from the sinner to the sanctuary. The cleansing of the sanctuary required two goats and on the Day of Atonement the high priest chose two goats (Leviticus 15:5). The high priest cast lots. One goat was chosen for the Lord and the other was the scapegoat (Leviticus 1:8). The high priest killed the goat on which the Lord lot fell. The high priest sprinkled the blood of the slain goat (the Lord's goat) on the mercy set which is the cover of the ark containing the Ten Commandments, God's eternal moral law. This was only permitted on one day of the year; the blood of the Lord's goat was sprinkled on the mercy seat located in the Most Holy Place, representing Jesus' sacrifice for sin. The Lord takes responsibility for the sins of his people. The blood of the animal could not take away sins, these services merely pointed to the great sin bearer, Jesus. These symbols all represent the ministry of Jesus (see Heb 10:1, 2, 4, and Matt 26:28). When the high priest came out of the Most Holy Place, he removed the sins accumulated in the holy place all year. The sins removed are confessed over the head of the goat and he is sent away in the wilderness (Lev.16: 20 and 21). The sanctuary was now cleansed (Lev16: 16 and 19). The scape goat represent Satan, he is the author of sin and he is ultimately responsible for sin and he will be banished here in the wilderness of this barren earth by a chain of circumstances with no one to tempt for 1000 years. He and his wicked angels will eventually die in a lake of fire.

The live goat or scapegoat is not slain, he is ultimately responsible for sin and the sins of the people are confessed over his head, representing Satan as ultimately responsible for sins. In order to remove the sins of the people from the sanctuary, a work of judgment was needed; this is the Day of Atonement, the most holy day of the year (Yom Kippur) when the sins of the people were removed and they were reconciled or atoned (at-one-ment) with God. On this day both the sanctuary and people were cleansed. Yom Kippur is symbolic of Judgment day. It was a day of solemn prayer and atonement for sins. Whosoever did not confess their sins on the Day of Atonement they were cut-off from the people (Lev 23:29). Jesus death on Calvary ended the earthly sanctuary and its services including Yom Kippur but the more serious reality is the sanctuary services are now going on in Heaven and we now live in the antitypical day of atonement when we should search our hearts and make sure they are right with God and was done on the typical day of atonement, Yom Kippur. Atonement with God is only possible through the shed blood of the lamb, Christ Jesus.

The cleansing of the sanctuary or the Day of Atonement foreshadows the removal of sin from the Heavenly sanctuary. When Jesus is finished with his work in the Most Holy Place of the Heavenly sanctuary, and every case is decided on, the pronouncement will be made he that is holy let him be holy still and he that is filthy let him be filthy still. Jesus our High Priest, because of His precious blood shed on Calvary cleanses the Heavenly sanctuary of all the sins of the people of all ages. These sins will be placed on Satan, and he will eventually bear the penalty for our sins if we are saved.

Once Jesus takes off these priestly robes, he is no longer interceding for sinners; it is over. Sinful man now stands before a righteous God without a mediator. Jesus is getting ready to return as conquering king no longer a lamb or a priest. There is a time for everything and this is a very serious time. This is the time of trouble that Daniel 12:1 speaks about that never was since there was a nation; make sure that your sins have been taken care of by Jesus before He closes his high priestly ministry for us. At this point Jesus is ready to step into his role as returning conquering King of Kings and Lord of Lords. He is Michael the archangel of Daniel 12:1 who is coming to deliver his saints from Planet Earth. Think back to what we discussed in Daniel 7 and 8, Daniel is told unto 2300 days/years then shall the sanctuary be cleansed. It could only be referring to the cleansing of the Heavenly sanctuary where the work of judgment is taking place. The 2300 years ended in 1844 and the Day of Atonement fell on 10/22/1844. Since the earthly sanctuary was no longer in existence in 1844, the only other sanctuary is the Heavenly sanctuary and the antitypical Day of Atonement began in the Heavenly sanctuary on 10/22/1844. This is the pre-advent judgment that we studied in Daniel. It is the same judgment we read about in Rev 14:6, Rev 20:12 that tells that the name of every person who has ever lived is recorded in the books of Heaven. Not only are our names in the books of Heaven but in Matthew 12:36–37 Jesus says "That every idle word that men shall speak, they shall give an account thereof in the day of Judgment. For by thy words thou shall be justified, and by thy words thou shall be condemned." Heaven keeps accurate records but Jesus is faithful and just to forgive all of our confessed sins and cleanse us from all unrighteousness. In Daniel 7:10 we read the judgment was set and the books were opened. We are saved by grace but we are judged by our works good or bad that is written in those books (See James 2:10–12). Our works show forth our faith. Our works reflect our choice in life. Did we choose to do the will of God? Jesus words in Matt 7:21 the only ones entering Heaven are those who do the will of the father. Rev 3:5 tells us that Christ confesses these names before the father. Many will come in that day calling Lord, Lord and prophesying about their great works that they have done on earth and the huge churches that they have pastored, the bestselling books they have written, the great radio and TV programs, and the millions of people they have preached to all over the world, but great works cannot save anyone; they are the result of a saved life. Jesus in Rev 22:12, 13 says "Behold I come quickly; and my reward is with me to give every man according as his work shall be. I am the alpha and the omega the beginning and the end the first and the last." In order for Jesus to give his rewards, the judgment would have to convene prior to his return. The angel of Revelation 14:7 warns us "Fear God and give glory to him for the hour of his judgment _is_ come." Judgment began in the Heavenly courts in 1844, at the end of the 2300-year prophecy. Connecting the dots this coincides with the time period of the final church period of Laodicea mentioned in the book of Revelation. Laodicea means the Judging of the people. John 5:22 states "that the father judges no man, but has committed all judgment to his son."

The Bible teaches that those who do not accept Jesus and confess their sins, their names will be blotted out from the book of life. An example is the story of King Saul and King David. The sins of David seem more heinous than Saul. David coveted another man's wife (breaking the tenth commandment, he then committed adultery with her (7th commandment), then he bore false witness against the woman's husband and had him killed breaking the 10 and 6th commandment. When the prophet Nathan revealed David's sin to him, David was truly sorry and deeply repented and wrote Psalms 51 and the Lord in mercy forgave sin but King Saul did not confess his sins and so he died in his sins.

Each one of us has a case that is being tried in the courts of Heaven. Our prosecuting attorney is Satan and he has thousands of years of experience on us, and he knows just how to get us to sin and he knows the sins that we have committed. He makes the charge before the court that we are guilty and deserves to be in hell. When our adversary that old devil accuses us, Jesus, our lawyer and public defender will say they have confessed their sins and have accepted my sacrifice of Calvary on their behalf therefore they are vindicated. 1 John 2:1 states "My little children, these things I write unto you that ye sin not. And if any man sin, we have an advocate with the father, Jesus Christ the righteous." Jesus is our High Priest and advocate in the courts of Heaven. He is quite familiar with this court and because of his sinless life and his atoning sacrifice for our sins he is qualified to be our advocate in the Heavenly courts. If we come clean, admit to our shortcomings, confess all our sins, rely wholly on Jesus and throw ourselves on the mercy of the court we cannot lose our case because he is faithful and just to forgive us of all our sins and cleanse us from all unrighteousness. Jesus, our heavenly advocate, has the nail prints on his hands and feet to show the price he paid for our redemption. When Satan accuses us Jesus shows the nail prints in his palm and say forgiven. He earned that right at Calvary. As much as Satan tries to hide this reality, Jesus is performing a most important work in the Heavenly sanctuary today.

The sanctuary represents the three phases of Christ ministry 1. His sacrificial work on the cross, (2) his mediatory or intercessory work in the holy place (Revelation 8:3 and 4, Revelation: 11:19 and Revelation 5: 8, and (3)the final work of Judgment in the Most Holy Place, completing the cleansing of the Heavenly sanctuary. The Heavenly sanctuary reveals to all beings in the entire universe that God deals with sin in an open and fair way. Sin began in Heaven and God will deal with it in the Heavenly sanctuary. Now that we have studied the Sanctuary we can now better understand the judgment that is taking place in the Heavenly sanctuary.

The Judgment

Satan has obscured the judgment that is taking place now and as a result the Christian Church does not have a clear concept of the judgment. God's judgment is one of the most important but most neglected and misunderstood subject in the Bible and therefore we should study it carefully. In the model of the Earthly sanctuary the Day of Atonement was associated with the work of judgment. The same holds true for the Heavenly sanctuary. The angel Gabriel introduces the topic of the judgment and the Heavenly sanctuary to Daniel in Daniel 8:14. The name Daniel means God is my judge. Daniel is given the time of the start of the Heavenly judgment. The angel said to Daniel "Unto 2300 days (years) then shall the sanctuary be cleansed". We will repeat and enlarge on what we have studied before. Daniel is concerned and did not understand the vision of the 2300 days so the angel Gabriel who stands in the presence of God (Luke 1:19) was sent to help Daniel understand this vision. Gabriel told him in Daniel 8:17 that this vision will extend to the time of the end and he further assures Daniel in verse 26 that this vision is true. The angel Gabriel gives Daniel the answer in chapter 9:25 and 26. Here Gabriel tells Daniel that the starting point for seventieth week and the 2300-day prophecy is the time when the decree is given to restore and rebuild Jerusalem.

The seventy weeks prophecy

Daniel 9:24: The seventy weeks or 490 years were determined or cut off from the 2300 years. The angel Gabriel tells Daniel that the seventy weeks or 490 years were specifically cut off for the Jewish people. The angel told Daniel what would happen during the 70-weeks/490 years and what will take place during the 2300 years. During the 490 years time prophecy God gave the Jews this specific time period to make an end of sins, to reign in everlasting righteousness and to seal up the vision and the prophecy and to anoint the most Holy, Jesus Christ. The Jews, God's chosen people to spread the truth to a lost and dying world, had a most solemn responsibility to anoint the Most Holy that is to prepare the world for the first coming of Jesus Christ. This was the role for which they were chosen as God's people. Daniel was shown in Daniel 7:24/25 that this time period started in 457 BC add 2300 years to that it takes us to 1844 AD This is a very important date in history; this is the start of the great Day of Atonement that is symbolized as the Day of Atonement or the yearly (Yom Kippur) in the earthly sanctuary. Daniel is shown that the cleansing of the Heavenly sanctuary takes place at this time. This is the meaning of the vision of Daniel 8:14 "Unto 2300 years then shall the sanctuary be cleansed." This sanctuary is the Heavenly sanctuary. There are 2 sanctuaries mentioned in the Bible the Heavenly sanctuary and the earthly sanctuary. Moses was told to build the earthly sanctuary like the model of the Heavenly shown to him in the mountain. There were 3 earthly sanctuaries mentioned in the Bible the first was the portable sanctuary or tabernacle built by Moses in the wilderness, the second was the permanent one built by Solomon and destroyed by Nebuchadnezzar, the 3rd was the post exile sanctuary built by Ezra and later refurbished by Herod the great. Titus and the Roman army destroyed the physical structure of the earthly sanctuary in AD 70. The services in the earthly sanctuary lost their significance in AD31 when Christ was crucified. The angel Gabriel says in Daniel 9:27 the death of the Messiah will cause the sacrifice and ablation to cease. When Jesus died on the cross and he uttered the words "It is finished", the veil of the temple separating the Holy from the Most Holy Place was torn asunder by an unseen hand. The Most Holy Place of the Earthly Sanctuary was no longer sacred. As the priest was about to sacrifice the Lamb that was brought to the sanctuary representing Christ, the lamb escaped because the true lamb of God had given his life on Calvary thus causing the sacrifices and ablation to cease bringing the sacrificial system to an end. They lost their significance because the true sacrifice to which all of these sacrifices pointed to had arrived in the reality of Jesus Christ. There was no more purpose for the earthly sanctuary and the Levitical priesthood designed to operate until the death of the Messiah came to an end and Christ our High Priest move the operation to the Heavenly sanctuary (Hebrews 9:11). Therefore the prophecy given to Daniel unto 2300 prophetic days is referring to the only sanctuary in operation now and that is the Heavenly Sanctuary. The earthly sanctuary and its services were merely shadows of Heavenly realities. Substance arrived and shadows disappeared. The Jewish Nation did not recognize the messiah and continued with the sacrificial services until the temple was destroyed in AD70 when the temple was totally destroyed by the Romans.

These two time prophecies revealed that in the midst of 70th week the Messiah was crucified and at the end of the 2300-day/year prophecy the sanctuary would be cleansed. We accept that Jesus was crucified at sixty nine and a half weeks (in AD 27) and the seventieth week ended in AD 34. How about the longer time prophecy which Daniel was shown as extending to the end of time? When would the cleansing of the sanctuary begin? Daniel was shown that at the end of the 2300 years in 1844 that the cleansing of the sanctuary or the pre-advent judgment began. Using the earthly sanctuary model on the Day of Atonement the High Priest went into the Most Holy Place and the sanctuary was cleansed from the sins of the people that had accumulated there all year. This earthly model was a symbol of the true Day of Atonement in the Heavenly sanctuary. Therefore the work of Jesus in the Heavenly sanctuary since 1844 is the reality symbolized by the earthly Day of Atonement. In 1844 Jesus Christ went into the Most Holy Place of the Heavenly Sanctuary and the cleansing of sins that have accumulated there since Adam began. This is the investigate judgment being carried out by Jesus our High Priest. In this phase of the judgment the books of Heaven are reviewed (see Revelation 3:5, Revelation 20:12, and Malachi 3:16). The judgment means good news for God's people. Since 1844 we have been living in the time of Heavenly atonement and our Heavenly High Priest has been pleading his shed blood for our sins. This is how sinful human beings can pass the judgment bar of God. When we confess our sins, ask for forgiveness and turn from our sins; Christ righteousness is applied to us by faith. We put our sinful unworthy lives in the hands of our redeemer. Jesus gets us through the judgment but he has a process. The earthly sanctuary service is a pictorial model of the process.

Jesus death spelled the end of the earthly process. The Bible teaches that the only way to atone for sins is through the blood of Jesus. The blood of Jesus shed at Calvary is the supreme sacrifice of all ages. It is this blood that Jesus presents on the mercy seat in the Most Holy Place of the Heavenly sanctuary. In the mercy seat is God's unchangeable law. However there is mercy for the repentant sinner who breaks God's law. This judgment process is a solemn process that every Bible believing Christian should be aware of and it is mind boggling that this all-important subject matter is not taught in the churches of Christendom today.

God's people need to know these biblical truths that Satan has hidden. The result of this judgment determines the saved from the lost. The records of Heaven will be reviewed (see Revelation 20:12) and every man's character will come up in judgment and a decision will be made before Jesus returns with his reward to give everyman according to his work (2 Corinthians 5:10). We are judged by our works but saved by our faith in Jesus; a faith that is manifested by good works. Every person who has ever lived on Planet Earth will be judged. Jesus is presiding over this pre-advent judgment now. On the earthly Day of Atonement the people of God should be searching their hearts and preparing their souls for this solemn event and making sure that all their sins were confessed so they could be forgiven. Similarly we are living in the time of the Heavenly judgment and we should be doing the same thing. The angel Gabriel told Daniel in the prophecy that the Little Horn Power would cast down the place of the sanctuary and so today Satan has obscured this sanctuary biblical doctrine in the Christian churches today.

Revelation 22:12 says "behold I come quickly and my reward is with me to give every man according as his work shall be." This is the final result of the work of the judgment. This judgment is sound Bible teaching and not a man made invention. The concept of God's judgment is all over the Bible, it's inescapable yet so many do not understand it.

Every human being will face God's judgment. Hebrews 9:27 states that it is appointed unto man once to die and after death the judgment. Ecclesiastes 12:14 states "for God shall bring every work into judgment, with every secret thing, whether it be good, or whether it be evil." In 1Peter 4:17, the Apostle Peter writes, "For the time has come for judgment to begin at the house of God; and if it begins with us first, what will be the end of those who do not obey the gospel of God?" The question can be asked why does God who knows everything needs an investigative judgment pre-advent judgment prior to his second coming. God is a God of order, a righteous judge who keeps accurate records. It should not come as a surprise that he has a judicial process. God is very precise. Satan and his angels have accused God before the entire universe of being unjust and unfair and his law is arbitrary. In the great controversy between good and evil, Satan has rebelled against God and his law and has challenged the character of God before the Heavenly beings and the entire universe. Since 1844 the judgment has begun and at the end of it the results will show that God is just and fair. He will have a remnant that have honored his law and they will be a living testimony that God is just and fair. The record will be there to be seen by the entire universe including the saints and the angels as to why his judgments are correct and just and fair. God is a God of order; He is a righteous, mighty, and a just judge and he has a judicial process that he follows to deal with the eradication of sin. It is called the pre-advent judgment taking place in the Heavenly sanctuary. During this phase of the judgment every soul who has lived from Adam to the last person to be judged will be judged; every secret sin will be brought to light so that sin could be eradicated. Every injustice will be dealt with; many times we are unhappy with justice in this world but a righteous God now sits in judgment and one day judgment day is coming for those who have sinned against God's law. No one is going to get away with sin. During this phase of the judgment the decision next to each name will be made, saved or lost. This has to be done before the 2nd advent of Christ who states "Behold I come quickly and my reward is with me to give every man according to his work." In this first phase of the judgment, God investigates what we have done and he pronounces judgment. The concept that God investigates sin prior to judgment is well documented throughout scripture. Take the example of Adam and Eve, God knew what they had done; yet he investigated before he punished. In Genesis 3: 9–13 God asked Adam "where art thou? Who told you that you were naked? What is it that you have done?' Similarly with Sodom and Gomorrah, God came down and investigated before making his final judgment on Sodom and Gomorrah. In Genesis 18:25 Abraham recognizes God as the righteous judge of all the earth. Did an omniscient God not know every detail about these events? Similarly in the parable of the wedding Banquet in Matthew 22 Jesus tells a parable of the king inspecting the wedding clothes of the guests prior to the banquet and there was one guest who chose to wear his own garment instead of the robe of righteousness provided by King Jesus. The king decided or judged that this man was unfit to attend the banquet and cast him into darkness or with the unsaved where there will be weeping and gnashing of teeth. God who determines who can attend the banquet wants us to develop a Christ like character so that we can be fit to attend the Heavenly banquet. God will destroy sin from this planet and the judgment process is the process that he has established to accomplish this. Psalms 96:13 states "For the Lord cometh to judge the world with righteousness, and the people with his truth. God has a standard of righteousness and truth laid out for us in the Bible. God wants us to know his truth and establish a right relationship with him so that by his grace we will be covered with his robe of righteousness. The Bible is far from silent on the judgment that is taking place now.

The prophet Daniel is shown that this judgment began shortly after the 1260 years of Papal domination and this judgment is going to last until just before the second coming of Jesus to set up his eternal kingdom. The deceiver of this world Satan has succeeded in masking one of the most important events going on in Heaven now and that is the judgment. The reality of this judgment is revealed throughout the Bible. The Bible has given us ample warning of God's judgment In Revelation 20:12 "And I saw the dead small and great stand before God; and the books were opened and another book was opened which is the book of life and the dead were judged out of those things that were written in those books according to their works." Malachi 3:16 tells us of a book of remembrance is kept for them that reverence the Lord and speak about his name. God really wants to know about the ongoing judgment. It is to Satan's advantage to keep the judgment a secret but the Bible is not silent on this important event. This is a biblical doctrine and one that the Lord wants to know about.

Revelation 14:6 "fear God and give glory to him for the hour of his judgment is come."

Acts 17:31 states "that God hath appointed a day in which he would judge the world in righteousness by that man whom he hath ordained whereof he hath given assurance unto all men, in that he hath raised him from the dead." While living in the first century Paul refers to the judgment as a future event.

Matthew 25:31–33 clearly tells us of a judgment process when Jesus separates the saved from the lost, the saved to eternal life and the lost to everlasting punishment.

This Heavenly judgment process is best described in the book of Daniel. Daniel 7:9 and 10 tell us that the judgment is set and the books are opened. Here Daniel describes the pre-advent Heavenly judgment scene taking place in the Most Holy Place of the Heavenly sanctuary. Daniel is shown the convening of the Heavenly judgment court where thrones were set up and God the father, the Ancient of Days sat down. No one has seen God so symbolically Daniel sees this scene in vision and he writes down the event as humanly possible in words we can understand. He sees God the father in garment as white as snow. In this judgment scene thousand thousands ministered unto him and ten thousand times ten thousand stood before him and the books were opened. Our sovereign God is conducting an open, just investigative judgment in front of all of Heaven and the entire universe. Satan has accused God before the universe of being unfair and has an arbitrary law. God is going to show to the entire universe his decisions in the judgment and why he is fair and just. In the Supreme Court of the United States the judges swear to uphold the constitution. The God of the universe has a law in the Ark of the Covenant and our sovereign God will uphold his law. In the earthly tabernacle the law was placed in the Most Holy Place in the Ark of the Covenant this was a copy of the great original in the Holy of Holies in the Heavenly sanctuary. In the earthly sanctuary the children of Israel could not go into the Most Holy place and change the commandments for any reason. When they sinned against the Law of God, they repented and ask for forgiveness the law was not changed to accommodate sin. Similarly in the Heavenly Sanctuary God original Law stands in the Ark of the Covenant. God does not change his law to accommodate our sins. When we sin against any commandment in that law we have to repent, seek forgiveness and turn away from our sins and our High Priest pleads our case before the righteous judge of the universe.

Daniel 7:11 tells us that as a result of the findings during the judgment the little horn power will lose and judgment will be pronounced against this power.

Daniel 12: 2 states the result of the judgment many that are sleeping (that is the definition of death) in the dust of the earth shall awake, some to everlasting life and some to shame and everlasting contempt.

Revelation 22:12 and behold, I come quickly, and my reward is with me to give every man according as his work shall be. It is pretty obvious from this text that before Christ second coming, a pre-advent investigation and a decision must have been made to determine the reward and who gets it.

John 5:22 "For the father judges no man but hath committed all judgment to the son."

Hebrews 9:27 "For it is appointed for men once to die, but after this the judgment."

2 Corinthians 5:10 "For we must all appear before the judgment seat of Christ."

Matt 12:36 "But I say unto you that every idle word that men shall speak they shall give an account in the Day of Judgment."

Acts 10:42 "And he commanded us to preach unto the people, and to testify that it is he which was ordained of God to be judge of quick and dead."

Revelation 22:12 "And behold I come quickly and my reward is with me to give every man according as his work shall be."

Job 34:10 and 11 "Therefore hearken unto me, ye men of understanding: far be it from me God, that he should do wickedness; and from the Almighty, that he should commit iniquity. For the work of a man shall he render unto him, and cause every man to find according to his ways."

Jeremiah 17:10 "I the Lord search the heart, I try the reins, even to give every man according to his ways, and according to the fruit of his doings."

Revelation 2:23 "And I will kill her children with death; and all the churches shall know that I am he which searches the reins and hearts: and I will give every one of you according to your works."

Job 15:5 and 6 "For thy mouth uttereth thine iniquity, and thou choosest the tongue of the crafty. Thine own mouth condemneth thee, and not I: yea, thine own lips testify against thee."

Even our own words and actions are judged. For out of the abundance of the heart the mouth speaks.

The Bible reveals that judgment is taking place in the Heavenly sanctuary and the righteous judge of the universe will dispense judgment and everyman will give an account of their sinful deeds, the controversy between good and evil will be resolved and the character of God throughout the universe will be vindicated.

Revelation 20:4 and 5 in the first resurrection, the saints go to their reward in Heaven and live and reign with Christ for a thousand years. Blessed is he that hath a part in the first resurrection. The wicked dead live not again until the thousand years were finished. The Bible teaches here that the wicked are dead during this thousand years and verse five they will be resurrected at the end of the thousand years to face their reward. The concept of an eternal hell burning somewhere is not biblical it is a misunderstanding of the biblical references. When a wicked person dies and they are determined lost in the pre-advent judgment process they do not come up in the first resurrection as John describes they are awakened at the end of the thousand years or the 2nd resurrection and they are judged from what is recorded in those books and they will be consumed by the fires of the final death. According to this text in Revelation the wicked are not now in an eternal burning hell as is taught in many churches today. Revelation 19:5 states but the rest of the dead or those who are judged to be lost will not rise in the first resurrection to eternal life but will not live again until the thousand years are finished, then they will be raised to face the second death into the lake of fire. These are very solemn circumstances. We want to be in the first resurrection.

John describes a great white throne judgment in Rev 20:12 "And I saw the dead small and great stand before God and the book was opened which is the book of life and the dead were judged out of those things which were written in the books, according to their works, in this phase of the judgment the wicked will understand why they were lost." As we stand before a righteous God whose judgments are infallible every tongue will be silenced, there will be no excuses. Justice would have been served equally on everyone and only those who are covered by the blood of Jesus will receive mercy and forgiveness of their sins. In the Most Holy Place of the Heavenly sanctuary, where the work of judgment is going on, is located the mercy seat. God's judgment is a mixture of justice and mercy. There is mercy for the repentant sinner and justice for the rebellious sinner.

The writer to the Hebrews describes the Heavenly sanctuary. John the Revelator was also shown the Heavenly Sanctuary. So when did Jesus begin this phase of his final ministry, the work of Judgment, which is the time of the cleansing of the sanctuary. Rev 11:19 states "that the temple of God was opened in Heaven and there was seen in his temple the ark of his testament." In the ark is contained the 10 commandments located in the second apartment of the sanctuary. A replica of the same Ten Commandments was placed in the earthly sanctuary. God instructed Moses to make the earthly sanctuary just like the Heavenly sanctuary. When Christ completes this final phase of his Heavenly ministry in the Holy of Holies he will declare as stated in Rev 22:11 and 12 "he that is filthy let him be filthy still, he that is righteous let him be righteous still he that is holy let him be holy still." In the end Christ will appear without sin unto salvation and save his waiting church. The realities of the Sanctuary and the Judgment are two topics that need serious study because of their significance to Christ believers. I hope I have opened your appetite for a deeper study of the sanctuary and the judgment. There is a lot more to study but we need to move on to Daniel 10.

Chapter Ten

DANIEL 10

Verse 1. In the 3rd year of King Cyrus of Persia 536/535 BC Daniel whose Babylonian name was Belteshazzar received another true vision in his seventieth year in Babylon. The time period for this vision was a long way off, and Daniel understood this vision.

Verse 2. Daniel was mourning for 3 full weeks.

Verse 3. He ate no pleasant food; neither flesh nor wine fasted for 3 weeks and did not even anoint himself. He was fasting and mourning because there was opposition to the Jews returning to Jerusalem.

Verse 4. On the 24th day of the first month he was standing by the side of the great Hiddekel or Tigris River.

Verse 5. He looked up and had a vision, and he saw a man clothed in linen, and around his waist he was girded with fine gold of Upaz.

Verse 6. His body was like beryl, face like lightening, eyes as lamps of fire, and his arms and feet like polished brass, and the voice of his words like the voice of a multitude. This is a similar description of Jesus given to the prophet John in Revelation 1: 12–18.

Verse 7. Although Daniel was in the presence of other men, only Daniel saw this vision. The other men felt a great quaking, they became terrified and they fled to hide themselves.

Verse 8. Daniel was then left alone when he saw this great vision, he lost all strength. His comeliness was turned into corruption.

Verse 9. Yet he heard the voice of his words, and when he heard the words he was in deep sleep on his face and his face was on the ground. (This supernatural experience often occurs to a prophet is in vision.)

Verse 10. Then a hand touched me and set him to his knees and upon the palm of his hands.

Verse 11. And the being said to Daniel, O Daniel, a man greatly beloved, understand what I say to you; stand upright, for I was sent to you. Daniel stood up trembling.

Verse 12. Then he said to Daniel, Fear not Daniel: for from the first day that you set your heart to understand and to humble yourself before God, that the Lord heard you and I am sent to give the understanding.

Verse 13. For 21 days Gabriel was engaged in a spiritual battle with the powers of darkness, which influenced King Cyrus of Persia, Michael the archangel - Jesus came to help. Here again, Jesus when in direct conflict with Satan is referred to as Michael the archangel. Satan was trying to stop Daniel's prayer from being answered. The Samaritans tried to stop the reestablishment of the nation of Judah. God allowed the king of Persia to exhibit the free will of decision for good, and then he answered Daniel's prayer. Artaxerxes, the king of Persia, passes favorable judgment so Jews can go on and build Jerusalem.

Verse 14. Now I am come to make you understand what will happen to your people in the future, for the vision is for the latter days or the time of the end.

Verse 15. And when he had spoken these words unto me, I set my face to the ground and couldn't speak.

Verse 16. And behold one who look similar to the sons of men touched my lips, then I opened my mouth and spoke and said unto him that stood before me, O my Lord by the vision my sorrows are turned upon me and I have retained no strength.

Verse 17. For how can the servant of this my Lord talk with this my Lord? Daniel was left breathless and without strength. This is characteristic of a prophet in vision.

Verse 18. Gabriel touched him and he regained strength.

Verse 19. And said fear not O greatly beloved man, peace be unto thee be strong, yea be strong and when he had spoken unto me, I was strengthened, and said Let my Lord speak for thou has strengthened me.

Verse 20. Gabriel said to Daniel, do you know that I have come to help you to understand the vision and now I will return to fight with the prince of Persia and when I am gone forth the Prince of Greece will come. Here we are given a glimpse behind the scenes in the struggle of good versus evil. Apparently the forces of Satan was working on the King of Persia preventing the Jewish exiles from returning home and so Gabriel was wrestling on the forces of evil that influenced the king.

Verse 21. But I will show you that what is written in the scriptures is true. And no one is assisting me in contending with the forces that control these earth's empires except for Michael your Prince or Jesus.

Chapter Eleven
DANIEL 11

– Gabriel continues to speak to Daniel and Daniel is shown the same sequence of powers as Daniel 2 and Daniel 7 and 8. The symbols used to describe these powers are the king of the North and the King of the South. We expect this prophecy to expand and enlarge on the previous prophecies. Here again Gabriel shows Daniel the sequence of kingdoms from Medo-Persia to the kingdom of Christ.

This is one of the most challenging chapters in the Bible to understand and a lot of it is very difficult to interpret. Caution is needed in the interpretation of the latter end of this chapter particularly because the final verses are unfulfilled prophecy. We will interpret the parts that we can. This chapter needs fervent prayer and study for the full understanding of it.

Verse 1: The angel Gabriel continues speaking to Daniel. This is a continuation of his speech in Chapter 10. The time is about 536/535 BC. He tells Daniel that after the fall of Babylon, in the first year of Darius the Mede, ruler of the Medo-Persian Empire, even I confirmed and strengthened him. Gabriel tells Daniel that Heaven helped King Darius the Mede during the first year of his administration. Darius is now dead and Gabriel tells Daniel future events.

2. I will now show you the truth. After the death of Cyrus, three more kings are to rule Persia. The fourth shall be richer than the previous three and by his strength through his riches he shall stir up all against Greece. Here God enlarged on previous prophecies and gives more details.

3. History revealed that after the death of Cyrus (539–530 BC), who was reigning when the vision was given to Daniel, the three kings who ruled Persia were Cambyses, the son of Cyrus (530–522 BC), Cambyses killed his brother Smerdis and Bardiyya (False Smerdis) pretended to be Smerdis and reigned for nine months in 522 BC while Cambyses was away. The third king was Darius I Hystaspes (522–486 BC). The fourth king was Xerxes known in the Bible as King Ahasuerus, the husband

of Queen Esther. He was on a campaign to conquer all of Europe and became wealthier in the process. As the prophecy said he used his wealth to keep the Greek states at war with each other. He attacked Greek and was successful at the battle of Thermophylae in 480 BC but his fleet was later defeated at the battle of Salamis in 480 BC. This was one of the last Persian-Greek battles and he was the last Persian king to attack Greece. Xerxes is the king who in 457 BC gave the decree to restore and rebuild Jerusalem, which marked the beginning of the 70-week prophecy and the 2300-year prophecy. Xerxes died in 424 BC. *The first two verses of Daniel 11 deal with the Medo-Persian Empire, Babylon having fallen. Gabriel now shows Daniel a new empire and so we skip over a few Persian rulers and we move on to the Grecian Empire and the four divisions of that empire.* The prophecy now takes us to a mighty king that shall arise, and rule will great dominion, and do according to his will. Alexander the Great, son of King Philip of Macedonia was that mighty king. He overthrew the Persian Empire and conquered many lands. This is the same power shown in Daniel 8:8 and 21 where Greece is described as the he goat whose horn was broken.

4. And when he shall stand up or at the height of his power, his kingdom shall be broken and the divided kingdoms shall point to the four winds of the Heaven-North, South, East and West of Palestine, but not to his descendants or to the dominion in which he ruled, his kingdom will be given to others.

Alexander died suddenly in 323 BC at age 32 and the height of power and his power was broken. His kingdom was jealously fought for and about 301 BC his four main generals divided his kingdom; Cassander got the west of Palestine (Macedon and Greece), Seleucus the east of Palestine (Syria and Babylon,) Lysimachus the North (Trace and Bithynia) and Ptolemy the South (Egypt, Libya). Seleucus later defeated Lysimachus. The Hellenistic kingdoms resulted from the disintegration of Alexander's kingdom. In relation to the Jews living in Palestine the eventual consolidation of these kingdoms led to the two powerful kingdoms of Syria and Egypt referred to as the King of the North of Palestine (Seleucid) and the king of the South of Palestine (Ptolemy). The Seleucids of the North and the Ptolemy's of the South. The Seleucid Empire was much larger and stronger than the Ptolemic Empire of the South.

5. The king of the South shall be strong, and one of his princes shall be stronger than he and have dominion and his dominion shall be a great dominion.

The king of the south at this time in history is Ptolemy I (Soter). He ruled Egypt from 323–285 BC. One of his princes was Seleucus I Nicator (312–281 BC) a general in Alexander's army. He fled to Egypt from Syria and he captured Syrian territories from Antigonus, the Syrian ruler. He had a great dominion and became stronger than Ptolemy 1 Soter, the king of the south.

6. After a few years, the King of the North and the King of the South will make peace and the king of the South's daughter (Egypt) shall come to the king of the North (Syria) to make peace, but she shall not retain the power of the arm, neither shall he stand, nor his arm, but she shall be given up, and they that brought her, and he that begat her, and he that strengthened her in these times.

The prophecy now takes us 75 years after the death of Alexander the great and the offspring's of Kings of the North, the Seleucids, and the Kings of the south, the Ptolemies, were constantly at war. On this occasion about 248 BC in an attempt to broker a lasting peace between these two powers a marriage was arranged between Berenice, the daughter of Ptolemy II Philadelphus (285–246 BC) King of the South and the Seleucid king of the North, Antiochus II Theos (262–246 BC). The king of the North had to divorce his wife Laodice and disinherit their two sons in order to marry Berenice. The prophecy states that Berenice did not retain the power of the arm because when Berenice father died, Antiochus II divorced Berenice and took back his wife Laodice. Laodice made sure that this did not happen again by poisoning and killing Antiochus, Berenice, her young son and all her entourage. Laodice then had her son Seleucus II Callinicus (246–227 BC) succeed his father. Hundreds of years (about 300) before this actually happened God revealed this to the prophet Daniel. This gives us confidence in God who reveals the future in his word.

Verse 7. But out of a branch of her roots shall arise in his place; he shall come with an army and shall enter the fortress of the King of the North and shall deal against them and prevail.

The next king of Egypt, Ptolemy III Eugertes (246–221 BC) the brother of Berenice, a branch of her roots assembled an army and attacked Syria in order to avenge the death of his sister; he successfully captured many of the countries of the king of the North, he killed Laodice and cleaned out the King of the North's treasury.

8. And he shall carry off to Egypt their gods, with their princes, and with their precious vessels of silver and of gold; and he shall continue more years than the king of the North.

After a while the king of Egypt Ptolemy III Euergetes (246–221 BC), the brother of Berenice returned to Egypt with much of the precious treasures of Syria. He outlived the Syrian King Seleucus Callinicus (246–225 BC) who died in exile.

9. So the king of the south shall come into his kingdom, and shall return into his own land.

So the King of the South returned to his own land with a great booty.

10. But his sons shall be stirred up, and shall assembly a multitude of great forces: for one shall certainly come, and overflow, and pass through: then shall he return, and be stirred up even to his fortress.

It is now 223 BC, one hundred years after the death of Alexander the great, Seleucus III Ceraunus 225–223 BC and Antiochus III Magnus the Great 223–187 BC, the sons of Anthiochus Callinicus were stirred up to avenge what happened to their father and their country. Seleucus III Ceraunus first became the king but he died shortly and the other son Antiochus III became king for a long time. About 219 BC he attacked Egypt retaking captured territories.

11. Then the king of the South (Egypt) Ptolemy IV Philopator (221–203 BC) shall be angry and will come out to fight with King of the North Antiochus III Magnus who will raise a huge army but it shall be given into Ptolemy's hand.

Ptolemy IV Philopator (221–203 BC) succeeded his father Ptolemy III Euergetes (246–221 BC). He was angry with the King of Syria, Antiochus III Magnus and assembled a large army; this war in 217 BC, called the battle of Raphia, despite Syria's vast army, Ptolemy of Egypt defeated Antiochus III Magnus and took many captives.

12. And when he (Ptolemy IV) had taken away the multitudes, his heart shall be lifted up; for he shall cast down many ten thousands; but he shall not be strengthened by it.

The King of Egypt heart was lifted up because of his exploits. He killed thousands people, but he was not strengthened by killing so many thousands of people. After the reign of Ptolemy IV, came Ptolemy V 203–181 BC Ptolemy V was only 6 years old when he began to reign.

13. For the king of the North shall return, and shall set forth a multitude greater than the former, he shall certainly come after certain years with a great army and much riches.

After his loss at the battle of Raphia in 217 BC, the king of the North Antiochus III regrouped and assembled a vast army and attacked the young king.

Daniel has taken us down to the rule of Anthiochus III Magnus from 223 BC to 187 BC. Are you wondering why Gabriel is revealing all of these historical information to Daniel? Do you think it is for Daniel or for us who live in the end of time so that we can know end time events and have confidence in God's foreknowledge? I hope that you are appreciating how God reveals more details of prophecy and he expands and enlarges on the previous prophecies. He reveals details of the rule of the Ptolemy's the kings of the South, Egypt which is south of Jerusalem and the rule of the kings of the North of Jerusalem or the Seleucids or Syrian Kings.

Verses 3 to 13 dealt with the Grecian Empire of Alexander the great and the 4 divisions of that empire. The prophecy of Daniel 11 takes another jump to a new world power and now we are further along in the history of this world to the next world ruling empire: Imperial Rome.

Verse 14. And in those times there shall many stand up against the king of the south: also the robbers of thy people, shall exalt themselves to establish the vision; but they shall fail.

There was a lot of internal unrest in Egypt, in addition there were external forces threatening Egypt; Philip of Macedon and Antiochus III Epiphanes of Syria formed an alliance in an attempt to divide some of the territories of Egypt between them. The father of the young Egyptian king had left him under the guardianship of Rome and so in 200 BC Rome became involved to protect the young King (Ptolemy IV) Epiphanes (204–181 BC). Here the prophecy becomes intriguing and more difficult to interpret. Who are the robbers of thy people? Rome now comes into this prophetic picture. It appears as if Rome comes into view now as we are shown the succession of kingdoms from Babylon to the second coming of Jesus.

Antiochus III Magnus (223–187 BC) the king of the North waged war against Egypt, captured the fenced city of Gaza about 201 BC defeated the Egyptian army led by General Scopas. We know that Rome has entered the picture because the Roman Senate appointed the guardianship of the young king of Egypt to Aristomenes, an old minister of the court. He then set up an army to contain the threat of Antiochus III Magnus and Philip of Macedon. General Scopas led the army. Antiochus III defeated the army and captured Judea. In 190 BC Rome defeated Antiochus III Magnus in the battle of Magnesia.

Verse 15. So the King of the North shall come and cast a mount and take the most fenced cities: and the arms of the South shall not withstand, neither his chosen people, neither shall there be any strength to withstand.

Antiochus III Magnus died about 187 BC He was succeeded by Seleceus IV Philopator (187–176 BC). He was followed by Antiochus III Epiphanes and ruled from 175 BC to 164 BC. This new king of the North captured the fenced cities guarding Egypt. Egypt was defeated and there was persecution of the Jews. Antiochus III Epiphanes tried to spread Hellenistic culture to the Jews and he attacked desecrated the temple and tried to destroy the Jewish religion. This resulted in the Maccabean revolt when the Jews stood up and fought back and drove him out of Jerusalem putting an end to the spread of Hellenistic Greek culture in Jerusalem. Some say that Antiochus III Epiphanes is the Little Horn Power. Note here that he cannot be the little Horn power, which Daniel was shown will come after imperial Rome disintegrates. Antiochus III is way before the time of Christ and is therefore not the abomination of desolation that Jesus spoke about in Matthew 24:15. Jesus clearly states that would be in the future.

Verse 16. But he that cometh against him shall do according to his own will, and none shall stand before him: and he shall stand in the glorious land, which by his hand shall be consumed.

After the success of the Maccabean revolt that disposed of Antiochus Epiphanes a new world power is arising and we no longer hear about the king of the North and South for a while. The new rising powerful kingdom of Imperial Rome is in control and the kingdoms of North and South is silenced. There is a new powerful kingdom that no one can stand before. Rome is quickly gaining power. In AD 65 Pompey captured Syria and in AD 63 Jerusalem and brought them under the control of Rome. Rome having already captured Macedon and Thrace captures Jerusalem and now stands in the glorious land of Palestine.

Verse 17. He shall also set his face to enter with the strength of his whole kingdom, and upright ones with him; thus shall he do: and he shall give him the daughter of women, corrupting her; but she shall not stand on his side, neither be for him.

Rome now enters with the strength of his whole kingdom. Rome having control of Syria and Jerusalem in the North now moves south to control Egypt. The king of Egypt Ptolemy XI Auletes died in 51 BC and he left Egypt to his two young children Ptolemy XII about 9 years old and Cleopatra. They were placed under the guardianship of Rome. Pompey was assigned their guardian. Pompey and Julius Caesar quarreled and fought each other. Pompey fled to Egypt and was murdered there. Julius Caesar was now the guardian of Ptolemy and Cleopatra. Ptolemy XII and Cleopatra were feuding. Julius Caesar attempted to settle the dispute and a battle ensued and Ptolemy XII died, Julius Caesar won. The Jews helped Julius Caesar and the Roman army to succeed. Julius Caesar had an affair with Cleopatra of Egypt, the daughter of women. She did not stand by his side; she turned to Mark Anthony, the rival of Octavian, Caesar's heir. In 31 BC Octavian defeated Cleopatra and Anthony's army. Mark Anthony committed Suicide and later Cleopatra committed suicide. She did not stand on the side of Caesar. Verse 17 is clearly referring to Julius Caesar. With the death of Cleopatra VI in 30 BC the Ptolemy dynasty ended and from about 30 BC onward Egypt became a Roman province. At this point in history Rome has control and has conquered the territories once controlled by Greece. Egypt the once great world ruling power before Assyria now becomes the lowest of kingdoms and it shall never again rule over the nations fulfilling the prophecy of Ezekiel 29:13–15. *Surely the Lord God does nothing unless he reveals his secrets to his servants the prophets.*

Verse 18. After this shall he turn his face unto the isles, and shall take many: but a prince for his own behalf shall cause the reproach offered by him to cease; without his own reproach he shall cause it to turn upon him.

This is a difficult text to interpret but is again referring to Julius Caesar. War in the coastlands caused Julius Caesar to leave Egypt and go to the isles or the coastlands of North Africa and Spain.

Verse 19. Then he shall turn his face toward the fort of his own land: but he shall stumble and fall, and not be found.

Verse 19 foretold the death of Julius Caesar. After all his exploits, he returned home and was assassinated by his own men. Julius Caesar was killed in 44 BC, Ides of March. At the death of Julius Caesar, Rome's first triumvirate consisting of Octavius, Mark Anthony and Lepidus was formed.

Verse 20. Then shall stand up in his estate a raiser of taxes in the glory of the kingdom: but within few days he shall be destroyed, neither in anger, nor in battle. Somewhere here we are making the transition from BC to AD This verse foretold the arrival of Augustus Caesar. Julius Caesar was followed by Augustus Caesar. Augustus Caesar, born Octavius, was the nephew of Julius Caesar. He was adopted as the son of Julius Caesar and succeeded him on the throne. The prophet Daniel was shown that he would be a raiser of Taxes. This is supported in Luke 2:1 which states "and it came to pass in those days that there went out a decree from Caesar Augustus that all the world should be taxed." He raised taxes to support his kingdom, Rome was at the height of its glory at this time. The prophecy states that he would not die in battle, so Augustus Caesar died peacefully in bed in AD 14 at age 76. There should be no question now that the prophecy of Daniel 11 has taken us down to AD 14 to an established Roman Empire that followed the kingdom of Greece.

Verse 21. And in his estate shall stand up a vile person, to whom they shall not give the honor of the kingdom: but he shall come in peaceably, and obtain the kingdom by flatteries.

Tiberius Caesar (AD 14–37) followed Augustus Caesar. He was a vile person and was not respected. He was the stepson of Augustus Caesar. His mother Livia became Augustus Caesar's wife. He did not seem like a qualified candidate for the job as Caesar but his mother Livia got him on the throne by flatteries and he came to the throne peaceably.

Verse 22. And with the arms of a flood shall they be overflown from before him, and shall be broken, yea, also the prince of the covenant.

This prophecy that God gave to Daniel in the fifth century BC now takes us to the death of Jesus in AD 33. Rome continued her conquest and controlled many countries and the Prince of the Covenant who is Jesus who was put to death under the rule of Tiberius Caesar. The Prince of the Covenant is the same Messiah the Prince who made a covenant with Israel on Mt. Sinai. He confirmed the covenant as stated in Daniel 9: 25–27. In the fifteenth reign of Tiberius, Pontius Pilate was governor of Judea, and Herod was tetrarch of Galilee, John the Baptist began his ministry (see Luke 3:1). In AD 31 in the eighteenth year of the reign of Tiberius Caesar, Jesus was crucified on a Roman Cross on a hill called Golgotha by order of Pontius Pilate of Judea. In AD 31 Christ, the Prince of the covenant, was broken under Roman authority by Emperor Tiberius Caesar. Tiberius had a large army and had many military conquests. He was violently killed in AD 37. Take note how God has revealed to us the kingdoms from Babylon to the second coming of Jesus. In Daniel 11:4 He revealed Greece and now Daniel 11:21 and 22 He reveals Rome. In Daniel 9 we are told the time line of Jesus baptism and crucifixion and now we are told the leaders that would kill him. These are truly amazing prophecies. No wonder Satan tries to distort them. The fact that in Daniel 11 we are given so much details about the history of the world from Daniel's time to the end of time is amazing and should be enough to disprove the false assertion by Satan that the book of Daniel is a historical book that was written in the second century BC Satan is an avid Bible student and he has studied these prophecies and knows how to distort them but God loves us enough to reveal the truth to us. The truth is that we have been revealed the history of God's people now down to the leaders of the Roman Empire and now down to the death of Jesus. *God's truth is marching on to eternity. Surely the Lord God will do nothing unless he reveals his secrets to his servants the prophets.*

The rest of the chapter becomes more difficult to interpret, it is just not so clear the exact events mentioned. It appears as though verses 23–30 is referring to physical actions of the Papacy and the remainder the spiritual actions. I'm still praying for the enlightenment of the Holy Spirit on these verses.

Verse 23. And after the league made with him he shall work deceitfully; for he shall come up and become strong with a small people.

The prophecy and history moves from imperial Rome to Papal Rome. The papacy came up and was strong with a small people – difficult to understand.

Verse 24. He shall enter peaceably even upon the fattest places of the province; and he shall do that which his fathers have not done, nor his fathers' fathers; he shall scatter among them the prey, and spoil, and riches, yea, and he shall forecast devices against the strong hold even for a time.

This describes exploits of Medieval Rome maybe the crusades.

Verse 25. And he shall stir up his power and courage against the king of the South with a great army; and the king of the South shall be stirred up to battle with a very great and mighty army; but he shall not stand: for they shall forecast devices against him. With imperial Rome out of the way we are back to the King of the North and South. We know that the new king of the North's crusaders conquered Jerusalem and now Egypt is fighting against the crusaders. They were defeated in 1099.

Verse 26. Yea, they that feed on the portion of his meat shall destroy him, and his army shall overflow: and many shall fall down slain.

Verse 27. And both these kings shall be able to do mischief, and they shall speak lies at one table; but it shall not prosper: for yet the end shall be at the time appointed.

Verse 28. Then shall he return into his own land with great riches; and his heart shall be against the covenant; and he shall do exploits and return to his own land.

Verse 29. At the time appointed he shall return, and come toward the south; but it shall not be as the former, or as the latter.

Verse 30. For the ships of Chittin shall come up against him: therefore he shall be grieved: and return, and have indignation against the holy covenant: so shall he do; he shall even return, and have intelligence with them that forsake the holy covenant.

Verses 23–30 seem to describe physical political activities of papal or Medieval Rome. I refrain from speculating.

Verse 31. And arms shall stand on his part, and they shall pollute the sanctuary of strength, and shall take away the daily sacrifice, and they shall place the abomination that make desolate.

The prophet here describes some of the spiritual activities of papal Rome. The church using the power of the state creates an abomination that makes desolate. Papal Rome will use arms or force to pollute the sanctuary of strength and take away the daily sacrifice. Very early in the history of Papal Rome, Clovis the king of France assisted the Papal Rome in destroying the three horns the Heruli, the vandals and the Ostrogoths. The Papacy used the power of the state to do its exploits. God expands and enlarges on previous prophecies. The spiritual characteristics of this power was shown to us in Daniel 8:11 where we saw that the Little Horn Power takes away the daily sacrifices by reason of transgression. This power that shall obscure Christ intercessory ministry in the Heavenly sanctuary and set up an earthly priesthood system and set up the abomination of desolation. In Matthew 24:15 Jesus spoke of this abomination of desolation that was prophesied by the prophet Daniel in Daniel 8:13. In AD 30 Jesus said it would be in the future and the prophecy takes us there. This abomination of desolation have a dual application it refers to the Roman destruction of Jerusalem in AD 70 as well as the work of this new power, Papal Rome. He that have an ear let him hear the abomination of desolation cannot be Antiochus Epiphanes who was a minor Seleucid king from 175–164 AD before Jesus was born. Jesus refers to this abomination of desolation as in the future.

Verse 32. And such do wickedly against the covenant shall be corrupt by flatteries: but the people that do know their God shall be strong; and do exploits.

People like to hear smooth things that do not require much change in behavior. This power will corrupt with flatteries those who do wicked things against the covenant of God. The majority of Christendom will believe and follow after this power but God has always had a faithful few who stood for the truth even in perilous times and they taught others the pure Gospel. Back in the dark ages men like Lucian 250–312 AD, Virgilantius (304–368 AD), Patrick (360–420 AD), in the Middle Ages the Waldenses, the Albigenses, etc. who lived in the mountains of Italy memorized the scriptures and refuse to mix compromise their Christianity.

Verse 33. And they that understand among the people shall instruct many, yet they shall fall by the sword, and by flame and by captivity and by spoil many days.

This is a persecuting power that kills by the sword. For 1260 years of Papal supremacy (538 AD–1798 AD) the church persecuted God's people who were trying to share the truth. They burned martyrs at the stake. Millions of Christians across Europe lost their lives for not following the dictates of the Church of Rome. The Celtic church tried to hold on to the sacred scriptures and kept the Bible Sabbath for a while until they were taken over by the Church of Rome. The crusaders attacked and killed many Christians like the Albigensians of France, and the Waldensians of Italian alps. These people died by the sword and by flame and were captives for trying to hold on to the pure Christian faith of the Bible.

Verse 34. Now when they shall fall, they shall be holpen with a little help: but many shall cleave to them with flatteries.

Amid the bitter persecution, God raised up various leaders some from within the Catholic Church e.g. John Wycliffe and John Huss. These men spoke out about the false practices of the Roman Church and in so doing they were helpful to these persecuted believers. Many of these leaders were killed. In 1415 John Huss was burned at the stake. God did not deliver them from the vicious persecution of the Roman Church but he would provide a little help by raising up another voice. This was the initial spark of the Protestant reformation that produced men like Martin Luther, John Calvin, Ulric Zwigli, John Knox of Scotland, etc. These men tried to put the Bible back in its rightful place among God's people. They rejected papal supremacy over the Bible. The church fought back and thousands were martyred for their faith, the church charged them with heresy and called herself the corrector of heretics. There were many enemies of the early reformers Protestant reformation e.g. bloody queen Mary of England persecuted the reformers. Some Protestants fled to America which helped the reformation.

Verse 35. And some of them of understanding shall fall, to try them, and to purge, and to make them white, even to the time of the end: because it yet for a time appointed.

These verses describe the fate of God's true believers even to the time of the end. The fires of persecution purged these true believers and purified them. Although the fell to the sword of persecution their characters were refined by this process. The church persecuted for 1260 years or until the appointed time of the end at 1798. This is the same time period described in Daniel 7:25 which states that this power will reign for time, times and half a time or 1260 years. This same time period is described in Revelation 12:6 and 14 and Revelation 13:5. God has appointed this period as the beginning of time of the end. This end time period ends with Jesus second coming.

Verse 36. And the king shall do according to his will, and he shall exalt himself, and magnify himself above every god and speak marvelous things against the God of gods, and shall prosper till the indignation be accomplished: for that this is determined shall be done.

This power that is now the king of the north will do things according to his own will and will exalt himself above all that is called God and will speak marvelous things against God and will be successful for a time. This is the same power described in Daniel 8:11. Papal Rome now in the picture has exalted and magnified itself above every other God and is prosperous.

This power has done according to its own will by changing God's law as prophesied in Daniel 7:25. She changed the fourth commandment from 94 words to 8 words and changing the Sabbath from Saturday to Sunday. She omitted the 2nd commandment that forbids the worship of image and divided the 10th into two. This power has exalted himself by trying to intercede between God and man when the scriptures plainly teach that Jesus if the only intercessor between God and man, the Catholic Mass has replaced the Lord's supper and the bread and wine has been changed into the very blood and body of Christ; the veneration of saints, these and many more practices are alien to scripture and fulfills this prophecy. If you read the Catechism you will find many more statements like the pope has the power to change times, abrogate and dispense with all things even the precepts of Christ.

The apostle Paul describes this same power in 2 Thessalonians 2:3–4 when he writes Let no man deceive you for that day (the second coming of Jesus) will not come, except there come a falling away (from the true teachings of the scripture) first, and that man of sin be revealed, the son of perdition; who opposes and exalts himself above all that is called God, showing himself that he is God. In the first century the apostle Paul writing under the influence of the Holy Spirit reveals this to the believers in Thessalonica.

Verse 37. Neither shall he regard the God of his fathers, nor the desire of women, nor regard any god: for he shall magnify himself above all.

Verse 38. But in his estate shall he honor the God of forces: and a God whom his fathers knew not shall he honor with gold, and silver, and with precious stones, and pleasant things.

Verse 39. Then shall he do in the most strongholds with a strange god, whom he shall acknowledge and increase with glory: and he shall cause them to rule over many, and shall divide the land for gain.

The papacy became not only a powerful religious force but a powerful political force.

Verses 36–39 are referring to this King of the North as Papal Rome; these verses describe the final demise of this power. Verses 40 to 45 are very difficult to understand and caution in interpretation is warranted because these events are in the future and we are not sure how these things would fit into place but when they do we will know. We anticipate the fulfillment of these verses with great curiosity.

Verse 40. And at the time of the end shall the king of the south push at him: and the king of the North shall come against him like a whirlwind, with chariots and with horsemen, and with many ships; and he shall enter into his countries, and shall overflow and pass over.

Verse 41. He shall enter also into the glorious land, and many countries shall be overthrow: but these shall escape out of his hand, even Edom, and Moab, and the chief of the children of Ammon.

Verse 42. He shall stretch forth his hand upon the countries: and the land of Egypt shall not escape.

Verse 43. But he shall have power over the treasures of gold and silver, and over the precious things of Egypt: and the Libyans and the Ethiopians shall be at his steps.

Verse 44 But tidings out of the east and out of the north shall trouble him: therefore he shall go forth with great fury to *destroy, and utterly to make away many.*

Verse 45. And he shall plant the tabernacles of his palace between the seas and the glorious holy mountain, yet he shall come to his end and none shall help him.

Verses 40–45 are very challenging to interpret and they are various possible interpretations. We know that the king of the North and the King of the South fought over Judah. Judah is now the Christian church. Who are the final attackers of the Church in this final drama? These are unfulfilled prophecies therefore caution is need in the interpretation. We may have to wait and see the fulfillment before we truly understand these verses.

Chapter Twelve
DANIEL 12

Verses 1 to 3 refer to future events.

Verse 1. And at that time shall Michael stand up, the great prince which stands for the children of thy people: and there shall be a time of trouble, such as never was since there was a nation even to that same time: and at that time thy people shall be delivered, every one that shall be found written in the book.

We are now at the very end of time, the history of this world is over and at the end of the events described in Daniel 11: 40–45, Michael, the great prince or (Jesus) stands up. When Michael our great prince who stands for the children of thy people stands up it is all over. Hebrews 10:10 and 11 describes Jesus as our High priest in the Heavenly sanctuary sitting at the right hand of God, the father. The prophet Daniel now tells us that at that appointed time in history, Jesus, our high priest, having completed the investigative phase of the judgment in the Heavenly sanctuary will stand up to deliver his children. At this time the last warning of the three angels of Revelation 14 will have been given. The last person has had an opportunity to accept or reject God's plan of salvation. God's people are sealed. Jesus stops pleading for sinful man and He stands up and with a loud voice and uplifted hands He says the most solemn statement as told in Revelation 22:11 "It is done, he that is filthy let him be filthy still and he that is holy let him be holy still." Sinful man now stands before God without a mediator; God's spirit is withdrawn from the earth and now there is a time of trouble all over the world such as never was since there was a nation. During this time of trouble the seven last plagues will be poured out on this earth. Judgment has been decided against the Little Horn and the stone that Daniel was shown is about to strike the image and the kingdom is God is about to begin and the people of God whose names are written in the book of Heaven will be saved for eternity. *A brief discussion on Michael.* We read in the book of Revelation that Michael and his angels fought against the devil and his angels. The name Michael, the archangel has come up several times in the book of Daniel and Revelation. Who is Michael? Revelation states that Michael and his angels fought against the devil and his angels. Millions of sincere Christians today believe that Michael is an angel. Let us examine the evidence. There is much evidence to suggest that Michael is another name for Jesus. The name Michael in Hebrew means "who is as God." El is the short form of Elohim. It is the name of God.

Daniel 12:1 states "And at that time meaning the final time of trouble on Planet Earth Michael shall stand up, the great Prince, who stands for the children of thy people." This is referring to Jesus. At the end of the investigative judgment over which Jesus is presiding or sitting down at the right hand of the father; Jesus will stand up and declare that time is no longer; he will deliver his people. When Jesus stands up and no longer pleads for humanity, there will be a time of trouble as never was since there was a nation. No angel can stand up for the people of God; at the close of human probation Jesus will stand up and shortly thereafter come and deliver his people. In Daniel 9:25 the Messiah is referred to as a prince. In 1 Thessalonians 4:16 states that the Lord will descend with a shout, with the voice of the archangel. It is Jesus' voice that is heard from the Heavens when the dead is raised. The voice of the archangel is the voice of Jesus; the archangel must be Jesus. Arch means ruler or king. Jesus is the great prince that stands up for the children of thy people. This name Michael is often used at times when Jesus is in direct conflict with Satan. When the name Michael is used for Jesus, it to be referring to Jesus, the conquering leader and protector of his people.

In Joshua 5:13 and14 as Joshua was preparing to attack Jericho, he saw a man standing with a drawn sword and Joshua approached him saying, "are you for us or against us?" The man said to Joshua "I am the captain of the army of the Lord." Joshua recognized that this was the Lord himself and fell on his face and worshipped him and ask what does my Lord want me to do? The captain of the Lord's host also known as the Lord Jesus Christ said to Joshua what he said to Moses "take off thy shoe from off thy feet; for the ground where thou stand is holy ground. There can be no doubt here that the captain of the Lord's host is Jesus, the archangel, the highest messenger, the Holy God.

In Jude 1: 9, Satan is actually contending with Michael the Archangel who is Jesus, the resurrection and the life, for the body of Moses. Can you believe it? Jesus himself, not an angel, is going to resurrect Moses and the accuser of the brethren, Satan shows up claiming the body of Moses. Michael the archangel, was contending with the devil for the body of Moses and Jesus who is also known as Michael the archangel says to

Satan, "The Lord rebuke thee." We know that Jesus discretely buried Moses (Read Deuteronomy 34:5 and 6). We know that Jesus, the resurrection and the life won this battle with Satan because Moses was resurrected and later appeared on the Mount of Transfiguration with Jesus some 1500 years later (Matthew 17.3). Moses represented those who died and will be resurrected at the second coming, also present with Jesus was Elijah who never saw death and came back 900 years later to be with Jesus before his crucifixion representing those who will be translated without seeing death. This story of Salvation gives us the assurance of such a wonderful future.

Jesus, it appears from scripture, has myriads of different titles, responsibilities, among them Jesus in battle is sometimes referred to as Michael. Jesus is the commander in chief of the Heavenly host. There is enough evidence here to support the fact that Michael is Jesus. Jesus' position is the head of all the angels. He created them (see Colossians 1:16 and 17). Jesus is the leader of the angelic hosts and sometimes He is referred to as The Prince of Angels, or the archangel. The President of the United States is often referred to as commander-in-chief of the armed forces, that does not make him a soldier and not president; it is one of his titles. Jesus is often referred to as a lamb, a shepherd, a rock etc. These are symbolic terms. Michael is Jesus who is altogether lovely but he is awesome in battle. No one wins Michael in battle.

Verse 1 describes the end of it all when Michael stands up and delivers His people, everyone whose name is written in the book of Heaven. When Michael comes the following happens:

Verse 2. And many of them that sleep in the dust of the earth shall awake, some to everlasting life, and some to shame and everlasting contempt.

This text alone should settle the state of the dead and that is death is like sleep; there is a cessation of awareness. When Michael stands up and deliver his people, those whose names are written in the book of life are raised to everlasting life. The wicked dead remain in the grave for another 1000 years when they will wake up to their punishment (Revelation 20:5). In order for some to wake up to contempt there will be a special resurrection for some (probably those who mocked and crucified Jesus (see Revelation 1:7) to shame and everlasting contempt. The judgment determines the final result truth will finally be vindicated and just rewards will be given to all.

Verse 3. And they that are wise shall shine as the brightness of the firmament, and they that turn many to righteousness as the stars forever and ever.

Those who study and teach the truth to others, as enlightened by the Holy Spirit, will shine as the stars forever.

Verse 4. But you, O Daniel, shut up the words, and seal the book, even to the time of the end: many shall run to and fro, and knowledge shall be increased.

Daniel is told to stop writing and seal the book of Daniel until the end of time, at that time knowledge shall increase and these end time prophecies would be studied and understood. Some of the events that Daniel saw in vision pertains to the end of time and would be better understood at that time. Note that the time of the end is different than the end of time. The end of time is when Michael stands up and delivers his saints. The time of the end prophetically began about 1798 and will last until the end of time when Jesus comes. This prophecy has been fulfilled because since 1798 onward there has been greater interest in the study of the book of Daniel. Believers around the world from many beliefs have been studying these prophecies. The book of Daniel has been unsealed and we now have a better understanding of Daniel than before. We still have more to learn about the final two chapters. Both secular and Biblical knowledge has increased tremendously since the time of the end and today we are running to and from the earth. We can get around the world in one day.

5. Then I Daniel looked, and behold there stood other two, the one on this side of the bank of the river, and the other on that side of the bank of the river.

After this angel gives Daniel this long prophecy, two other Heavenly beings appeared to be standing on each side of the Tigris River.

6. And one of them said to the man clothe in linen that Daniel had seen at the beginning of this vision (Daniel 10:6), who was standing upon the waters of the river, how long shall it be to the end of these wonders that I was shown?

The man clothe in linen standing upon the waters is Jesus.

7. And I heard the man clothed in linen, who was standing upon the waters of the river, when he held up his right hand and his left hand unto Heaven, and swore by him that lives forever that it shall be for a time, times, and a half; and when he shall have accomplished to scatter the power of the holy people, all these things shall be finished.

The man clothe in linen (Jesus) lifts up both hands and swears by him that lives forever that the persecution and scattering of the power of God's people would last for, time, times and half a time or 1260 years. This is the same time period referred to in Daniel 7:25 – and he shall speak great words against the most high and shall wear out the saints of the most high and think to change times and laws; and they shall be given into his hand until time, times and dividing of time.

8. And I heard, but I understood not: then said I, O my Lord, what shall be the end of these things? Daniel does not understand and still wants to know what will happen at the end of these things.

9. And he said, go thy way, Daniel: for the words are closed up and sealed till the time of the end. Jesus said to Daniel, go your way, the words of this little book of Daniel will be sealed until the time of the end. When that time in history comes under the influence of

the Holy Spirit men would start studying their Bibles diligently and knowledge about the book of Daniel will increase and these prophecies in the book of Daniel will be studied and understood. Daniel would not be alive to see these prophecies fulfilled and he was not allowed to understand the time prophecies but the people of the time of the end will see and understand these time prophecies as they are or have been fulfilled. These prophecies were given to Daniel primarily for those living at the time of the end.

Verse 10. At that time many shall be purified and made white and tried; but the wicked will continue to do wickedly; and none of the wicked shall understand; but the wise shall understand.

Those in the last days who study God's word devoutly will understand God's messages for their times and will be made pure by the outpouring of the Holy Spirit but the wicked will continue to ignore these messages and would not be wise unto salvation.

Verse 11. And from the time that the daily sacrifice shall be taken away, and the abomination that makes desolate set up, there shall be 1290 days.

These appear to be symbolic times and the day to year principle should be applied here. The 1290 days ended in 1798 therefore they begin in 508 AD In 508 AD the king of France Clovis defeated the Ostrogoths and paved the way for the establishment of the Papacy which took away the daily sacrifice or true worship of God. This same power will deal a deadly wound to the Papacy in 1798.

Verse 12. Blessed is he that waiteth, and cometh to the thousand three hundred and thirty five days or years. From 508 to 1844 is 1335 years. This is the beginning of the time of the end when these prophecies began to be understood. Judgment started in 1844.

Verse 13. But go thy way till the end be: for thou shall rest, and stand in thy lot at the end of the days.

Note that Gabriel does not tell Daniel that at death he will be going to Heaven; instead he tells Daniel that he will be sleeping in the grave or resting in the grave, but he will be resurrected and stand in his lot in the end of time. In other words Daniel will be resurrected at the end of time and did not go on to his reward at death contrary to popular teaching.

We have come to the end of the book of Daniel and most of it has been unsealed. There is still some unfulfilled prophecy that we need to understand but there is a lot that we understood. God wants us to study and understand the book of Daniel and make it a regular part of our Bible study. There are many truths that you will discover. I hope I have peeked your interest in the study of this important prophetic book.

Prophecy did not end with the prophet Daniel it will continue until the end of time. These prophecies in Daniel are key to the understanding the book of Revelation and vice versa. These prophecies given to the apostle John were given after Jesus came and returned to Heaven. The true prophetic gift among God's people will continue until the end of time.

Prophecy continues with Jesus

Since Jesus is the embodiment of all the biblical prophecies and He sends these prophecies to us through his chosen prophets it is important to study some of the prophecies He gave us during His earthly sojourn. After centuries of warnings from the prophets, Jesus the fulfillment of all the messianic prophecies of the Old Testament came to earth and warned us himself.

Almost two thousand years ago, Jesus outlined some of the events that will precede his second coming. In AD 33 as Jesus left the temple in Jerusalem for the last time, his disciples showed him the magnificent beautiful buildings of the temple in Jerusalem. It had massive white stonewalls that glistened in the sun. It was the pride of the Jewish nation. "Master," they say, "see what manner of stones and what buildings are here! Jesus prophesied to them by saying that the temple would be completely destroyed and not one of these massive stone will be left on another.

Mark 13:3 says that Jesus and at least four of his disciples ascended up the Mount of Olives that overlooked the temple and the city of Jerusalem. While there four of his disciples Peter, Andrew, James and John came to him privately and asked him to tell them when will the temple would be destroyed and what would be the signs of his second coming and the end of the world? These disciples were asking Jesus to tell them the signs of the end of the world. In every age believers have thought that the second coming would happen during their lifetime and perhaps the disciples thought that the destruction of the temple and the second coming would happen at the same time. Jesus' response is most interesting and reveals that He is God and knows the future. In his answer to the disciples Jesus tied the two important events together and combined many of the signs that were common to both the destruction of Jerusalem and its' magnificent temple by the Romans in AD 70, and the second coming at the end of the world. His admonitions were not only for his followers at that time but also for everyone especially people living at the end of time.

Jesus told them events that would happen in their lifetime and also those things that would happen in the distant future at the end of the world. Quoting from the book the desire of Ages, page 628 "Jesus did not answer his disciples by taking up separately the destruction of Jerusalem and the great day of his coming. He mingled the description of these two events. Had he opened to his disciples future events as He beheld them, they would have been unable to endure the sight. In mercy to them he blended the description of the two great crises, leaving the disciples to study out the meaning for themselves. When he referred to the destruction of Jerusalem, His prophetic words reached beyond that event to the final conflagration in that day when the Lord shall rise out of his place to punish the world for their iniquity, when the earth shell disclose her blood, and shall no more cover her slain. The entire discourse was given, not for the disciples only, but for those who shall live in the closing scenes of this earth's history."

Jesus then warned his disciples about Satan's deceptions. He told them about the appearance of False Christs' "Take heed that no man deceive you. For many shall come in my name, saying, I am Christ and shall deceive many." This was not only for the disciples' time but we have certainly seen the fulfillment of this prophecy in our lifetime. There are many impostors saying that they are Jesus Christ and have deceived many. He warned them that there would be wars and rumor of wars but do not let that trouble them because these things must happen but the end is not yet. He told them that nation would rise against nation and kingdom against kingdom. Jesus said that there will be famines, pestilences, and earthquakes in many different places. These things happened before the destruction of Jerusalem. We are certainly seeing these things happening again before the return of Jesus and I cannot imagine that it was worse than that now. We have seen more wars, pestilences, unusual weather patterns (tornadoes, hurricanes, cyclones, etc.), floods, mudslides, fires, famines, poverty, and disasters by land and by sea. Fierce diseases like Aids, cancer, drug abuse, cardiovascular diseases are snuffing out the lives of millions of people around the world. Alcohol and other drugs are destroying the lives of countless people; heroin, cocaine, amphetamines, marijuana and countless other drugs are available everywhere in our neighborhoods, our schools, and our homes. Earthquakes are occurring with alarming frequency these days, tsunami is now part of our vocabulary.

These destructive weather patterns are a common occurrence. Nature is crying out loud warning us that the end is nearer than we think. There are millions of people in the world who are homeless and starving. Violence fills our land and innocent people even babies are losing their lives at the hands of wicked people. Our children are not safe even when sleeping in their beds at home. These things Jesus said are the beginning of sorrows but they are not the very end. He told them that they will suffer persecution, they will be arrested, tried, delivered up to be afflicted, killed and be hated of all nations for his sake. He warned about false prophets that will arise and deceive many. These things occurred before the fall of Jerusalem in AD 70 and will be repeated before the end of time. Many people are going to be offended and hate each other. Many who once loved the truth will grow cold but those who are faithful until the end will be saved. He further states that while these things are going on the gospel of the kingdom of Heaven will be preached in all the world for a witness unto all nations and when this gospel shall have reach the world and warn everyone then shall the end come. The gospel was preached to the then known world and this prophecy is currently being fulfilled with the use of television, the internet, door to door and personal missionary work. This gospel has almost reached earth's remotest bounds.

Jesus gave them ample warning about what to do to escape the destruction of Jerusalem. He gave then a sign that would alert them when to flee Jerusalem. He told them when they see the abomination of desolation, spoken of by the prophet Daniel (in Daniel 9:27, 11:31 and 12:11) stand in the holy place, whoso readeth, let him understand. He told them that when they see the abomination of desolation stand in the Holy Place that tells you that the destruction of Jerusalem is imminent. Luke 21:20 makes it clearer and tells us the sign—when you see Jerusalem surrounded by the Roman armies, know that the desolation is near. Jesus then gave them instructions as to how to survive the desolation of Jerusalem. Those in Judea flee to the mountains. Do not be concerned about your personal belongings. He mentions the difficulties that pregnant and nursing mothers would face and told them to pray that their flight would not be in the cold winter or on the Sabbath day; it would be difficult to keep the Sabbath under those circumstances. So forty years in advance Jesus warns his followers that they should pray that they do not have to flee on the Sabbath because that would make it difficult to keep the Sabbath holy. Similarly in the end of time when we see *the abomination that causes desolate as prophesied by Daniel* places itself in God's place know that the end is also imminent and pray also that your flight be not on the Sabbath or in the winter again. Those Christians who followed his advice had ample time to get to safety and were not destroyed when Jerusalem was destroyed. Similarly those who at the end of time follow his instructions will escape destruction. Here Jesus gives us an important helpful clue to look for at the very end of time.

Jesus then describes a period of great tribulation for the church and except the length of the tribulation is shortened no one will escape. He warns of false Christs, false prophets deceiving many with their miracles. Many would lose faith and apostatize. Jesus warns his followers about the false teachings about his second coming that would deceive many people. False teachers are going to tell them about his secret coming but do not believe them. When he returns to take his children home it would not be a secret event. He warns do not go looking for him in the desert or secret chambers. His return is a visible worldwide event that no one will miss. "For as the lightening cometh out of the east and shines even unto the west so shall the coming of the son of man be." The entire world would see this dramatic event. Do not believe anyone who states that Christ came in one part of the world. His second coming is a cataclysmic worldwide event. Notice that

Jesus never promised us there will be a time of peace on this earth before his return; He tells that the opposite is true. Jesus then describes cosmic events that will appear before his coming, the sun shall be darkened, the moon would not give her light, falling of the stars from Heaven and the powers of Heavens will be shaken then He will appear in the clouds of Heaven with power and great glory. His angels who will make a great trumpet sound and gather his saints from the four corners of the earth. He prophesies that the tribes of the earth would mourn at his second coming.

In His answer Jesus did not give the exact date and time of his second coming. Matter of fact he said of the day and the hour no man knows not even the angels in Heaven but his father only. No one knows the exact day or hour of Jesus second coming. However, He gave us an idea of the season in the parable of the fig tree. He told us that when the branch is still tender, and it put forth leaves know that summer is nigh, so likewise when you see these things know that the end is near, even at the doors. Sadly Jesus warns us that the conditions that occurred during the time of Noah will again prevail at the end of time. People were caught up with the cares of life and when the flood came they were all destroyed. Similarly people today are absorbed with the here and now and have little time to spend preparing for eternity. The truth is that the end is near, time is running out and Satan is aware that he has little time left and he is making the most of the time he has left. What about you? In Revelation 12:12 God warns us "Woe to the inhabitants of the earth and of the sea for the devil is come down unto you, having great wrath because he knows that he hath but a short time. Satan realizes that his short time is fast running out and he is like a ravenous lion wreaking havoc and destruction everywhere. Satan knows that he has lost the battle for Planet Earth and he is soon to be punished for his rebellion against God. He knows that his end is near and had decided to go out in a blaze of fire taking as many as he could with him.

Why did Jesus give us these warnings of the events surrounding his second coming? He did not give us these events so that we can develop a checklist to see when he is coming but rather as a warning to live in constant readiness for His return and to share these truths with others. He warns us "Therefore be ye also ready for in such an hour as ye think not the son of man cometh". The chapters of Matthew 24 and 25 are full of warnings and admonitions for us. These warnings are for our benefit but warnings are useless unless people pay attention and heed them. Jesus warns us in Matthew 24 that as it was in the days of Noah so shall it be when He comes. In Noah's time people were seeking temporary gains of pleasure, money, fame and fortune when the flood came and washed them all away and only eight people were saved. He said the same thing is going to happen when He comes the second time, people will again be caught up with the cares of this life and ignore these solemn warnings given by God and that day will catch them unaware.

These ominous signs that Jesus described to His disciples over 2000 years ago are all around us today indicating that things are winding down. The majority of society do not act as though this is a matter to be taken seriously. The Bible in 2 Peter 3 tells us that in these last days some people will be scoffers saying "where is the promise of his coming for since the fathers fell asleep, all things continue as they were from the beginning of the creation." So today there are many scoffers are saying we have always had wars, climate changes and natural disasters, these things occur in cycles, so I am not convinced that these things are suggestive of the second coming of Christ. 2 Peter 3:9 warns us that the Lord is not slack concerning his promise of returning, as some men count slackness; but is long-suffering to us, not willing that any should perish, but that all should come to repentance. God is giving us time to repent but there is a time limit to his forbearance. The Bible states that "the day of the Lord shall come as a thief in the night; in which the Heavens shall pass away with a great noise, and the elements shall melt with fervent heat, the earth also and the works that are therein shall be burned up."

In Matthew 24:15 Jesus authenticates the apocalyptic prophecies of Daniel and He later enlarges and expands on these prophecies through the Prophet John.

Prophecy is one of God's tools that he uses to prepare us for his soon return. God established the prophetic ministry way back in Old Testament times and it will be present in the church until His second coming. The prophet Joel tells us in Joel 2:28–31 that before the second coming of Jesus the Holy Spirit will be poured out and your sons and daughters will prophecy, Pentecost is one manifestation of this prophecy. In Matthew 24:11 and 24 Jesus warns us against the false prophets that will arise in the last days; the text does not say that all the last day prophets would be false. We need to know God's word so that we will be able to discern the true prophets from the false ones. Prophets are God's messengers to us. They bring us warnings and messages from God. Some of the messages are encouraging; some are warnings of impending judgments. God's people have steered off course and have deviated from biblical truth. Just look at the many interpretations of biblical truth practiced in the many denominations of the world today. Satan, the master deceiver, has led many to misinterpret the Holy Scriptures that is why we have so much deviation from the biblical standard of truth. God lovingly sends his prophets to correct those who are in error from misinterpretations of biblical truth but sadly the people reject the prophets and continue in their own ways. Surely the Lord does nothing unless He reveals His secrets to his servants the prophets.

Throughout the entire Bible from the advent of sin on this planet to this current end time generation, God has been sending us warnings and admonitions through his prophets but only a few have heeded the words of the prophets. God's people have ridiculed, stoned and killed his prophets. The Eternal God of the ages who sent the prophets became a man and lived on earth for 33 years. He left us many prophecies and He bridged the gap between the Old Testament prophets and the New Testament prophets. He too like so many of His prophets was rejected and killed. Satan is the mastermind behind the deceptions but God has exposed his deceptions in the many prophecies of the Bible and has so concealed these prophecies in symbols that Satan could not destroy them all.

God revealed His divine plan of Redemption to his prophets

Since the fall of man God initiated his plan of redemption and he has chosen messengers or prophets to communicate this plan to us. In every major event in history God has sent His prophets to warn His people. He chose Noah to warn the world about a worldwide flood, He chose Abraham and He revealed to Abraham His entire plan of redemption including His second coming and Abraham's eternal home in that city whose builder and maker is God. He revealed the captivity in Egypt to Abraham and rose up Moses to lead his people out of the Egyptian Captivity. He chose Jeremiah to warn about the Babylonian Captivity and He chose Daniel during the captivity. He chose the Jewish nation to be his representative in this world to spread the Good news that the Messiah was coming and that there is Salvation in Jesus Christ. God sent numerous messianic prophecies foretelling His first coming (Read Isaiah 53). The Old Testament prophet Isaiah foretold He would be rejected and despised especially by the very people who were chosen to prepare the world for His coming. The prophet Daniel revealed the exact time of His first coming. God raised up John the Baptist to prepare the way for His first coming. Only a few listened to His warnings. These warnings were for most part ignored by God's people and the world at large and as a result His first coming was not a reality for the masses of society. Despite the many messianic prophecies regarding His first coming Jesus Christ was rejected by the very people who were suppose to prepare the world for His first coming. The world instead of welcoming our creator and redeemer rejected and killed Him. He died a cruel death at the hands of cruel men on a cruel cross in order to redeem us and save us from the penalty of our sins.

Despite His rejection by the masses of society then, the plan of salvation is still alive and His truth is marching on. God's plan of salvation did not stop because His chosen nation did not fulfill their assignment. God is God and He has many ways to accomplish His plans but He has chosen us who are sinners saved by grace to tell other sinners about His saving grace. Not only has He chosen prophets He has also chosen us to be partakers in this important work of redemption. God is always seeking people to spread the good news of Salvation. The plan must go on. After the rejection of Christ by the very people who were supposed to prepare the world for His first coming, Jesus chose twelve disciples and for three and a half years He trained them for the life saving work of spreading the everlasting gospel to the world. After His death and resurrection he stayed with them for forty days strengthening their faith and outlining the great commission that He had for them to do. From this core group the early church was formed. This New Testament Christian church consisted of a body of like-minded believers with a special commission to spread the good news that Christ is risen and there is salvation in Jesus Christ. The church although initially composed of mostly Jewish Christian believers was inclusive of all believers and to them He entrusted the work of spreading the gospel. Although the Jews as a nation rejected Him and forfeited their position as God's chosen to prepare the world for His coming, individual Jews embraced Jesus and were pivotal in the establishment of the early church. Today God has no special nation if you are a true believer in Christ you are Abraham's seed and heirs of the promises made to Abraham.

God came to earth and demonstrated to us the plan of salvation. He was rejected and killed. He is God and He came out of the tomb.

Jesus' resurrection from the tomb is the pivotal event in our history. After his resurrection He stayed with his disciples forty days, establishing them in the faith and preparing them to spread the everlasting gospel to the world. From this core group of disciples the early church was formed. This newly organized church impressively spread the gospel, and, as a result, they suffered much persecution from the authorities and in particular from the priests and rulers of Jerusalem who rejected the Messiah. Under heavy persecution, some of these early believers sought refuge in Damascus about 150 miles from Jerusalem.

From its very inception God's true church has been under heavy persecution. Saul of Tarsus, a rabbi in Jerusalem, aggressively persecuted the early church leaders. He was present when an early church leader, Stephen, was stoned to death. Stephen was the last prophet sent to the nation of Israel, and just before he was stoned to death, he gave the Jewish nation a review of their history. It is recorded in Acts chapter 7. In verse 52 Stephen asked the question, "which of the prophets has not your father's persecuted?" They took him out of the city and stoned him. Saul was present when Stephen uttered his last words, "Lord lay not this sin to their charge." Saul went around wreaking havoc of the church and imprisoning its members. One day Saul asked the high priest in Jerusalem for permission to go to Damascus to find more Christians that he could imprison in Jerusalem. He began the seven-day journey from Jerusalem to Damascus, where he intended to persecute more Christians and stop the work of the gospel. As he neared Damascus there was a dramatic show down. Suddenly a light from heaven shone around him. He fell to the ground blind and he heard a voice saying, "Saul, Saul, why are you persecuting me?" Saul then inquired, "who are you Lord." And the voice said "I am Jesus who you are persecuting. It is hard for you to fight against the pricks." Trembling and astonished Saul asked "Lord what do you want me to do?" He was told what to do. He obeyed and made a total surrender to God. Saul had been fighting against the promptings of the Holy Spirit which was convicting him since he witnessed the events at Stephen's death. He rejected the promptings of the Spirit by continuing to persecute the followers of Jesus. Saul was zealous for Yahweh, but did not accept the truth that Jesus was the Messiah and Lord of all. Saul no doubt studied the prophecies again and realized that they pointed to Jesus as the Messiah. He now saw in the scriptures what his previously prejudiced mind would not allow him to see. Saul had a total conversion. He continued on to Damascus, where his eyesight was restored and he was baptized. Saul's name was changed to Paul. God chose Paul as an apostle to the Gentiles, as well as to kings and the nation of Israel. It is important to note here that the 490 years allotted to the Jewish people to make an end to sins and reign in everlasting righteousness ended here at the death of Stephen, and now the gospel went out to the gentiles. This is what the Bible teaches so anyone who teaches that the Jewish nation will again to be chosen by God to fulfill his purposes is teaching doctrines that are contrary to scriptures.

The Prophetic Gifts of Apostle Paul

The Apostle Paul's calling is most encouraging. We do not know who God would choose to champion his cause. Saul was Zealous about his beliefs but after his Damascus Road encounter with Jesus; his eyes became opened to the truth as it is in Jesus. Paul boldly went forth declaring that Jesus was indeed the Messiah. He became a tremendous leader in the early church and one of the greatest Christian leaders of all times. He was chosen by God and placed in the early church. What a blessing he was in unifying the truths in this early church period. God used Paul mightily. He wrote about the gifts that God has given to the church. One of those gifts is the gift of prophecy. Blessed is the church in which God has placed the prophetic gift. Paul acknowledges the role of prophecy in the church. After his encounter with Jesus, he went back and studied the Messianic prophecies and realized that Jesus was indeed the Messiah. This is what the study of prophecy does: it reveals vital truths about Jesus, the author and finisher of our faith.

Paul wrote in Ephesians 4:11–14 that prophecy perfects the saints for the work of the ministry; it *edifies* the body of Christ so that there is *unity* of faith and belief in the church, and there is unity in the knowledge of Jesus. Prophecy *protects* Christian believers from false doctrines so that believers are not tossed about by every wind of doctrine. Satan the great deceiver is lurking at every opportunity to lead the church astray. The rejection of true prophecy in the Christian churches has led to major divisions in beliefs as well as the myriads of interpretations of scripture that are so evident in the Christian churches today. God placed the spirit of prophecy in his church to protect the believers from false doctrines. Paul tells us that these gifts, including prophecy, will be needed in the church until the saints are perfected, so we see clearly that these gifts are needed until the very return of Jesus. Only then will the saints will be perfected.

God has a standard of Truth

Since Jesus returned to Heaven, the church has strayed from the pure gospel taught by Jesus. Look at the practice in your church today and in the early church that Christ started and see how and if your church has strayed from the fundamental doctrines established by Jesus. Today there are variations of the gospel from preacher to preacher, teacher to teacher, church to church, culture to culture, locale to locale, and time to time. There seems to be a multiplicity of truths, and it is difficult for many people who are earnestly seeking truth to discern who is closest to the true gospel of Jesus Christ.

God wants us to be unified in the truth. It is not his will that there should be 500 plus denominations. If God's people would stick to the Bible and its teachings instead of their favorite radio, TV, or internet interpreter, their cassette tapes and CDs, we would not have the divisions that we have today. Satan can use whatever means he can to deceive people and keep them away from the truths of the Bible.

One thing we know for sure is that Jesus did not leave us with a multiplicity of truths. He established the early church and gave one body of truth.

If you have any doubts about truth, go back to the early church and review the truths established by Jesus. Follow in the footsteps of Jesus, pray for discernment, and the Holy Spirit will lead you into all truth. In Matthew 28:18–20 Jesus told his disciples, "All power is given to me in heaven and earth; go you therefore and teach all nations, baptizing them in the name of the father, and of the son and of the Holy Ghost. Teaching them to observe all things whatsoever *I have commanded you*: and lo I am with you always even unto the end of the world." He explicitly and exclusively declare declared in John 14:6 that He is the Way, The Truth and the Life; no one can come to God the Father unless they come through Him. Today there are many liberal interpretations of scripture, and some teach that there are many ways to God. Ephesians 4:4–5 tells us that there aren't several different ways to heaven: there is only one body and one spirit, and you are called into one hope, one Lord, one faith, and one baptism, and only one God and Father of all. Jesus further states in John 14:6 that "I am the way, the truth and the life no man come to the father but by me". We must be very careful about the truth that we settle for and what we teach. It matters what we believe and it matters what we try to teach others.

How Can the Body of Christ Achieve Unity in its Teachings?

Throughout the history of God's people, the presence of the prophetic gift among them has provided a unifying effect. Prophecy prevents the church from being tossed about by every wind of doctrine. There are so many well- educated, talented, gifted, convincing, brilliant voices on all the airwaves proclaiming that they have truth, and they understand the Bible best and they can best interpret what the essential Christian doctrines of the Bible.

How can you discern who is teaching what sounds good to the ear or someone's honest but false interpretation of scripture versus the true gospel of Jesus? You must know Biblical truth to know when your favorite speaker, though sincere, is not interpreting the Word of God correctly. Today the airwaves are filled with so many gifted, talented, entertaining, convincing preachers and speakers. Many of them are exciting to listen to and you can learn something from anyone. But how can you tell when they are preaching half-truths?

The gift of prophecy among God's church has been a guide and protection against deviant teachings claiming to be Biblically based. True prophecy interprets the Bible correctly and leads to more diligent study of the Bible. By diligently studying the scriptures and praying to God for enlightenment; God will give you knowledge, wisdom, and understanding so that you will know truth for yourself so that you are not tossed about by false interpretation of scripture as good as it may seem. This is an important issue and one day we will all stand before God's judgment bar and answer for ourselves. Our favorite speaker or pastor cannot be answer for us, so we need to study God's Word for ourselves and not be carried away by impressive but false teachers. Jesus specifically warned about these false teachers that will lead the church astray. He identified them as an end-time sign.

Safeguarding Truth

God cares that we know His truth. God knew that Satan would distort truth using the most brilliant minds at times. God has many ways of protecting His truth. One important gift that God has used to protect and impart truth to His people has been the true gift of prophecy. The prophetic gift in the midst of the body of Christ is an important means of disseminating truth, and it has been present at critical times throughout the history of God's people.

Most of the Bible is God speaking to us through His chosen prophets. God has lovingly revealed truth to us in His Holy word and very often through His prophets. He wants us to share this truth to others in love. God does not want us to condemn or to judge others. We are all God's children and should treat each other like brothers and sisters regardless of our perceived differences. We are not sent to condemn others, but to share our faith with them. Some will accept and some will reject. We leave all judgment to God. In the final analysis it is God and God alone who justifies and determines who is saved.

God is the ultimate source of all wisdom and knowledge and often equips even the weakest of the weak to proclaim His salvation plan. He chose teachable people who are willing to be led by the Holy Spirit.

The same Holy Spirit who inspired these prophets is available to us to help us to understand the Bible. The function of the Holy Spirit is to guide us into truth. The Holy Spirit will lead us to God, the source of truth. An important sign that someone is filled with the Holy Spirit is that they will lead you to Jesus and His great atoning sacrifice at Calvary. The central theme of the Bible is Jesus, our great Redeemer. Prophecy leads us to Jesus, the true source of wisdom and knowledge.

Colossians 2:3 tells us that in God are hid all the treasures of wisdom and knowledge. Only in God do we find absolute truth and absolute knowledge. The deep truths that are found in the Bible require much prayer and study. They are not gained by a superficial encounter with spiritual ideas. They require diligent study of the Bible, comparing scripture with scripture. Since the scriptures were inspired by the Holy Spirit we should pray earnestly for the guidance of the Holy Spirit in order to properly understand truth and most importantly have a willingness to accept truth.

God wants us to know and study these truths for ourselves. He does not want us to be deceived by false teachers, and there are numerous false teachers of the Bible are all around us. They play on our emotions and do not lead us to a deep understanding of Gods' word. God does not want us to accept false teachings with blind faith. God is not honored by unthinking blind faith. The deep spiritual and philosophical issues of the Bible cannot be understood by a casual encounter. The Holy Spirit is an educator. He leads us to study the word of God diligently. Studying the word of God should be our daily experience. We are admonished in 2 Timothy 2:15 to study the Bible to show ourselves approved unto God that we are workmen who are not ashamed, correctly interpreting the word of truth. God wants us to search the scriptures diligently and the Holy Spirit will lead us to truth and when we have found truth we should turn away from false teachings. God wants to sanctity us through the truth in his word. God does not want us to practice false beliefs. He is light and truth and He will do all he can to bring truth to us. God wants everyone to know truth. If you are sincere and diligent in finding truth, God will lead you to His truth.

God hears our prayers and leads us into His truth. A good example of this is found in the book of Acts, chapter 10. Cornelius was a rich Roman Army centurion who loved and feared the Lord. He prayed regularly and was very generous to the poor. Although he was a very devout, religious man, he did not have a true knowledge of God. He was a sincere seeker for truth and prayed fervently. It mattered to God that Cornelius should come to the truth.

One day an angel sent by God told Cornelius in a vision that God had heard his prayers and had noticed his generosity to the poor. The angel did not give Cornelius the gospel, but instructed Cornelius to send for the apostle Peter, who was staying by the seaside in Joppa in the house of a man named Simon the tanner. In the meantime God was preparing Peter for this mission to spread the gospel to the gentiles. Peter was in Joppa on the housetop of Simon who lived by the seaside. He was hungry and while he was waiting for the food to be ready, God gave him a vision. He saw heaven opened. He saw a sheet filled with many unclean animals. He heard a voice telling him, "Rise Peter, kill and eat."

Peter refused, citing that he had never eaten anything unclean. The voice then said to Peter, "What God hath cleansed, you should not call unclean." This happened three times and then the sheet was taken up to heaven. While Peter was still on the rooftop trying to understand the meaning of the vision, Cornelius' servants arrived. The Holy Spirit revealed to Peter that he should return with them and so Peter returned with them to Caesarea the next day. When Peter arrived at Cornelius home, he found a house full of people waiting to hear the gospel. Cornelius greeted Peter and fell down at his feet to worship him but Peter forbade him, saying that he was just a man like Cornelius. He told Cornelius that it is unlawful for a Jew to keep company or enter the house of a non-Jew because they are unclean but God has showed Peter that he should not call any man common or unclean.

Peter then understood the vision clearly that it was not about God giving him permission to eat unclean animals. Prior to this vision Peter believed that the gospel was only for the Jews. God revealed to Peter that he is no respecter of persons. He wanted Peter, a Jew to take the message to the Gentiles and that no one should look down on another and call them unclean because Jesus has made us all one in him. The Holy Spirit was poured out on these Gentile brethren and they got *baptized* in the name of the Lord Jesus Christ.

The Lord knows His children, He knows where they are and he often sends more vital truth that everyone may accept and do God's will. Cornelius had an open willing mind and accepted the truth when he heard it. Peter, a Jewish man, declared that he could see that God does not does not discriminate. He is the God of all people and He has an open door policy for every human being but we must be willing to accept vital truth. The gospel commission is for everyone.

One important lesson to learn here is the sincerity of Cornelius; he truly wanted to follow God and exhibited a willingness to understand. He had an open heart and mind and he prayed to God for understanding. The Holy Spirit led the way, and he discerned truth. He accepted it and became a follower of Christ in spirit and in truth. Cornelius could then teach the truth to others. This is the essence of the gospel. It liberates us spiritually and let us be one in Christ Jesus to preach His everlasting, untarnished gospel.

This is the mystery of the Gospel that Paul speaks about in Ephesians 3 where he says that the gospel was given to the Jews that it should be made known to all men. God made the Jewish nation custodian of his law and keeper of the oracles of God. God did not give this responsibility to the Jews because they were a superior nation. The opposite was true. They were a nation just released from slavery when he chose them for this important task. He entrusted them with His truth so that they could communicate or demonstrate His truth to the world. As a nation they failed in doing this most important work and Christ set up the Christian church made up of people from every nation, kindred, tongue, and people who are engaged in spreading the everlasting gospel to earth's remotest areas. God is able to raise up stones to finish His work, and He often chooses the least among us and equips us with the necessary tools to spread this gospel. It is under these circumstances that His grace could be best demonstrated.

God has no grandchildren. We are all His children from every denomination, every culture, and every tongue from all peoples of the earth. He wants the best for all of his creation. He does not want us to believe and practice false traditions, He wants us to reject false teachings and do exactly what he asks us to. This is not a New Testament phenomenon. This has always been God's position.

About 2000 BC God called Abraham out of the Ur of the Chaldees to leave his old way of life behind and follow him. Abraham left his family with their wealth and followed God not knowing where he was going. God still calls us today to leave false teachings, leave the crowd, leave the worldly ways behind and follow him. If you hear His voice and understand His will, do what He asks you to do. God wants a unified body of believers. In John 17:20–21 Jesus prays that all believers in Him may be one as He is one with the Father. It is the great longing in the heart of the Father that all His children should be gathered home under one fold and one banner.

How Can God's Church Achieve Unity?

The church today has become such a profitable business institution that truth is no longer the driving force or the cornerstone of the church. The culture of the world has invaded the church. The entertainment industry is now part of the church. How does this square up with the simple gospel church that Jesus started? Sometimes what sells is not the true gospel, but the popular variety of whatever people want to hear and what can sell and entertain? Do you go to a church because you like the music or do you go there because the Word of God is taught? How do you find the right church? This poses a challenge for the sincere searcher of truth.

How does God protect the truth from the popular merchandizing of it? What important safeguard has God given to us in the Bible that helps to unify the church and solidify truth? The Apostle Paul gave us some of the answers in Ephesians 4. The placement of Prophecy in the God's church is helpful in unifying and solidifying truth. It has always been and will always be a distinguishing feature of God's true church. Down through the centuries God placed the prophetic gift among His people to protect the integrity of the truth. God did not stop this practice in New Testament times. A careful study of the Bible reveals that God has *always* had a prophet or prophets among His people and that God has chosen to communicate His will to us through these prophets is an undeniable fact for any Bible believing Christian. Prophets are men or women called by God who receive special messages from God to for His people. It is a serious and dangerous thing to claim that God has called you to be a prophet if He has not. It is also dangerous not to heed the words of God's chosen prophet. Prophets are not self-proclaimed or man appointed. They are called to the prophetic office by God. Prophets tell the story of Jesus. Prophecy is all about Jesus and his salvation plan for us. The story is not about the prophet. The prophets should lead us back to God.

What is the issue with prophecy and the Christianity today?

Prophecy exposes Satan and his many deceptions. His most effective weapon against prophecy is to destroy and distort it and confuse people by raising up so many false prophets. Whenever God raises up a true prophet Satan raises up many false prophets so that people do not listen to the true prophet. Today, so many people claim that the Lord called them and gave them the prophetic gift? How can you distinguish the false prophets from the true prophets? How does God use the prophetic gift? It is very important to know who God's true prophets are. Is it possible that you are ignoring vital messages sent by God to you through His prophets because you do not recognize His prophets? In 2 Chronicles 20:20 "God's people were admonished to "Believe in the Lord your God so shall you be established; believe in his prophets, so you shall prosper." In 1 Corinthians 14:1 we are admonished to follow after charity, and desire spiritual gifts, especially the gift of prophecy. Here Paul admonishes us to seek after the best gifts, especially the gift of prophecy. Paul would not admonish us to seek the gift of prophecy if God had stopped imparting this gift among His people.

The significance of Prophecy in the divine plan of salvation

Since the fall of Adam and Eve, God has communicated to us through His prophets. This is clear throughout the Bible. God chooses both men and women to be His messenger or prophet. The Bible is God speaking to us through His prophets. In the Old Testament there were four major and twelve Minor Prophets. In the New Testament there is one major prophetic book, but there are prophecies in other books (e.g. Matthew 24). God sends vital messages to His people through His prophets. The prophet Amos assures in Amos 3:7 that "surely the Lord God *does nothing, unless He reveals His secrets to His servants the prophets*."

This is true even down to the very end of time. The prophetic gift is going to be part of the church until Jesus comes. We know this from careful interpretation of the Bible. The Apostle John in Revelation 19:10 told us that the devil is angry at the church, and makes war with the final remnant church. The final remnant church is characterized as the final church that keeps the commandments of God and has the testimony of Jesus. Revelation 19:10 tells us that the testimony of Jesus is the Spirit of Prophecy. This clearly indicates that the prophetic gift is going to be a part of the final church just as it was in the beginning of the New Testament church and in Old Testament times. The prophetic gift to God's people did not end after the book of Revelation was given. The Spirit of God who has inspired the prophets from the beginning will do so until Jesus comes.

The Apostle Paul in Ephesians 4:8–12 indicates that when Jesus ascended to heaven, He left the church with gifts. To some apostles, to *some prophets*, to some evangelists, and to some pastors. These gifts, including the prophetic gift, will be in the church until Jesus comes. They are necessary for the perfecting of the saints, for the work of the ministry and the edifying of the church. These gifts will remain in the church until we all come to the *unity* of faith, the knowledge of the son of God, to a perfect man, to the measure of the stature of the fullness of Christ. We will no longer be children, tossed to and fro about by deceptive teachers and by every wind of doctrine that blows by us.

1 Corinthians 12:28–30 states that God has set some in the church, first apostles, secondarily prophets, thirdly teachers, After those were miracles, and then gifts of healings, helps, governments, and diversities of tongues. Jesus is the Head of the Church and the members represent the body. He gives these gifts to the church so that as believers come into the Church they will become more like Jesus. These gifts are clearly needed in the body of Christ until he comes again. They are for the up building of the church in many ways (1) The gift of prophecy in the church unifies the church and help the believers to mature and be grounded in truth so that they won't be tossed to and fro by false doctrines and false teachers (2) The gifts direct the missionary work of the church (3) The prophet edifies, exhorts, and comforts the church. (See 1 Corinthians 14:3).

The prophetic gift among God's church continues with God's warnings through the Prophet John

We have traced God's plan of salvation since the fall of man in Genesis and we have fast forwarded to the final book of the Bible Revelation. The book of Revelation is a very relevant book in the life of God's people. God has revealed a lot of information in this book. Satan has opposed God's redemption plan from the beginning of time. We have seen how he has opposed God's word and despised his prophets. Satan is going to continue these attacks and they are going to get much worse as we approach the end of time. Despite his ingenious attacks, the plan of Salvation is still moving forward because God is greater than any attack Satan can muster against his plan.

God is consistent and changes not. He has a plan of salvation that He has been executing for centuries now. Some seven hundred years later God expands and enlarges on the prophecies revealed in the book of Daniel. He does so with the prophet John in the book of Revelation. Daniel holds the key to a better understanding of Revelation and vice versa. God has revealed a lot of important end time information in both books. The book of Revelation expands and enlarges on the prophecies revealed in Daniel. This consistency is the work of the Holy Spirit. 2 Peter 1:20–21 states that "knowing this that no prophecy is of private interpretation. For prophecy came not in old time by the will of man: but holy men spoke as they were moved by the Holy Ghost." This is why the true prophets of God do not contradict each other. The same Holy Spirit inspires the prophets. Therefore their messages are consistent. God's prophets from beginning to end will not contradict each other.

The prophetic gift in New Testament times

The author of the book of Revelation is the Apostle John, the last of the 12 original disciples of Jesus. The emperor Caesar Domitian commanded worship for himself and punished dissenters. The Apostle John along with many other Christians was banished on the barren Isle of Patmos in the Aegean Sea. The Christian church was under great persecution from Roman authority. It was during this time that God sent his angel Gabriel to the prophet John while in exile for his faith on the lonely Isle of Patmos and gave him the apocalyptic prophecies of Revelation. This book, as its name suggests, is a revealing of events that will take place culminating in the second coming of Jesus. Here God enlarges and expands on the details of some of the apocalyptic prophecies that he showed to Daniel in the 6th Century BC. A verse-by-verse study of Revelation is an enormous undertaking, so we will just study the prophecies that expand and enlarge on those given to Daniel. Let us begin with Revelation 13 since it enlarges and expands on the prophecies of Daniel 7. Here God elaborates on the prophecies of Daniel and introduces a new power.

Chapter Thirteen
REVELATION

Verse 1: "And I stand upon the sand of the sea, and saw a beast rise up out of the sea, having seven heads and ten horns, and upon his horns ten crowns, and upon his head the name of blasphemy."

It is well over 600 hundred years since the prophecies of Daniel 7, and now in Revelation 13:1 God gives a vision to his exiled prophet John. It is similar to the one He gave to Daniel. Notice a pattern here; John is shown the same prophetic scenes. God is expanding and enlarging on the prophecies shown to Daniel. God wants us to know these prophecies, and He repeats them. In this vision John was stands on the seashore and sees a beast/nation coming out of the sea with seven heads, 10 horns and has 10 crowns (kingly crowns), and on each head was the word "blasphemy."

The same principle of prophetic interpretation that we used in the studied of the book of Daniel holds true here. The beast represents a nation or kingdom, while the sea represents multitudes of peoples. The prophet is shown a seven-headed beast nation described as coming out of the sea of humanity or a populated area of the world. Daniel 7:7 describes this same dreadful and terrible beast coming out of the sea and having 10 horns. The seven heads probably represent the seven kingdoms that have opposed God's people. They are Egypt, Assyria, Babylon, Medo-Persia, Greece, Pagan Rome and Papal Rome. The ten horns represent the ten political kingdoms into which the 4th beast of Daniel (Pagan Rome) was divided into. Remember Daniel was shown a Little Horn kingdom of Papal Rome that came up among the 10 horns. The leopard-like composite beast shown to John and the Little Horn Kingdom shown to Daniel have similar characteristics. God reveals the same power to both prophets 600 years apart.

Verse 2: "And the beast which I saw was like unto a leopard, and his feet were as the feet of a bear, and his mouth as the mouth of a lion: and the dragon gave him his power, his seat, and great authority."

Satan is depicted as standing on the sands of the seashore and as this power comes out of the sea Satan gives him his power, seat and great authority. John, living in the time of the Roman Empire (which is the 4th beast power shown to Daniel), is looking backwards and is shown these beasts in the reverse order that Daniel saw them. John describes this beast as having characteristics similar to the first three beasts of Daniel 7. It has the body of a leopard, the feet of a bear and the mouth of a lion - its body resembled a leopard. The leopard beast of Daniel represents Greece; the feet like a bear represent Medo-Persia; and the mouth of a lion is Babylon. This leopard-like composite beast shown to John had characteristics of all three beasts described in Daniel 7. In 603 BC Daniel was shown the lion, then the bear, and then the leopard. These were the great dominant powers of Babylon, Medo-Persia and Greece. These powers have dominated history just as that prophecy predicted. John is living in the days of Daniel's 4th beast power Rome in its Pagan form before its demise. Daniel was shown the Little Horn power that is Papal Rome. John is also shown this power as a leopard-like beast.

John is shown that the dragon gives his power, seat, and great authority to this beast. In this great controversy between Satan and God, in order for Satan's deceptions to work, he must disguise them. Satan has long tried to exterminate God's people and God's church. He has failed and so he now infiltrates the Church and carries out his plan from within. This method has been very successful for him. Satan, having lost every battle against Christ, continues to wage war by disguising himself behind these powers. The dragon here is Satan working behind the scenes. He gave to this power - his power, his seat, and great authority to this beast power.

History supports this interpretation. The great Roman Empire began to disintegrate after recurrent invasions by various tribes. Constantine, the Roman emperor, moved the capital east from Rome to Constantinople, which bears his name. He gave his seat to the Roman Pontiff.

LaBlanca, professor of history at the University of Rome, wrote "When Constantine left Rome, he gave his seat to the Pontiff." Constantine accepted Christianity as his religion, and the devil, working through pagan Rome gave this new power- Papal Rome -his power, his seat and great authority. This leopard-like composite beast is a mixture of paganism and Christianity. Look closely at all of its teachings and see which came from paganism and which came from Christianity.

In his book, The History of the Eastern Church, Arthur P. Stanley wrote "The pope filled the place of the vacant Emperors of Rome, inheriting their power, prestige, and titles from paganism. The papacy is but the ghost of the deceasing Roman Empire sitting crowned upon its grave."

Alexander Flick wrote in his book, The Rise of the Medieval Church (1900) "Out of the ruins of political Rome, arose the great moral empire in the 'giant form' of the Roman Church." The Roman Emperor Justinian made the bishop of Rome the legal head of all churches. The Roman Church consolidated power in 538 after the defeat of the Ostrogoths. The Pope became the head of all churches. For 1260 years the Catholic Church had great authority over people; emperors and kings were subject to its authority.

Verse 3: "And I saw one of his heads as it was wounded to death; and his deadly wound was healed: and all the world wondered after the beast."

God reveals more and more details about this beast. John is shown the history of this beast. It was wounded to death politically, but it recovers from this wound and in the very end of time all the world would follow this restored beast. In the year 538AD the papacy solidified its power after the destruction of the final Arian power of the Ostrogoths. The power of the papacy grew and dominated the secular and religious world for 1260 years. This is the same time as little horn beast of Daniel 7:25, Revelation 12:4 and 14. The reformation of the 16th century weakened the power of the papacy. The papacy was still a dominant power at the time of the French Revolution. The French revolted against the Papacy. Napoleon, a major world leader at the time wanted to rule all of Europe, but couldn't do it because of the strength and power of the papacy.

In 1796 Napoleon invaded Italy, and on February 15, 1798 he sent the French Army General Berthier to abduct the Pope Pious VI and declare the political rule of the papacy ended. He removed the pope from the Sistine chapel in Rome and took the pope prisoner to France where he died in exile on August 29, 1799. The papacy received the deadly wound that was shown to the prophet John. It lost its great political power and it was felt that the papacy was over. The Papal States were later absorbed by Italy in 1870, and the power of the papacy almost came to an end. The deadly wound was inflicted. This ended the 1260 years of papal domination from 538AD to 1798 AD This is the same power described in Daniel 7:25 as having wearing out the saints of the most High and the saints shall be given into his hand for time, times, and a dividing of time or 1260 years.

In 1870AD the Papal States were taken just as the prophecy states almost 1800 years before. Thus began the Roman question. The Roman Question was a political dispute between the Papacy and the Italian government about the problems that arose when the sovereignty of the papacy was restricted. The Roman Question began when Rome was declared the capital of Italy, the power of the papacy was severely restricted and the popes felt they were prisoners in the Vatican. The deadly wound was healed and in 1929 Benito Mussolini and First Cardinal Gusparri signed the Roman Pact. Mussolini entered the picture and decided to settle the Roman Question. In 1929 the Lateran treaty restored the power to the papacy and Mussolini paid the papacy 21 million and gave the papacy Vatican City 108.7 acres thus settling the Roman Question. "The Roman question tonight was a thing of the past and the Vatican was at peace with Italy. The formal accomplishment of this today was the exchange of signatures in the historic palace of St. John Lateran by two noteworthy plenipotentiaries, Cardinal Gasparri for Pope Pius XI and premier Mussolini for King Victor Emmanuel III." (Associated Press, 1929)

The San Francisco Chronicle, a secular paper, on February 11, 1929 stated that "the Roman Question tonight is a thing of the past and the Vatican is at peace with Italy, thus healing the deadly wound. Extreme cordiality was displayed by both sides." So in 1929 religious and civil powers, and land was handed back to the Vatican, thus healing the deadly wound.

It happened just as the prophecy said over 1800 hundred years before. The wound has healed completely, and today the papacy stands as the major religion of this world. The Vatican is a sovereign government with ambassadors from all over the world. No other religious body has ambassadors from all over the world to their headquarters. The United States has an ambassador to the Vatican. This power is admired worldwide. The prophet was shown that this power's deadly wound would heal and the whole world would roam after this sea beast power, indicating that it is a universal system of worship. The papacy today is the dominant religious body, and the pope is considered the most important religious voice in the world today.

Verse 4: "And they worshipped the dragon, which gave power unto the beast: and they worshipped the beast, saying. Who is like unto the beast? Who is able to make war with him?"

Satan wants worship and he gets it by deception. The devil gave power to this beast. The dragon is disguised in this beast power. The devil unites with this power and form a counterfeit union that is so cleverly deceptive that it is worshipped. The text says, "They worshipped the beast." Clearly this is a religious counterfeit power that receives worship. Satan wants worship and he gets it by deception.

Verse 4 asks "who is able to make war with this beast?" Resistance to this beast would be met by force. No one except God can make war and overcome this power.

Verse 5: "And there was given unto him a mouth speaking great things and blasphemies; and power was given unto him to continue for forty and two months." When the day-to-year principle is applied here this prophecy tells the length of time the papacy would dominate for 42 months or 1260 years (See Daniel 7:25).

Verse 6: "And he opened his mouth in blasphemy against God, to blaspheme against God, to blaspheme his name, and his tabernacle, and them that dwell in heaven."

This power is boastful and speaks great things and is accused of blasphemies. What is blasphemy? Blasphemy occurs when one assumes divine functions. This is a biblical definition of blasphemy. Here is an example: In Mark 2, Jesus was in Capernaum, preaching and healing, when a man was let down through the roof for Jesus to heal. When Jesus saw their faith, He said, "Son thy sins be forgiven thee." The scribes then accused him of blasphemy because only God can forgive sins.

In John 10:33: "Then the Jews answered him, saying, for a good work we stone thee not; but for blasphemy; and because that thou, being a man, making thyself God." So blasphemy is when a man makes himself God.

This power claims the ability to forgive sins. When a priest says "ego te absolve," or "I absolve thee," he is blaspheming. Only God can do this. This is assuming the function of God. This power is obscuring Jesus' mediatory work in heaven. It is counterfeiting on earth what Jesus is doing now in the heavenly sanctuary.

In Daniel chapter 8 this power is also accused of blaspheming God's sanctuary and casting truth to the ground and prospering in the process. The importance of the heavenly sanctuary and Christ's mediatory work for us is obscured by elaborate earthly religious systems. The heavenly ministry of Christ at the right hand of the father has not gained the attention of God's people because this power has substituted its own earthly mediatory system.

Verse 7: "And it was given unto him to make war with the saints, and to overcome them: And power was given over all kindred, and tongue and nations." This is a power with world wide political and religious authority.

This power made war with the saints and overcame them. This is the same description given of the beast of Daniel 7:25. It is the same beast. It should be emphasized that the prophecy is referring to a power and not an individual.

Verse 8: "And all that dwell upon the earth shall worship him, whose names are not written in the book of life of the lamb slain from the foundation of the world."

The crux of the matter is really worship. Satan wants the worship that belongs to God, and in his battle against God he sets up a system whereby the true worship of God is eclipsed by an earthly system that he has set up. He is extremely clever in this deception and makes the deception look like the right thing to do.

Verse 9: "If you have ears, you should listen." God is saying pay attention to what He is revealing to you.

Verse 10: "He that leadeth into captivity shall go into captivity: He that killeth with the sword must be killed by the sword. Here is the patience and the faith of the saints."

Eventually God will vindicate his saints and will execute judgment on all including this beast power. If you lead others into captivity, you shall go into captivity. If you kill by the sword, you shall be killed by the sword.

Before going on to the second beast that was shown to the prophet John in Revelation 13, let us review some of the *Characteristics of the 1st beast of Rev 13*. (They are similar to those shown in Daniel 7)

1. It came out of the sea, which represents the populated area of Western Europe. (Rev 13:1, Daniel 7:2)

2. Had seven heads and 10 horns and upon his horn 10 crowns and the name of 'blasphemy' on its head. (Rev 13:2; Daniel 7: 8 and 20). On the heads of this beast was the name Blasphemy meaning this beast power blasphemes against God. It assumes titles that belong only to God.

3. It has a composite body-leopard body, bear feet, lion mouth (Rev 13:2)

4. The dragon or Satan gave him his power, his seat, and great authority. (Revelation 13:2)

5. One of his heads was wounded to death. (Rev 13:3)

6. The deadly wound was healed (Rev 13:3)

7. All the world roamed after this beast power (Rev 13:3)

8. It receives worldwide worship (Rev 13:4).

    The whole world worships this beast. The world is led astray by the teachings of this beast. It commands worship; it is definitely a religious political power.

9. It has a mouth speaking great things and blasphemy against God, His name, His tabernacle, and everyone that dwells in Heaven. (Rev 13:6)

10. This power is allowed to dominate for 42 months or 1260 years. (Rev 13:5).

11. It made war with the saints and overcome them (Rev 13:7)

12. It received power over all kindreds, tongues and nations.

13. All them that dwell upon the earth shall worship the beast. Those who worship him will not have their names written in the book of life. Rev 13: 8.

14. It killed with the sword (Rev 13:10)

15. It went into captivity (Rev13:10)

16. Another power will force others to worship the dictates of this beast. (Rev 13:12).

17. The number of this beast is 666. (Rev.13: 18).

18. She has a political alliance; all the kings of the earth do business with her. It has worldwide influence. (Rev 17:2).

19. It is the same beast as Daniel's Little Horn.

At the time this beast power is taken into captivity; the prophet John is shown a second beast power arising at the same time that the first beast is wounded. Both beasts have a major role in the apocalypse or the revealing of end- time events. God gave this information to us via his prophets. *Surely the Lord God does nothing before he reveals his secret to his servants the prophets.*

The characteristics of the second beast of Revelation 13

Verse 11: "And I beheld another beast coming out of the earth; and he had two horns like a lamb, and he spoke as a dragon."

John is still in vision and he sees a new beast coming out of the earth; and he had two horns like a lamb and he spoke as a dragon. John is given a few identifying characteristics and is shown a nation with lamb-like and dragon like characteristics. Let us look at the characteristics in detail in order to identify this beast correctly.

1. Time of arrival

2. Location of arrival

3. What are the characteristics of this nation?

4. What will it do in the end?

1. Time of arrival – In Revelation 13:10 John sees the first beast receiving its deadly wound in 1798 and going into captivity. As the sea beast goes into captivity, in verse 10, he is shown a new beast is coming up out of the earth in verse 11. The time of the arrival of this second beast nation is given to us. It arises at the time of the captivity of the first beast. Revelation 13:10 states that he that killeth with the sword must be killed with the sword and he that leadeth into captivity shall go into captivity. So as this first beast that killed so many of God's people went into captivity, the second beast came up. It came to prominence about the time of the captivity of the other beast about 1798. God revealed to John living in the first century the time of Papal dominance and that it will receive a deadly wound. It happened in 1798 when Napoleon's general Berthier abducted the pope and he died in exile in France. At the time this power receives this wound another power is on the rise. Note the fulfillment of the prophecy given to John that this power would reign for 1260 years before receiving its deadly wound.

What nation was coming into power about 1798 when the other beast went into captivity after receiving it's deadly wound? What nation was coming up out of the earth- or an unpopulated area of the world -in 1798? There is only one nation that arose at this time and fits the characteristics of this new beast. It is the USA. The USA plays a major role in Biblical end time prophecies of the Bible. The declaration of independence was signed in 1776. The birthday of the USA is July 4, 1776. The constitution was ratified in 1787 and the Bill of Rights in 1791. There is no denying that God has revealed to us the major world powers and how they have impacted on his people. It is quite consistent with prophecy to reveal the last great world ruling power and its major role in end time events. It would be strange that God would show all the world powers and their impact on his people and not mention one of the greatest world powers, the USA that will be the last world ruling power with major impact on God's people just before his second coming.

2. Location of arrival – The first beast mentioned in Revelation 13:1 came out of the sea. All of the other prophetic beasts that we studied in Daniel came out of the sea too. The sea represents well-populated area with peoples; the Bible tells us so in Rev 17:1, 15. In this context the sea represents the densely populated areas of Western Europe or the Old World. About this time, John sees a new beast/nation, very different from the other beasts, and this time it is coming out of the earth – a relatively unpopulated area. Unlike Babylon, Medo-Persia, Greece, and Rome that came up in the populated areas of Europe, this nation sprung up in a new uninhabited place. The other kingdoms arose where there was a nation before, not this one. This second beast nation God raised in the unpopulated area of the New World.

3. What are the characteristics of this nation?

The prophet was shown that it had two horns like a lamb, suggesting that it is lamb like in its beginnings. When compared to the way the other nations came into power, this nation is described as peaceful and gentle in its beginning. It did not have to overthrow any other kingdom to establish itself. It was a new and youthful nation. This beast power was not ferocious like the preceding ones. It was different; it is lamb-like and more humane. When compared to the other nations that rose to power, this beast had no crown on its head or and no crown on its horns denoting that it has no king or queen or monarchy or earthly dominant religious leader. It rose to power quietly without a king, a queen or a dominant religious leader. As compared to the warlike way the other beast/ nations came to power, this nation in its beginnings was raised up by God as gentle as a lamb and it has respect for religious liberties. Numerous religions blossomed in the USA and they are tax exempted.

Remember the first beast nation described in Revelation 13:1 had crowns on its horns denoting leadership by a king, queen, pope, or some form of monarchy. This power has no such leadership because it is a democratic form of government. The two horns on this beast nation represent its civil and religious liberty. This is the foundation that this nation was built on. The people of the USA rule this country via representatives they choose to speak for them in the Congress and the House of Representatives. No one can make the laws of this country unilaterally.

This lamb-like beast nation began as a peaceful haven for the oppressed from every nation who came to these shores. Having experienced religious and political persecution and oppression in their homeland, they were determined to establish a government free from religious control, hence the Declaration of Independence guaranteeing the greatest freedom to worship God, free from the dictates of the church and state. This is quite different from the religious practices of Europe, where political or religious authorities dictated worship. Millions were killed because they dare to worship according to the dictates of their conscience; examples of these martyrs are the Huguenots, the Waldensians, and the Albigenses.

Many of the inhabitants of this new kingdom were exiles who suffered political and religious oppression in their homeland and they were seeking independence from these oppressive forces in Europe. Their views are reflected in the Declaration of Independence that all men are created equal and are endowed with inalienable right to life, liberty, and the pursuit of happiness, and in the constitution that guarantees, among other things, the freedom to worship as guided by religious conscience. The stated principles of the US Constitution guarantees civil and religious freedom. As a result of these principles, millions of poor oppressed people from all over the world flocked to the shores of America, seeking freedom from all kinds of persecution: some from religious persecution, some from persecution of dictatorships.

Millions found this freedom in America, and this second beast power described in Revelation 13:11 has risen to become the most powerful nation on earth. When communism fell in 1991 with the help of President Reagan and the pope, the USA became an unrivaled super power, a prophetic fulfillment. In order for her to fulfill the role that was shown to the prophet John, she would have to be a world superpower.

4. What will it do in the end? The prophecy does not show a glorious ending for this nation. It shows a rather disappointing end. Despite her rise to the pinnacle of world power, the prophecy clearly states that in the end of time, or immediately before the coming of the Lord, she would speak like a dragon, become a false prophet and become a persecuting power to God's true followers. How can that happen? How does this change from her lamb-like beginnings to her dragon like state in the end of time and allow its power to be used by Satan to fulfill his purposes? How can this lamb like horned beast speak with the voice of the dragon?

On July4, 1776 the Declaration of Independence was signed. In her lamb-like stage the founding fathers, George Washington, Thomas Jefferson, Patrick Henry, James Madison, and Benjamin Franklin wrote the constitution, opposing any legislation that would endanger the freedom to worship God according to the dictate of one's conscience. These principles have made America a great nation. The amendments to the Constitution read that Congress shall make no law respecting an establishment of religion, or prohibiting the free exercise thereof. Article six states that no religious test shall ever be required as qualification to any office or public trust in the United States.

The prophecy tells us that in the end of time, these freedoms that made her great will be revoked. This beast, that the exiled prophet John was shown, that this power with its two horns like a lamb, which started out like a lamb, young and gentle, will become a world power and in the end of time will speak as a dragon. The prophet is shown how the USA will speak as a dragon and have a dominant role in the persecution of God's people in the very end of time. She will be led by those who believe they have the truth and so the final battle would be those who think that they are God's people imposing their beliefs over God's.

Verse 12: "She would exercise all the power of the first beast before it, and cause the earth and them which dwell therein to worship the first beast, whose deadly wound was healed."

From this passage of scripture we see that these two beast nations are in existence at the same time in history and both have worldwide influence. It tells us clearly that the first beast nation was wounded but the wound healed and she regained worldwide power. The second beast does her prophetic thing after the deadly wound of the first beast is healed. The deadly wound was healed in 1929.

This means that America, the second beast nation shown to John in Revelation 13:11, will enforce the power of the first beast, Papal Rome, revealed in Revelation 13:1. How would the USA promote the Papacy's cause? In order for the second beast to cause a worldwide worship to the first beast she would have to be a dominant world power. How would the lamb-like beast force her people to worship after the dictates of the leopard-like beast power? The prophecy states that the USA will force the world to worship according to the dictates of Papal Rome. How can this lamb-like beast with no king, no pope, and no dominant religious leader, with a Constitution that guarantees religious freedom and a Bill of Rights, deny its people civil and religious freedoms? In order to enforce worship of the first beast, the USA will have to repudiate civil and religious liberty and break down the separation of church and state and dictate religious worship just like the first beast did in Europe for centuries. During the 1260-year period (538AD–1798AD) the first beast was a religious political power with no separation of church and state. If you dissented from the dominant belief, you were killed, that is a historical fact and the fulfillment of prophecy shown to Daniel.

God revealed to the prophet John that this lamb-like beast with the two horns will in the end of time and at the height of her power loose this lamb-like quality and *speak like a dragon*. It is quite obvious that the USA is no longer a lamb-like nation. Since the fall of communism in 1991, the USA has been the sole world ruling power and has the world's attention. She is going to change and is already changing rapidly. The events of September 11, 2001 have fast tracked these changes. The prophet John was shown that she will support what the first beast did and she will cause the whole world to worship the first beast that was wounded but recovered. How does this nation speak like a dragon? She will enforce by legislation the man-made laws that the first beast has enacted.

What is the characteristic mark of the 1st beast?

It is clear from history that the Papacy forced conscience in the Old World and dissenters from popular beliefs were punished. Millions were killed for not going along with the dictates of the church during the inquisitions, the crusades etc. Satan working behind the scenes, and attempting to gain the worship of this world, caused the first beast to changed God's law. This is a major issue with God, but Satan causes man to think that it is not important. God came and died because his law could not be changed to accommodate sin, yet some people cannot see the dangerous consequences of changing the law of God. The prophecy in Revelation states that the second beast will cause the world to worship according to the dictates of the first beast. God showed the prophet Daniel in Daniel 7:25 that a religious political power would come along and think to change his 10 commandment law. Centuries later, human history has recorded that this power has attempted to change God's law and the entire world except a few have followed this beast power.

The second beast power arises after the first beast was wounded; it has 2 horns like a lamb, but in the end will speak as a dragon. One of the most dangerous things that this power would do is to convince the whole world to worship after the dictates of the first beast power that was wounded and was healed. The second beast, arising after the first beast received its deadly wound, has become a dominant world power, with the political, military, and economic power enough to convince the world to worship what the first beast instituted. The USA is a dominant world power and her relationship with the papacy, the first beast, is getting better and better. These two powers were instrumental in the fall of communism in 1991. The deadly wound inflicted on the Papacy has healed and today the Papacy is again a powerful force to contend with. There are ambassadors for all over the world in Vatican City. The USA has an ambassador to the headquarters of this power. In the end, the USA the second beast of Revelation will exercise the power of the first beast by enforcing that which is the hallmark of the first beast.

In order for the second beast of Revelation to enact the change that the first beast instituted the separation of church and state, part of the early foundation of the USA, will be broken down. This is currently happening before our very eyes. The first amendment to the Constitution states, "Congress shall make no law respecting an establishment of religion, or prohibiting the free exercise thereof, no religious test shall ever be required as a qualification to any office of public trust under the United States." The Declaration of Independence states, "We hold these truths to be self-evident that all men are created equal; that they are endowed by their creator with certain unalienable rights; among which are life, liberty, and the pursuit of happiness." These statements endorsing individual rights and freedoms have made America the greatest country in the world. It is a glorious land blessed by God, and people from all over the world clamor to get here to be part of the American dream. It is a great land of opportunity and it is obvious that God has blessed America.

The prophecy of Revelation warns us that these freedoms that we take for granted will not last forever. We are seeing the fulfillment of these prophecies. The wall of separation between Church and State will be broken down and these freedoms will be lost. Here is an interesting statement by the late chief justice of the United States William Rehnquist: "The wall of separation between church and state is a metaphor based on bad history, a metaphor which has proved useless as a guide to judging. It should be frankly and explicitly abandoned." When the Supreme Court, the third branch of government, no longer endorses the separation of Church and State, you know that we are well on our way to set up the final drama when liberty of conscience will be threatened.

Some religious leaders of this country support the dismantling of the separation of church and state. It is interesting to note that the Protestant churches of America are leading the fight. The stage is now being set to make possible the final events of the prophecies of Daniel and Revelation. The events of September 11, 2001 have been a major turning point in recent history and it has significant effect on our liberties. The events of September 11/2001 have given the US government more power and control over individual rights. The magnitude of this event and its effects seem prophetic in nature.

The separation of Church and State is a serious matter. Just look at governments around the world today that do not separate Church and State and see the restriction of individual freedom that exists. You can lose your life for professing to be a Christian in some countries.

This magnificent land of freedom will soon repudiate religious freedom and will force people to worship according to the dictates of the first beast. The first beast used its political and religious powers to force conscience; the second beast will do likewise. They will force worship. God doesn't force worship. He gives us freedom to make our own decisions. Therefore any power that forces worship is not of God. The prophecy states that in the very end of time, this glorious, magnificent land of freedom will force worship and command worship according to the dictates of the first beast. The forces that cause this to happen will do so perhaps innocently, thinking they are doing God's will. Conditions in this country will deteriorate to the point that the religious leaders will dictate the political climate to correspond to their religious ideologies.

In the very end of time, the law of God will be an issue. The Protestant churches of America, who have long stopped protesting against the spiritual practices of Catholicism, are joining forces with each other and with Catholicism, and will be foremost in leading "the get America back to God movement." Their goal is to get America back to keeping God's law. The problem is that the law they will be enforcing is the law that was changed by the Papacy. These events will eventually lead to laws mandating Sunday as the day of worship.

Many Bible believing Christians sincerely take a stand on what they believe to be right. Many of these leaders are sincere Christian believers who stand up for many Christian principles. These leaders are convinced that truth is on their side. When the elected leaders of this great land subscribe to these beliefs, the stage is easily set for the final showdown in the history of planet earth. America's final leaders will think they are doing God's will, and they will have their minds made up about what truth is. According to the prophecy, they will influence the final decisions of this country. In order for the final aspect of the Bible prophecy that states that she will speak like a dragon to take place, America's final leaders will be deeply influenced by religious ideology. More and more politicians today and judicial leaders are appointed according to religious ideology. As we approach the end of time, America's political and government leaders will listen to and be influenced by various religious leaders. The leaders will be in position of influence and their influence will be seen in legislative halls throughout this land. Their religious beliefs will also get them elected to the highest positions of this great country. There is no question that moral values and religious ideology has shaped the outcome of elections and appointments to the highest courts of this land.

What is wrong with good religious ideology? Isn't this a Christian nation? Herein lies the problem; these leaders practice beliefs that they believe are consistent with the Bible. These leaders have a lot of biblical truth, but they don't realize that they are dealing with a subtle impostor, Satan who will inject just enough error to cause deception in such a subtle way that it is dismissed.

What will the USA do in the end? See Revelation 13:12–17. The prophecy states that this second beast power will cause the earth and them that dwell therein to worship the first beast. In other words she will use her power to enforce what the first beast did: the worship on a day that the first beast enacted. Simply put, the USA in the end of time will enforce the change of God's law that the first beast did by forcing the worship of Sunday, using economic sanctions, and in the very end the threat of death.

How will it happen?

This is the future and so we thread with caution. As conditions around the world deteriorate, and disaster after disaster begins to wear us out. As trouble surrounds us, there will be those crying out the reason for the trouble is that we have strayed away from God's law. The religious and political leaders of this nation will demand that this nation return to God, and the law of God will be a forefront issue. They will eventually legislate a Sunday law, requiring that all worship on Sunday, thus using her power to enforce what the first beast did. The church and the state will unite again and will force conscience. The final showdown in history will be over the law of God and the true worship of God.

The great controversy began in heaven over the true worship of God and it will finally come to an end over the true worship of God. Revelation 22:14 states that God will win and He will have a remnant. He will say, "Blessed are they that do his commandments that they may have right to the tree of life and enter into the gates of the city."

All of us should want to be part of that remnant. When the time comes for you to make that decision for truth, will you be able to stand up for the truth. Do you know God's word enough to discern the truth?

Verse 13: "And he doeth great wonders, so that he make fire come down from heaven on the earth in the sight of men."

Revelation 16:13, 19:20, and 20:10 says that this lamb-like beast will become a false prophet and perform miracles as she commands worship to the first beast. In order for Satan to convince the world that this sequence of end time events is ordained by God, he has to perform extraordinary miracles that appear to come from God. Satan, through these end time powers, will perform great wonders that will mesmerize believers. Spiritualism will play a major role in aiding this power to convince people. What convinces the world to go along with the beasts' powers? This verse tells us that many great wonders will be performed; fire will come down out of heaven. Remember the story of Elijah on Mt. Carmel when God sent fire down to consume Elijah's sacrifice. They will try to impersonate this to convince the world that this is of God. These miracles will be seen by the world and would further deceive men into believing that this new organization is from God. These miracles will be so powerful that they will deceive many. The world is being primed for these miracles now; there are television shows where people contact the dead and Satan and his angels impersonate dead relatives. People communicating with Satan will try to convince you that God is revealing things to them. Satan will appear as an angel of light stating he is God and he changed the law.

At this time in history, Satan has a very narrow window of time left before it's all over and he is making the most of it. Satan has a lot of wiggle room to work with in the area of miracles; people are fascinated by them and often think that they are miracles from God when in reality they are from the devil.

The prophecy here implies that the combined forces Apostate Protestantism, Spiritualism (the miracles) and the Papacy will combine forces in the very end of time to secure the worship of men. This strong union will punish dissenters. The two grave errors of the church will make this union possible. These are the immortality of the soul, which gave rise to spiritualism, and the change of God's Sabbath to Sunday.

Verse 14: "And deceives them that dwell on the earth by the means of those miracles which he had power to do in the sight of the beast; saying to them that dwell on the earth, that they should make an image to the beast, which had the wound by a sword, and did live."

Many will be deceived into making an image or a likeness to this beast that was wounded by the sword and did live. In order to understand what an image to the beast is, you must first understand the beast. We have established that the first beast power is the Papal Rome. The beast changed God's eternal law as prophesied in Daniel 7:25. The USA will enforce this change of day by calling on the entire world to worship on Sunday. The protestant churches will seek the aid of the civil government to enforce this change.

Protestant America will religiously influence the USA or the second beast power, and she will unite with the first beast the papacy to promote the first beast's cause. These prophecies of Revelation are being fulfilled around us. Today the great Protestant churches of America, as well as other religious bodies, are uniting with the Catholic Church. Today these protestant groups have an important political voice, in all areas of government. Many who think that what they believe is God's truth, and when trouble comes, they are the ones that the political leaders of this country will turn to. Dissenters from the established plan will be punished. In effect the individual practice of religion and conscience will be severely threatened. This country, which is described as a lamb in its early beginnings, will lose its lamb-like features and become dragon like in the very end of time. She will be influenced by dominant religious denominations and enforce their beliefs. The most dangerous of these changes will herald the very end of time when the worship of the wrong day will be enforced thus setting up the stage for the *mark of the first beast. In the end of time, the legal enforcement of Sunday as the Sabbath and the acceptance of this constitute the mark of the beast.*

As conditions around the world deteriorate, there will be those who will proclaim (and some have already said) that we need to get back to Godly principles, as they understand them. Church and state will unite, and Sunday observance will be enforced in the USA and around the world. The majority of this world keeps Sunday as God's day and the minority dissenters will be punished. The majority believes that what they are doing is God's will. This was the practice of the first beast nation for 1260 years.

The prophecies of Revelation 13 predict a church and state will again unite and will persecute God's people similar to what occurred during the 1260 years of Papal domination. An image to the beast will be formed. People will have made a choice between the law of man and the Law of God. This is exactly the choice that Daniel had to make while captive in Babylon. Sunday observance will be enforced under the threat of persecution and death (See Revelation 13:15.) Economic sanctions will be imposed to enforce the mark of the first beast. Revelation 13:17 states that "no man will be able to buy or sell save he that has the mark or the name of the beast or the number of his name." The commandments of the man will be upheld in the USA over the law of God, and in God's sight this will constitute national apostasy from God's Word. The rest of the world experiencing serious economic and political strife, will follow the lead of the USA.

Are there forces at work today trying to unite church and state and trying to bring America back to their understanding of Gods law? At that time in history when the USA, the second beast with the lamb-like horns, shall enforce Sunday worship, the prophecy of the second beast, speaking like a dragon by enforcing the change of the first beast will be fully realized. The first beast power changed God's law. According to the Catholic Encyclopedia, the boldest change the church made occurred in the first century when it changed the Sabbath from Saturday. The change is not from scripture, but from the church's sense of its own power.

Verse: 15 "And he had power to give life unto the image of the beast, that the image of the beast should both speak, and cause that as many as would not worship the image of the beast should be killed."

The practice of the medieval church killing dissenters will be revived in the very end. The final showdown in history will be about worship. For 6000 years Satan has been the great deceiver and has distorted the true worship of God. The true worship of God versus the worship of Satan is about to be decided. Satan is working behind these earthly powers and distorting the true worship of God. This end-time power would order anyone who would not worship this beast to be killed. This is what happened to the Daniel and his three companions in Babylon.

In order for this to happen, this country must get to a point where there is no longer a separation of church and state, and liberty of conscience to worship according to the dictates of one's conscience will no longer be allowed. Clearly we are heading to this point in history. We are seeing a breaking down of the separation between church and state. The judicial and legislative branches of government will legislate in favor of a national Sunday Law. When that occurs the make up of the Supreme Court will be favorable to that decision. The religious ideology of the Supreme Court justices will be important in the end of time. The wall of separation between church and state will come down as was shown to the prophet John in the first century. Today we see religious movements in the USA calling for the breakdown of the separation of church and state and to get America back to God. As conditions become worse in our country, this will lead to the easy passage of these laws.

It is obvious that some parts of this prophecy have not come to pass yet, but look at so much of it that has. Daniel's prophecies have almost all been fulfilled. John recorded these prophecies 2000 years ago, and here we are with the United States as the dominant world power and no longer gentle as a lamb. Need I say more? The admonition is to stay on the side of truth because it cannot fail. Millions around the world proclaim these truths. It is not popular to tell the truth that God has revealed to us but truth is truth and it will never fail.

Verse 16: "And this end-time power causes all, small and great, rich and poor, free and bond, to receive the mark in their right hand, or in their foreheads."

Everyone will be forced to receive the mark of this beast. At that time in history everyone will have to choose the worship of the beast and its mark, which is Sunday observance, or the worship of the God and his true Sabbath. So in the end there will be only two classes of people: those who receive the mark of the beast and those who receive God's seal of approval. Sadly, despite all the warnings and the prophecies, there will only be a remnant that will receive God's seal. The majority will receive the mark of the beast. They will keep the commandments of men, and they will have the beast's mark on their foreheads. John saw this as happening all over the world.

2000 years ago Jesus came to earth and showed us how to live. His self-sacrificing love for us drove him to a cruel Roman cross on Calvary's Hill. Jesus never forced his will on anyone. His invitation was to everyone, and he forced no one. God does not force worship so any power that enforces worship is not of God. Before the mark of the beast can be enforced, the commandments of God will be brought before the inhabitants of this world. Interesting, on Sunday May 7th 2006, the first annual Ten Commandments weekend was celebrated in the USA. The Ten Commandment commission is broad coalition of pastors in the USA, and it has worldwide plans for this endeavor.

Verse 17: "And that no man might buy or sell, save he that had the mark, or the name of the beast, or the number of his name"

This worldwide end time religious and political alliance will not allow anyone to buy or sell if you do not go along with their dictates.

Verse 18: "Here is wisdom. It is the number of a man. Let him that has understanding count the number of the beast: for it is the number of a man. And his number is 666.

In addition to the other identifying marks of the beast here is another identifying feature that requires divine wisdom to interpret. Seven is God's perfect number; it represents perfection examples are the seventh day Sabbath after the completion of his work in the creation week, the seven candlesticks, the seven stars, and we could go on and on. The number six falls short of seven and represents the number of a man. This is a difficult symbol to interpret. The SDA Church, in its official publication, *The Sabbath School Quarterly* for July 2002, suggested that it may represent symbolism for rebellion and total independence from God.

Let us review the characteristics of the *second beast* in Revelation 13.

1. It comes up out of the earth in an unpopulated area at a time when the first beast is wounded and going into captivity. This gives us the location and time (in the New World at about 1798).

2. It has one head and two horns. Like a lamb it starts out peacefully and as a Christian nation with its government promoting civil and religious freedom (its two horns). In its lamb-like state it does not force worship.

3. It will speak as a dragon. It will change from a lamb-like beast to a dragon-like beast and will speak for Satan by legislating laws contrary to the laws of God. It will force worship. Satan forces worship.

4. It will work great wonders or miracles—causing fire to come down from heaven on earth in the sight of men.

5. It will deceive the earth's inhabitants with these miracles.

6. It will force the entire world to worship the leopard-like beast nation/power who received a deadly wound by a sword in 1798 but healed in 1929.

7. It has the power to give life unto the image of the beast. It exercises the power of the first beast by enforcing Sunday worship in the very end of time. It has to be a dominating power to do this. Worsening world conditions will set up the conditions that will cause her to do this.

God has revealed the USA in prophecy and tells its prophetic role in the history of Planet Earth. This chapter reveals that at the very end of time the Roman Church, with the help of the USA, will attempt to impose religious worship and force conscience like the church did during the 1260 years of Papal domination. We know that the end is near because the USA will be the last world ruling power. These prophecies are true and will not fail.

The message of Revelation 12

This chapter begins with a great sign appearing in heaven. A woman (the pure church) is clothed with the Son of Righteousness, who is Christ. Under her feet is the moon reflecting the Son of Righteousness, and upon her head are twelve stars or the 12 apostles, representing the true apostolic church. This pure church is armed with the pure gospel of Jesus Christ. In many references in the Bible, God likens the church to a woman. In Isaiah 54:5 and Jeremiah 6:2 God likens his faithful church to good woman, and in Jeremiah 3:20 and Ezekiel 23:2–4 He likens the apostate church as a corrupt woman.

The woman is pregnant and travailed in pain for a while as waited to deliver. The woman is symbolically portrayed here as ready to give birth to Christ. Another sign appears in heaven a great red dragon having seven heads, and ten horns, and seven crowns upon its head. Satan works behind the scenes and uses political powers to accomplish his evil deeds.

Revelation 12:4: "And his tail drew one third of parts of the stars of heaven, and did cast them to the earth: and the dragon stood before the woman who was ready to be delivered, for to devour their child as soon as it was born." Satan rebelled against God's law in heaven, and a battle broke out. He and one third of the heavenly angels who sided with him were cast out of heaven. Satan caused Adam and Eve to sin, and God put His redemption plan in action. When the fullness of time was come God sent his son to die. Satan does not want God to redeem lost men, and so he and his evil angels have a master plan to sabotage God's plan. He used Herod, the Roman governor, to try to kill the baby Jesus as soon as He was born.

The woman delivered a son who grew up to judge and rule all the nations with a rod of iron: and her child was caught up unto God, and to his throne. Satan tried to kill Jesus as a baby but was unsuccessful. After his crucifixion, Christ ascended to his throne at the right hand of his Father in heaven.

And the woman who brought forth the child fled into the wilderness, where she had a place prepared for her by God. There she was. There she was nourished for 1260 years.

The devil, no longer able to get to Jesus, turned his fury on the faithful Christian church. The devil persecuted the church and the true church went into the wilderness or underground for 1260 years (538 AD–1798 AD).

The prophet John tells us that this great controversy between Jesus and Satan started in heaven before the creation of Planet earth. The devil and his angels lost the battle and no longer had any place in heaven. The great dragon, that old serpent also known as the devil and Satan, who is deceiving this whole world was cast into the earth and all his evil angels with him. This great controversy, which began in Heaven a long time ago, has continued on Planet Earth for over six thousand years now.

In Revelation 12:10 John hears a voice in heaven saying "Now is come Salvation, and strength, and the kingdom of our God, and the power of his Christ: for the accuser of our brethren is cast down, which accuses them before our God day and night."

This verse implies that because of Calvary our salvation is sure; we now have salvation and strength and Satan, the accuser of the brethren is "cast down," and there is victory because of Calvary. We prevail because of the blood of the Lamb. Jesus gained the victory and now is our High Priest in Heaven. This verse states that the devil was cast down and confined to the earth and can no longer destroy Christ or accuse the brethren day and night before God. Implied here is that when Satan was originally cast down to this earth, his access to heaven was not restricted. Evidently he has access to heaven until the showdown at Calvary when Christ emerged victorious. The text states that the accuser of our brethren is cast down that accuses them before God both day and night.

There is an account in the book of Job, where he showed up to represent earth at an intergalactic conference God held, showing that he was not initially restricted to planet earth. This seems to have changed at Calvary. The devil lost big time at Calvary, and his evil nature stood bare before an on-looking universe that saw their creator hung up on a cruel cross. When Jesus came from the tomb triumphant, saying "I am the resurrection and the Life," Satan had lost the great controversy. The Creator won and went back to heaven to begin his intercessory work for fallen humanity.

Revelation 12:11. "And they overcame him by the blood of the Lamb, and by the word of their testimony; and they loved not their lives unto the death." No matter the trial that Satan brings our way; the shed blood of Christ on Calvary gives overcoming power to God's people who would rather die than give up the truth that they have found in Jesus.

Revelation 12: 12. "Therefore rejoice, you heavens, and you that dwell in them. Woe to the inhabitants of the earth and the sea for the devil is come down to you having great wrath because he knows that his time is short." There was great rejoicing in heaven when

Satan and his evil angels were thrown out but a warning is given to the inhabitants of planet earth because an angry devil is on the loose for a while or a short time.

Revelation 12:13. *"And when the dragon saw that he was cast unto the earth, he persecuted the woman which brought forth the man child."* After Jesus' ascension, Satan was no longer able to attack God directly, and he turned his attention to the church: an indirect attack. Satan was unsuccessful in his war with Jesus in heaven. He was unsuccessful in his attempts to destroy Jesus during his earthly sojourn. Most importantly Christ defeated him at Calvary when he laid down His life to save lost humanity. Christ's resurrection on the third day sealed Satan's fate. Satan, knowing that he has limited time left, decided to destroy the Church that Christ started on earth. In Satan turned up the heat on the woman (the church), and great persecution began among God's people. Fierce persecution and death resulted. Working behind Pagan Rome, Satan killed thousands of Christians and fed many Christians to lions as a spectator sport in the Roman Coliseum.

Revelation 12:14, " *And to the woman were given two wings of a great eagle, that she might fly into the wilderness, into her place, where she is nourished for a time, and times, and half a time, from the face of the serpent."*

God intervened and gave the church wings of a great eagle so she can fly into the wilderness and there he protected her for time, times and half a time or 1260 years from the devil's persecution. Revelation 12:6 states that the woman or God's true church fled into the wilderness, where God had prepared a place for her and he protected her for 1260 years. God had to protect his true church from extinction. Satan hides behind powers and people. After using Pagan Rome to destroy God's church, he used Papal Rome to persecuted the true Church under the guise of Christianity. The Church made itself the corrector of heretics and killed a lot of Christians. Many of these people loved not their lives until death. Written in the books of heaven are the details of those saints who suffered. God cannot forget His people. They did not die in vain. Despite the dominance of the Church of Rome in the lives of people during these 1260 years, God rose up faithful people down through the centuries who would keep the light of truth burning.

Revelation 12:15, "*And the devil cast out of his mouth water as a flood after the woman, that it might cause her to be carried away by the flood.*" The devil was angry with the true church and cast out of his mouth water as a flood after the woman, that he might cause her to be carried away by the flood. For 1260 years the true church was in hiding, Christians who wanted to practice the pure apostolic faith were killed and the doctrines of the dominant church became corrupted with a flood of false doctrines.

Revelation 12:16. "*And the earth helped the woman, and the earth opened her mouth, and swallowed up the flood which the dragon cast out of his mouth.*" Under God's protection, the church survived and when the 1260 years were passed, she emerged from the Wilderness. God never permitted the devil to stamp out his people. He has always had a faithful few. When the church emerged from the wilderness in 1798, the devil was still angry at the church.

Revelation 12:17 states that "the devil was angry with the church and went to make war with the remnant or last day church, which keeps the commandment of God and have the testimony of Jesus Christ." The church emerged from the Wilderness with great help from the protestant reformation and great light was revealed to the church. God restored the truths that he started in the first century and the devil was angry and made war with the final church, which keeps the commandment of God and has the testimony of Jesus Christ.

The Remnant Last Day Church

In Revelation 12 the great controversy between Christ and Satan is portrayed. We learned that bad things would happen to the Christian Church and it would apostatize from truth but a remnant would be faithful to God's truth. This is similar to what happened to God's church in Old Testament times only a remnant church emerged to carry on God's work. God has a final remnant church and the devil has and will make war with this final remnant church. This final church will be the object of Satan's wrath. The concept of the remnant is best understood from the point of view of looking at a bolt of cloth or carpet; if you purchase the remnant you will notice that it is the same as the original piece of cloth or carpet. This is true of the remnant church: it will be the same in doctrine and practice as the early first century church that Christ started. As a Matter of fact, the remnant beliefs are the same throughout history. The message was the same for Israel of Old as well as Spiritual Israel today.

How do we identify this final remnant Church? The clues given in Revelation 12 are: (1) it arises after the 1260 years of Papal persecution, so it arises after 1798. (2). It teaches obedience to all of God's commandments. (3) It has the testimony of Jesus which is defined as the spirit of prophecy in Rev. 19:10.

Prophecy will be part of the remnant church. Revelation 12:14 tells us that God's true church fled in the wilderness or underground for 1260 years and there God protected her. How did the true church get out of the wilderness? Only in eternity will we know the whole story from beginning to end. Only when the books of heaven are revealed will we know the whole story of the reformation of God's church, but from what we know, we can see the hand of God leading the church back to the truth of the Gospel that Jesus gave.

At the appointed time in history, God began to restore truth on a large scale. He began to reform his church. It began with deep study of the Bible and its prophecies and it will end the same way.

The Reformation of God's True end- time Remnant Church

The Bible has shown us that down through the centuries God has always had a remnant people, just a few who chose to follow him in spirit and truth. We can begin with faithful Abel, Methuselah, Noah, and Abraham: the few in their generation who chose the Lord. God has never had the majority on his side. Paul in Romans 11:5 said even so then in Old Testament times as now at the present time, there was a remnant according to the election of grace. This trend continued in New Testament times, and despite grave persecution, God always had a faithful witness to the truth. During the dark ages of Christianity, when the Bible was stifled and was not available to the masses, God had a faithful few who kept his word.

Little has been recorded in the history books about the fate of God's true followers down through the centuries, but God who sees and knows everything has the record in heaven where everything that has happened on Planet Earth has been recorded. God's faithful martyrs will live again, and everyone will have their day in court with our Righteous Judge.

The mastermind behind all the evil on Planet Earth is Satan. He uses people, political powers, and institutions to perpetrate his evil, and one day he will pay big time for it. If we peek at the back of the book we will see in Revelation 20 that at the end of the judgment when God's saints are in heaven, Satan will be bound for 1000 years on Planet Earth desolate after its destruction from the second coming of Jesus. He and his evil angels will be bound by a chain of circumstances in that there will be no one to tempt and no one to perpetrate evil on, and he will be here looking over the evil he has caused.

In Matthew 24:9 as Jesus stood on the Mount of Olives. He said to His disciples, "They will deliver you up to be afflicted, and will kill you: and you will be hated of all men for my name's sake." It happened Just as Jesus foretold. The Roman Empire persecuted Christians. The Roman Emperors (i.e. Nero and Diocletian) killed thousands of Christians. In the Roman Coliseum Christians were fed to animals that tore them to pieces to the excitement of the spectators. The early church was terrorized as symbolically described in Revelation 1 and 2. Still many held on to the pure faith of the apostles.

Apostle Paul, who suffered many persecutions and eventual death for the cause of Christ, wrote in 2 Thessalonians 2:2–7 that there would be a great apostasy from biblical truth (a falling away from righteousness first) led by the man of sin who opposes God's law and rule and sits in the temple of God and speaks for God. This mystery of iniquity is already at work in the Church. At this early stage in the Christian church, Paul is saying that the stage is being set for the great apostasy from truth. This apostasy occurred gradually over the early centuries of the Christian church. About the early 4th

century, Paganism and Christianity merged when Emperor Constantine, a former pagan, converted to Christianity. This opened the door for the rapid spread of paganism in the Christian church. This was a means of attracting more Pagans to Christianity and for the Christian church to gain more favor with pagans.

Satan brings his people into the Christian church by getting the church to adapt worldly standards to accommodate them and call it God's standards. Satan is still successful today, using that method that has worked for him. In 321 AD Constantine formally enacted the first Sunday keeping law. Sunday, the day that the pagans worshipped the sun, was made into a day to honor the resurrection. Jesus did not tell us to keep Sunday in honor of his resurrection. Jesus said that the communion supper should be used as a symbol to remember his death, burial, and resurrection, and if we truly love Jesus we would do what he commands.

Conditions within the Roman Empire and Jewish revolts and persecutions made Christians reluctant to identify with Jews, and the Sabbath was eventually labeled a Jewish institution and Sunday became the Christian Sabbath. As pagan Rome disintegrated, Papal Rome took its seat and power and its great authority. From 538–1798 Papal Rome ruled the lives of people in Europe. During this time the Medieval Church called the shots. Church and state were united and the priests and monks practiced a religion apart from biblical doctrine. God's truth was cast to the ground, and a lot of traditional beliefs entered the church that cannot be found anywhere in the Bible. Some of these practices are the veneration of saints, the worship of images, infant baptism, purgatory, the communion bread and wine becomes the actual flesh and blood of Christ, Sunday sacredness, penance, confession to an earthly priest, worship of the Virgin Mary, etc. The simplicity of the early apostolic church was lost except for a faithful few.

The Medieval church practiced a religion unknown to the church that Christ started. The church went on pilgrimages, offered indulgences, visited the statues of certain saints, etc., as a means of obtaining salvation. The Bible was not read and followed and consequently there was a great apostasy from biblical truth. Manmade tradition was practiced instead. It was obvious that the medieval church needed a serious reformation. There were many attempts down the centuries protesting the unbiblical practices of the church, but the Church put out those fires easily.

Amid widespread apostasy from the word of God, God has always had a faithful few. An example is Claudius the Bishop of Turin, who believed in justification by faith and taught the biblical doctrines around 817 AD. The Church was so dominant for 1260 years that if you wanted to practice the pure apostolic religion of the Bible you had to hide and do it or you will be killed.

The Protestant Reformation

Something had to be done to restore the church to its original Bible based beliefs and so God began the Protestant Reformation. The Roman Church did all it could to stifle the Reformation, and there were major persecution of the reformers. But the time had come for the Reformation to take hold.

We can formally trace the Reformation back to John Wycliffe (1320–1384), known as the morning star of the Reformation. At Oxford, Wycliffe studied the Bible and learned about justification by faith in Christ alone. Wycliffe called for the reformation of the church and he began to write about the problems of the church, the lavish lifestyles of the friars and monks at the time, the dominant role of the church in political affairs. He became a professor at Oxford and taught his students the Bible. He translated the Bible into English so the English people can read God's word for themselves.

The church labeled him as a heretic and emissaries were sent from Rome to silence him. Pope Gregory XI ordered his trial, but the church became distracted because two rival popes were elected at the same time—Pope John XXIII in Avignon, France and Pope Gregory XII in Rome. These Papal issues occupied the Papacy, and so Wycliffe work continued. Wycliffe died in 1384 and he left a great legacy. He made the word of God available to his people and placed the word of God above human tradition. He was God's man for his time and God used him at a time when conditions were more favorable for the promotion of biblical truths. Forty years after his death the Council of Constance ordered his remains dug up. His bones were burned and his ashes thrown into the river.

This early reformer's work did not die. It reached Czechoslovakia and the University of Prague, to an early reformer named John Huss. This Catholic priest began reading Wycliffe's work. This Catholic priest began to follow the promptings of the Holy Spirit; he took up the baton and translated Wycliffe writings into Czech. He began reading the Bible and taught that the Bible was the supreme authority. He protested against the teachings of the Roman Church that were inconsistent with scripture. Pope John XXIII excommunicated Huss. His stand against the errors of the church caused him his life. He was summoned to appear before the Council of Constance. On his arrival to Constance he was thrown in jail and brought up on charges of heresy before Roman Catholic Church Council of Constance (Germany) in 1415. (This council met from 1414–1418). Here he defended his beliefs based on the word of God. He was convicted of heresy and burned at the stake on June 6, 1415. He died a faithful martyr's death, joining the long list of God's faithful killed for daring to follow their conscience and sticking to the principles and commands God outlined in the Bible. Another reformer, Jerome, a citizen of Prague and a faithful colleague of Huss, was also imprisoned and burned at the stake too. These men had done their work enlightening Germany about God's truth. They laid the groundwork and now that God's word was being read, the church no longer had full power over the conscience of people. Christian believers started to follow God's word and not the traditions of the Church.

In every dispensation of history God, has had just a faithful few that would stand up for his truth even when faced with death. Martin Luther was one such reformer. He was an Augustinian monk who became a professor in Wittenberg, Germany in early 1500. Luther loved the Lord and studied the scriptures.

On a pilgrimage to Rome, he was climbing some steps when he heard a voice say "the just shall live by faith." This text has its impact, and he began to study the scriptures diligently. He understood the Apostle Paul teachings of justification by faith and that forgiveness of sins is a gift from God that cannot be bought. Luther could no longer believe in the mass, penance, purgatory, confession and many of the teachings of the Church of Rome that were placed above the scripture. He openly challenged these practices and on October 31, 1517 on the eve on All Saints Day when pilgrims came to the church at Wittenberg, Germany, he nailed his 95 theses against the non-biblical practices of the church to the church door.

The Church tried to silence Luther, and Luther was summoned by Charles V to appear before the Diet of Worms in front of kings, prelates, ambassadors, clergymen, etc. He was asked to recant, but said, "Unless I am convicted by Scripture and plain reason, I do not accept the authority of popes and councils, for they have contradicted each other – my conscience is captive to the word of God. I cannot and I will not recant anything, for to go against conscience is neither right nor safe. God help me." He studied the book of Daniel and along with so many of these early reformers he believed that the Little Horn Power of Daniel was the Papal Church and many of its activities were anti-Christ. The church excommunicated Luther and tried to kill him, but the Lord protected him. Luther translated the Bible into German making it available to the people. Luther was God's man for that hour, and his work was the cornerstone of the Reformation.

In Zurich, Switzerland a priest named Ulric Zwingli carried on the reform movement in Switzerland. He spoke out against the traditions of the church (e.g. the sale of indulgences), but he too was killed in 1531. Despite the death of these early reformers, the Reformation was here to stay, and numerous people joined the reformation.

God worked with reformers in France. A notable French reformer was John Calvin. He was well educated and knew about the Reformation in Germany, Switzerland, etc., and he was determined to bring the truth to France. The Church tried hard to stamp out the Reformation and regain control of Christendom. The French reformer John Calvin was forced to flee to Geneva, Switzerland. Geneva became the home of Calvinism, and from there the reformed doctrines were sent out to various parts of Europe. Calvin took the reformation even further than Luther had.

In 1545 John Knox, a Scottish Catholic priest rejected the practices of the Roman Catholic Church and joined the Protestant Reformation that was sweeping across Europe. He was a close friend of George Wishart, a prominent reformer who was deemed a heretic and burned to the stake in 1546. John Knox was fearless and determined in his beliefs and became a student of Calvinism. He was instrumental in the formation of the Scottish Presbyterian Movement.

I could go on and on about the Protestant Reformation, but will instead refer you to books about the protestant reformation such as J. H. Merle D'Aubigne's *History of the Reformation of the Sixteenth Century*. The point is that the time had come for the church to reform. It is fascinating to see how the church made its way back out of the wilderness and how these movements are spreading throughout Europe.

The important issue here is that God's true church is making its way out of the wilderness. God's true followers had to hide in caves and mountains to avoid being killed for reading and practicing biblical doctrines that the dominant church did not approve. An example of the Church in the Wilderness is the history of the Waldensians. These Christian believers like the Waldensians who held on to the pure word of scripture and were hunted and killed in the wilderness or mountains and Piedmont valleys of Northwest Italy. As far back as the 1200AD these Christians were hunted down and massacred for believing and practicing biblical truths. The Roman Catholic Church sent crusaders into the wilderness of these valleys, namely the Angrogna valley where they had taken refuge. Here they were hunted down, and Men, women and children were massacred. Although they were constantly on the run for their lives, the Waldensians were active evangelists. The copied the scriptures and had a Bible college named Collegio dei Barba, where they trained pastors. Pra del Torno was the center of the Waldensians' operations, and they often retreated to the valleys here when attacked. They would memorize the Bible and translate into French by hand. When they came into contact with receptive people, they would give out copies of the Bible. They held on to that good old missionary spirit through fiercest persecutions and death during the era of papal domination. I hope that you are appreciating the battle of the great controversy between Satan and Christ and how the devil used one of his great arsenals, the deceived apostate church, to do his biddings. In 1655 an army went into the valleys, and a major slaughter of the Waldensians took place. Many in Europe reacted with sorrow at their massacre. The blind poet Milton penned these words:

> "Avenge, O Lord, thy slaughtered Saints, whose bones
> Lie scattered on the Alpine mountains cold;
> Even them who kept thy truth so pure of old,
> When all our fathers worshiped stocks and stones,

Forget not: in thy book record their groans
Who were thy sheep, and in their ancient fold
Slain by the bloody Piemontese, that rolled
Mother with infant down the rocks. Their moans
The vales redoubled to the hills, and they
To heaven. Their martyred blood and ashes sow
O'er all the Italian fields, where still doth sway
The triple Tyrant that from these may grow
A hundredfold, who, having learnt thy way,
Early may fly the Babylonian woe."

The Waldensians are representative of the church in the wilderness during the 1260 years of Papal persecution. Despite great persecution, hunger, and cold, they held on to the pure gospel taught by Jesus. They gave up their lives for the truth. One great morning, when the cares of this life are passed away, the Waldensians will live again in that home above the wilderness of this world. They will live peacefully on the mountains of God, never to be hunted and killed for serving God as conscientiously as they knew how to.

The early protestant reformers began to put the pure word of God above tradition, and God began to reveal more and more light to these reformers. The Protestant Reformation took hold, and the church began to emerge from centuries of spiritual darkness.

It is obvious that these early protestant reformers did not grasp all the truths of the Bible: hence their various interpretations of the Bible. However, but they believed with all their hearts and they died for their faith. God was leading this reformation movement back to His word as He gradually restored truth as it could be handled at the time.

The Protestant Reformation gave rise to many denominations. From Luther came the Lutherans about 1522AD The Calvinists followed the theology of Calvin and formed the Presbyterian Church. The Anglican Church was founded by King Henry VIII in 1534 after the Church of Rome would not give him permission to divorce his wife Catherine of Aragon. The Baptist Church was formed 1606 when the biblical doctrine of baptism was rediscovered. In 1774 John and Charles Wesley founded the Methodist church, with an emphasis on the perfection of worship. Many more reform movements were formed as the early reformers studied the Bible and discovered new truths.

The church of the wilderness was making its way out of gross darkness and light was discovered step by step. God was revealing truths to them. One of the problems of the Reformation that led to the formation of individual religions was that the people refused any more light than their leader had obtained and they tried to protect what their leaders believed by protecting their unique beliefs and shutting out any other light. They were afraid they would lose the truths they had obtained.

God used the protestant reformation to restore the lost truths, and each movement contributed greatly to the restoration. The Protestant movement, however, was not a united movement because people began to form groups around the beliefs of a particular leader. This gave rise to various bodies of movement (e.g., the people who believed what Calvin taught, those who believed Martin Luther, and those who followed John Wesley). Distinct denominations were formed and believers stuck to one movement or another.

These men were not God's prophets but God used them in miraculous ways to begin the restoration of truth.

The Reformation in the USA

The English Reformation gave rise to the Puritan movement. After persecution in England, the Puritans fled to Holland and then to the United States.

These early immigrant reformers, enjoying the freedom of early America, laid the background for the framing of the Constitution guaranteeing freedom of conscience to serve God, and the Bill of Rights. Thousands came to the shores of the United States, where the Bible was available and widely circulated.

God prepared a country for the nurturing and propagation of the Protestant Reformation. The spreading of the Reformation to the United States has profound significance and biblical implications. God had this special country prepared to shelter the fleeing reformers and to play a major role in the end time events on Planet Earth.

At the end of the 1260 years God's church began to emerge from the wilderness. God restored truth to a church that had gone astray from the pure gospel of the Bible. These changes are occurred as there arose a worldwide study of the Bible and its many prophecies.

This period, known as the time of the end, saw a great increase in knowledge as prophesied in Daniel 12:4. The little book of Daniel that was sealed until the time of the end will now be understood. People in various continents began to study the prophecies of Daniel and Revelation. With more understanding of the Bible, there became an obvious need to reform religion to confirm with the principles of the Bible, and the Protestant Reformation progressed.

This did not happen by chance. God worked out his purposes and began setting up his final movement to spread the everlasting gospel to the entire world. He had greater light to reveal to the reformers and here in the USA God established the final remnant church which anchored the reformation and reestablished the standards of the apostolic church that Jesus started. The doctrines of this remnant church are the same as the pure apostolic church of the first century.

Let us look at the biblical evidence for the characteristics of this church. It has to have its origin after 1798, the time of the end when God's church emerged from the wilderness. In Revelation 12:14–17 we see that God's church was underground for 1260 years (from 538AD to 1798 AD). During that time God nourished her and protected her. The devil tried to destroy God's church and drown the church with false teachings. Then came the Protestant Reformation, and the light of God's word helped the Church and she came out of the Wilderness. Revelation 12:16 indicates that the earth helped the woman by swallowing up the flood that the devil cast after the woman. The USA helped the church as it emerged from the wilderness. The pilgrims fled here for freedom of religion and Bibles were available.

Rev. 12:17 states then the devil was angry at God's church and went to make war with the remnant church defined as the one that keeps the commandments of God and has the testimony of Jesus Christ. Which church is this remnant Church of Revelation 12:17? God cuts to the chase and gives us two characteristics here. Which church was organized after 1798 (as identified in Revelation 12:14–17), kept all of God's commandments and had the Spirit of prophecy in their midst?

In 1798 the church came out of the wilderness and the final remnant church, the church that the devil is angry with, has not yet been formed. The remnant of the apostolic church must arise after 1798 when the church in the wilderness becomes visible at the end of the 1260 years. According to Revelation 12:17, God is going to raise up a final movement or church that teaches obedience to all of his commandments and have the spirit of prophecy in their midst. This Church is going to anchor the Protestant Reformation and the devil is going to be very angry with this church.

Which church can make that bold claim that they arise after 1798, preaches adherence to all of God's commandments and have the spirit of prophecy in their midst. In addition this church was given the responsibility of spreading God's last warning to planet earth inhabitants. This final warning is found in the 3 angel's message of Revelation 14: 6–12. Is there a church today that claims that understands the messages given in Revelation 14: 6–12 and is equipped to spread this end time message to the world? Let us look at the evidence in Revelation for the formation of this final remnant group from all beliefs and from all nations, tongue and people.

Revelation 10:1 "And I saw a mighty angel come down from heaven, clothed with a cloud: and a rainbow was upon his head, and his face was as it were the sun, and his face as pillars of fire:"

2. "And he had in his hand a little book open: and he set his right foot upon the sea, and his left foot on the earth." This mighty angel whose description is similar to the being the prophet John described in Revelation 1 came down from heaven with a world-

wide message and he had a little book in his hand. Setting one foot on the sea and the other on the earth he held a book in his hand.

3. "And cried with a loud voice, as when a lion roareth: and when he had cried, seven thunders uttered their voices."

4. "And when the seven thunders had uttered their voices, I was about to write: and I heard a voice from heaven saying unto me, seal up those things which the seven thunders uttered and do not record them."

5. "And the angel which I saw stand upon the sea and upon the earth lifted up his hand to heaven." John sees an angel standing on the sea and the earth and the angel raised his hand to heaven.

6. "And swore by him that lives forever and ever, who created heaven, and the things that therein are, and the earth, and the things that therein are, and the sea, and the things which are therein, that time shall be no longer." The meaning here is that after 1844 there will be no more prophetic time given to us. Prophetic time has ended and we are now living in the end of time. The 2300-day prophecy ended in 1844 and there is no more time prophecy after that.

A similar vision is described in Daniel 10:5–7, two beings appeared, one on each bank of the Tigris River and one of the being asked the man clothed in linen and standing above the waters how long it will be before the end of these things. The being that appeared to Daniel in Daniel 10:5–7 was clothed in linen with a belt of gold. His face was like lightening and his eyes like flaming torches and his arms and legs gleamed like polished bronze, a description similar to the being John described in Revelation 1: 13–15. He held up both hands to heaven and swore by him who lives forever and ever that the time when this power shall persecute and scatter the power of the holy people will be for time, times and half a time or 1260 years. The 1260 years ended in 1798 and since 1798 we have been living in the time of the end.

7. "But in the days of the voice of the seventh angel, when he shall begin to sound, the mystery of God shall be finished, as he has declared to his servants the prophets."

In other words when the seventh angel begins to sound this whole plan of redemption that he has revealed to his prophets down through the centuries will be over. I hope that you can appreciate that the time mentioned by the angel who stood on the sea declaring (prophetic) time shall be no longer (verse 6) and the time when the voice of the seventh angel will sound (verse 7) are two different historic and prophetic times.

8. "And the voice which I heard spake unto me again, and said, Go and take the little book which is open in the hand of the angel which standeth upon the sea and upon the earth."

Here John is told to go and take the little book, which is open in the hand of the angel who is standing upon the sea and upon the earth.

9. "And I went unto the angel, and said unto him, give me the little book. And he

said unto me, take it, and eat it up; and it shall make thy belly bitter, but it shall be in thy mouth sweet as honey."

John asked the angel for the little book. The angel told John to take the book and eat it up or understand the message; it will be sweet as honey in thy mouth but bitter in thy belly.

9. "And I took the little book out of the angel's hand, and ate it up: and it was in my mouth sweet as honey: and as soon as I had eaten it, my belly was bitter."

What is this book that the mighty angel has in his hand? The only book that we know that is closed until the time of the end is the book of Daniel (See Dan12: 4, 9).

10. "And I took the little book out of the angel's hand, and ate it up: and it was in my mouth sweet as honey: and as soon as I had eaten it, my belly was bitter."

John is placed in this verse as representing these end time advent believers who took the book of Daniel and began to study it and it was sweet as honey in their mouth but as soon as they had eaten it, it was bitter in their belly. What does this mean? The book of Daniel that was sealed until the time of the end was now being avidly studied worldwide. This was prophesied in Daniel 12:9, 10 that the words of the prophecy of Daniel will be sealed until the time of the end when knowledge will increase and many will be purified and the wise shall study, restudy and understand these prophecies but none of the wicked will. Remember all of the prophecies that we studied in the book of Daniel; it is in this book that the 2300day/year prophecy which ended in 1844 is introduced. At the end of this 2300-year prophetic time in 1844 an amazing phenomenon happened. The spirit of the Lord was working with people in various parts of the world and there arose a great awakening to the study of the Bible and its prophecies. Bible students independently began to study the 2300 day prophecy of Daniel 8:14 with great interest. Some of these avid Bible students were Joseph Wolfe in Europe: A Catholic priest in Chile, South America, Manuel de Lacunza who used the pseudonym of Juan Ben-Ezra: Edward Irving of England: Johann Benger of Germany.

In the USA about the early 1800's Christian believers from every denomination avidly began to study the little book of Daniel. The angel told Daniel to shut up the words and seal the book of Daniel until the time of the end. At the appointed prophesied time the angel gives John to take the book and eat it up; it will be sweet as honey in his mouth but as soon as he eats it, it will be bitter in his belly. The angel bids the Prophet John who is representing these believers do not give up even after you eat the book and it becomes bitter in your belly.

11. "And he said unto me, thou must prophesy again before many peoples, and nations, and tongues, and kings."

Although John experience bitterness in his belly he was reassured and told that he must prophecy again. Don't give up, he must go back and restudy the prophecies again so that he can understand the prophecy and assume his responsibility to spread the message to every nation, kindred, tongue and people. So these early advent believers heeded the admonition given by the prophet John and they studied the prophecies again and understood the meaning of the prophecy.

The message given to John continues in Revelation 11

Verse 1. "And there was given unto me a red like unto a rod: and the angel stood saying, Rise, and measure the temple of God, and the altar, and them that worship therein."

John was given a measuring rod and was told to measure the temple of God in heaven, and the altar, and the worshippers. John was shown the heavenly sanctuary where Christ began his high priestly work of judgment in 1844. Attention was now drawn to the heavenly sanctuary. God's people must know the truth about the sanctuary and the important judgment scene that is taking place there.

Verse 2 "But the court which is without the temple leave out, and measure it not; for it is given unto the Gentiles: and the holy city shall they tread under foot forty and two months."

God tells John do not measure the outer court which is given to the gentiles who do not believe in the heavenly sanctuary and have trampled it under their feet for 42 prophetic months or 1260 years. The hidden Sanctuary truth will now be brought to light at the end of the 42 months or 1260 years.

Verse 3 "And I will give power unto my two witnesses, and they shall prophesy a thousand two hundred and threescore days, clothed in sackcloth."

God tells John that he would give power to his word; the New and Old Testaments are his witnesses who for 1260 years were clothed in sackcloth while human tradition flourished.

God's final remnant

As a result of the Protestant Reformation a church would arise that is in direct fulfillment of prophecy and capable of anchoring the protestant reformation and like John the Baptist prepare a people for the coming of the Messiah. This last day church was given the necessary tools to prepare a people for the second coming of Jesus. Let us take a closer look at the movement in the United States that rose up in direct fulfillment of the prophecies of Daniel and Revelation. The United States has a major role to play in the final events of earth's history and it is no accident that it is the birthplace of God's final movement that anchored the Protestant Reformation. I'll give a very brief history of the beginning of this movement. It is a miraculous story and although much of it has been written in many books the whole has not been told but God has recorded this fascinating movement in the scrolls of heaven and one day we will know the whole story. Here is a very brief synopsis of what is known. By 1844 the protestant reformation had been deeply rooted in the still youthful nation called the USA. The protestant movement which began in Europe was not a united movement because people began to form religious movements around the beliefs of a particular leader and this gave rise to various bodies of movement e.g. the people who believed what Calvin taught became Presbyterians, those who believe Martin Luther became Lutherans, and those who followed John Wesley became Methodists, some discovered the biblical doctrine of baptism and became Baptists etc. Distinct denominations were formed around the teachings of these leaders and believers stuck to one movement or another and the reformation fragmented. A divided church cannot make progress effectively. It was clear that the Protestant Reformation was a process and God was revealing truth in stages. Apostasy occurred gradually and truth was being restored gradually. God had a lot more light to reveal to his people but God cannot take you any further that you are willing to be led by him. God who has been the guiding light for this reformation was still guiding it and so in the United States there arose a mighty awakening centered on the study of the Bible.

God chose a man in the USA to move the reformation forward.

The Protestant Reformation continued in the USA with a man named William Miller. William Miller was born in Pittsfield, Massachusetts in 1782. He was a captain in the US army and fought in the war of 1812. After serving his time in the US army he moved to Low Hampton, New York and became a farmer. William Miller was an intellectual who studied the works of Hume, Voltaire, Ethan Allen and others. He became attracted to Deism (a belief that God created the world and withdrew from it). He practiced Deism from about 1804–1816. In his study of Deism, Miller could find no light, no hope beyond death. Miller's wife was a Christian believer and he often accompanied her to his uncle's Baptist Church. One Sunday under the influence of the Holy Spirit he surrendered his life to Christ. He now found hope in Jesus and began to study the Bible. His deist friends questioned his newfound beliefs. He promised his friends that he would return to Deism if he found that the Bible was not true. For several years Miller set out on an intensive study of the Bible. He studied text upon text, precept upon precept and found out that the Bible had all the answers. It made sense. It had unity. It interpreted itself and it could be understood. He also found out that he could understand the symbolic language of some of the chapters of the Bible. Miller found out from his studies that Jesus would return to earth soon. At that time no one preached about the soon coming of Jesus. There were gross misinterpretations of the Bible and most Christians were pre-millennialists. (They believed that this world was getting better, and after a thousand years of peace Jesus would come.) The soon second coming of Jesus was not a common belief as it is today. William Miller laid the foundation for this fundamental, now universal, Christian belief.

Miller was particularly fascinated with the prophecies in the book of Daniel. Miller focused on Daniel 8:14 "unto two thousand and three hundred days; then shall the sanctuary be cleansed." He believed that the 2300 days/years spoken of here would end in 1843 or 1844. It was also the common belief then that this earth was God's sanctuary. He therefore concluded that Christ would return to the earth at that time and cleanse the earth with fire.

William Miller was not the only person to come to this conclusion from studying the Bible. In the book, *The Prophetic Faith of Our Fathers*, 1946, LeRoy Froom indicates that in the libraries of Europe he found at least 43 books about this 2300 day prophecy and 26 of them place the end of the 2300 days about 1843, 1844, or 1847. Many Biblical Scholars and prominent church leaders before William Miller believed from the study of Daniel 8:14 that some great event would take place at the conclusion of the 2300 days. A few were Joseph Wolfe in England, Archibald Mason in Scotland, William Davis in South Carolina, and Alexander Campbell, the founder of the Disciples of Christ.

William Miller was more definitive about his conclusions. He felt that the 2300 days of Daniel 8:14 would end in the second coming of Jesus in 1844. Miller believed that this was the hour of God's judgment mentioned in Revelation 14:6. He also felt that the cleansing of the sanctuary would occur at this time. He was initially reluctant to go public with his beliefs. Over the ensuing years (about 1831), Miller did go public with his beliefs, and he attracted many converts, including prominent preachers from other Protestant denominations.

In 1839 Joshua Himes, a prominent pastor of the Charlton Street Church in Boston, was impressed by Miller's preaching about the imminent return of Jesus and became Miller's promoter and publicist. He published two pamphlets Signs of the Times and the Midnight Cry. Soon William Miller's message was heard and read in many large cities throughout the USA. The organized Christian churches at the time rejected the teachings of Miller and soon did not allow the teachings of William Miller in their churches. The Millerite movement was formed and they went everywhere with the teaching that Jesus return was imminent about 1843. The midnight cry went out throughout New England and New York: "Behold the bridegroom cometh on the Jewish Day of Atonement on the 10th day of the seventh month," which fell on October 22, 1843. Soon there were advent believers from every denomination. These believers were disfellowshipped from their various protestant churches. There were Millerite advent believers who were Quaker, Methodist, Baptist, Presbyterian, Congregationalists, etc. They called themselves advent believers because they believed in the imminent return of Jesus in 1843 or 1844.

Miller was initially reluctant to set a date but Samuel Snow another Millerite preacher set the date of 10/22/1844. At a camp meeting in Exeter, New Hampshire the dynamic preacher Samuel Snow preached that these prophecies pointed to the close of probation and Jesus would return on October 22, 1843. In the audience that day were James White, age 23, and Joseph Bates, age 52. They accepted these teachings and expected the Lord to come in 1843. They realized that there was no year 0, the Millerites settled on the date for the cleansing of the sanctuary at the time of Yom Kippur, the 10th day of the seventh month, and so the date was set for October 22, 1844. The Millerites sold their earthly possessions, preparing for the return of Jesus on October 22, 1844. When Jesus did not return to earth that day they were very disappointed. The groups in England and around the world were disappointed too. This became known as the Great Disappointment, and the Millerite movement disintegrated into many splinter groups.

William Miller though very disappointed, did not lose hope. He encouraged his followers by saying "Brethren, hold fast; let no man take your crown. I have fixed my mind upon another time, and here I mean to stand until God gives me more light. And that is today, today, today until he comes, and I see him for whom my soul yearns" (Miller, 1844). Five years later on December 10, 1849 Miller died. As He did with Martin Luther, God used a Protestant reformer William Miller to lay a foundation that He will build on. I do not know why truth is revealed in stages; maybe it is possible that God reveals to people according to their ability to understand and follow His will.

After the great disappointment in 1844 a group of Millerite believers went to a barn to pray about the great disappointment. They wanted to know what had gone wrong. After a night of prayer, some members of the prayer group, namely Hiram Edson, a Methodist Millerite farmer from Port Gibson, New York, and Owen Crosier another Millerite decided to walk through a cornfield,. They were probably trying to avoid the disdain of the crowd, on his way to encourage some of the disappointed Millerites on December 23, 1844. Suddenly in the middle of the cornfield Hiram Edson felt the heavens open up and he envisioned that the sanctuary to be cleansed was the heavenly sanctuary. He saw Jesus leaving the Holy Place for the Most Holy Place.

God placed a vivid impression in the mind of Hiram Edson and he went back and shared it with members of the prayer group. Hiram Edson, Owen Crozier and Franklin Hahn regrouped and began studying the prophecies of Daniel with renewed vigor. They realized that the sanctuary of Daniel 8:14 was the heavenly sanctuary. They learned that at the end of the 2300 days our High Priest Jesus, instead of coming to this earth as was previously misunderstood, Jesus entered the second apartment of the heavenly sanctuary. They realized their mistake that Jesus did not come to earth as they had expected but instead he came to the ancient of days in the Most Holy Place of the heavenly sanctuary to commence the judgment and cleanse the heavenly sanctuary.

Their attention was also directed to Revelation 10, where the prophet John was shown that when the book was opened, it was sweet in the mouth, but bitter in the belly. John was also told to go back and prophesy again to many peoples, nations, tongues and kings. Edson told the vision to the Crozier and Hahn and they went back and studied these prophecies again with renewed vigor. They realized that the Millerites had the date correct but the event wrong. The sanctuary being referred to in Daniel 8:14 was the heavenly sanctuary. The correct interpretation of the prophecy should have given them the date on which Jesus enter the Most Holy Place of the Heavenly Sanctuary to complete the second and final phase of his High Priestly intercessory ministry in heaven.

After His ascension to heaven in AD 33 he began his work in the Holy Place. They realize that there was a heavenly sanctuary and the earthly sanctuary was a replica of it. They saw that Jesus would not come back to earth until He had completed the second phase of His heavenly ministry. They saw the connection between the judgment shown in Daniel 7 and the simultaneous cleansing of the heavenly sanctuary from sin. The heavenly sanctuary that had long been obscured was now brought to light in the most unusual way. For generations from 1844 on to the end of time, the Great Disappointment will always be associated and stands as a reminder of this most important event in heaven the start of the heavenly judgment. Having understood the judgment scene in heaven they saw themselves as that final remnant charged with the responsibility to preach the everlasting gospel of Revelation 14:6–12, known as the three angels' message, telling the world that the hour of God's final judgment has come. This group did not distance themselves from Millerite teachings, but went back and restudied these teachings. Like the reformers who built on the foundation laid before them these reformers continued to build on the doctrines discovered before as more light was revealed to them. They did not revert to their former churches and draw a circle around their beliefs. In addition to preaching the soon coming of Jesus they discovered the heavenly sanctuary and could teach about the judgment. This theology laid the foundation of the Seventh-day Adventist doctrine.

It is a misconception to say that the Seventh-day Adventist Church predicted the great disappointment because the SDA church was founded later. William Miller and many of these early Millerite believers never heard of the Seventh-day Adventist Church although their work laid the groundwork for the church. We cannot say that these men were not chosen by God and they were instrumental in laying the foundation of this final movement even though they died not knowing the result of what they started. Similarly

God chose the early protestant reformers even though they did not have the full understanding of the Bible. God restored truth in stages.

This movement started from those who went back and studied the prophecies again. Men like Edson, Crosier and Hahn studied the prophecies again and again and more light was added. A biblical point here is to be careful not to discard truth with error but before discarding things prove all things and hold fast to that which is good. Test these things to see whether they come from God. God works in mysterious ways. God often reveals truth in stages and we often do not understand the truth clearly at first but God works with us if we let him and the more we study his word the more we will learn. These early advent believers did not give up despite their great disappointment. They were on the right track and they prayed for understanding and God did not disappoint them.

The early advent believers discovers the Sabbath truth

The early advent believers, having understood the judgment and the sanctuary, still had more truth to learn. They did not fully understand the seventh-day Sabbath and its relationship to the law of God. Throughout history God had to continually re-educate His people about His Sabbath. This movement is fulfilling what God expects of his people as described in Isaiah 58:11–14. "And the Lord shall guide thee continually, and satisfy thy soul in drought, and make fat thy bones: and thou shall be like a watered garden, and like a spring of water, whose waters fail not. And they that shall be of thee shall build the old waste places. Thou shalt raise up the foundations of many generations; and thou will be called, The repairer of the breach, The restorer of paths to dwell in. If thou will turn away your foot from the Sabbath, from doing thy pleasure on my holy day; and call the Sabbath a delight, the holy of the LORD, honorable; and shalt honor him, not doing thine own ways, nor finding thine own pleasure, nor speaking thine own words: Then shall thou delight thyself in the Lord; and I will cause thee to ride upon the high places of the earth, and feed thee with the heritage of Jacob thy father: for the mouth of the LORD hath spoken it".

The Lord is serious about the breach in His commandment. The Sabbath was instituted on the seventh day of creation week. It was lost during the exile in Egypt and reinforced at Sinai. During the 208- year reign of the kings of Israel, there was disregard and careless keeping of the Sabbath. This disregard for the commandments of God led to the 70- year Babylonian captivity. After the captivity, particularly in the days of the prophet Nehemiah, strict Sabbath keeping was enforced. When Jesus came he found the Jews had burdened the Sabbath with so many rituals. Jesus restored proper Sabbath keeping (See Luke 4). By the second and third centuries most practicing Christians had abandoned God's Sabbath that was established during the first week of creation. In every century God has always had a few who held on to this truth (e.g., the Waldensians during the time of Papal domination, the Anabaptists, the Seventh Day Baptists who had been keeping the original Sabbath of God's commandment). There are enclaves of people throughout the world who have never heard of the change of the Sabbath and they have been keeping the original Sabbath (e.g., in Abyssinia, Ethiopia, Ghana, etc.). Dr. Peter Chamberlain, a physician and commonwealth speaker, was a Seventh Day Baptist who kept the Sabbath in the 1600's.

The Sabbath Revival

A Seventh Day Baptist woman named Rachael Oakes (1809–1865) played a very important role in the reintroduction of God's true Sabbath to his end time church. She was a Methodist woman from Vermont. She joined the Seventh Day Baptist church of Verona in Oneida County New York around 1837. The Seventh Day Baptists had rediscovered the Sabbath of the fourth commandment from the English Puritans. Rachael Oakes moved to Washington, New Hampshire to be close to her 18-year-old daughter Delight, who was a school teacher there. There was no Sabbath keeping churches close by so Rachael Oakes went to the Sunday church. She tried to introduce the Sabbath to these advent believers who were awaiting the imminent return of Jesus on October 22, 1844, but no one took the time to pay any attention to her. After the Great Disappointment, while attending church one Sunday, she heard Frederick Wheeler from Washington, New Hampshire (the Methodist preacher who became a Millerite minister) encouraging his congregation to keep God's commandments. When he visited her later, she told him that he needed to keep all of God's commandments including the fourth. He listened to her, studied the Bible again and decided to keep the Sabbath. The Sabbath truth was catching on and many people accepted it. Thomas Preble, a free-will Baptist church preacher-turned-Mellerite accepted it. Preble wrote an article about the Sabbath in a Millerite paper called the hope of Israel. In 1845 Joseph Bates, a former sea captain read it and was convinced that the seventh -day was still the Sabbath and he accepted the Sabbath truth. Joseph Bates published a pamphlet about the Sabbath, called "The Seventh-day Sabbath: A perpetual sign." This pamphlet was read by many of the Millerite Adventists, and many of them accepted the seventh-day Sabbath.

Someone met one of the early advent reformers Joseph Bates one day and asked him what is the news? He responded "the news is the seventh day is still the Sabbath." In 1846 James and Ellen White heard the seventh-day Sabbath message from Joseph Bates.

Edson and Crosier were Millerites who shared the significance of the sanctuary with Bates and he introduced them to the Sabbath truth. Edson accepted the Sabbath but Crosier was tentative. He accepted it for a year and then he rejected it. We have now seen how the biblical Sabbath has been reintroduced among God's people. The bottom line is that God's ten commandment Sabbath will stand forever, and no human can change that. Throughout history man has attempted to discard the Sabbath and have failed and God has reestablished it time and time again.

More truths discovered

In 1840 George Storrs, a Methodist minister was studying his Bible and became convicted that the soul is not immortal. The souls of people who die do not live on in heaven, or go to an eternally burning hell. Immortality is granted only at the resurrection, so the doctrine of soul immortality is not biblical. He joined the Millerite movement in 1842 and the biblical teaching that the soul was not immortal was accepted by the Millerites.

By 1847, four important lost biblical truths were reintroduced into God's final movement. They are (1) The Second Advent; (2) The sanctuary Services; (3) The Sabbath Truth; and (4) The State of the Dead.

God distinguished his final movement

Two months after the Great Disappointment in December of 1844 during a prayer meeting, the prophetic gift that was seemingly silent among God's church for centuries was again restored. *God gave this special gift to firmly establish his final remnant church.* God used the prophetic gift to confirm the interpretation of these believers who went back and studied again. The prophetic gift or the spirit of prophecy was given to these believers to confirm that they were on the right track in their understanding of the Bible. In December 1844, a remarkable vision was given to a 17-year-old girl named Ellen Harmon, who along with her family was disfellowshipped from the Methodist Church for joining the Millerite movement. While she was praying in the company of other women at the home of a Mrs. Raines, the Holy Spirit came over her. In the vision she was rising higher and higher from the earth. She looked for the advent people but could not find them. A voice told her to look again. She looked higher up and she was shown these advent believers traveling to the heavenly city. The pathway was straight and narrow, leading them to the heavenly city at the end of the path. At the beginning of the pathway, a bright light shone behind them. The angel told her that was the midnight cry.

This confirmed that the Great Disappointment was part of their prophetic history. The light shone all around the saints and provided light so they would not stumble. Some of the believers denied that the light behind them was from God and that he was leading them; others grew tired and felt that the city was too far away and so their light went out and they fell off the path down into the dark and wicked world below. Like that pillar of fire that led the Israelites, Jesus was the light that was leading his people out of darkness. In her first vision she was shown that Jesus was the great light that was leading His people toward the heavenly city. They were to keep their eyes on Jesus and do not deny that their movement was of God. This was the first vision given to the 17- year- old girl. For the next 70 years she was God's messenger to his remnant church.

Like all of God's messengers Ellen White was been ridiculed, criticized, and rejected, but her 70 years of prophetic ministry manifested by her untiring hard work to earth's inhabitants has left such a witness with tremendous relevancy to God's end- time people. Critic after critic has been silenced but these powerful admonitions from the Lord which will last until the end of time.

If you want to continue in your beliefs in spite of the warnings from God's prophet you naturally find ways to discredit the prophet. This has been the case throughout the history of God's people. This story is told in 1 Kings 22 - In 853 BC wicked King Ahab of the Northern Kingdom asked King Jehoshaphat of Judah to join him in battle. Ahab the wicked king asked the advice of 400 false prophets if he should go to battle and they told him what he wanted to hear—yes, the Lord will give Ramoth Gilead to him. King Jehoshaphat of Judah worshiped Yahweh and wanted the Lord's advice so he asked King Ahab, "Is there not a true prophet from the Lord that we can consult?"

Ahab replied, "Yes, there is Micaiah, the son of Imlah but he never prophesies anything good about me."

The prophet was summoned and he did not go along with what the other 400 prophets who told Ahab what he wanted to hear. He told Ahab what the Lord showed him: Israel would be defeated. Ahab turned to Jehoshaphat and said, "I told you he never prophecies anything good about me. "The majority of society would not accept the prophet of the Lord who prophesies things that are contrary to their beliefs even if is sent from the Lord to correct error.

Ellen Harmon White – God's Chosen Messenger

I want to talk just a little about the messenger that God placed in their midst of his end-time movement. Ellen Harmon was that messenger. She was born in Gorham, Maine on November 26, 1827. Ellen White had very little education. In 1836 at the age of 9 while walking home from school she was struck by a thrown rock and sustained significant head and facial trauma. She was in a coma for weeks. Her injuries prevented her from ever attending school again. This incident changed her life and led her to find total dependence, comfort and joy in God. This injury made her long for heaven and she placed her life in God's hands. She became a person that Jesus can use for his cause. He chose her as his end time messenger. She has faithfully delivered his messages. These messages are so devastating to Satan's deceptions that he has vigorously attacked her but God has preserved these messages and they are accomplishing his purposes.

She lived for 87 years as an exemplary Christian. She wrote many books and spent her money in the cause of God. She did not capitalize on her calling. God used the unique circumstances of this young woman's life to show the world what He can accomplish using the weakest of the weak. Read Ellen White's writings for yourself and ask the Holy Spirit to lead you in understanding the message God sent to his end time movement.

Ellen Harmon was a Methodist Christian, who along with her family, attended one of William Miller's meetings in Portland Maine about 1840. She heard William Miller's exposition on the prophecies of Daniel. She and her family joined the Millerite movement in 1843. They were subsequently dis-fellowshipped from the Methodist Church. On October 22, 1844, they all suffered the Great Disappointment. Ellen Harmon was only 17 years old and was in poor health. She was weak and frail and suffering from tuberculosis. Two months after the Great Disappointment, she received her first vision and in that vision God gave her admonition and encouragement for this little flock of disappointed believers. It is important to note that this young woman at age 17 with a 3rd grade education was not a Bible scholar. As she followed God's instructions, she understood more of His will and she better understood more the visions He showed her. Today her writings are in schools of higher education.

God's Other End-time Messengers

Shortly before God chose Ellen Harmon to be his end time messenger to his remnant end time church, it appears that there were others to whom God gave important messages. The history of this Advent movement reveals that in 1842 a young, educated black man named William Foy moved to Beacon Hill in Boston to prepare for the ministry. He was a member of the Freewill black Baptist Church. God gave him several visions regarding the Advent movement. Two of his visions were reportedly given in 1842 two years before the great disappointment. These visions revealed information about the investigative judgment and the three angels messages of Revelation 14. In 1844, shortly after the great disappointment he received a third vision which he did not understand. He was shown the path God's people would travel to the heavenly city. William Foy's visions were also given under supernatural circumstances similar to the ones described by the prophet Daniel. He was examined by physicians who noted the supernatural phenomenon.

A doctor Cummings examined William Foy and noted that it was a supernatural experience. He showed no signs of life during the vision except for a pulse. In his second vision he was shown scenes of the judgment. William Foy was initially reluctant to share his visions partly because of the existing racial prejudice at that time. After the great disappointment no more visions were given to him. He became a noted speaker and later told these visions to his congregations. It appears as though William Foy only received about four visions. I wonder if they understood Foy's visions about the pre-advent judgment if the great disappointment would have happened. In December 1844 William Foy was in the congregation when this 17-year-old girl gave her first vision. He jumped up saying "that is the same vision the Lord gave to me." Now the critics of God's prophet hearing her tell the same vision would call this plagiarism, a modern day term, but we know that this is the work of a consistent unchanging God who gives similar messages to his prophets and that is why the Old Testament repeats so much of the language of the Old Testament.

Subsequent to William Foy, God chose an educated Millerite man by the name of Hazen Foss. It is reported that he received his first vision shortly before the Great Disappointment. He was shown the pathway that the people of God would travel to the Holy City. He was shown the problems that he would encounter as he carried these messages. He did not understand the vision regarding the pathway to heaven. He declined to give these messages to them. After the disappointment, he was given another vision. The Great Disappointment made it even more difficult to share the vision. He could not bear to live with the rejection and criticisms that God's messengers have to deal with. He was told that if he did not relay the vision, someone else with fewer abilities would be called upon. He was reluctant and did not accept the task. The Great Disappointment and its aftereffects were too much for him, and he did not accept the responsibility to be the messenger of the Lord. In his third vision he was told that if he did not relate the visions they would be given to someone else. He declined still and the spirit of the Lord left him. He was no longer interested in religion or spiritual things.

The Lord called a 17-year-old, uneducated, frail young woman stricken with Tuberculosis. In 1844, God called Ellen Gould Harmon to be his end time messenger and he bestowed on her the prophetic gift and gave her supernatural strength to accomplish the task. In 1846, Ellen Gould Harmon married a Millerite Advent preacher named James White. Gould and Harmon are her ancestral names.

Hazen Foss heard her tell her early vision in Poland, Maine, and he told her this: "The Lord gave me a message to bear to his people. And I refused after being told the consequences; I was proud; I was unreconciled to the disappointment. I heard you talk last night. I believe the visions are taken from me and given to you. Do not refuse to obey God, for it will be at the peril of your soul. I am a lost man. You are chosen of God;

be faithful in doing your work, and the crown I might have had, you will receive." (*SDA Encyclopedia Review and Herald,* volume 2, page 562).

At the appointed time in history, God sent a messenger to the group of advent believers who were on the right track in understanding the Bible and the prophecies of Daniel and Revelation. The prophecies were not only for these believers, but also for God's people living at the end of time. Ellen Harmon was very helpful in assuring these dejected Millerites who went back and restudied the prophecies that they were on the right track. Why did the Lord send an end time messenger? God needed to guide his end-time remnant movement down through the closing scenes of this earth's history and prepare a people for His second coming.

As an identifying mark of the remnant church, God restored the prophetic gift among his people. Prophecy is one of the gifts of the Holy Spirit. God sent this messenger to his end time church and gave her the gift of prophecy. This gift of the Holy Spirit is for instruction, correction of errors, guidance, reassurance, and comfort. God's messenger to his end-time people has provided a unified message to the world and this is evident today. God gave this messenger with only a 3rd grade education instructions on every aspect of Christian living needed to prepare a people for the second coming of Jesus.

History has shown, both in Old Testament times and in modern times, that when the church did not follow the instructions given to the prophets, disastrous things happen. We see a similar pattern during the ministry of Ellen White. For example when the publishing House in Battle Creek started printing commercial materials, the Lord instructed her to tell them not to. They refused, and the publishing house burned as the Lord had shown the prophet.

I cannot tell you that every church that uses the SDA name follows the guidelines set down by God; nonetheless, God has sent instructions for the final movement chronicled in the volumes of material that this prophet left for us. Satan has been trying to drown out these messages, and he has had a lot of success. This messenger's work is largely obscured and has been the object of Satan's fiercest attacks. As has been the story of all of God's prophets' down through the centuries of time, this prophetic voice was not embraced by most of these early Adventist believers but God reassured her that He would be there for her and uphold her and strengthen her for this task. This messenger wrote in Spiritual Gifts, vol.2, 35–36, "The Lord showed me the trials I must pass through; that I must go and relate to others what he revealed to me; that I should meet with great opposition and suffer anguish of spirit… the vision troubled me exceedingly. My health was very poor and I was only 17 years old. I looked with desire to the grave. Death appeared to me preferable to the responsibilities I should have to bear."

After prayer and encouragement from some of the brethren, she surrendered her will to God and for the next 70 years had over 2000 dreams and visions and God restored the prophetic gift among his people in a most remarkable way. The prophetic voice that seemed to have been silent for a long time was again present among God's people. At this time in the history of the reformation, God chose a messenger to help to prepare his people for the final phase of the earth's history.

This final movement, Seventh-day Adventism, it is a prophetic movement established by God to be the church that will be the final anchor for this great movement in the great plan of Salvation. God has been leading a people from the beginning and despite numerous pitfalls and snares set by the devil, the plan is marching on to its conclusion. Despite Satan's deceptions and man's failures, God has not deserted us. God rose up men and women around the world and enlightened them with this specific message at this particular time in history. God revealed to them the lost biblical truths that he wants to re-establish among his people. God placed his true prophet among them to show that he is leading this movement. The prophetic gift upholds the Bible; it is present truth that contemporizes the church in many ways.

Many of Ellen White's visions were given to confirm what the advent believers had discovered from their study of the Bible. Her vision of the heavenly sanctuary came after the brethren had studied it. Her visions often confirmed the results of Bible study. This prophetic gift was essential in unifying the church to do its God-ordained mission to preach the everlasting untarnished gospel, which includes the three angels' message of Revelation 14:6–12, to all the world. This is God's final warning to the inhabitants of planet earth, and God has chosen an end-time remnant people for this great work.

After the great disappointment, the majority of believers left the Millerite Advent movement. Many groups splintered off this movement. The group with the prophetic gift in their midst became the Seventh-day Adventist Church. The Seventh-day Adventist movement was officially organized as a Church in 1863. This church is accomplishing God's mission of preaching the gospel everywhere. Of the 230 countries in this world as recognized by the UN, the SDA church has a presence in almost all of these countries. The church has 13 world divisions carrying this gospel around the world. For the past five years more than one million members have joined the Adventist Church each year. The following is a quote from one of the vice presidents of the SDA church. "Church officials estimate almost 3,000 people join the church daily, meaning there is now one Seventh-day Adventist per 429 people around the globe. More than one million of those members joined the Adventist Church between July 2006 and June 2007, making the year in review the fifth consecutive to net such a measurable response to the Adventist message.

God's truth is marching on and millions around the world are joining God's end time movement.

Satan has been very angry with this church and is constantly raising up critics from within and without, but this work of the gospel has been circling earth's remotest bounds and accomplishing that which God intends. Like He did with Old Testament Israel, God is leading this movement and he has deposited a body of truth to be heralded to the world.

SDAs feel that they are a movement of prophecy called to proclaim God's final message to the inhabitants of planet earth, and as the prophetess was told in her first vision, they are to keep their eyes on Jesus. He will be the leader in accomplishing this daunting mission of proclaiming the gospel, which includes three angels' message given in Revelation 14:6–12.

The prophetic gift given to Ellen White is a revelation of the story of Jesus. That is the purpose of true prophecy. This is clearly seen in her book, The Desire of Ages, a remarkable book on the life of Jesus. Many misunderstand the work of Ellen White. It is not the Bible and does not replace it. Let me repeat that. The messages given to Ellen White for the remnant church did not replace the Bible; the Bible and the Bible only holds a pre-eminent position in God's church. The prophetic gift is a gift to the Church and it helps immensely in the correct understanding of the Bible. God want us to study and understand the Bible. He added the prophetic gifts to these believers who were engrossed in studying the scriptures, and it was crucial in assisting the final movement in affirming the correct interpretation of the scriptures. It helped greatly in every aspect of Christian living and the work of the Church. It has guided the publishing ministry, the health ministry, education, evangelism, theology, stewardship, marriage, child guidance, messages to young people, the mission of the church, particularly in the mission of preaching the three angels messages throughout the world; and this message has circled the globe. The prophetic gift enabled the church to build mission outreach projects in specific areas; it edifies the church; it unites the church, and guides the church when specific issues arise that would divide the church. Her writings comfort the church and help us to understand the Bible better.

She wrote, "I recommend to you, dear reader, the Word of God as the rule of your faith and practice. God has, in that Word, promised to give visions in the last days; not for a new rule of faith, but for the comfort of His people, and to correct those who err from Bible truth" (*Early Writings*, 1802).

The second coming of Christ is V-day for the Christian and the event of all events for planet earth. The church, the bride of Christ, must be ready for his return on this day. While our Kinsman Redeemer, the Heavenly Bridegroom tarries, the church cannot sleep. It must be on its God-given mission. It cannot accomplish this mission with the myriads of false teachers with so many different messages. God has given His end-time message and has chosen His messenger to help His church to understand His word.

These messages specifically prepares the church for the Second Advent of Jesus by telling the church specifically what to expect and how to prepare for the final crisis that God's people must face before the second coming.

The great reformation of the 16th, 17th, and 18th centuries started us on our way, but splintered into many denominations that settled for the truths that their leaders taught and now refuse to let in more truth. God had a lot more truth to reveal to the reformation, and God has chosen this final reformation to complete the work of restoring lost biblical truths.

So why is the Seventh-day Adventist church different from the other churches?

Why did God choose the SDA church at this time in history? Note that I am not speaking about individuals. This is not about individualism; God has decent Christian people in every denomination. I regularly listen to preachers and to music from non-SDA speakers and I am blessed. Matter of fact my favorite radio station for music is non-SDA and the music is heavenly. I do not agree with the teachings, but the music lifts me up spiritually. My message is not about criticizing people because God loves all of us and wants to see us all saved. In every denomination there are those who join the church and apostatize for whatever reason. That does not define the church. Apostasy has been present from the entrance of sin on Planet Earth. It is one of Satan's weapons of deception and distorting truth. My message is one of being aware of God's truth and deciding for yourself what you accept as truth. It is clearly not about individual people, but it is the role that the church is called to play in the final events of Earth's history.

What has Seventh-day Adventism brought to the table? Nothing else than what God has revealed in the Bible. Some of the truths that this final movement brings to the attention of inhabitants of Planet Earth are 1. *To repair the breach in God's law and restore the correct Sabbath day and keep it holy. 2. To place Jesus in his rightful place as High Priest in the heavenly sanctuary presiding over the ongoing judgment in the heavenly sanctuary. 3. Preach the three angels message of Revelation 14:6–12. 4. Restore fundamental lost biblical truths like the dead are asleep or in an unconscious state until the resurrection (Ecclesiastes 9:5, John 11:11, 14) 5. The-non immortality of the soul. 6. The wicked will not burn eternally, but will be burned up (Malachi 4: 1–3). 7. The ordinances of humility and the Lord's supper (John 13:4–17; 1 Corinthians 11:23–26). The church practices communion service with foot washing just as Jesus taught his disciples. 8. Baptism by immersion (Mark 1:9). 9. A healthy lifestyle no alcohol, tobacco, unclean meats, illegal or bad drugs. 10. They were to continue the preaching of the imminent return of Jesus. 11. To reveal to this world the great deceptions of Satan, especially among the apostolic church. 12. The need to study the scriptures fervently to guard against Satan's deceptions. 13. Take the gospel to earths remotest bounds.* Therefore you would expect this final remnant to be in every part of the world preparing a people for the second coming of Jesus. The SDA Church are millions of believers in thousands of churches and congregations all over planet earth, in some of the most desolate places and working to spread the gospel to earth's remotest bounds. Jesus is the center of this movement and every member counts and is important in spreading this gospel. In addition to the distinct biblical based doctrines that we teach, this final movement hold many biblical doctrines in common with other denominations (e.g., Salvation is a gift of God; Jesus is the divine Son of God and our Savior; righteousness by faith not by works: Our works reveal our faith, etc).

The second coming of Christ is the most anticipated and awesome event in history. Before every major event in history, God provided a messenger for His people. The evidence is clear that He has done so again and He gave His end-time messenger volumes of information to prepare a people for that final event of all events, the second coming of Jesus.

The writings of this messenger should be studied carefully. As a prophetess she has passed all the biblical tests of a true prophet. She has faithfully recorded God's admonitions for his end-time people. It is Satan's job to call her a false prophet and discredit her work. He has done so with all of God's prophets.

Ellen Harmon White was chosen to be the messenger of the Lord and after reassurances of God's protection for this task she accepted the call. The Lord showed her that her ministry would meet with great criticisms and rejection, but He sustained her despite the devil's most aggressive demonic led attacks.

Why does God need an end time messenger?

There are over 500 denominations preaching divergent beliefs. God lovingly sent a messenger to his end time church to lead us back to his will as outlined in the Bible. God has a standard of righteousness that we must strive for by his grace. In Matthew 22 the parable of the wedding feast depicts the kingdom of heaven as a king who made a wedding feast for his son. The invited guests of the Jewish nation did not come, so he sent his servants everywhere to invite whosoever would come (the Gentiles). When the king came to examine the guests (which represents Judgment), there was one guest who did not have on the wedding garment or the robe of righteousness. The king could not let him into the banquet because he did not meet the standard of righteousness required. The parable warns that there will be weeping and gnashing of teeth, for many are called to the banquet but few are chosen. God wants everyone to be ready for the banquet.

God's messenger and the Bible

Many people have the wrong impression that the SDA Church put more emphasis on Ellen White's writings that the Bible. Nothing could be further from the truth. In 1871, God's messenger wrote that the *Testimonies* are given so we can order our lives in accordance with the Bible's teachings: "You are not familiar with the Scriptures. If you had made God's word your study, with a desire to reach the Bible standard and attain to Christian perfection, you would not have needed the *Testimonies.* It is because you have neglected to acquaint yourselves with God's inspired Book that He has sought to reach you by simple, direct testimonies, calling your attention to the words of inspiration which you had neglected to obey, and urging you to fashion your lives in accordance with its pure and elevated teachings." (Ibid., 2:605).

Ellen White is the listed as the fourth most translated writer in history. She wrote and published more books, articles, and other publications than any other woman in history. Through the light that God has revealed to her, the SDA church has about 65 publishing houses around the world. She wrote in Testimonies for the Church Volume 8 and page 87 "Years ago the Lord gave me special directions that buildings should be erected in various places in America, Europe, and other lands for the publication of literature containing the light of present truth."

It has been almost 100 years since she has been asleep in Jesus, and the publishing houses around the world are still circulating God's messages to us. She left us with 100,000 pages of information. She has left a tremendous paper trail. Her book, The Desire of Ages, was classified as one of the best books ever written on the life of Jesus. I highly recommend the reading of that book. It's a masterpiece that has circulated the globe. Her books written in the 1800's are still used and taught in colleges today because they are timeless messages given to her by God for those of us living at the very end of time. Her writings lead us to study the scriptures for the truths that are hidden therein. Interestingly Ellen White never called herself a prophet; she called herself the messenger of the Lord. Her work covered so much more ground than prophecy. Prophecy is a small part of her work. Here are some quotations from Ellen White on her calling:

"Early in my youth I was asked several times, 'Are you a prophet?' I have ever responded, 'I am the Lord's messenger.' I know that many have called me a prophet, but I have made no claim to this title. My Savior declared me to be His messenger. 'Your work,' He instructed me, 'is to bear my word. Strange things will arise, and in your youth I set you apart to bear the message to the erring ones, to carry the word before unbelievers, and with pen and voice to reprove from the Word actions that are not right. Exhort from the Word. I will make My Word open to you. It shall not be as a strange language. In the true eloquence of simplicity, with voice and pen, the messages that I give shall be heard from one who has never learned in the schools. My Spirit and My power shall be with you.'

"Why have I not claimed to be a prophet?–Because in these days many who boldly claim that they are prophets are a reproach to the cause of Christ; and because my work includes much more than the word 'prophet' signifies." .

"To claim to be a prophetess is something that I have never done. If others call me by that name, I have no controversy with them. But my work has covered so many lines that I cannot call myself other than a messenger, sent to bear a message from the Lord to His people, and to take up work in any line that He points out."

"When I was last in Battle Creek, I said before a large congregation that I did not claim to be a prophetess. Twice I referred to this matter, intending each time to make the statement, 'I do not claim to be a prophetess.' If I spoke otherwise than this, let all now understand that what I had in mind to say was that I do not claim the title of prophet or prophetess" (*Review and Herald,* July 26, 1906, reprinted in *Selected Messages,* book 1, pp. 31–35).

"During the discourse, I said that I did not claim to be a prophetess. Some were surprised at this statement, and as much is being said in regard to it, I will make an explanation. Others have called me a prophetess, but I have never assumed that title. I have not felt that it was my duty thus to designate myself. Those who boldly assume that they are prophets in this our day are often a reproach to the cause of Christ."

"My work includes much more than this name signifies. I regard myself as a messenger, entrusted by the Lord with messages for His people" (Letter 55, 1905; quoted in *Selected Messages,* book 1, pp. 35).

The Lord gave Ellen White the courage needed to proclaim His messages. Imagine a 17-year-old girl telling the early advent believers, fresh from the experience of the Great Disappointment, that she has visions from God at a time when these early believers after their Albany New York conference in 1845 wrote in the Morning Watch of May 5, 1845 that they have no confidence whatsoever in any new messages, visions, dreams, tongues, miracles, extraordinary gifts, revelations, impressions, discerning of spirits or teachings, etc., not in accordance with the unadulterated word of God. You can only imagine how skeptical these early advent believers were of her. She has had critics from the very beginning of her ministry and will have them until the end of time. Despite criticisms, God gave her a successful seventy-year prophetic ministry.

She received some 2,000 visions of varying lengths. During the first 30 years, her visions were often accompanied by a similar physical phenomenon as described by many of the biblical prophets in vision. Her early critics were silenced by the physical phenomenon that accompanied her earliest visions. J.N. Loughborough, an early church pioneer, saw Ellen White in vision about 50 times. He described her in vision in his book, *The Great Second Advent Movement*. He stated that she would begin her visions by saying "glory" three times. (When you have a true vision of God, magnificent glory surrounds you). At the end of her visions, Ellen would say 'dark' as she was "transported" back to earth. Many of her visions were given in public, and she was examined by doctors who documented the supernatural phenomenon that accompanied her visions. He recorded that a Dr. Drummond who did not believe in her visions examined her during a vision and after examination remarked "she doesn't breathe!" During her visions she exhibited supernatural strength, lost consciousness, lost vision, and could walk around the room, with her eyes open but gazing. Sometimes her arms and hands made gestures as she walked around. She did not breathe but was alive. During one of her visions, she held up a heavy Bible in one hand for over 30 minutes, a sign of supernatural strength. After the vision she could not do that.

There are numerous descriptions from people who have observed her in vision. I will briefly mention a few. Here is one by another physician: "I am quite certain that she did not breathe at that time while in vision, or in any of the others which she had when I was present. The coming out of the vision was as marked as her going into it. The first indication we had that the vision was ended, was in her again beginning to breathe. She drew her first breath deep, long, and full, in a manner showing that her lungs had been entirely empty of air. After drawing the first breath, several minutes passed before she drew the second, which filled the lungs precisely as did the first; then a pause of two minutes, and a third inhalation, after which the breathing became natural." Signed, M.G. Kellogg, M.D., Battle Creek, Mich., Dec. 28, 1890.

Another eye witness to her visions was Daniel T. Bourdeau. He did not believe that she was really in vision and so he examined her. He wrote: and writes that "on June 28, 1857, I saw Sister Ellen G. White in vision for the first time. I was an unbeliever in the visions; but one circumstance among others that I might mention convinced me that her visions were of God. To satisfy my mind as to whether she breathed or not, I first put my hand on her chest sufficiently long to know that there was no more heaving of the lungs than there would have been had she been a corpse. I then took my hand and placed it over her mouth, pinching her nostrils between my thumb and forefinger, so that it was impossible for her to exhale or inhale air, even if she had desired to do so. I held her thus with my hand about 10 minutes, long enough for her to suffocate under ordinary circumstances. She was not in the least affected by the ordeal.

Several people, including physicians, have evaluated her in vision, and she was totally under supernatural power as she received these visions. She was not having a seizure or any other illness. When she emerged from these visions, some lasting hours, the Holy Spirit would help her to remember these visions so she could write down what the Lord had shown her. Sometimes it took a long time to record great books like the Great Controversy and The Desire of Ages. Satan could never inspire books like these. They are classics that are relevant now for over 100 plus years. Read them for yourself and see. Millions of people have been inspired to a closer relationship with God through these books.

Her messages have provided tremendous encouragement, guidance and comfort to God's last day movement. She clearly states that her writings are not to replace the scriptures; they are instructions that God has sent to his last day people to prepare the world for his second coming. It is evident from her writings, however, that she had extensive knowledge of the Bible. In eight of her leading books, she quoted the Bible 14,000 times. She claimed that her writings are a lesser light that leads up to the greater light, the Bible.

How should we regard the writings of Ellen White?

Only the Bible is the gold standard of instruction. The writings of Ellen White are not the Bible and should not be placed on the same level. Her writings can lead you to a deeper study and understanding of the Bible. They are not the Bible, but they are not ordinary writings. They are inspired writings.

If people understood the Bible and its prophecies, they would not need the lesser light. However, they do not understand the Bible, as evidenced by the confusion and diversity of beliefs practiced in the world today. These messages are for everyone. Here is a quotation by *E.G. White:* "The Bible itself is totally sufficient to enlighten the most beclouded mind. But some still live in opposition to the plainest teachings of the Bible. So to leave men and women without excuse, God gives a plain and pointed testimony which brings them back to the Word that they have neglected to follow." She has left us a legacy of biblically sound messages and her writings help us to understand the Bible better.

Here is an interview with E.G. White about her writings and the Bible taken from Memoirs of Adventist History.

Interviewer: "Mrs. White, a lot of people seem to be confused regarding the relation of your writings to the Bible. Can you help me on this point?"

E.G. White: "I am glad you asked. This is the most misunderstood areas of my work. My husband had it straight back in 1847. He wrote this in our first little book (*A Word to the Little Flock*, p. 13).

(She reads.) 'The Bible is a perfect and complete revelation. It is our only rule of faith and practice.'

I said much the same thing in my 1851 autobiography. (She reads.) 'I recommend to you, dear reader, the word of God as the rule of your faith and practice.' (*Early Writings*, p. 78).

And throughout my ministry I repeatedly emphasized that we want Bible evidence for every point we advance. "The Bible is the only rule of faith and doctrine" (*Review and Herald*, July 17, 1888).

Interviewer: "If the Bible is the only authority for faith and doctrine, Sister White, then why do we need your writings?"

E.G. White: "Certainly not for doctrine! All of our early believers were too biblically literate to ever rely on my writings for doctrine."

Interviewer: "Pardon me for interrupting, but you are not answering my question."

E.G. White: "You are right. It seems to me that God has given me messages for several reasons. First to lead people back to the Bible, which all too many have neglected. James put it very nicely back in 1868. (She reads.)

'Let the gifts have their proper place in the church. God has never set them in the very front, and commanded us to look to them to lead us in the path of truth, and the way to heaven. His word he has magnified. The scriptures of the Old and New Testament are man's lamp to light up his path to the kingdom. Follow that. But if you err from Bible truth, and are in danger of being lost, it may be that God will in the time of his choice correct you (through the gift of prophecy), and bring you back to the Bible.' (*Review and Herald*, Feb. 25, 1868).

"This is the point that you want to catch."

Interviewer: "What point?"

E. G. White: "That is a primary function of my writings is to lead people back to the Bible. I said the same thing myself in volume five of The Testimonies. If our people had studied the Bible as they should have, they wouldn't need my writings. My writings were given to bring them back to the Bible."

Interviewer: "I'm afraid that a great number of Adventists haven't got your position straight."

E.G. White: "I had to fight misconceptions regarding the relationship of my work to the Bible all my life. This is why I have written so frequently on the topic. I wrote one of my clearest statements in 1903: 'Little heed is given to the Bible, and the Lord has given a lesser light to lead men and women to the greater light'" (*Colporteur Ministry*, p. 125).

Interviewer: "That makes it quite clear!"

E.G. White: "Yes, it is! Without meaning to do so they have made my writings into the greater light. Some even get their theology from my writings. Some people have not only misunderstood me, for they frustrated me beyond measure."

Interviewer: "I can see why. Earlier you noted that there were several reasons why God gave messages to you for his people. What are the other reasons?"

E.G. White: "I will briefly state that I believe that God desires my writings to help people apply biblical principles to their lives and to enlighten people on some of the difficulties they face as they prepare for the Second Advent."

Ellen White clearly stated that her writings are not to replace the Bible. In her book, Evangelism, (page 257) she says they are the lesser light to lead men and women to the greater light. This is true. Her writings are divinely inspired and hence do not contradict the Bible. They do not add to the Bible; she wrote, "The Lord designs to warn you, to reprove, to counsel, through the testimonies given, and to impress your minds with the importance of the truth of His word. The written testimonies are not to give new light, but to impress vividly upon the heart the truths of inspiration already revealed. Man's duty to God and to His fellow man has been distinctly specified in God's word, yet but few of you are obedient to the light given. Additional truth is not brought out; but God has through the *Testimonies* simplified the great truths already given and in His own chosen way brought them before the people to awaken and impress the mind with them, that all may be left without excuse." (Ibid., p. 665).

These messages were given to Ellen White by the Holy Spirit. The messages are tailored for the time in history for which they are sent. Ellen White could not have originated these powerful, poignant messages geared to prepare a people for the second coming of Jesus. Here is a statement from Ellen White and there are so many of them.

"The Lord has sent his people much instruction, line upon line, precept upon precept, here a little, and there a little. Little heed is given to the Bible, and the Lord has given a lesser light to lead men and women to the greater light. O, how much good would be accomplished if the books containing this light were read with a determination to carry out the principles they contain! There would be a thousand fold greater vigilance, a thousand fold more self-denial and resolute effort. And many more would now be rejoicing in the light of present truth."(Ellen G. White, Review and Herald, 20th January 1903 'An open letter')

A study of Ellen White's admonitions inevitably leads you to a deeper study of the Bible. In the Review and Herald, 1903, she wrote, "Little heed is given to the Bible; the Lord has given a lesser light to lead men and women to the greater light." In 1870, she wrote in volume 5 of the Testimonies to the Church that "the word of God is sufficient to enlighten the most beclouded mind and may be understood by those who have any desire to understand it. But notwithstanding all this, some who profess to make the word of God their study are found living in direct opposition to its plainest teachings. Then, to leave men with out excuse, God gives plain and pointed testimonies, bringing them back to the word that they have neglected to follow." Her work is not an addition to the Bible it explains a lot of the Bible. Her work helps tremendously in understanding the Bible. It guides and edifies the church in every aspect of church growth. It guides in every aspect of Christian living, health, education, marriage, home and family, etc.

Ellen White, God's messenger to us in these final moments of Earth's history, has important messages for us today. We all need to read them. In 2 Chronicles 36:15, 16 "And the Lord God of their fathers sent to them by his messengers rising up be times and sending because he had compassion on his people and on his dwelling place but they mocked the messengers of God and despised his words and misused the prophets until the wrath of the Lord arose against his people till there was no remedy." This has been the history of God's prophets and E. G. White is no exception. Her writings have been ignored, taken out of context, misinterpreted, and sometimes early beliefs that she had before her remarkable calling are brought to the forefront and her 70 years of prophetic experience and ministry discarded.

God revealed a lot to Ellen White over 70 years. If she were a false prophet, one should find volumes of false information in her writings. There is a 70-year paper trail of her writings. Her life has been an exemplary faithful, God-fearing Christian woman. She faithfully and tirelessly recorded the information God gave her into books, manuscripts, letters, etc., and she did not profit from them. She lived a humble, godly life and used her money to promote God's cause.

God revealed light in stages and this is true for Ellen White. Ellen Harmon, still a teenager when she was called to the prophetic ministry. She had a Methodist background and did not initially see the significance of the Sabbath in God's law. In 1845 Joseph Bates read an article that T.M. Preble wrote on the Sabbath in a Millerite paper the hope of Israel. He was convinced that the seventh day was still the Sabbath. Joseph Bates published a pamphlet on the Sabbath called the Seventh Day Sabbath a perpetual sign. James and Ellen White read the publication and were convinced that the seventh day was still the Sabbath. In April 1847 she received her first vision about the Sabbath and its importance. Note that Ellen White did not present the Sabbath truth through a vision; the brethren studied the scriptures and were convicted. Her vision confirmed that their interpretation of scripture was correct.

Three individuals Joseph Bates, James and Ellen White became nucleus of what is now today the Seventh-day Adventist Church. As we study God's word and accept his truth he reveals more to us. The more we study and accept God's word the more we are enlightened. When the children of Israel were released from Egyptian captivity they had to be taught God's way. God restored his law and he reinforced the keeping of the Sabbath; we see a similar picture here as the church emerges from the dark ages when God's word was suppressed God began to restore lost truths to sincere men and women from diverse denominations who were avidly seeking truth by studying the Bible.

God gave Ellen White visions about the need for the publishing ministry to spread the messages he gave her. She told of a vision that from the small beginning the publishing ministry would send beams of light around the world. The publishing ministry developed rapidly and the Adventist Review a journal that her husband started before 1850 is still in publication today. Her vision about literature evangelism greatly helped literature evangelism or the colporteur work that has spread throughout the world.

Like most of God's prophets she has be ridiculed, rejected, and Satan has thrown all manner of accusations against her but she has done her job; it is up to us to read, pray and study for yourself. In the final analysis God will vindicate all of His prophets. Her work speak for itself; despite her critics, Today E.G. White remains one of the most translated American author in history; her works on a wide range of spiritual and health issues written over 150 years ago are quite relevant to God's end time church. Her masterpiece the desire of Ages is critically acclaimed by the Library of Congress as one of the best book ever written on the life of Christ. God has inspired her to write numerous books that are just incredible. Some of these books are *Steps to Christ, The Desire of Ages, The Great Controversy, Education, The Ministry of Healing, Diet and Health, Patriarchs and Prophets, Prophet and Kings, The Acts of the Apostles, Child Rearing, The Adventist Home, 9 Volumes of Testimonies to the Church, Counsels to Parents, Teachers and Students, Thoughts from the Mount of Blessings*, just to name a few of her books. Many of these were the result of visions God gave her. Here is a quotation from *SDA Encyclopedia*—"At the time of her death her literary productions consisted of well over 100,000 pages: 24 books in current circulation; 2 book manuscripts ready for publication; 4600 periodical articles in the journals of the church; 200 or more out-of-print tracts and pamphlets; 6000 typewritten manuscript documents consisting of letters and general manuscripts, aggregating approximately 40,000 typewritten pages; 2000 handwritten letters and documents and diaries, journals et cetera, when copied comprising 20,000 typewritten pages." (*Seventh-day Adventist Encyclopedia*, 1966 edition page 1413)

God's final remnant church with a messenger in their midst is accomplishing that which God wants it to, and that is to advance His kingdom throughout planet earth. The accomplishments of this movement can only be the effort of a God-led movement. Many of our medical and educational institutions today came about as a direct result of the visions that God gave her. The SDA Church has thousands of institutions of higher education throughout the world. The SDA Church operates about 175 hospitals throughout the world. God showed her the property on which Loma Linda University was to be established and the property was obtained for a fraction of its original cost. Loma Linda has been the beacon for sending missionaries around the world and runs numerous clinics and hospitals overseas. God's messenger has traveled to many continents to carry His messages. In 1891 she traveled to Australia and was influential in establishing Avondale College and their church on 1450 acres of land 75 miles North of Sydney. She and her son James Edson White were instrumental in spreading the gospel to Southern Blacks. Through her influence, the site was bought in Huntsville, Alabama. Oakwood was a large slave plantation before it became Oakwood College, and now Oakwood University. At its inception, the same concepts were employed as at Avondale: a work-study program was instituted in which the students worked on the many industries located on the grounds of the campus.

Many errors have occurred, and the task of accomplishing the task of spreading the three angels' message of Revelation 14 has lost speed when the Church leadership did not closely follow the instructions given to her by God. When the Church followed her God-given instructions, it prospered. When they did not, the work was impeded.

In the 1890s pantheistic ideas embraced by Dr. Kellogg invaded the Church, and God sent specific information through her that this was not His way. He also sent messages through her to decentralize the Church and build smaller churches in different areas. The Church leaders did not initially follow the Lord's leadings, and the large central church, the dime tabernacle went up in smoke. So did the Battle Creek sanatorium when they refused to follow God's messenger. There is a rich history of God establishing this movement and the steps God took to get His people on the right track. Time and time again Satan gets the Church off, track and he will do so until Jesus returns. There are libraries full of experiences that people had with this messenger of the Lord. She was real. Dr. Archibald Truman was an eyewitness to a prophecy revealed to Ellen White and he records it. (See Seventh-day.org website.)

Ellen White was indeed God's messenger to His end-time people and in 1863 and 1865, Ellen White received a series of health reform visions from God, and that has laid the groundwork for health reform among God's end-time people. This church has pioneered health reform 150 before the popular health conscious reform movements of today. She received her first vision about health reform in June of 1863. She went on to write extensively about health reform among God's people. A compilation of her writings can be found in the book diet and health. Her book, *The Ministry of Healing*, is still widely used today, mainly in Adventist institutions as a model for health care workers. In 1863 she urged the Church to start the Health Reform Institute in Battle Creek, Michigan. In 1877 John Harvey Kellogg renamed it the Battle Creek Sanitarium. This institution became the Mayo clinic of its time. The rich and the famous came to this institution, names like Thomas Edison, Henry Ford, John D. Rockefeller, and Dr. Morris Fishbein, the editor of the AMA. Dr. Kellogg, later separated from the church and interestingly that institution did not survive.

This woman with a 3rd grade education brought the light of health reform to the world leading medical doctors in her era. The health principles that God gave her, when followed, could eliminate the health crisis that the world is experiencing today. Those in the SDA Church, who follow her advice, live longer, healthier lives than those who do not. There is research data to support this.

God has used the weakest of the weak, a woman who sustained severe head trauma at age 9 and was in poor health from TB at an early age, to recover from ill-health and spread his health message to the world. She was over a hundred years ahead of her time; today thousands of people are spreading this health awareness message that God revealed to her in the 1800's. The fact that her messages are still relevant today is supportive of the fact that she is indeed God's end-time messenger. Many successful health reform institutions today operate on the principles of health reform that God showed her. These institutions offer a model of healthcare and health reform that is missing in many of the world's leading medical facilities. The health reform message that God gave her has largely been ignored by the major medical institutions until recently when the ballooning costs of health care has brought the realization that preventive medicine is the answer.

In the last 10 to 20 years we have become a more health conscious nation and there is a lot of research and up-to-date information available to the earnest seeker of truth. The fact that Seventh-day Adventists who follow her instructions live longer, healthier lives can be attributed to the numerous health messages that God gave her. The world has benefited from them even though they would not admit to it.

Modern medical science today is just now catching up to many of the revelations that God gave to her over 150 years ago. She wrote about preventive medicine and warned against the use of tobacco, alcohol and other foods that are harmful. It was only in 1960 that the Surgeon General put the danger warning on cigarette boxes.

She wrote about God's natural remedies for maintaining good health. These are the natural remedies that he gave to Adam and Eve at creation. They are good nutrition, exercise, water, sunlight, temperance or self-control, fresh air, rest, and trust in God's guidance. They lead to a longer, healthier life. God gave this health law to the children of Israel and in Exodus 15:26 he told them that if they diligently kept His statutes and His commandments, then he would not allow any of these diseases to afflict them. The Egyptians were dying from the same diseases that afflict us today: atherosclerotic vascular diseases, sexually transmitted diseases, arthritic diseases, cancer. God revealed to Ellen White the benefit of the simple lifestyle that he instituted in Eden.

The Health reform message that God gave her is just one of the wide array of information that this humble, woman brought to the early advent reform movement and to the world.

The early advent reform movement gave rise to the Seventh-day Adventist Church in 1863. A church formed on the principles of the Bible. A movement formed from the understanding of prophecy. God reveals light in stages and to this movement that has anchored the protestant reformation he revealed much of the biblical truths that were lost from the church e.g. the lost Sabbath truth, the state of the dead, the sanctuary services, the non-immortality of the soul, the 3 angels message, the Health Reform movement, the imminent return of Christ, the judgment, the significance of the sanctuary in heaven. God revealed many of these biblical truths to Ellen White. Many of these truths were lost while the church was in the wilderness. The same Holy Spirit that inspired the prophets inspired Ellen White too and her messages are in harmony with what is in the Bible, a lot of what is written in the New Testament is in the old and we do not accuse the new testament prophets of copying from the old because it is the same spirit that is still speaking to the prophets. Ellen White's writing is reflecting what the Holy Spirit reveals to her and they are consistent with what is in the Bible.

Satan hates the writings of Ellen White and he has been successful in sabotaging them. Her writings are truly helpful in preparing a people for the second coming of Jesus. Satan does not want us to do the work of preparation and to help others to prepare for the second coming. The longer he keeps us in this world of misery, the longer he gets to tempt us into sin. It is interesting that there are so many bestselling books by people to whom God has not given any message for his people, while His true messenger's books have not been recognize by the majority of professed Christians. I would dare say that the majority of her critics have not read these life transforming books that God inspired her to write. If God's people had been listening to his messengers, we would have finished the work that God has entrusted us with.

Most of Ellen White's messages are geared towards preparing God's end-time people for the second coming of Jesus. Her prophetic predictions are few but some of them have been fulfilled so far. She predicted that Catholics and Protestants would in the end of time bridge their differences and unify on points of faith that are common between them. This is happening today in the form of the great ecumenical movement and the Vatican councils.

She also predicted the rise of modern spiritualism. She warned about the deception of spiritualism in the last days. It is now accepted as part of many people's religious beliefs and it has become a worldwide phenomenon. There are television shows where people are attempting to contact the dead. There are children who are having psychic phenomenon and seeing dead people. Satan and his evil angels are ready and willing to impersonate the dead. Unless you are aware of these end-time deceptions, you will be deceived by Satan who is much more clever that human beings. God warned us over a hundred years ago that these things will happen in the end of time. These predictions are given to prepare God's people living at the end of time for the events that will usher in the second coming.

Despite severe oppositions to her messages from within and outside the Church, the work of the Lord has progressed amazingly, and when the Church follows the instruction of God's messenger, the Church has prospered. Despite her critics, she faithfully discharged her duties and she has unified the beliefs of God's end-time church, enabling it to spread to gospel to earth's remotest bounds. This Church has risen from less than 60 members in the 1840s and 30,000 members in 1888 to over 16 million members worldwide and billions have heard God's end-time message.

It is the fastest growing Protestant church in the world with about 2500 daily baptisms. The truth that God has revealed to her is marching on despite Satan's aggressive attacks for over 160 years now. God has given this prophet so much information for his final movement that the information is astounding and jaw dropping. It will be difficult to deny the existence of this prophet and it would take a lifetime of diligent study to master this information.

The church has its many critics, and we know that the devil is wrought with the Final Church and is seeking to destroy it, but he cannot. The Seventh-day Adventist Church is not perfect, but God is. There are no perfect churches because we are all sinners. If you find the perfect church it is no longer perfect when you join it. The Church is God's instrument to spread the everlasting gospel. You cannot rely on your senses and how you feel in a church service. Many churches have services that are quite moving and reverent, but they do not all preach the biblical truths.

I have also gone to many SDA churches whose leadership clearly has strayed from their mission of preaching and teaching the everlasting gospel. You must know the truth for yourself because Satan is alive and well in every church and that includes the SDA church. There are many people in the SDA Church, including preachers, who do not fully understand and do not follow the pathway that God has instructed his final movement to follow. This was the case with ancient Israel; they continually strayed from God's instructions. There are many people in other churches who preach and teach a different interpretation of the Bible from SDAs. Many of them are sincere in their worship and serve the lord in sincerity to the best of their knowledge. I am not criticizing them; I love and admire these wonderful Christian people. God loves and cares for them and wants to save all of us. He does not discriminate. His heart breaks when we fall short of His will for us. God did not ask us to judge anyone but to love and respect each other. He is the only righteous judge. Regardless of which church we attend, we are all sinners in need of God's love and forgiveness, so let us share our understanding of the Bible with others and love and respect their beliefs too. Let me add that no church is perfect only God is. We are all striving for his perfection. Whatever our beliefs are, we need to be humble, knowing that only God has the final say and only God knows it all.

Let us not judge each other and don't judge God's end-time movement by what you see in the Church sometimes. Study the word and look to Jesus as your example. He is our perfect example. Do not go to a church because it has great choirs and the music is good, the church is large and affluent, they have a gifted preacher, etc. Go to the church chosen by God to finish his work in all the world and where the true word of God from the Bible is the main menu.

Why did God raise up the Seventh-day Adventist Church?

Just like God called the Jewish nation and made them custodians of His law and keepers of the oracles of God. He has again done that with this final end-time movement. I am not saying that SDAs are the only Christians or it is the perfect Church. God has his people in every Church and he is appealing to them to follow him. The SDA church is composed of members who have left various churches and have heeded the call of the three angels' messages. This should not be interpreted that if you are a SDA you are saved or you are a superior Christian or if you are the member of another church you are lost. God chose the Jewish nation and entrusted them with the information to prepare the world for his first coming. He did not choose them because they were a superior nation. He chose them to do a task. Similarly God has an end-time message that the world needs to hear and get ready for His second coming and He has chosen this Church to spread this message.

To the Seventh-day Adventist Church, God has given an understanding of the end-time messages of Daniel and Revelation and the final events of earth's history. This end-time message transcends the individual church or person. God has His children in these churches, and to them He sent the final warning to get out of Babylon because she teaches many false doctrines. Babylon has mixed up truth and error. The Protestant Reformation was not in vain. It was part of God's plan of restoring lost truths. The early reformers did not grasp the full truth of the Bible, but they stood up for the truths that they understood and they laid the groundwork for the full restoration of truth.

Although the SDA Church shares many Christian beliefs with other protestant denominations, God has given it a distinct task to do in these final movements of earth's history and he has chosen it at a particular time in history and prophecy. God's final movement is a movement of prophecy and those who have taken the time to study these prophecies are blessed.

Ellen White's revelations regarding the USA in Prophecy

Ellen White was shown that the USA has an important role in end-time prophecy. Here are a few of the things that she wrote regarding the USA in prophecy.

"To secure popularity and patronage, legislators will yield to the demand for a Sunday law ....By the decree enforcing the institution of the papacy in violation of the law of God our nation will disconnect herself fully from righteousness" (Testimonies to the church, 1885)

"The people of the United States have been favored people, but when they restrict religious liberty, surrender Protestantism, and give countenance to popery, the measure of their guilt will be full, and "national apostasy" will be registered in the books of heaven." (Review & Herald, 1893).

"When our nation, in its legislative councils, shall enact laws to bind the consciences of men in regard to their religious privileges, enforcing Sunday observance, and bringing oppressive power to bear against those who keep the seventh-day Sabbath, the law of God will to all intents and purposes, will be made void in our land, and national apostasy will be followed by national ruin."(White, 1888)

"The substitution of the false for the true is the last act in the drama. When this substitution becomes universal God will reveal himself. When the laws of men are exalted above the laws of God, when the powers of this earth try to force men to keep the first day of the week, know that the time has come for God to work." (White, 1901)

"The substitution of the laws of men for the law of God, the exaltation, by merely human authority, of Sunday in place of the Bible Sabbath, is the last act in the drama. When this substitution becomes universal God will reveal himself. He will arise in his majesty to shake terrible the earth" Testimonies to the Church, 1902)

"As America, the land of religious liberty shall unite with the Papacy in forcing the conscience and compelling men to honor the false Sabbath, the people of every country on the globe will be led to follow her example". (Testimonies, 1901)

"The fast fulfilling signs of the times declare that the coming of Christ is near at hand. The days in which we live are solemn and important… The calamities by land and by sea, the unsettled state of society, the alarm of war, are portentous. They forecast approaching events of the greatest magnitude. The agencies of evil are combining their forces, and consolidating. They are strengthening for the last great crises. Great changes are soon to take place in our world, and the final movements will be rapid ones. The conditions of things in the world shows that troublous times are right upon us. The daily papers are full of indicators of a terrible conflict in the near future. The world is stirred with the spirit of war. The Prophecy of the eleventh chapter of Daniel has nearly reached its complete fulfillment. Soon the scenes of trouble spoken of in the prophecies will take place" Testimonies to the church, 1904)

"When Sunday observance shall be enforced by law, and the world shall be enlightened concerning the obligation of the true Sabbath, then whoever shall transgress the command of God, to obey a precept that has no higher authority than that of Rome, will therefore honor popery over God. He is paying homage to Rome and the power, which enforces the institution ordained by Rome. He is worshipping the beast and his image.... And it is not until the issue is thus plainly set before the people, and they are brought to choose between the commandments of God and the commandments of men, that those who continue in transgression will receive the mark of the beast" Great Controversy, 1888)

"In the time of the end, every divine institution is to be restored. The breach made in the law at the time the Sabbath was changed by man, is to be repaired. God's remnant people, standing before the world as reformers, are to show that the law of God is the foundation of all enduring reform, and that the Sabbath of the fourth commandment is to stand as a memorial of creation, a constant reminder of the power of God. In clear, distinct lines they are to present the necessity of obedience to all the precepts of the Decalogue. Constrained by the love of Christ, they are to cooperate with Him in building up the waste places. They are to be repairers of the breach, restorers of paths to dwell in." (*Prophets and Kings*, 1917)

Down through the centuries God has had a chosen people to whom he deposited his commandments, his precepts and his laws. This prophet has written volumes on the subject of the end time and her work has gone a long way in preparing God's end time people for his soon appearing. God has sent us warnings by his prophets and it is up to us to heed these messages. To be forewarned is to be forearmed. In the symbolic language, the prophecies of Daniel and Revelation have revealed to us what will happen in the end of time. In these last days of this world's history God chose a woman, E.G. White, living in the last great World Power, to be his end time messenger. She has delivered God's end time message is plain language, no symbols and it is very detailed and easy to understand. It covers all aspects of Christian living that is necessary in preparing a people for the second coming of Jesus.

Only a handful of people have believed the true prophets down through the ages. In Noah's day, only Noah's family went into the ark of safety. Jesus said as it was in the days of Noah so shall it be in the coming of the son of man. Satan will close even professed Christians' eyes to God's true prophets. As the angels holding back the winds of strife start to loosen up their grip, disaster after disaster will plague planet earth and the conditions will be set up for the final fulfillment of these prophecies that God has shown to her.

The Protestant Reformation led to the formation of many different Churches who made a circle around the beliefs of their leaders and settled for that belief. God had a lot more truth to restore and the movement went on and culminated in this final remnant Church described in Revelation 12:17.

How do we find God's end-time remnant that keep the commandments of God and have the testimony of Jesus?

Just as John the Baptist did in preparing a people for the first coming of Jesus, similarly God prepared an end-time movement armed with the everlasting gospel to prepare a people for the second coming of Jesus. The beliefs of this church are the same as the beliefs of the first century Church that Jesus started. That defines the remnant church. These believers heeded the call to leave Babylon and its apostate teachings and follow the pure teachings of the scripture. This final remnant movement is composed of members from all denominations and belief systems. To this remnant church, God has an urgent end time message that must be proclaimed by all means possible as rapidly as possible to all the inhabitants of this earth. It is the three angels' message of Revelation 14: 6–12.

This three part message is given in Revelation 14:6–12. *Three angels are symbolically seen flying in the midst of heaven with a final warning to the inhabitants of planet earth.* To proclaim this final message fully you must understand and believe it. God has chosen a people to spread this end-time message of Revelation 14:6–12. He put in their midst the prophetic gift to ensure that there would be unity of faith and belief, such that this end time message of salvation can be preached effectively to the world. The spreading of this message requires humility, consecration, dedication, and the total guidance of the Holy Spirit. I believe if all of God's professed people on earth understood and accepted this message and spread it to others we would have been home by now.

We have looked at many of the previous warnings that God has given to generations before, and we have seen the consequences of ignoring his warnings. We have now come to the most solemn message ever given by God to the inhabitants of planet earth; it is recorded in Revelation 14:6–12. The prophet John here is given this fearsome message in a symbolic form. The angels are the messengers of God proclaiming this three-fold message to all the earth's inhabitants. These messages are sent to the generations of people living at the end of time.

The angels of Revelation 14:6–12 have been heralding God's last warnings to the world. God is telling us that we are not recognizing our condition in Babylon. We are comfortable and think everything is alright, but they are not. He wants us to come out of Babylon. God's judgment is against Babylon and we will partake of Babylon's punishment if we remain in Babylon and insist on promoting Babylon's false doctrines. We have convinced ourselves that we are fine in Babylon. Babylon is like Sodom it is about to blow up with us in it. God cannot save us in Babylon so come out of it. Rev 2:19 "I know your works, and charity, and service, and faith, and patience." God is telling us that He knows that there are good works and many good things taking place in Babylon but nonetheless He has a few things against us, so come out of Babylon. Babylon is a mixture of truth and error and many of God's saints are still caught up in Babylon. He desperately want to save us, so leave Babylon now.

The prophet John here is given this fearsome message in a symbolic form. The angels are the messengers of God proclaiming this three-fold message to all of earth's inhabitants. These are sent to the generations of people living at the end of time. In these messages given in Revelation 14, God is pleading with his people to flee Babylon. Disastrous consequences await the worshippers of Babylon. Why is the wrath of God directed at Babylon? She has not practiced biblical truth and has led countless people away from the true worship of God. Such a solemn warning deserves our full attention. Her disobedience will no longer be tolerated. God has dealt long enough with her and now its judgment time.

God cannot let sin go on forever. As time is wrapping up, He sends a final warning to his people intoxicated with the wine of Babylon. Babylon stands for rebellion against God's truth. God's people refuse to listen to truth and refuse to heed the call to leave Babylon. They would rather defend Babylon than leave it. Babylon represents confusion as a result of apostasy from God's truth. Despite of the apostasy of Babylon, God has many of his beloved people in Babylon and he sends them a final warning. God is patient and long suffering with us. We are almost to the end of this world's history and God's beloved people are still in Babylon and would not heed the call of God to get out of Babylon. They are convinced that Babylon is the truth.

Chapter Fourteen

God sends His final warning in Revelation 14

THESE ARE THE MOST SOLEMN WARNINGS EVER GIVEN TO MANKIND ON PLANET EARTH. THESE ARE GOD'S FINAL WARNING TO THE INHABITANTS OF PLANET EARTH.

Revelation 14:1–5 depicts a scene that takes place after the second coming of Jesus. Just before this occurs God gives a final warning to the world through his end-time movement.

The First Angel's Message

Rev 14:6: "And I saw another angel fly in the midst of heaven, having the everlasting gospel to preach to all the earth, and to every nation, and kindred and tongue and people."

An angel is a messenger and the angel in this text is symbolic for God's end time people taking *the everlasting gospel* to the entire world. God had called forth a people and he is working with them to boldly spread his everlasting gospel to every person on planet earth. The angel is seen flying in the midst of heaven rapidly spreading this everlasting gospel. God's messengers are armed with the untarnished everlasting gospel of the love, mercy, redemption, and the righteousness of God.

Rev 14:7: "Saying with a loud voice, 'Fear God and give glory to him for the hour of his judgment is come; and worship him that made heaven and earth, and the fountain of waters.'"

Why a loud voice? A loud voice is used when you really want someone to hear what you are saying; it's a very important message. Reverence, love, and respect God and make a full surrender to his sovereign will, which includes his law. The first angel announces that the hour of God's judgment is come and calls on the inhabitants of planet earth back to the true worship of the Creator of heaven and earth and everything.

Pay attention to what God is saying because the hour of his judgment is come. Jesus is in the Most Holy Place of the heavenly sanctuary and has convened the judgment. The judgment process involves everyone who ever lived. God will show to the entire universe that his judgments are fair and just. Satan has accused God of being unfair and arbitrary and creating a law that cannot be kept. The judgment will vindicate God's character before the entire universe.

The first angel's message is a call back to the true worship of the creator; implied here is the warning to leave false teachings alone and get back to the everlasting gospel of Jesus Christ. The first angel announces the start of the judgment. God's judgment has started and the angel or God's end-time messenger must hasten around the world to warn the inhabitants of planet earth that God's judgment has begun and there is time to come back to the true worship of God. Time has not yet ended. We have a probationary period, but the judgment has started. This message, heralded by the first angel, will be carried by God's end-time people from 1844, when the judgment began, to the second coming of Jesus.

Rev 14:8: "And there followed another angel, saying, Babylon is fallen, is fallen, that great city, because she made all nations drink of the wine of the wrath of her fornication."

A second angel joins the first angel with another urgent, solemn message: Babylon is fallen. This is not referring to that ancient Babylon that was destroyed centuries before John. This text refers to spiritual Babylon. Babylon here represents false teachings in many churches today, many of which have roots in ancient Babylon. Babylon refers to apostate Christianity that is teaching a message that is not consistent with God's sovereign will. This is serious business. God has made a solemn judgment against Babylon. God does not make mistakes, and He has determined that His people should be aware of Babylon's false system of worship and leave.

False doctrines are taught and practiced by God's people in Babylon. Many in Babylon hear God's last call but refuse to repent and follow God's will. God's people in Babylon refuse to accept the first angel's message and separate from Babylon. The 2nd angel charges Babylon with making all nations drink of the wrath of her fornication. She has fornicated with earthly powers and become idolatrous, mixing truth and error.

Spiritual Babylon is practicing a religion that is in opposition to God's will. God considers these errors very serious and rebellious. These errors have corrupted his people. They are deceptive errors and God is pleading with his people to recognize these errors and flee Babylon.

The prophet John reveals a lot of information about spiritual Babylon in Revelation 17 and 18. One of the seven plague-bearing angels said to John, "come and I will show you the judgment of the great whore which sits on many waters." Here in Revelation 17:1 Babylon is depicted as a whore with whom the powers of the world have committed fornication. Fornication here is the illicit relationship depicted by the false doctrines that this power has used to deceive the world. Satan uses Babylon to create rebellion against God in a very deceptive way. In Verse 2 the angel tells John that the kings of the earth have an illicit relationship with her and the inhabitants of the earth are drunk with the wine of her fornication. They are too drunk to perceive her errors. The 3rd angel of Revelation 14:8 declares that she made the whole world drink of the wine of the wrath of her fornication.

In verse 3 John is shown the woman as she sits on a scarlet beast full of names of Blasphemy, having seven heads and 10 horns. In Rev. 17:4, she has a golden cup in her hand full of abominations and filthiness of fornication. This golden cup is deceptive. Her doctrines are corrupt.

In verse 5, she is the mother of harlots, meaning that her daughters are the churches that join her in her opposition to God's truth. Revelation 18:4 give a serious warning to Gods people to leave Babylon and her erroneous teachings. This is the final message and proclamation of Rev 14:6–12. The message of the 2nd angel is warning about false worship and begging God's people to leave Babylon. God has judged Babylon, and she will fall. If you are still in Babylon when she falls, so will you.

3rd Angels' message

Rev 14:9, 10 states: "And the third angel followed them, saying with a loud voice, if any man worship the beast and his image, and receive his mark in his forehead, or in his hand, the same shall drink of the wine of the wrath of God, which is poured our without mixture into the cup of his indignation and he shall be tormented with fire and brimstone in the presence of the holy angels, and in the presence of the Lamb:"

The image of the beast is the eventual enforcement of Sunday sacredness. This is a violation of the supreme law of God and against His sovereign will. As we approach the very end of time, there are going to be two sets of people: those who worship the beast and his image and receive his mark and those who worship Christ and receive His seal. The seal of God is wrapped around his Sabbath. This is found in the fourth commandment that states that the seventh day is the Sabbath of the Lord thy God. The seal of God gives *His name* – the Lord, thy God, *His title*- the Creator, *His territory*- heaven and earth. The 3rd angel gives a stern fearsome warning for God's people to leave Babylon which represents a system of worship that is rebellious to God's will. The message of this angel is clear: everyone at this time must decide whether they are going to choose the true worship of God or worship according to a false system, which constitutes Babylon. A decision must be made. The worship of God is the major theme of these three angels' messages. Satan has usurped the true worship of the Creator and has gotten the church to stray away from the true gospel; finally it is time for the final restoration. God says if you truly love Him keep His commandments.

God rose up a final people from every denomination who began to read and understand these three angel's messages. God knew that the majority of believers would not believe these messages and many teachers, preachers and followers would insist on staying in Babylon despite these fearsome warnings. God also foresaw the millions who would heed these fearsome warnings and leave Babylon. God gives the warning, "come out of her My people that ye be not partakers of her sins and receive not her plagues." John was shown those who heed the warnings and wrote "Here is the patience of the saints: here are they that keep the commandments of God, and the faith of Jesus."

Revelation 15 and 16 describes the judgment of God against those who reject this final call. The seven last plagues will be poured out on the human race that rejected the final call. These plagues are awesome. God's people must heed the final call of Revelation 14 to avoid these plagues.

These amazing prophecies of the Bible help us to appreciate that we serve an awesome God. These prophecies should leave no doubt in our minds that there is an omnipotent God who is totally in control of events, and he is working out his eternal plan of salvation. Revelation 1:3 states, "Blessed is he that reads, and hears the words of this prophecy, and keep those things, which are written therein, for the time is at hand."

God's amazing and redeeming love is the central theme of these prophecies. He gave us these prophecies because he loves us and wants to save us. He does not want the end to come as a surprise, although we are told that this will sadly be the case for most people. Matthew 24:37 tell us that as it was in the days of Noah, so shall it be when Jesus comes. In those days people continued their daily lives, paying little attention to God's warnings until the flood came and swept them all away. Similarly today people will be occupied with the daily routines of life and that great day of the Lord will catch them unaware, like a thief in the night.

Signs of his coming

The second coming of Jesus is the most anticipated and one of the most important events in the history of Planet earth. It brings the end of the great controversy of the ages between Satan and God. Since sin entered this planet man has been looking forward to the second coming of Jesus. Jude 1:14 tells us that Enoch the seventh generation from Adam prophesied saying "Behold, the Lord comes with ten thousands of His saints to execute judgment upon all, and to convince all that are ungodly among them of their ungodly deeds that they have committed." Jesus and His second coming is the central theme of the Bible. The Bible has shown that down throughout the history of man on this planet, from the time man sinned to the second coming of Jesus, God has been working out His plan of Salvation. In John 5:39 Jesus says "Search the scriptures for in them you think in them you have eternal life, but they testify of Me."

The second coming of Jesus is real, literal, and imminent. This is an event will be seen by everyone on planet earth and it will affect everyone. Accompanied by an innumerable host from heaven, Jesus Christ is coming in the clouds of heaven with great power and great glory to redeem his faithful children from this doomed planet. Jesus is returning with the armies of heaven as King of King and Lord of Lords. The prophet Isaiah states in Isaiah. 25:9 that God's children will say "This is our God. We have waited for Him, and He will save us. We have waited for Him and We will be glad and rejoice in His salvation."

It is an event that we have long waited for and we are excited. In John 14:2–3 Jesus promised us "Let not your heart be troubled; you believe in God believe also in me. In my father's house are many mansions; if it were not so I would have told you. And I go and prepare a place for you, I will come again and receive you to Myself; that where I am there you may be also." God has great plans for his redeemed children. What a bright future and a great hope that awaits those who have made the necessary preparation for this event.

Everything on Planet Earth indicates that we are slowly but surely getting there and that is good news for those who are looking forward to this glorious event. This grand and glorious event brings us face-to-face communion with God again. That which was lost in Eden will be restored. The Bible is our guide, authority, and main source of information regarding this event. It informs us that this is one event that you must be prepared for. It will be the greatest disappointment of one's life to be unprepared for this event. The results will be catastrophic, if you are unprepared.

God does not want anyone to be destroyed by His second coming, so for more than 6000 years now He has patiently given us plenty of warnings and instructions so that we could be ready for this most important event.

The Lord is coming are you ready?

God wants us to be ready for His coming, and as we have seen from this study, God has been constantly at work preparing us for this grand event when He will restore lost humanity. Throughout history He has sent us warnings by His chosen messengers to help prepare us for this event. It is extremely important that we follow God's instructions so that we could be ready for His coming. He has given us the Bible and all of its prophecies so that we can be fully informed and be ready for His second coming. The Bible did not reveal to us the exact date and time when He would come and no one knows the day or hour of His second coming. We do, however, have signs that the Bible tells us would happen just before He comes, and the Apocalyptic prophecies of the Bible give us great insight about the nearness of His second coming. To those who have been anxiously watching and waiting for this event the signs of our times indicating that His coming is near are very reassuring. After a long trip away from home the signs along the way that tells us we are nearing home are very helpful and welcoming. Similarly, the Bible has identified many of the signs along the course of history that indicates we are almost home. The Bible with its many stories and apocalyptic prophecies is very helpful in pointing us in the right direction toward the second coming of Jesus and our eternal destiny.

Jesus isn't coming back until the gospel of the kingdom has been preached in the entire world, and everyone has an opportunity to make a choice. God has been patiently waiting, but when the door of probation closes, the end will come and there will be no second chance after that.

Today is the day of salvation. When Jesus returns the saints that are alive will be caught up by Jesus. The saints in the grave will awake to immortal life. 1 Thessalonians 4 indicates that the saved living and the saved dead will meet Jesus in the air at His second coming. The unsaved will be killed by the brightness of his coming and the unsaved dead will not be raised for their final punishment for 1000 years. For 1000 years Satan who has been busy tempting saints and deceiving the lost will have nothing to do. He has plenty of time to look over the chaos He caused for thousands of years.

This is the beginning of the 1000 years. In Revelation we read that an angel came down from heaven and took hold of the devil and bound him for a thousand years then he will be let loose for a little season. During this thousand years Satan is bound by a change of circumstances and can't tempt anyone because there is no one alive on this planet to be tempted. His reign of terror is over.

Rev 20:6 states "blessed and holy is he that wakes in the first resurrection: on such the second death hath no power, but they shall be priests of God and of Christ, and shall reign with him a thousand years." For 1000 years the righteous will live in heaven with God. At the end of the thousand years, the wicked dead will be raised. You do not want any part of this resurrection. Satan will be loosed from his chain of circumstances because he now has people to tempt again for a little season. The prophet John was shown in Revelation 21 that the holy city of God, the New Jerusalem, that Great city that God has prepared for his saints, will descend from heaven, prepared as a bride adorned for her husband. God himself will accompany His saints back to earth. Revelation 20:8 and

9 states that Satan will gather an innumerable host, probably the world's greatest generals and surround the New Jerusalem. God will destroy them with a final cleansing fire. This is the second death that will completely destroy leaving nothing behind. John is shown a new heaven and new Earth where righteousness dwells.

The second coming of Jesus is soon to take place. Jesus the commander and chief of the heavenly army will return as a conquering King soon. On his vesture and thigh is written King of Kings and Lord of Lords. Accompanying him will be the armies of heaven, thousands and ten thousands of angels. He will return with his glory, with the glory of the father and all the angels. Can you even begin to imagine this awesome sight? No man can withstand brightness of his second coming.

About 2000 years ago Jesus left the throne room of the universe, where he dwells in light, that mortal cannot approach, and came to live in this dark world with the shadow of death and curse. He forsook the adoration of angels to suffer shame, insult, humiliation, rejection, hatred and death to redeem us from sin and its consequences, which is death. Time is fast running out and the second coming of Jesus is imminent. I end with three statements. Two from God's end time messenger to us, E.G. White and one from King Solomon, the wisest man who ever lived.

In the book Great Controversy, Ellen White writes: "We are living in the most solemn period of earth's history. The destiny of earths teeming multitudes is about to be decided. Our own future well-being and also the salvation of other souls depend on the course, which we now pursue. We need to be guided by the spirit of truth. We have a fight to be fought and a battle to win. Each follower of Christ should earnestly inquire Lord what wilt thou have me do? We need to humble ourselves before the lord with fasting and prayer and meditate much upon the word especially upon the scenes of the judgment. We should seek a deep and living experience in the things of God. We have not a moment to lose. Events of vital importance are taking place around us; we are on Satan's enchanted ground. Sleep not sentinels of God, the foe is lurking near, ready at any moment should you become laxed and drowsy to spring upon you and make you his prey. We must be on the offensive in this battle and fortify our minds with the word of God; the intensification of Satan's forces against us must be met by the intensification of our faith. These times demand that we do the will of our master."

In Steps to Christ, she writes: "There is nothing more calculated to strengthen the intellect than the study of the Scriptures. No other book is so potent to elevate the thoughts, to give vigor to the faculties, as the broad, ennobling truths of the Bible. If God's word were studied as it should be, men would have a breadth of mind, a nobility of character, and a stability of purpose that is rarely seen in these times."

Finally, I conclude from Ecclesiastes 12:13 and 14 "Let us hear the conclusion of the whole matter: Fear God, and keep his commandments: for this is the whole duty of man. For God will bring every work into judgment, with every secret thing, whether it is good or whether it is evil.

THE END

ADDITIONAL STUDY TOPICS.

(1). The Immortality of the Soul

The majority of Christians today believe in the teaching of the immortality of the soul and that when you die you automatically go to heaven or hell and sometimes to purgatory.

Time and time again, The Bible defines death as a sleep. Throughout the books of Kings we read that the king died and slept with his father's. See 1 Kings 1:21; 2:10, 15:24; 22:40–50; and 2 Kings 8:24; 10:35:13:9 and numerous other references in the book of kings. Deuteronomy 31:16 states "Moses shall sleep with his fathers." Numerous writers in the Bible refer to death as a sleep. This is consistent with Jesus teaching. In John 11 the account is given of the death of Lazarus, a man whom Jesus loved dearly. When Jesus heard of the death of Lazarus, he said to his disciples in John 11:11, "Our friend Lazarus sleeping I go that I may awake him out of sleep. In Verse 12, the disciples misunderstood what Jesus was saying and they said to Jesus, "If he sleep he doeth well." Jesus explained to them that Lazarus was sleeping the sleep of death, but because they didn't understand, he made it plain by saying that Lazarus was dead. In verse 23 Jesus said to Martha, "Thy brother shall rise again." Martha said to Jesus, "I know that he shall rise again in the resurrection at the last day." Martha understood it the correct way. Jesus did not teach the false doctrine of the immortality of the soul. Martha was a student at the feet of Jesus and understood death the correct way as Jesus taught. Jesus did not tell her that her brother was in heaven but reassured her that "I am the resurrection and the life and he that believeth in me though he were dead yet *shall* he live. Jesus was taken to the grave where Lazarus lay; he had been dead four days and no doubt was decomposing. The creator of this universe called on God the Father and then with a loud voice shouted, "Lazarus came forth" and Lazarus came forth from the grave. Jesus did not call up to heaven for Lazarus to come down. Lazarus did not come forth with any grand stories about heaven because he was not there. He came forth just as though he was sleeping.

Daniel 12:1 and 2 indicates that "there is coming a time of trouble in this world such as never was since there was a nation; it will be a terrible time for God's people but Michael (Jesus) the great prince will come and deliver his people every one that is written in the book in heaven. And on his return many of them that *sleep in the dust of the earth shall awake,* some to everlasting life, and some to shame and everlasting contempt." Daniel makes it clear when people receive their reward or punishment. It is clearly not at death. It is at the time of the resurrection when Jesus returns. The Bible does not teach that at death people go on to their reward or punishment. The concept that the soul lives on at death is a continuation of the same lie that Satan told to Eve in the Garden of Eden that she would not die but will live on forever.

Job 14:10 states that "But man dies, and wastes away: yes, man gives up the ghost, and where is he?" verse 12 "So man lieth down, and riseth not: till the heavens be no more, they shall not awake, nor be raised out of their sleep." Verse 13 "Oh that thou would hide me in the grave that thou would keep me secret, until thy wrath be past, that thou would appoint me a set time, and remember me!" The set time mentioned here is at the second coming of Jesus. Job is saying that he will wait in the grave until he is changed from mortal to immortal. Verse 21 "His sons come to honor, and he knoweth it not; and they are brought low, but he perceiveth it not of them." In other words if his children become successful or they are failures he does not know. When your parents are dead they do not know what befalls you. Nowhere does Job gives the impression that when he dies he will be in heaven. The biblical teaching here is clear, man sleeps in the grave awaiting the resurrection. The belief that you go to heaven when you die is alien to Job.

In Acts 2:29,34 the Apostle Peter writes: "Men and brethren, let me freely speak unto you of the patriarch David, that he is both dead and buried here, and his remains is with us unto this day." Verse 34 "For David is not ascended into the heavens; but he saith himself, the Lord said unto my Lord. Sit down on my right hand." David here understood the death, resurrection and the priestly work of Jesus, his Lord.

In Ecclesiastes 9:5, 6 King Solomon answers the question of what does man knows when he dies. He writes: "For the living know that they shall die but the dead does not know anything. Neither have they any more a reward; for the memory of them is forgotten. Also their love, and their hatred, and their envy, is now perished; neither have they any more a portion forever in anything that is done under the sun." Solomon makes it plain and clear. The dead knows nothing. Not until the resurrection. They are not in heaven looking down at you and they do not know what is going on. They are no longer conscious. This teaching that you go to heaven at death is clearly a deviation from biblical teaching.

In Psalms 6: 5 King David writes: "For in death there is no remembrance of thee: in the grave who shall give the thanks?

Psalms 146:4 His breath goes forth he returns to his earth in that very day his thoughts perish.

In 1 Thessalonians 4:13 the Apostle Paul enlightens us regarding the state of the dead. He writes: "But I would not have you to be ignorant, brethren, concerning them which are asleep that you sorrow not, even as others which have no hope. For if we believe that Jesus died and rose again, even so them also which sleep in Jesus will God bring with him. For this we say unto you by the word of the Lord, that we which are alive and remain unto the coming of the Lord, shall not prevent them which are asleep. For the Lord himself will descend from heaven with a shout, with the voice of the archangel, and with the trump of God, and the dead in Christ shall rise first. Then we which are alive and remain shall be caught up with them in the clouds, to meet the Lord in the air: and so shall we ever be with the Lord. Wherefore comfort one another with these words." To paraphrase Paul is saying that the dead is Christ are sleeping, but sorrow not as those with no hope they will be resurrected when Jesus comes. In Verse 15 he makes it clear that we who are alive when Jesus comes will not go to heaven before those who are sleeping in the graves. Verse 16 he states that when Jesus descends his archangel voice will sound as a trumpet and the dead in Christ shall rise first. Then those who are alive will be caught up to meet him in the air and so shall all both the resurrected and the dead shall be with the lord as he takes them back to heaven. Paul has clearly enlightened us here about the state of the dead.

1 Corinthians 15:51–54 Paul also writes "Behold I show you a mystery; we shall not all sleep, but we shall all be changed in a moment in the twinkling of an eye at the last trump: for the trumpet shall sound and the dead shall be raised incorruptible, and we shall be changed. For this incorruptible must put on incorruption and this mortal must put on immortality then shall be brought to pass the saying that is written; Death is swallowed up in victory."

1 Cor. 15: 13–18 Paul here teaches the essential doctrine of the Christian faith and that is the resurrection. If Christ be not raised then those who are fallen asleep in Christ are perished. Everlasting life follows the resurrection. Jesus is coming back to resurrect his children. If you are already in heaven, He does not need to come back. There is the exception of Elijah who was translated and there will be those who will be alive at Christ coming who will be translated. But for the rest of us the way to eternal life is through the resurrection. This is the time when immortality will be given. The soul is not immortal. 1 Timothy 6:15 and 16 teaches that only God has immortality.

Frankly speaking the concept of the immortal soul is foreign to the bible and has its roots in Ancient Paganism and Greek mythology. There is no immortal soul. The bible clearly states in Ezekiel 18:20 that the soul that sinneth shall die. The immortality of the soul is another deception of Satan. This deception began in the Garden of Eden when God said to Adam and Eve in Geneses 2:17 that in the day that they eat of the fruit of the tree they shall surely die. Satan told Eve No you will not surely die for God know that in the day that you eat thereof. Then your eyes shall be opened. Satan was successful then and by masterful deception he is successful again. God says that the soul that sinneth shall die and that is the truth. Today people are trying to contact the dead not realizing that they are dealing with Satan who is impersonating their dead loved ones. The bible states that the dead knows nothing.

Luke 23:43 is one of the most misinterpreted texts in the Bible. Some believer's state that Jesus told the thief on the cross. "Verily I say unto thee, today thou shall be with me in Paradise. This translation in the KJV is incorrect; the comma was placed incorrectly during translation. It reflects the belief of the translator. The comma was not in the original biblical text. It was added later. It should read. "Verily I say unto thee today, thou shall be with me in Paradise." It means, "Today, this day that I am hanging on this cross, I say unto you, when all the redeemed are gathered in Paradise, you along with them will be with me in Paradise." The events surrounding the crucifixion reveal that Jesus did not go to Paradise that day. He went to the grave. The following Sunday, the first day of the week, Jesus said to Mary Magdalene: "Touch me not; for I have not yet ascended to my father John 20:17." Mary and the thief understood the words of Jesus better than many today. The thief knew that he wasn't dying and going to heaven immediately, so he said, "I believe in you Lord and when you set up your kingdom, remember me."

The parable of the rich man and Lazarus in Luke 16:19–31 is often used to justify the claim of those who state that the dead go to heaven at death. This parable was used by Jesus to show the difference between the rich who do not depend on God and the poor who depend on God.

Here Jesus tells the parable of a certain rich man who lived it up every day with his fine clothes. This poor beggar named Lazarus was full of sores and begged outside the rich man's gate. The poor man wished he could get the crumbs that fell from the rich man's table. The dogs would go and lick the poor man's sores. The rich man did not help the poor man even though he did not prevent him from sitting at his gate. The rich man went about his daily living in luxury, totally ignoring the poor man. The day came when the beggar died and was carried by the angels into Abraham's bosom: the rich man died also and was buried. This rich man in hell looked up and beheld the beggar sitting in Abraham's bosom.

It is easy to misinterpret this one, but remember it is a parable that cannot be taken literally. The saved do not go to Abraham's bosom. He would have to have a large bosom. Those in hell cannot look up and see heaven. Jesus was using the common belief of the day that that is consciousness in death to explain the results of not obeying the truth. Jesus was not using this parable to explain the state of the dead. He says if they hear not Moses and the prophets neither will they be persuaded even though one raise from the dead.

There are many lessons in this parable. Once dead, there is no 2nd chance. Jesus was asking here what will it profit a man if he gains the whole world and lose his soul. Christ was talking to the Jewish nation. Many who were rich in this worldly goods.

In verse 26 Abraham said, "between you and us there is a great gulf fixed." Though he was Jewish, he was not obedient and did not live the life Abraham was. Today there are many in this class who live for pleasure and wealth and ignore the poor and therefore would not be in the same class as Abraham.

Jesus uses current events or beliefs in parables to teach eternal truths. This is one of those times. The big lesson here is that by the life you live you determine your destiny. There is no second chance. Make use of your opportunities and accept Gods grace freely now to live according to His will. Do not create an impassable gulf between you and your God. A parable is an earthly story with a heavenly meaning and should not be taken literally. There is an overwhelming amount of biblical information to support the fact that the dead are asleep until the resurrection

People burn forever and forever- Eternal Torment.

Here is another deception of Satan. He portrays God as an evil God who burns people forever and ever. This eternal burning hell is a doctrine of paganism that the devil brought into the church. Some teach that the dead either go to heaven or to an ever-burning hell. Not so God is just and fair. Why should Cain burn for thousands of years for killing one man and Hitler who died 6000 years later should burn for less time for killing millions? It doesn't make sense. God is a righteous judge and has a fair judicial system. This is another misunderstanding of biblical truth. What is the Biblical truth?

Malachi 4:1 "For, behold the day cometh that shall burn as an oven, and all the proud, yea, and all that do wickedly, shall be stubble; and the day that cometh shall burn them up, saith the Lord of Hosts that it shall leave them neither root nor branch. Here the Bible teaches that the wicked will not be burning forever and ever somewhere that no one can say because the bible does not teach that but it teaches that the wicked will be totally destroyed leaving neither root nor branch.

Verse 3 "And ye shall tread down the wicked; for they shall be ashes under the soles of your feet in the day that I shall do this saith the Lord of Hosts. "Ashes" suggests total destruction. The prophet here says that the only thing left of the wicked will be their ashes.

The misinterpretation of this part of scripture has to do with the word forever. "Forever" must be interpreted correctly. It has different meanings. For example, Jude 1:7: "Even as Sodom and Gomorrah and the cities about them in like manner giving themselves over to fornication and going after strange flesh are set forth for an example suffering the vengeance of eternal fire." The effects of the fire are eternal not the fire itself. These cities have burned up and are no longer burning. Archeologists have unearthed the remains of these cities. The fires of Sodom and Gomorrah have had their eternal effects were extinguished a long time ago.

There are many instances in the Bible where "forever" had different meanings. 1 Samuel 1:22 states that when the child Samuel was weaned, Hannah his mother brought him to the temple that he may appear before the Lord and there abide forever. "Forever" here means "as long as the child lives."

Ezekiel 28:19: "I will bring thee as ashes upon the earth. After God has destroyed sin and sinners in hell fire."

Ps 37:10 yet in a little while and the wicked shall not be. The bible teaches that death and destruction is the end result of sin, if you are dead why would you be roasting forever and ever. It makes no sense to roast a dead person forever and ever. Eternal torment is the doctrine of the devil. Our God is too loving and just for this. He will eradicate sin from this universe but the punishment for sin cannot be eternal hellfire, because Jesus took on our sins but didn't burn eternally.

Nahum 1:9 states that affliction will not rise up a second time. Sin will never again happen in all of God's universe.

We invite you to view the complete
selection of titles we publish at:

www.TEACHServices.com

Scan with your mobile device
to go directly to our website.

Please write or email us your praises, reactions, or
thoughts about this or any other book we publish at:

P.O. Box 954
Ringgold, GA 30736
info@TEACHServices.com

TEACH Services, Inc., titles may be purchased in bulk for
educational, business, fund-raising, or sales promotional use.
For information, please e-mail:

BulkSales@TEACHServices.com

Finally, if you are interested in seeing
your own book in print, please contact us at

publishing@TEACHServices.com

We would be happy to review your manuscript for free.

www.ingramcontent.com/pod-product-compliance
Lightning Source LLC
Chambersburg PA
CBHW080725230426
43665CB00020B/2616